Provisional Avant-Gardes

Little Magazine Communities

Sophie Seita

Stanford University Press

Stanford, California

Stanford University Press
Stanford, California

Parts of Chapter 1 first appeared in the introductory essay to *The Blind Man* (New York: Ugly Duckling Presse, 2017), facsimile reprint. Reprinted with permission.

Part of Chapter 4 was previously published as "The Politics of the Forum in Feminist Avant-Garde Magazines After 1980," *Journal of Modern Literature* 42, no. 1 (Fall 2018): 163–82. Reprinted with permission.

An earlier version of Chapter 5 was published as "Thinking the Unprintable in Contemporary Post-Digital Publishing," in *Chicago Review* 60, no. 4 / 61, no. 1 (2018): 175–94. Reprinted with permission.

Printed in the United States of America on acid-free, archival-quality paper

Library of Congress Cataloging-in-Publication Data

Names: Seita, Sophie (Poet), author.
Title: Provisional avant-gardes : little magazine communities from Dada to digital / Sophie Seita.
Description: Stanford, California : Stanford University Press, 2019. | Series: Post-45 | Includes bibliographical references and index.
Identifiers: LCCN 2018053068 (print) | LCCN 2018056649 (ebook) | ISBN 9781503609587 | ISBN 9781503608719 (cloth : alk. paper) | ISBN 9781503609570 (pbk. : alk. paper)
Subjects: LCSH: Little magazines—Publishing—United States—History. | Literature, Experimental—Publishing—United States—History. | Periodicals—Publishing—United States—History. | Avant-garde (Aesthetics)—United States—History. | Arts, Modern—20th century. | Arts, Modern—21st century.
Classification: LCC PN4878.3 (ebook) | LCC PN4878.3 .S45 2019 (print) | DDC 051—dc23
LC record available at https://lccn.loc.gov/2018053068

Cover design: Jason Alejandro

Contents

Illustrations

Acknowledgments

In homage to *The Little Review*, I'd like to follow Jane Heap's goodbye to her magazine by, like her, distributing metaphorical "wreaths" to those who in some shape or other were important to me in the making of this book.

Many colleagues and friends read and commented on my work at various stages, and their ideas, generosity, and care resonate throughout my writing. I'm particularly indebted to Andrea Brady, whose rigor and never-tiring attention to detail, as well as her activities and interventions as a scholar, poet, publisher, and organizer, have been and continue to be an inspiration. In addition to being a superb reader, kitt price's cheerfulness always reminded me of the joy that brought me to this project in the first place—a joy that is necessary for a sane relation to any work. Michael Tencer's careful and extraordinarily detailed thoughts on the manuscript have been invaluable. Some intellectual debts also predate the writing of this book, so immeasurable thanks are owed to Ian Patterson, without whose encouragement and support I would not be where I am today. His commitment to the politics of experimental writing have shaped my thinking and writing in more ways than I can acknowledge.

I'm also tremendously grateful for the invitations and opportunities to present my work in countless formal and informal settings, for the inspiring and thoughtful conversations with colleagues and friends, many of whom made introductions and other life and art things possible: Lee Ann Brown, Eric Bulson, Kate Crowcroft, Lisa Gitelman, Alan Golding, Robert Hampson, Kaplan Page Harris, Sarah Hayden, David James, Paolo Javier, Josh Kotin, Wendy Lotterman, Karen Mac Cormack, Steve McCaffery, Jacob McGuinn, Adam McKible, Peter Middleton, Anna Moser, Stephen Motika, Francis Naumann, Yates Norton, Andrew Peart, Danny Snelson, Paul Stephens, Emma Stirling, Tony Torn, Dorothy Wang, Rachel Warriner, Lucy van de Wiel, Uljana Wolf, Matvei Yankelevich, and Yvonne Zivkovic. Many thanks, in particular, to Andreas Huyssen and Peter Nicholls for hosting me as a Visiting Scholar at Columbia University and New York University, respectively, and for their support of my project; and to Clifford Wulfman and Natalia Ermolaev at Princeton's Blue Mountain Project for inviting me to collaborate on their fantastic modernist digitization project between 2014 and 2015.

At Stanford, Emily-Jane Cohen and Faith Wilson Stein shepherded this book to completion in the most responsive and meticulous way one could wish for. I also greatly appreciated the helpful and enthusiastic feedback from the series editors, Loren Glass and Kate Marshall, and from my two anonymous readers. My colleagues at Queens' College and the University of Cambridge, in turn, were lovely lunch companions and provided a supportive and stimulating environment in which to think and write.

Several institutions supported this project financially: Queens' College, University of Cambridge; Queen Mary University of London; the Beinecke Rare Book and Manuscript Library, Yale University; Princeton University Library; the Poetry Collection at SUNY Buffalo; New York University; and Archive of the Now. I want to thank the many curators of the above archives, as well as those at Columbia University, Fales (NYU), and the New York Public Library, especially Jay Barksdale, Michael Basinski, Karen Gisonny, James Maynard, Karla Nielsen, and Charlotte Priddle, for help with finding materials, for granting me residence in the NYPL's Wertheim Room, and for supplying high-resolution scans for this book. For the latter, I also thank Ugly Duckling Presse.

I owe much to many of the poets and editors discussed in the following pages who readily answered my queries and, in some cases, dug up treasures for me: Susan Bee, Charles Bernstein, Abigail Child, Steve Clay, Jean Day, Thom Donovan, Johanna Drucker, Ken Edwards, Kathleen Fraser, Erica Hunt, Lucy Ives, Kevin Killian and Dodie Bellamy, Alison Knowles, Kimberly Lyons, Bernadette Mayer, Holly Melgard, Jerome Rothenberg, Carolee Schneemann, and James Sherry.

Of course, profound thanks to my family for sending vegan treats in the mail and for unfailing presence, grounding, and cheer, always. Luke McMullan deserves my greatest gratitude: his patience, equanimity, sharp mind, and love sustained me throughout.

Finally, I would not have written this book in the way I did if I wasn't also a poet and artist, so I want to reserve a special wreath for the community of poets and artists whose readings or performances I attended or organized, whose poems or reviews I read, who collaborated on feminist and queer performances with me over the last few years, and who taught me—in theory and practice—real avant-garde hospitality.

Provisional Avant-Gardes

INTRODUCTION
A Theory of the Avant-Garde Today

Avant-Garde Proto-Forms

Whether the avant-garde is declared dead, of only historical interest, or still urgently necessary and contemporary, critical responses to an (or the) avant-garde are as divided and diverse as the practices they seek to address. In late 2012, when I began this project, I set up a Google Scholar alert for the word *avant-garde* and—as was to be expected—received a barrage of irrelevant emails. While the sheer abundance of hits showed me that the concept was anything but obsolete, the vagueness surrounding its application became the initial problem this project attempted to remedy. I believed that there was, in fact, a tried-and-true formula of avant-gardism based on the untried nature of experimental form and leftist political commitment—a formula that I needed to resurrect from the shambles of critical infighting. Very quickly, however, my research led me to little magazines, and my preconceptions had to be thrown overboard.

If this sounds like a neat conversion narrative, why is it not more common? Much of the persistence of a fixed version of avant-gardism (according to which one could be right or wrong) at the expense of provisionality has to do with the specific stakes of an avant-garde's identity. One tempting response to the definitional question would be to enumerate characteristics, dates, and names. This is, of course, how the avant-garde has tended to be defined ever since its supposed inception in the 1910s. The word *avant-garde* is popularly understood to refer to an individual or a group with an anti-institutional attitude, producing stylistically innovative work, often with political aims in mind, sometimes articulated aggressively against previous generations or against tradition more broadly. This understanding has led to a seemingly coherent set of now-canonical and historical avant-garde movements with key players, clear manifestos, and an identifiable style. But what about those practices and groups that do not fit predetermined characteristics? And what about practitioners who traverse several social groups, aesthetics, and "periods"? Could avant-garde groups be described with a sensibility that emerges from material objects and the publishing contexts of their work and with an approach that remains open to multiple definitions? If we do not safely relegate the avant-garde to a more authentic long-gone past or a utopian future that we will never experience, how can we reclaim the avant-garde as a contemporary phenomenon that speaks to us as scholars, writers, and readers? These are some of the central questions this book tries to answer.

To take the avant-garde into the present in an inclusive fashion, the *Boston Review* hosted a forum called "Race and the Poetic Avant-Garde" in 2015. For Mónica de la Torre, to write from the position of a Mexican American avant-garde feminist poet means *not* to "speak for a collectivity," assuming homogeneity among a "minority" group, but to "perform a polymorphous subjectivity that undermines essentializing notions of identity." This performance requires an avant-garde "form" that responds to a social reality by "critiqu[ing] hegemonic, exclusionary discourses, including those pertaining to identity politics."[1] To forge a new interpretation of the avant-garde, this book therefore attends to precisely such forums and questions surrounding form, politics, and identity. Forums, reviews, and letters to the editor often democratize a poetry community, enabling it to weigh opinions and to determine new or necessary directions. At other times, such discursive interventions show an avant-garde community its own limits. Since the 1970s, feminist, queer, and intersectional critics have confronted the limited and normative understanding of the avant-garde, as well as "the literary." Much of this challenging of the canon and of supposedly universal tastes, values, and social and aesthetic expressions has taken place in magazines.

Provisional Avant-Gardes offers a new, diachronic study of twentieth- and twenty-first-century literary avant-gardes by focusing on little magazines as media that capture and create provisional and heterogeneous communities. It is driven by the need for a dynamic model of avant-gardism that accounts for contemporary networks and that pays close attention to the actual practices of writers, editors, and readers, however contradictory, variable, and historically specific they are or may have been. This book focuses on several Anglophone magazines published in the United States, many in New York, and places them within their cultural and material contexts. The majority of them are located on the peripheries of frequently theorized avant-gardes. The following chapters cover proto-Dada (~1914–29), proto-conceptual (~1965–75), proto-Language and queer New Narrative (~1971–89), feminist (~1983–2009), and contemporary digital magazine communities (~2008–17), with particular considerations of their provisionality, materiality, canonical omissions, and diachronic connections.[2]

My concept of avant-garde "proto-forms" conceives of avant-gardes as provisional networks of affiliation rather than rigidly demarcated groups, where *proto-* suggests provisionality and heterogeneity, while *forms* stresses media, genres, and groups. I take this term from artist, writer, and frequent magazine contributor Mina Loy, who intimated the complexity and uncertainty at the heart of communal projects when she wondered in the little magazine *Others* "what guaranty / For the proto-form / We fumble / Our souvenir ethics to."[3] Indeed, what does community mean for individual writers across time? By considering the inclusiveness, hierarchies, and gift-exchange of magazine communities, I posit hospitality as a useful metaphor for the complex interactions within literary communities and as one possible way of understanding them.[4] How is hospitality furthered or denied within or outside a magazine, and how does a pedagogy or poetics develop in avant-gardes through the magazine medium?

Virginia Woolf's remark in *Three Guineas* reads like a guiding principle for the publishing communities in this book: "By using these cheap and so far unforbidden instruments [that is, the private printing press, typewriters, duplicators] you can at once rid yourself of the pressure of boards, policies and editors. They will speak your own mind, in your own words, at your own time, at your own length, at your own bidding. And that, we are agreed, is our definition of 'intellectual liberty.'"[5] The self-reliance, democratic access, and independent thinking promised by small-press publishing and little magazines motivated many avant-garde editors throughout the twentieth century and continue to do so in the twenty-first. Again and again, editors and contributors have remembered their magazines fondly and considered self-publishing to be empowering. A former co-editor of the feminist magazine *HOW(ever)*, Susan Gevirtz, reminisces: "As an institution that is not a home or house, *HOW(ever)* has been a sanctuary in which to hone, flex, inquire, from which to venture out."[6]

Editors and contributors were the first to see their magazines as objects worthy of study. William Carlos Williams, a contributor to many magazines, wrote in the first issue of the revived *Contact*, which he co-edited and published in 1932: "The 'small magazine' must, in its many phases, be taken as one expression. It represents the originality of our generation thoroughly free of an economic burden. . . . Nothing could be more useful to the present-day writer, the alert critic than to read and re-read the actual work produced by those who have made the 'small magazine' during the past thirty years."[7] Editors and contributors, like Williams, became and still are theoreticians and pedagogues of the little magazine and remedied canonical exclusions outside the university context long before the important work of professional scholars. Taking Williams's injunction "to read and re-read" to heart entails, as another early commentator noted, "trac[ing] the ebb and flow of ideas" across time.[8]

Previous avant-garde theorists, such as Benjamin Buchloh, Peter Bürger, Matei Calinescu, Clement Greenberg, Hal Foster, Paul Mann, Richard Murphy, Marjorie Perloff, and Renato Poggioli, have tended to consider avant-gardes as monolithic, homogeneous, and historical entities outside their material and social contexts.[9] They have either tended to repeat the self-theorizations of avant-garde writers or have based their interpretations on a very selective range of documents and objects. Rather than extracting the most hermeneutically promising examples, I treat little magazines as avant-garde communities and art objects in themselves. I demonstrate how avant-garde magazine networks sometimes subvert or strategically shape the institutional discourses and labels that have entered the canon. By "canon," I mean the processes of aesthetic judgments that lead to a sanctioned body of "great" literature and art according to prevailing academic and popular accounts, as well as the alternative, putatively anti-canonical, but equally sanctioned, avant-garde canon, erected by practitioners and critics wishing to differentiate avant-gardism from the so-called mainstream.[10] Challenging avant-garde theorists' focus on canonicity, as well as anti-canonicity, requires encountering texts in their original publication contexts rather than as canonized and decontextualized objects of study. What Jerome McGann terms the "bibliographical code" of a text (whether in print or online), which might include layout, design, ink, paper, binding, screen size, display of images, and typography, must be incorporated in a study of avant-garde publishing communities.[11]

Given how influential the material turn and periodical studies have been in literary studies, and modernist studies in particular, it is surprising how little research has been done, comparatively speaking, on the material and cultural contexts and objects that supposedly gave rise to generally accepted truths about particular avant-garde groups or individual writers within them.[12] While periodical studies and the new modernist studies have remedied avant-garde theory's lack of historicist and material considerations and have expanded modernism's geographical, temporal, and medial range, these approaches remain focused on the modernist period.[13] *Provisional Avant-Gardes* fills this gap by offering an extensive diachronic study of avant-garde print communities beyond modernism. Rather than following the negative view that later avant-garde communities have ridden on the coattails of modernist innovation, this book reveals how they have often reinvented the periodical form for their own concerns or engaged in a textual conversation with previous magazine communities, as did avant-gardes before them. Avant-gardes simply do not have singular, historical existences that clearly separate them from each other by period, practice, or social affiliation. This networked and diachronic view of avant-garde groups provides a more nuanced reading of the "old vs. new" debate and the avant-garde's supposed revolt against tradition, because it locates revolt as well as the continuation of tradition within the magazine medium.

Little magazine contributors are often republished in subsequent magazines. They may appear in the form of a reprint, write new work, or be discussed by other poets, whether for contrast or for legitimation. Each time, that contributor may appear contemporary—a fact that calls for a radical revision of our understanding of avant-gardes. The Gertrude Stein in the 1922 Picabia issue of *The Little Review* (the anarchist feminist magazine run by two lesbians, who had, in the previous year, been sued in an obscenity trial for publishing excerpts of James Joyce's *Ulysses*), in the eight-volume Yale University edition of her posthumous works in the 1950s, in the proto-conceptual *0 to 9* in the 1960s, in the theory-heavy *L=A=N=G=U=A=G=E* in the 1970s, in the feminist *HOW(ever)* and *HOW2* in the 1990s and early 2000s, or in Holly Melgard's 2012 PDF publication *The Making of the Americans* (which rids Stein's *The Making of Americans* of all repeated words) always appears in a new social, aesthetic, and institutional setting. Each time, she is "contemporary" in a different way, and each publication, in turn, is avant-garde in a different way.

Generations of practitioners cannot be clearly separated from one another; writers do not just cease to publish when a movement is supposed to have ended. Sometimes writers change their practice or their affiliation, or they belong to several groupings simultaneously. David Antin's genealogical metaphor of his magazine's "kinship," with "remote ancestors or merely peripheral relatives," illustrates how magazines often refer to other magazines in order to be legible as part of a network.[14] *The Little Review* editor Margaret Anderson, for example, presented the Pre-Raphaelite *Germ* as an antecedent to her new magazine,[15] as did Macgregor Card and Andrew Maxwell, who published a contemporary *Germ* between 1997 and 2005 both in print and online as the "PRB," an abbreviation that pays homage to the Pre-Raphaelite Brotherhood but also stands for "Poetic Research Bloc." Williams, in turn, wrote the first bibliography of "the advance guard magazine" for his magazine *Contact*—a project of making the marginal visible. Such projects today are considered both aesthetic and political, as in the annual "VIDA Count," in which the online feminist organization VIDA: Women in Literary Arts publishes statistics of the disparities of race, ethnicity, gender, sexuality, and ability in American publishing, reviews, and prizes. In 1976, *Studio International*, a reinvention of the 1893-founded *The Studio*, sent a questionnaire to other magazines in its special "Art Magazines" issue and listed a London reprinting service for such avant-garde magazines as *291*, *The Blind Man*, and *Broom*.[16] In 2006, *Frieze* sent the *Studio International* questionnaire to thirty-one contemporary magazines to find out if the questions posed thirty years ago were still relevant to magazine editors and artists today.

Diachronic reading has also become easier over time. Access to limited-run publications by a wide range of readers was facilitated by the emergence of cheap distribution and reprint services in the 1960s and 1970s, such as Bookpeople and Small Press Distribution in Berkeley, the Inland Book Company in Connecticut, and Printed Matter, the Segue Foundation, and the *L=A=N=G=U=A=G=E* Distributing Service in New York. In 1967 the Coordinating Council of Literary Magazines was founded, and it supported the launch of the Print Center in New York, which was set up to help magazines produce their issues cheaply. Beginning in the 1960s, the Kraus Reprint Corporation issued reprints of out-of-print little magazines, among them *The Little Review* and *The Dial*, making them more affordable. Today, historical magazine communities have a second life in archives, classrooms, and reprints or as PDFs and JPEGs on personal blogs and on private computers and, occasionally, as expensive collectors' items (a single issue of *some/thing* with its famous Andy Warhol cover, for example, now sells for more than $1,000). Some avant-garde practitioners see the archival and institutional survival of magazines and avant-garde work as a sign of co-optation. Others who archive, write through, or teach with these collections see it as an extension of their political, aesthetic, and pedagogical practice.

In *Provisional Avant-Gardes*, I ask how avant-garde groups form and dissolve, how they define themselves, and what kinds of roles they fulfill in later communities and academic scholarship. Asking these questions involves three particular subsets of inquiry that are mutually informing. First, I read poetic experiments alongside the materiality of magazines—their design, typography, and print technology. I examine how developments in print technology such as the letterpress, mimeography, xerography, and digital publishing change how magazine communities function. There are significant *material* considerations, from tangible letterpress impressions on the page, to mimeograph smudges, to the bureaucratic and activist associations of Xerox, to the assumed democracy of digital formats. Second, I consider the social contexts into and out of which groups grow, such as the events, salons, and readings they organize and attend, and who is included and excluded. Third, I read an avant-garde group's own statements, published in magazines or shared in correspondence, as well as contemporaneous reviews. Reviews at once serve a reviewer's own agenda and give us a unique, if mediated, insight into a history of reading. Taken together, these aspects can aid our understanding of editorial policies, changing tastes and values, sociality and friendship, and the institutionalization of a particular writer, group, or aesthetic practice. This inquiry—material, group-oriented, and textual—allows me to show how avant-garde vocabulary, such as radicalism, experiment, critique, anti-traditionalism, or innovation, becomes established, either as specific to one avant-garde group or as an avant-garde characteristic more broadly.

Beyond a Theory of the Historical Avant-Garde

Avant-garde is a label that most scholars of avant-garde work either leave unquestioned or theorize to the point of limiting its application. Since the appearance of Peter Bürger's seminal *Theory of the Avant-Garde*, critics have emphatically reiterated the avant-garde's institutional critique and drive to integrate art into life.[17] Bürger established a discourse, and while its key concepts have been bandied about or, when refuted, have served as the authority against which critics rebel, neither corroboration nor rejection has led to a new theory from the ground up. Given that extended critiques of Bürger's theory are numerous, I will not revisit them here, but some arguments from his work and avant-garde scholarship more broadly are worth rehearsing, as they have shaped contemporary critical discussion and avant-garde self-understanding.[18]

Scholars of the avant-garde tend to reflect one of three broad tendencies: there are those who emphasize the avant-garde's revolutionary politics, those who focus on aesthetics, and those who attempt to merge the two. For Bürger, the avant-garde is the most vocal opponent to bourgeois life and art and attempts to destroy their values by means of a radical negation of individual creation and reception. The avant-garde's institutional critique is not merely directed at the museum per se but at "the way art functions in society."[19] The notions of the "transformation of everyday life" and revolutionary utopia are still pervasive in the avant-garde discourse of critics and practitioners alike, and they continue to appear in magazines in many guises.[20]

Often paired with aesthetic categories of the "new," "modern," and "experimental," both avant-gardism and modernism are usually defined against the so-called mainstream or mass culture, where avant-gardism is understood to be the more aesthetically and politically radical of the two.[21] In 1939, Clement Greenberg presented the avant-garde as an heir to the Enlightenment, whereas kitsch, as the avant-garde's reverse image and the product of ever-expanding capitalism, provided only the "simulacra of genuine culture," easy pleasure and consumption.[22] For Theodor Adorno and Max Horkheimer, likewise, good art cannot be fun, since "amusement . . . is indeed escape, but not, as it claims, escape from bad reality but from the last thought of resisting that reality."[23] But such clear-cut distinctions between modernism and avant-gardism or avant-gardism and the "mainstream" are difficult to maintain. Many avant-gardes engaged with popular forms, as did avant-garde and media critics like Walter Benjamin.[24] In addition to political transformation and aesthetic originality, the notion of rupture appears regularly in theories of the avant-garde and modernity.[25] Avant-gardes are commonly defined by a "radical break with tradition" or critical consensus; some critics consider them literally unthinkable as a continuity.[26] Even formally the avant-garde possesses, in Marjorie Perloff's phrase, a "language of rupture."[27] Although the avant-garde's search for originality may be a myth that Rosalind Krauss has debunked, it is still a persistent one.[28]

Though the interrelatedness of the political and the aesthetic is not the sole purview of the avant-garde, the metaphoricity of the term *avant-garde* and its resulting vagueness have bestowed on it a distinct expectation, urgency, and promise of the superlative. Through its military etymology, denoting soldiers on the front lines of warfare, the avant-garde has been understood as a collective and mobile alliance of kindred spirits while retaining an association with conquest and violence.[29] This latter association is especially unhelpful when assessing contemporary avant-gardes, where an increasing dissatisfaction with that discourse can be felt in the face of actual racial, sexual, and gendered violence.

Like the manifesto, the avant-garde is often seen to "borrow its authority from the future," as Martin Puchner suggests.[30] Its association with revolutionary politics has led some critics to proclaim the avant-garde's inevitable failure. In Bürger's dialectical theory, his coinage of the "historical avant-garde," by which he meant primarily Dada, early surrealism, and Russian Futurism, already nominally excluded the possibility of a diachronic avant-garde or of lasting success.[31] In effect, Bürger wrote the history of the (supposed) failure of a particular historical avant-garde. While Bürger dismissed the post–Second World War "neo-avant-garde" as no true successor to the historical avant-garde, because it established the historical avant-garde as an institution, various critics rightly see postwar artists and writers as the equals of early twentieth-century practitioners in their innovations.[32] Sometimes, however, critics enlist features associated with Bürger's theory, like "parody" or "anti-aesthetics," to prove that this or that avant-garde is the legitimate heir of the historical avant-garde.[33] So the question remains how we can discuss not-yet-canonized avant-gardes or those on the avant-garde's periphery without recourse to Bürger's vocabulary. If prevalent discourses about avant-gardes have recurrent features, this is partly the result of an availability heuristic (a mental shortcut to the most easily remembered example) in debates about the avant-garde. Critics and artists expect certain outcomes of potential avant-gardes, expectations that are patterned by the narratives of previous avant-gardes and their critics. Many morticians of the avant-garde list as the cause of its death the political inefficacy of art, the evacuation of politics *from* art, or the impossibility of continuous shock and innovation.[34] Avant-gardes are expected to operate within a matrix defined by brief flares of success and eventual failures, embodied by an incorporation into the mainstream, the university, or the museum.

We can see how incompatible the avant-garde and institutions are still seen to be in Ben Hickman's 2015 statement that "an avant-garde in a university is a contradiction in terms," perhaps a nostalgic irony for a critic writing about the avant-garde in precisely such a university context.[35] Definitions based on an opposition between avant-gardes and institutions are inadequate once avant-gardes are viewed within their "complex social realities."[36] Many small presses, like John Rodker's and Mary Butts's Ovid Press, sold deluxe editions of their books, deliberately restricting supply and making their books valuable collectors' items (e.g., Sylvia Beach's fine edition of *Ulysses*), and many poets benefited from the institution of patronage or set up their own institutions (one might think of Marcel Duchamp, Katherine Dreier, and Man Ray's Société Anonyme Inc. or the Jack Kerouac School of Disembodied Poetics at Naropa). Indeed, there are, as poet and editor Charles Bernstein puts it, "provisional institutions" in the form of small presses, magazines, and reading series, or in the form of the modernist collection (as Jeremy Braddock has suggested for archives, private collecting, as well as collage as a stylistic example of a "collecting aesthetic"), that offer alternatives to more established or commercial institutions.[37] At the same time, many soi-disant anti-institutional avant-garde enterprises often served the institutional careers of men.[38] In response to the domination of avant-garde scholarship and practice by men, many critics have insisted rightly on using feminism to analyze avant-gardism and on regarding feminism itself as an avant-garde.

Importantly, the status of an artist is, as Hal Foster recognizes, "a retroactive effect of countless artistic responses and critical readings."[39] If we took such observations seriously, they would change the way we conceive of literary history. Being more aware of the provisionality of groups and of how critics have shaped the canon would be a step in that direction. We need to look beyond the search for an "effectiveness" understood as "the revolutionizing of the praxis of life," to instead look toward participants who debate such effectiveness in little magazines and to ask whether effectiveness is even a useful measure for success.[40] We also need to account for the minor and irregular social and aesthetic changes, what Gabriel Rockhill calls "metastatic transformations."[41] In other words, aesthetic or political practices do not change or spread abruptly, nor do the changes follow a simple cause-and-effect logic.

What many critics forget when they declare the avant-garde's lack of shock value or an end of the avant-garde altogether is that avant-garde works do, in fact, still shock readers. While I disagree with Rita Felski's definition of the avant-garde as "over the top" or "in-your-face," I agree wholeheartedly that we need to "account for the shock of the old" (or the quiet), be it an avant-garde or any other work.[42] Avant-garde works often continue to surprise, delight, or inspire after multiple readings or viewings. Felski calls for models that explain this "continuing timeliness," and this is my own point of departure.[43] To read historical and contemporary work side by side in a new temporal conjunction inside and across magazines can also helpfully undo the hierarchy between works that the terms *belatedness* and *afterlives* often imply.

Magazine Networks

Given that most avant-garde and modernist practitioners published their work initially or exclusively in magazines, modernist scholars and scholarly initiatives like the digital Modernist Journals Project have forcefully demonstrated that our notions of modernism and modernity need to be grounded in detailed material research.[44] Critics have investigated the material and cultural contexts of texts, their reception and circulation; they have found that modernist magazines shaped the discourses we now consider characteristically modernist; and they have treated periodicals as objects of literary and historical value in their own right.[45] But even the seminal three-volume *Oxford Critical and Cultural History of Modernist Magazines* ends in the 1960s, and while Eric Bulson's necessary revision of the magazine as a "world form" helpfully expands the field geographically and discusses digitizations, there is a big scholarly gap between the 1960s and the present.[46] It is simply scholarly hubris to consider the avant-garde a period, age, or era, or finite and originary, as the labels "historical avant-gardes" and "modernist magazines" imply. Victorianists discussed periodicals a decade before modernist studies focused on them, and avant-garde little magazines after 1960 remain rarely studied despite the concept of the avant-garde continuing to have contemporary critical purchase.[47]

Although magazines may look like little books, their mode of circulation aims toward periodicity, sometimes evident in a date and volume declaration or generic identifiers such as *monthly*, *quarterly*, or *review*. In theory, a magazine appears more than once, thus making each issue more unfinished than a book or anthology. Magazines also usually have multiple contributors, who produce heterogeneous contents. These features—provisionality, periodicity, multiple authorship, heterogeneity of contents—allow for a reflection on avant-garde community formation that is historically more variegated and less reductive than an emphasis on individual works or authors. From advertisements, illustrations, announcements, editorial statements, typography, and design, to accompanying archival materials (letters, receipts, mailing lists, etc.), magazines are stereoscopes that allow for an in-depth view of an avant-garde group. Although I am not the first to highlight the heterogeneity and provisionality of avant-garde magazines, these observations have not yet had the effect on critical analysis or wider reading practices that they merit.[48]

Definitions of the little magazine have been debated as hotly as those of the avant-garde, and these definitions resemble one another in telling ways. In the first extensive bibliography of little magazines, in 1946, Frederick J. Hoffman, Charles Allen, and Carolyn F. Ulrich described little magazines as standing "defiantly in the front ranks of the battle for a mature literature," thus echoing the avant-garde's supposed foray into new territory.[49] For Elliott Anderson and Mary Kinzie, little magazines "generally put experiment before ease," "can barely 'afford' to do anything," and "as a rule they do not, and cannot, expect to make money."[50] More recently, Suzanne Churchill and Adam McKible similarly foreground the little magazine's "aesthetic experimentation and political radicalism."[51] Little magazines are, indeed, usually anti-commercial, but we must not forget that many contributors and editors have been interested in accruing financial security, as well as cultural capital, or can simply afford not to worry about commercial viability.

Paying attention to the "sociology of texts," including print runs, price, and audience reception, means acknowledging overlaps between so-called mass-market or canonical publications and avant-garde, small-press publications, as Lawrence Rainey, Mark Morrisson, and others have shown—as well as rebutting Bürgerian critics who wish to maintain the distinction between mainstream and avant-garde.[52] Robert Scholes and Clifford Wulfman contend that "we must learn to stop talking, writing, and thinking as if the category of 'little magazines' represented something real in the textual world. It is a dream category, an attempt to unite periodicals of which the uniter approves and exclude those lacking such approval."[53] The same could, of course, be said of "the avant-garde." These two dream categories, then, meet in the rich material reality of print. I do not wish to give up on either category; instead, I want to take the dreaminess of the categories, or what I refer to as their "proto-ness," and lodge it at the center of their definitions.

While the oft-proclaimed avant-garde craving for newness seems perfectly suited to the built-in periodicity of the magazine, in which each issue surpasses the previous one, the apparent obsolescence of old issues is deceptive. Avant-garde magazines, unlike newspapers, are rarely out of date. In fact, as subsequent little magazines often attest, magazines retain interest and cultural value to other practitioners and readers long after they cease to publish. At the same time, the magazine's seriality and its usually multi-authored volumes offer instances of materially and historically specific collectivities that are often abstractly valued as the avant-garde's supposed demolition of individual authorship and genius. The dialogic and collective nature of magazines therefore requires integration into a theory of avant-garde groups.

Today, increasing critical attention is being paid to the role of community in experimental writing, to the social and institutional environments within which poets move, and to the poem itself as a site for sociality.[54] The magazine communities under discussion display ongoing processes of community building in their pages and beyond. They often reject programs, but they also want to create their own canons or institutions on their own terms. While most of these magazines never produced a so-called manifesto, they sometimes published work that partook of that sort of tone or was later read by critics as such. Benedict Anderson famously argued that imagining others simultaneously reading the newspaper helped readers conceive of themselves as members of a nation, thus fashioning "imagined communities."[55] For avant-garde magazines, these acts of imagination function similarly. Contributors and readers frequently thank editors for the "gift" of a magazine that makes them aware that there are others "at the outside edges" who share their feelings and opinions about literature, art, publishing, or politics.[56] Kathleen Fraser saw her feminist magazine *HOW(ever)* as part of an effort toward "building a much-needed community" for female writers and readers, viewing her publishing medium as conducive to her social aspirations.[57] Even so, we cannot presume that every community is therefore cohesive. Reflecting on community also entails recognizing its deficiencies, exclusions, and differences. Furthermore, avant-garde "interpretive communities" are composed of participants who belong to multiple reading communities and "who may disagree . . . fundamentally over the nature and purpose of reading itself" and, I would add, the purpose of an avant-garde.[58]

Ideally, a little magazine establishes a commons, with inclusive and distributed ownership. But most magazines and literary communities define themselves or are defined as much by their outsides as their insides. Not everyone who wants to take part actually can, and the commons are patrolled by editors and critics. The magazine communities in this book dealt with questions of inclusivity in a variety of ways, and I consider both contemporary and retrospective criticism by participants and readers, particularly in regard to some communities' "compulsory homosociality"[59] and to the often insufficient "racial dynamics of the avant-garde."[60] Many studies still assume conceptual unity among the groups they describe and often speak of "movements" or well-established figures within them, take a group's avant-gardeness for granted, or are still heavily author-focused, even though "the avant-garde is, we are told again and again, a communal enterprise by definition."[61] We still need to theorize the link between aesthetic practice, materiality, and group-formation across time and to examine how close-knit a community truly was or is.

One way of beginning to reconceptualize the avant-garde is to think of it as a network of "writing *communities*" rather than as a "school" or "movement."[62] In what follows, I introduce the concept of the "proto-form," which is intended to describe provisional avant-garde print communities that form in and around magazines. Although it is yet another label, the term implies a critique of previous conceptions of the avant-garde. This seems to me a simple and pragmatic solution. In my focus on avant-garde communities of print across time, I ask how it was and is possible to write and read a community today.

Provisional Communities of Print

The two principal arguments of this book are that the magazine is the medium through which we can analyze the collective and collaborative work of writers, editors, and readers across time and that artists on the periphery of an avant-garde group can revise our understanding of that group. But I also highlight that margin and center are often not so clearly separable. I track both self-identified avant-gardes and literary communities generally excluded from canonical versions of avant-gardism, for whom the little magazine became an important vehicle for politics, formal innovation, and social interaction. The majority of the selected avant-garde communities rethink the format of the magazine and the form of writing itself, often resulting from the impacts of changing print technologies on creative practice, reception, and sociality. The result is a new story about avant-gardes, one that reflects on cultural transmission, as well as on literary communities' negotiations of, say, gender, inclusivity, and formal experiment, as intimately tied to their chosen publishing medium.

Magazines, individual contributors, and specific aesthetic forms that diverged from the canonical version of particular avant-gardes may cease to participate in a wider print culture for a number of reasons. These range from an individual's change of career, affiliations, aesthetics, or politics; to low visibility brought about by a physical or published absence from poetry scenes; to lack of cultural capital, institutional support, or scholarly evaluation; to the individual's gender, sexuality, or race. Literary and art history privilege typicality, convenience, and already existing cultural capital. Postulating a coherent group with eloquent, rhetorically strong voices and memorable characteristics makes entry into a canon more likely, but we cannot construct a blueprint that is valid for all avant-gardes. When magazines or contributors do not construct their own taste or group belonging beyond the mere presentation of poetic material, recognition of the magazine's or contributor's innovation or impact is less likely, and the work is more susceptible to canonical attrition. Sometimes deliberately resisting programmaticity and endorsing provisionality prevented or slowed down incorporation into the avant-garde or mainstream canon. Many avant-garde magazine networks and participants within them are therefore excluded from literary and art history or from critical writing on a particular avant-garde, despite the strength and influence of their aesthetic, political, or social affiliations. This observation has far-reaching implications for an institutional pedagogy, especially for researching and teaching the avant-garde today.

Virginia Jackson's claim that "to be lyric is to be read as lyric" is instructive for a contemporary model of avant-gardism: modes of reading determine the understanding of their objects, even their material form and creative practice.[63] In the same way, to be avant-garde is to be read as avant-garde. This is no facile statement—the scholar throwing up her hands in the face of a definitional Möbius strip. Rather, it acknowledges changing tastes and affiliations and moves the inquiry away from aporia toward the discourses that have shaped what we understand avant-gardes to be. I analyze scholarly interventions and the avant-garde's own hermeneutic apparatus not to validate their authenticity but to understand self-theorization as one among many practices in which avant-gardes engaged and to show how critics had a hand in avant-garde history.

Magazines may help us discern how new work was experienced by readers, though letters to the editor are not always verifiable (were they written by readers or by the editors themselves? and who were these readers?), and much information about editing decisions, circulation figures, or reading habits is simply missing. The mutability and transience of the text, its unreliable and problematic transmission through history, need a place within theorizations of the avant-garde. Ralph Cohen's criticism of an essentialist view of genre is instructive here: "Classifications are empirical, not logical," he argues, because they are "constructed by authors, audiences, and critics in order to serve communicative [i.e., social] and aesthetic purposes."[64] As such, any theory of genres must recognize that such "groupings arise at particular historical moments, and as they include more and more members, they are subject to repeated redefinitions or abandonment."[65] *Avant-garde* as an adjective often means something different from *avant-garde* as a noun, and it rarely means exactly the same thing. It will become clear that any view of "the" avant-garde is as untenable as a definition based on key formal features. The new theory of the avant-garde put forward in this book will therefore posit four criteria: (1) the avant-garde is a print or publishing community consisting of multiple participants and heterogeneous materials; (2) it usually engages inventively with its medium of publication; (3) it is provisional in its aims, practices, and participants; and (4) the avant-garde is what is called avant-garde. It is a discursive and malleable construct within a not necessarily cohesive interpretive community.

Archival research is indispensable to rethinking these provisional avant-garde groups and practices. Magazine archives, editorial and private correspondence, as well as ephemera relating to events and the practicalities of publishing offer no simple window into the past, but they can restore some of the multiplicity of forms and voices that scholarship often lacks. *Provisional Avant-Gardes* engages with the many stories and voices from the archive and with those discourses that prepare, contradict, accompany, and shape avant-garde practices. Archival materials reveal that groups and practices are often more provisional than established accounts of avant-gardes admit, thus inviting us to rethink the inevitability and meaningfulness of canonization. We need abundant historical records in order to understand avant-garde group formations, an approach that is sensitive to materiality, reception, and the politics of the archive—what is preserved and what is not—and that reflects not only on archival materials themselves but on their circulation as cultural and historical objects with present stakes across time.

If avant-garde studies often neglect the material aspect of aesthetic practices and the provisionality of groups, periodical studies often forget to ask those broader questions about aesthetics, politics, and the value of experimental writing beyond literary modernism, questions that are the staples of many avant-garde studies. This book tries to answer the questions sidelined in those respective fields, adding that it is through magazines across time that we can rethink the avant-garde as more than a historical phenomenon. I am sympathetic to the provisionality and multiple uses of "descriptive reading," which has been a tenet of book history for a long time and is particularly suitable to contemporary magazines, in order to facilitate and empower a hospitable and dynamic contemporary community.[66] Little magazines make visible the missing connection between early twentieth-century avant-gardes and DIY print communities later in the century. They continue to offer avant-gardes the ideal form in which to imagine themselves as part of a network or group and to articulate their miscellaneous aesthetics and politics. The theory that I develop based on the provisionality and heterogeneity of avant-garde groups will be affirmed in each chapter, but the stories I tell to reach that conclusion will be different every time. Each magazine community possesses its own provisionalities and heterogeneities.

My project is based on the premise of historical recovery and on an intervention in the present, in both the scholarly and creative worlds I inhabit. When an object of study lies safely in the past, grand claims about it may be beyond rebuttal; but when the past has an active role in the present, critical appraisal and theorizing cannot be attempted without care and consideration for readers and practitioners across time. Although any recovery of neglected poets and issues is subject to the contingencies of individual taste and experience or the exigencies of the discipline, writing about the present entails additional nagging doubts. In our critical desire for exemplarity, why should this particular author or magazine matter to me or, indeed, to others? Analyzing and often criticizing the politics of inclusion in all my chapters, my own politics of inclusion, in particular for the present, has given me headaches. Selection is always necessary, but the case studies of the final chapter bear the additional weight of having been chosen from among my peers. I have selected magazines and publishing projects for their aesthetic and social links to previous magazine communities, for the ways in which they illuminate my recurrent interest in magazine hospitality and the self-conscious heritage of the small press or avant-garde, or because they engage in interesting ways with their publishing medium. I have largely refrained from writing about magazines in which I have published work, but in many cases I know editors and contributors, have published them, hosted readings for them, or have collaborated with them. As a participant-observer, I co-create an archive for the future, which comes with responsibility.

Bürger prioritized the avant-garde's politics and anti-institutional critique without questioning his own position within an institutional context that shaped his arguments. There is what Pierre Bourdieu calls a "cultural profit" to be gained for distinguished critics from their object of study's "rarity and from their discourse about it (after the show, over a drink, or in their lectures, their articles or their books), through which they will endeavour to appropriate part of its distinctive value."[67] The history of the avant-garde we have come to inherit is based on a history of reading innovative work in ways that capitalize on that work's distinctive quality. Thanks also to the New Critics' appraisal of difficult modernist poetry, and its incorporation into university syllabi, our own appreciation of the "difficult" as critics and poets has reinforced a striking difference from so-called mainstream and more accessible writing. These discourses of the experimental, often disguised as self-praise for either the critic or the poet, need to be interrogated alongside a reading of avant-garde practices. The avant-garde's supposed difficulty or inaccessibility has been called its democratic failure or its true democratic promise: either it fails to address the common reader, or, conversely, it emancipates that reader.[68] Ultimately, formal difficulty is a matter of taste and habit; in other words, if we are in the habit of reading difficult texts that are difficult in certain ways (say, they exhibit fragmented syntax), after a while they may no longer truly challenge us, because we are used to the intellectual and affective responses they ask us to perform. To understand how experiment, difficulty, and anti-institutional programs became established as avant-garde markers, we need to look at the little magazines that molded these discourses.

There are some high stakes in spending time with these avant-garde protoforms. The critical injunction to forever revise, add, qualify, and reread is, of course, the stuff that a scholar's career is made of. But a magazine's negotiation of hospitable editorship is also addressed to our own cultural and institutional present. It is my hope that this book not only speaks to the poets and readers within academia's increasingly precarious fold (by choice or circumstance) but that it is also informative, enjoyable, and useful for contemporary practitioners and editors of experimental work. In its investigation of historical and contemporary magazine trends from print to digital, *Provisional Avant-Gardes* argues that magazines demonstrate the culturally transformative power of print and generate lasting symbolic value for poetic communities. By studying avant-garde practices diachronically through little magazines, we apprehend the formations of our literary and political value systems, the developments of taste, the politics of inclusion and exclusion, and the potential roles of contemporary readers in attending to these issues.

1 The Magazine as Laboratory in New York Proto-Dada Communities

Proto-Dada Is Always Experimenting

Ezra Pound's essay "Small Magazines," published in *The English Journal* in 1930, established programmaticity and self-theorization as the signatures of the periodicals in which literary avant-gardes incubated: "periodicals in incubation can only be judged on their programs. . . . A review that can't announce a program probably doesn't know what it thinks or where it is going."[1] Indeed, magazines and groups that lacked programs have either been excluded from histories of the avant-garde or have been discussed within a framework that simply does not apply to those communities. Conversely, Alfred Stieglitz described *291*, a magazine that appeared through his gallery, by its very divergence from a consistent program: "'291' is always experimenting."[2] Dada is conventionally framed as a cohesive avant-garde movement that sports programmatic manifestos proclaimed by its most prominent figures—a narrative still dominated by originality myths despite the demolition of genius often ascribed to Dada. While Dawn Ades claims that "the centrality of [Dada's] little magazines to the many-headed phenomenon of Dada is well known," both studies and popular opinions of Dada tend to privilege the successful magazines, artists, and writers who have entered the canon, not necessarily questioning the ways in which we theorize avant-gardes around such figures and programmatic outlets.[3] The proto-Dada little magazine was a laboratory: it did not always "know what it thinks or where it is going."[4] As such, it serves as a test case for a new theory of the avant-garde: how can the avant-garde be adequately described as a print community in all its provisionality and complexity, and how can such an approach to Dada set a precedent for later and contemporary avant-gardes?

This allegedly ur-avant-garde movement may be examined afresh by reading four American magazines that were never entirely Dada: *291* (March 1915–Feb. 1916), *The Blind Man* (April–May 1917), *Others* (July 1915–July 1919), and *The*

Little Review (March 1914–May 1929).[5] All were published in New York City either exclusively or frequently, and they shared a number of contributors, some of whom would become known as Dadaists and many of whom frequented the same avant-garde circles, galleries, and salons. The convergence of proto-Dadaists in New York in the 1910s and early 1920s was no coincidence. A center for publishing since the nineteenth century, the city attracted artists, writers, intellectuals, and radicals from all over the world, especially those fleeing the war in Europe, creating an abundance of aesthetic practices—an abundance strikingly evident in little magazines.

Emerging from Stieglitz's 291 Gallery at 291 Fifth Avenue, Manhattan, the magazine *291* was the collaborative product of Marius de Zayas (a Mexican artist and caricaturist), Agnes Ernst Meyer (a journalist, poet, and art collector), Paul Haviland (a French American art critic and photographer), and Stieglitz (in the capacity of publisher). Alongside their own work, the editors published Guillaume Apollinaire, Georges Braque, Max Jacob, Pablo Picasso, Katharine Rhoades, Francis Picabia, Edward Steichen, Abraham Walkowitz, and others. The magazine promoted new photography, early collage work, visual poetry, and machine drawings.

The Blind Man emerged from another informal center of New York Dada—that of the Arensberg circle, based at 33 West Sixty-Seventh Street.[6] The editors Beatrice Wood (an actress, artist, and later ceramicist), French artist Henri-Pierre Roché, and Marcel Duchamp founded the magazine to support first the Society of Independent Artists' inaugural exhibition and then the rejected submission of R. Mutt's (in)famous *Fountain* to said exhibition. Its two issues published the editors, Walter Arensberg, Gabrielle Buffet, Charles Demuth, Charles Duncan, Mina Loy, Allen and Louise Norton, Francis Picabia, Erik Satie, Joseph Stella, Alfred Stieglitz, and Clara Tice, among others.

Others: A Magazine of the New Verse was edited by Alfred Kreymborg out of Ridgefield, New Jersey; New York; Chicago; and then again New York. Helen Hoyt, Lola Ridge, William Carlos Williams, and Maxwell Bodenheim variously acted as associate or guest editors. Other contributors included Djuna Barnes, H.D., T. S. Eliot, Amy Lowell, Marianne Moore, Ezra Pound, Man Ray, Carl Sandburg, and Wallace Stevens. *Others* is often compared to Chicago's *Poetry*, where Pound served as foreign editor and which he offered as an example of a functioning magazine thanks to his own intervention in the "Small Magazines" essay mentioned above. Unlike *Poetry*, *Others* quickly became known as one of the most politically and aesthetically radical magazines of its day. The contributors often met at Kreymborg's shack in Grantwood, New Jersey, and at avant-garde salons in Greenwich Village.

The Little Review advertised itself as "a magazine written for Intelligent People who can Feel, whose philosophy is Applied Anarchism."[7] This fiercely feminist periodical published experimental poetry, criticism, epistolary exchanges, and articles about marriage and birth control. Founding editor Margaret Anderson (previously a reviewer for Chicago magazines) was soon joined by her co-editor and lover Jane Heap (who had worked as an art teacher) and later by Ezra Pound as temporary foreign editor. Published first out of Chicago, then San Francisco, New York, and lastly Paris, the magazine included an impressive mix of American and European artists and writers, such as Guillaume Apollinaire, Hart Crane, H.D., T. S. Eliot, Emma Goldman, Ernest Hemingway, Wyndham Lewis, Elsa von Freytag-Loringhoven, Mina Loy, Francis Picabia, Man Ray, Gertrude Stein, Jean Toomer, Tristan Tzara, William Carlos Williams, and W. B. Yeats. It is well-known for its serialization of James Joyce's *Ulysses*.

These four magazines and their contributors have sometimes been grouped among the "first" American avant-garde. They have also sometimes been called, in constellation with other magazines, "New York Dada" or "proto-Dada."[8] Other terms, such as *Futurism*, *simultaneism*, *cubism*, *modernism*, and simply *modern*, were often used or ridiculed interchangeably by magazine contributors themselves.[9] By calling these magazines proto-Dada, I do not wish to imply a teleology toward the arrival of monolithic Dada but hope to identify a provisional network of practitioners with multiple affiliations who sometimes engaged critically and creatively with the practices of Dada, though not necessarily under that name.

The principal features of canonical Dada are often taken to be humor, chance, indeterminacy, irony, negativity, use of ready-mades or found objects, machine art, anti-art, irreverence toward the art world, rejection of the autonomous artwork, disgust, irrationality, and nonsense. Peter Bürger famously declared, "Dadaism, the most radical movement within the European avant-garde, no longer criticizes schools that preceded it, but criticizes art as an institution, and the course its development took in bourgeois society."[10] Bürger defined Dadaism by its intention, which was given material form in an (anti-)aesthetics of montage, collage, and chance procedures. Through close examination of the little magazines from the period, several of these posited political and aesthetic characteristics will prove flawed as historical descriptors; in other cases they make sense only when read as the products of collaboration, dialogue, or self-fashioning within magazines.

The Cabaret Voltaire is typically recognized as the birthplace of Dada and its venerable founders as the first Dadaists. As the contemporary American poet and painter Marjorie Welish puts it humorously in her poem "Wanted": "Dada 'was officially christened' on 5 February 1916. / vs / Yes but."[11] It is often argued that Dada was "largely a European phenomenon, which was transplanted into an American context," an account easily rectified when we observe that the group associated with New York Dada was active before Tzara's christening of "Dada" and when we trace its influence on the transatlantic avant-garde network through which magazines such as *291* traveled among groups.[12] When Francis Picabia contended that "Dadaism was invented by Marcel Duchamp and Francis Picabia—Huelsenbeck or Tzara found the word Dada," he offered an exemplary statement of self-fashioning Dada historiography and a purely male lineage.[13] Likewise, critics have described Duchamp as the "leader" of New York Dada.[14] Such playful origin myths highlight how the formation and canonization of group identities are based on selective inclusion. Putting the spotlight on these (often gendered) processes is important revisionist work necessary to a fuller understanding of every avant-garde group.[15] Sometimes the proto-Dada magazine community was—contrary to Pound's dictum—radically indecisive and nonprogrammatic; at other times it fashioned a narrative that has affected our understanding of Dada and the avant-garde ever since.

One way to describe proto-Dada print communities without taking group hierarchies as fixed, or taking programs at face value, is to return to their moments of "incubation" and explore the dynamics of group formation and self-definition in magazines. The magazines *291*, *The Blind Man*, *Others*, and *The Little Review* were laboratories—a term some magazines used themselves—for new typographies, verbal and visual collaborations, dialogues with each other and the public, and experiments that foregrounded the medium of the magazine itself. Editorial interventions, correspondence, and social gatherings contributed to the formation of a community of print and beyond. But communal longevity, inclusivity, or certainty was vexed. As many rude reviews and editorial rants imply, collectivity necessitated a willingness to disagree. By developing new critical languages to articulate their artistic innovations and views on group formation, these magazines allow us to reflect on our own reliance on these discourses today, setting the terms with which we now discuss avant-gardes, from experimentality, programmaticity (or lack thereof), provocation, and anti-institutionalism, to consistency. In this way, proto-Dada print communities help us trace an avant-garde lineage based on the medium of the magazine and to recalibrate avant-garde criticism.

Typography, Collaboration, and the Ready-Made Poem

Following Alfred Stieglitz's advancement of photography in *Camera Work* and 291 Gallery exhibitions, the first issue of *291* declared it would continue being "nothing but a laboratory, a place for experiments," but "with new problems to solve."[16] One such problem was the page as a terrain for typographical experimentation. While most commercial and large-circulation magazines kept text and illustrations separate, or printed text in neat columns, many avant-garde magazines mixed text and image and diverged from the rigid structures of the geometrically linear page. In particular, they mobilized, as Jay Bochner argues, the "double-page spread . . . [as] a privileged site for the avant-garde's battles, the more so for Dada."[17] Avant-garde communities increasingly conceived of the magazine medium as a space for dialogue between pieces, between art forms, where facing pages could function as an extended canvas—less battleground and more laboratory.

The first issue of *291* shows the magazine to be the test tube of the collaborative experiments with printing, design, and typography for which the historical avant-gardes, especially Dada, have become known. Though by no means widely discussed, *291* is often acknowledged as one of the first or "one of the most important early avant-garde magazines in America" that turned the magazine medium into an art form.[18] Its collaborative texts, typographical innovations, ironic machine drawings, collective approach to editing, artist statements, and interdisciplinary and aesthetically daring contributions make it an exemplary avant-garde production. Under 291 Gallery's wing nominally and financially, the magazine's editorial independence was visualized in the satirical depiction of Stieglitz on its first cover (fig. 1).

The parodic proto-Dada attitude of the cover's caricature jumps out at us like a jack-in-the-box or, more likely, a camera, referencing Stieglitz's leading role in the Photo-Secession movement. Unlike most American magazine covers of the period, which aimed for legibility and prioritized text and traditional typefaces, *291*'s cover declared its avant-garde ambitions with de Zayas's typographical

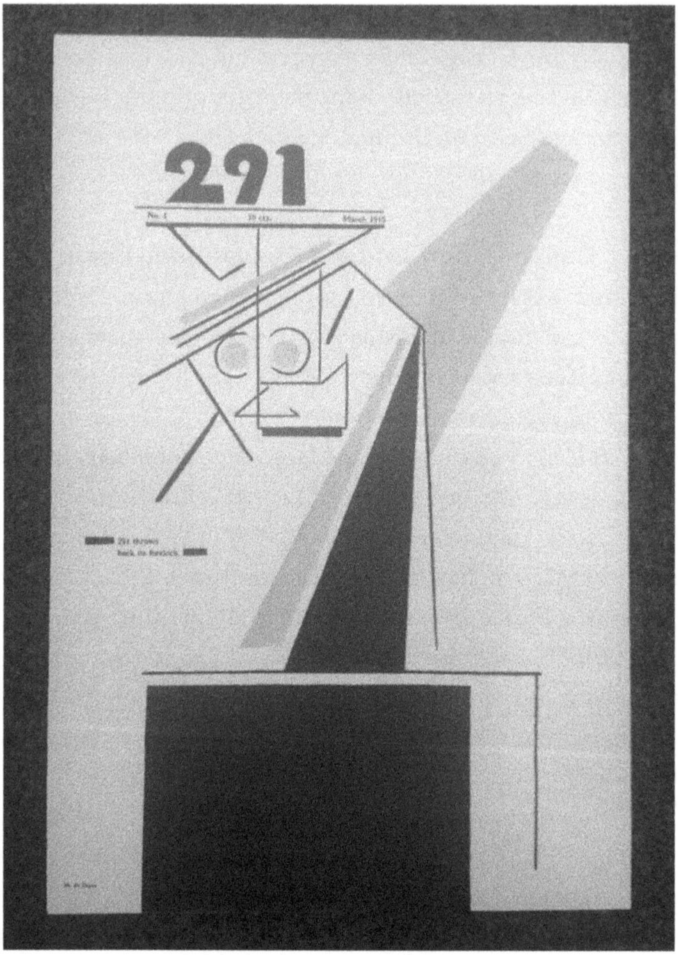

Figure 1. *291*, no. 1 (March 1915): cover. Courtesy of Marquand Library of Art and Archaeology, Princeton University.

"psychotype," an abstract caricature that integrated the bespoke and deliberately naive *291* logo (probably a linocut), as well as the bibliographical information of price and date into its architecture on the page.[19]

Replacing "FIXED laws" with "discoveries," *291* participated in the appropriation of scientific discourse that became popular among modernist and proto-Dada practitioners who used the language but not necessarily the method of scientific discourse. The magazine was even explicitly conceived as an experiment in print and typography, as advertised in *Camera Work*: "During 1915–1916, amongst other experiments, was a series with type-setting and printing. The experiments were based upon work which had been done with type and printers' ink, and paper, by Apollinaire in Paris, and by the Futurists in Italy. No work in this spirit had as yet been attempted in America."[20] In *Camera Work* and the 291 Gallery, Stieglitz had already emphasized experiment by calling his projects "laboratories," a label also claimed by *The Mask* for new experimental theater ventures since 1908, though the discourse of literary experiment began much earlier. In 1798, William Wordsworth called his *Lyrical Ballads* an experiment, describing his undertaking as a trial.[21] What was new about *291*'s (and other avant-gardes') concerted deployment of the term, however, was that the editors applied it to the print medium itself. Rather than using *experiment* as a synonym for a *new* project, *291* posited the pages of the magazine as a space for experimental activity.

The material encounter with the magazine is therefore important for understanding its production context (its innovations in printing, design, and typography) alongside its experimental content. Issues 1 and 5/6, for example, were six-page gatefolds (fig. 2)—where a sheet is folded into three panels, printed on both sides—making it a unique format among magazines of its time.[22] The abstract design of *291* anticipated many of the typographical experiments of European Dada magazines, preceded perhaps only by the odd trapezoidal shape of the one-off 1896 *Le petit journal des refusées*, published by Gelett Burgess out of San Francisco, with contributions (under female pseudonyms) by Burgess, Ernest Peixotto, Bruce Porter, and Porter Garnett. When looking at *291* in an archive, one immediately notices its size, which varied between 17 and 19 inches in height and 11 and 12.5 inches in width. Published in folio (except issues 1 and 5/6), the regular edition was printed on heavy buff paper, white paper, or heavy ivory paper; the deluxe version was printed on fine Japan vellum.[23] The first cover, like several pieces by de Zayas and Picabia throughout the run, combined black ink, graphite, and cut-and-paste typeset text on glossy paper that was glued to the cardboard, making it likely that the magazine was lithographed on an early offset press. While the size resembles newsprint, the paper's weight, similar to cover stock, gives the impression of a collation of drawings and thus of permanence and status. The deluxe edition, in name and material, indicates a richness of both content and financial backing (supplied by Agnes Ernst Meyer's husband); vellum, in turn—a material from traditional

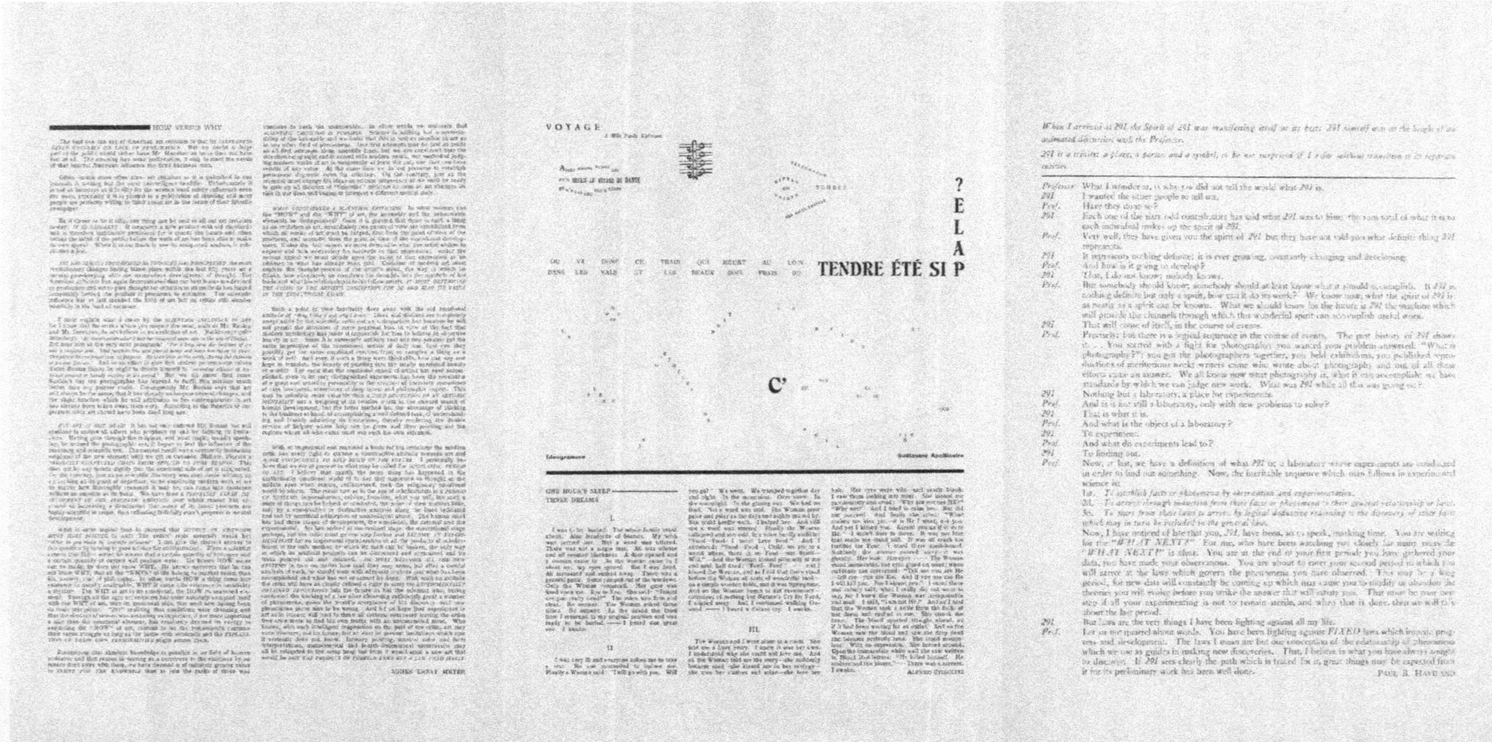
HOW VERSUS WHY
AGNES ERNST MEYER
VOYAGE
TENDRE ÉTÉ SI PALE ?
C'
Guillaume Apollinaire
ONE HOUR'S SLEEP —
THREE DREAMS
ALFRED STIEGLITZ
PAUL B. HAVILAND

Figure 2. *291*, no. 1 (March 1915): gatefold inside. Courtesy of Marquand Library of Art and Archaeology, Princeton University.

bookbinding—shows *291*'s connection to the past. Typographically decidedly modern, the magazine's high production values looked back to the book design of the Pre-Raphaelites and the *livres d'artistes* of fin de siècle aestheticism. Its design choices illustrate that the little magazine was a material object that invited attentive reading and needed to be distinguished from the low production values of mass-market printed matter, which had exploded in the nineteenth century.

Avant-garde magazines benefited from the typographical revolution of the 1910s, enabled by the increasingly widespread adoption of monotype technology and lithographic offset, which invited entirely new play with printing and typesetting, as well as faster production. More versatile than linotype (which printed a complete line), monotype, invented in 1884, enabled the mixing of typefaces within a word and irregular spacing. The rise of offset lithography and photolithography in the late nineteenth century, in turn, allowed typography to move beyond the seeming rigidity of metal-cast lines and facilitated the mixing of image and text. Concurrently, the invention of new typefaces gave type new expressive capacity. After all, typography had been dominated for almost four hundred years by the linearity and regularity introduced by movable type, continued in the nineteenth century by the linotype. New page design released syntactical possibilities and vice versa, but typographic innovations were primarily in *thinking* rather than a result of new technology per se.[24] Nevertheless, Dadaist and Futurist typographical innovations emerged out of experiments in advertising and were possible precisely because certain visual properties "had become sufficiently codified . . . [so] they could be manipulated" and used for the "subversive disruption" of authority and ideology.[25] For magazines like *291* to abandon strict adherence to vertical and horizontal axes and to mix text and image on the same page in complex ways was nothing less than radical, albeit not entirely new (Victorian literary periodicals had pioneered printing image and text on one page, and newspapers often exhibited the now-characteristic conglomeration of attention-seeking typefaces and type sizes).

The little magazine, then, became *the* medium in which experimental typography was developed, often as a collective and dialogic practice. Combining a poem by Meyer and graphic elements by de Zayas, "Mental Reactions" (fig. 3) was one of the first textual-visual collaborations that engaged with the new typography, to be published in an American avant-garde periodical.[26] The poem combines visual and syntactic experimentation with feminist critique:

> But is it fair
> to the woman? Parfumerie-de-Nice.
> Does it make her N-i-c-e.
> less—or more? Sunshine.
> Flowers.
> Color.
> Land of eternal loves.

The pun on "Parfumerie-de-Nice" and "N-i-c-e" is both funny and sharp; the typographical spacing ironizes the assumption that the female speaker cannot spell or pronounce the French "N-i-c-e." The things "woman" is expected to find "nice," such as flowers and eternal love, are reduced to boxes to be ticked. "Now if I were a man," the speaker sourly comments, "I should want to prove that I had lived even more dangerously. Being a woman, I am—silent"—a remark that reads as if the poem already anticipated its inferior place in a male-dominated canon. The formally innovative texture of the poem, in turn, is everything but silent.

The Dickinsonian dashes read both like the errant and not yet clearly articulated mental reactions of the speaker, but when they are overlaid by de Zayas, they also read like censored lines. Compared to the contemporaneous American free verse that appeared in *Poetry* and *The Little Review*, this March 1915 collaboration shows a rare emphasis on the mise-en-page. Sometimes de Zayas highlights the phrasal openness of Meyer's language with thicker dashes; sometimes Meyer's phrases such as "Clown," "Dancing buttons," and "Tilted hat" abandon the horizontal layout, thus disrupting linear reading and completing the abstract image on the page. De Zayas's graphic elements are in line with his abstract portraiture, which he exhibited at 291 Gallery, and, like the many typographically innovative texts in *291*, bear resemblance to the work of Apollinaire, whose "Idéogramme" appeared in the first issue, and to the Italian Futurists, whose magazine *Lacerba* would have been known to Stieglitz and his associates through Apollinaire. Meyer, in turn, was introduced to the French avant-garde in Paris through the Steins' salon.[27]

Looking back on these creative explorations in her 1953 memoir, Meyer remembers that "Stieglitz also encouraged the crazy experiments Marius de

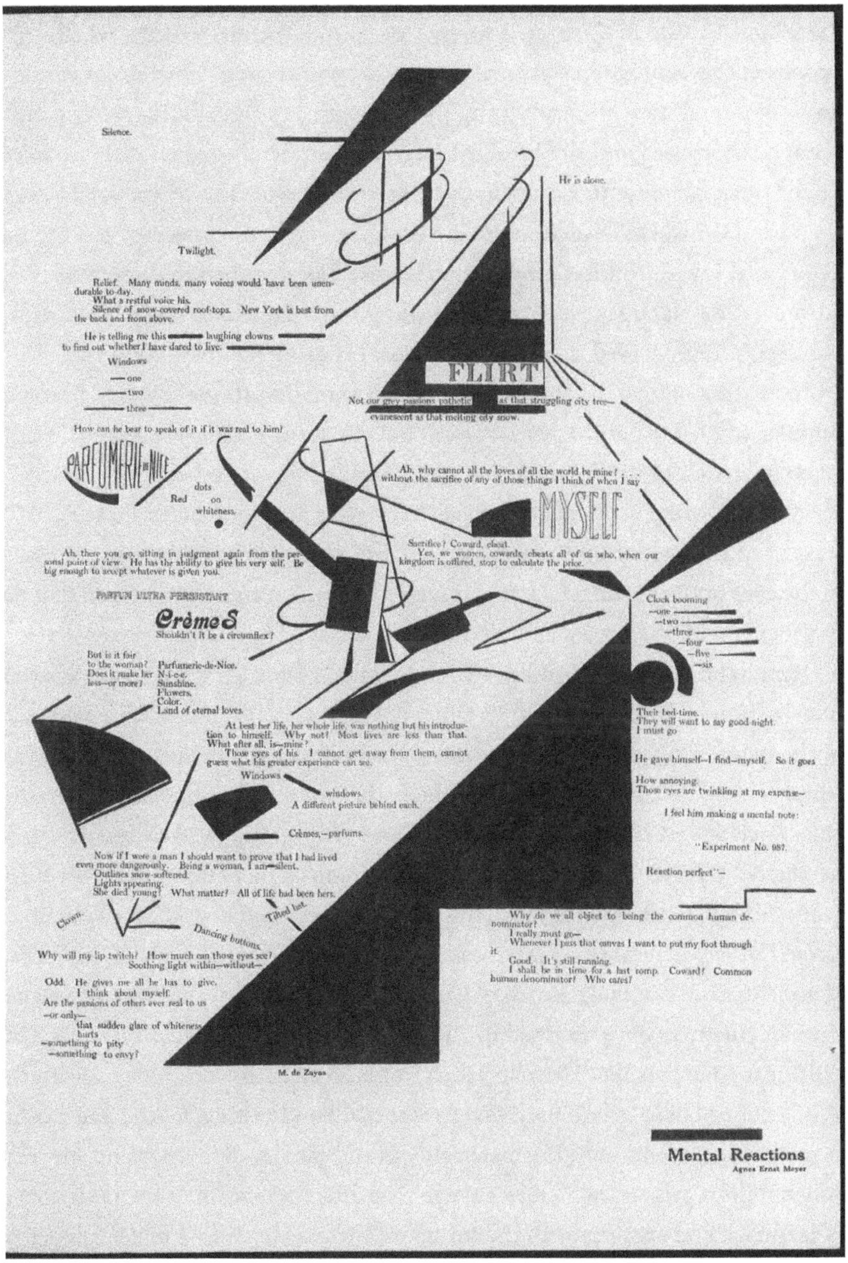

Figure 3. Agnes Ernst Meyer and Marius de Zayas, "Mental Reactions," *291*, no. 2 (April 1915). Courtesy of Marquand Library of Art and Archaeology, Princeton University.

Zayas and I made in illustrated 'stream-of-consciousness' writing, which was supposed to weld together the plastic and literary arts in a depiction of various levels of a total state of mind."[28] Highly aware of *291*'s contribution to contemporary literary and philosophical debates, she confidently asserts that "we were on the track of something only dimly understood before the crucial analyses of Freud and the works of such successful explorers of the unconscious as Virginia Woolf and Joyce."[29] Indeed, the poem's texture has absorbed multiple voices in such everyday language as "Ah, there you go" or "How annoying." De Zayas, correspondingly, called these typographical experiments "psychotypes."[30] This manipulation of type to express and visualize thought processes would become popular in Dadaist and Futurist work, but the term *psychotype* itself did not catch on as a description of the new typography that *291* so keenly endorsed.

"Mental Reactions" is also a collage. Its original maquette shows that "FLIRT" was cut-and-pasted from a magazine, then provocatively positioned in the place of the eyes of the profiled face.[31] This has led Francis Naumann to claim that de Zayas cut up Meyer's poem and rearranged it, collaged found text such as "Crème S," then hand-drew "Parfumerie-de-Nice" and "MYSELF."[32] Such an editorial intervention by de Zayas would certainly not be surprising, but we lack evidence of the typesetting and printing process. Naumann's explanation that de Zayas simply cut up the lines also seems unlikely when we look at a line like "Crème S" (in a thick advertising font that mimics handwriting) followed by the question of whether the French accent is correct—"Shouldn't it be a circumflex?"—which reads like a direct response to having found the collaged text. Meyer's memoir, quoted above, suggests a far more collaborative process at the heart of this piece. Naumann does not make much of the maquette's discovery, but it may well be the first cut-up poem published in America, and it even precedes the cutups of European Dadaists like Hannah Höch, John Heartfield, and Kurt Schwitters. While cubist collages had used text in stencils, handwriting, labels, and newsprint to draw attention to the materiality of the canvas, de Zayas's and Meyer's collaboration presents a literary collage that draws attention to the materiality of language and engages with the format of the magazine as a materially fixed form for representing simultaneous thoughts.

Collage, montage, and the fragmentary and nonorganic artwork are central tenets in Bürger's, Benjamin's, and Adorno's theories of modern art and literature. It would be easy to read *291* within the discourse of modernity as stipulated by those theories, and many avant-garde critics do just that: they apply specific features to a new set of avant-garde objects. One could, for instance, say that in Meyer's and de Zayas's collaboration neither text nor image is subservient to the other.[33] Such independence of parts is precisely what Bürger praised in the collages of Berlin Dadaist John Heartfield. Furthermore, "Mental Reactions" supports Bürger's claim that the historical avant-gardes negated individual production and reception. But unlike Benjamin, who reflects on media and new technology, Bürger does not consider magazines—a fact not to be dismissed lightly, given that most periodical studies scholars agree that magazines are not books, nor are they the products of single authors or artists. In *291*'s case, it is through attention to typography, layout, and, where available, editing and printing, in magazine collaborations like those described above, that we understand an avant-garde's working process as collective.

What Bürger called a "fragmentation of reality," or what is often considered a modernist fascination with representing consciousness, comes into play in the above collaboration's typographically innovative contribution to the discourse of "simultaneism."[34] From Apollinaire and Sonia and Robert Delaunay to Russian sound poems and experiments associated with Zurich Dada and Italian Futurist performance, simultaneist works explored the simultaneity of (sometimes discordant) voices, colors, and words, in an attempt to loosen temporal sequentiality and focus instead on presentness. Experiments with simultaneity in *291* might even have been an inspiration for other Dadaists and modernists.[35] In Europe, *291* was known thanks to its European contributors Apollinaire, Picasso, and Max Jacob—so much so that Ileana Leavens calls *291* an "almost certain" influence on *Cabaret Voltaire*.[36] Stieglitz also sent copies of *291* to Ezra Pound in 1915, and it is likely that the magazine introduced Pound to Dada.[37] But beyond its influence on other movements and writers, *291*'s simultaneism represented an experiment with and within the medium of the magazine.

According to the editorial notes in *291*'s first issue, "In literature the idea [of simultaneism] is expressed by the polyphony of simultaneous voices which say different things. Of course, printing is not an adequate medium, for succession in this medium is unavoidable and a phonograph is more suitable."[38] This inadequacy is then demonstrated in a rather tongue-in-cheek fashion:

> EXAMPLE:
> At the Arden Gallery, 599 Fifth Avenue
> "OH, COME ON, LETS GO TO
> MAILLARDS."

"I SAT NEXT REV.-AT GLADYS'
LUNCHEON."
"NOBODY COULD LOOK HUMAN
IN THESE FULL SKIRTS."
"DO YOU THINK HER HUSBAND
KNOWS IT?"
"SHE SAYS SHE'S A NEUTRAL
BUT–"

Here, *291* proves the limits of its medium by using that medium itself. Like a figure in a painting pointing to something beyond the frame, print can indicate but not represent. This rather inconspicuous note is also a clue to that issue's folding method: the gatefold is an attempt to create the semblance of simultaneity in the print medium. The short notice on simultaneism complements this experiment, inviting the reader to perform the lines—"All these phrases must be uttered simultaneously"—which is impossible unless they were read collectively. Here the materiality of print itself becomes central to the magazine's deliberately failing performance of simultaneity.

Incorporating a polyphony of voices into the texture of a piece became the core of a new poetic practice and a marker of a particular community. The discourse of experimentality entered proto-Dada magazines precisely through experiments with poetic form. When Mina Loy called Gertrude Stein the "Curie / of the Laboratory / of Vocabulary" in 1924, she transposed female scientific invention and discovery (the Nobel laureate Curie coined the term *radioactivity*) to specifically linguistic or poetic experiments.[39] Indeed, the case can be made that women like Loy, Stein, and Meyer were "the cause of modernism whatever that is," as Loy was introduced in an interview she gave in the *New York Evening Sun*, and little magazines were the venue for their innovations.[40] Although Loy is not generally considered a Dadaist, she contributed some of the most explicitly proto-Dada experiments to *The Blind Man*, engaging with "Dada notions of what the artist ought to be about" in "a mode of making that could be playful, provocative, and even political all at once."[41]

Loy's "O Marcel . . . Otherwise I Also Have Been to Louise's" (fig. 4) appeared in *The Blind Man* two years after *291*'s experiment with simultaneity.[42] Like *291*'s "Notes," Loy's simultaneist collage-poem quotes fragments of overheard conversation at an unspecified friendly gathering, mimicking everyday speech through paratactical insertions, non sequiturs, and prosodic variance (via capitalization), possibly modified for poetic effect or deformed by the dizziness of drink and the noisiness of simultaneous chatter. By mentioning her friends in a familiar manner—Marcel (Duchamp), Louise (Arensberg), Clara (Tice), and (Charles) Demuth—Loy not only signaled her membership within the Arensberg circle but wrote sociality into the poem's very texture—a feature famously taken up decades later by poets of the so-called New York School. Loy's poem is also a friendly jab at Duchamp, ironized in the title's apostrophe "O," which evokes the romantic ode but could also be read as an infantilizing exclamation, as if speaking to a child—"Oh, silly Marcel, you did it again . . ." In consonance with the teasing tone of the title, the slips and stutters easily read like the muddled speech and liberated (linguistic and erotic) play of a drunken party.

Critics have tried to attribute several sentences to Duchamp and debated which gathering Loy could have transcribed here, but the biographical detective work misses the point: Loy's appropriative method is a poetic translation of the ready-made.[43] Loy's found language shows an affinity with found objects, the most famous of which—*Fountain*—graced the same issue a few pages earlier. Signing her piece "Compiled by Mina Loy," Loy draws attention to her compositional method of *copying*, even withholding textual content via jokingly self-censoring ellipses, thus inviting readers to fill in the gaps or to see the lines as a visual composition. Laid out in columns in what looks like an early typewriter font (perhaps to mimic the note-taking of journalists and secretaries), Loy's device-laid-bare resembles, and may even have been influenced by, the insertion of clippings in different typefaces and the appropriation of speech in various Dada collages, and the simultaneist experiments in *291*, which Loy may have known, perhaps inspiring her to experiment with simultaneity and appropriation in little magazines. Tellingly, *The Blind Man*'s second issue added the subtitle "A Magazine of *Vers Art*." Borrowing from the French *vers libre*, the appellation combines the visual with the literary arts, while also evoking a sense of contrariness (*versus*). Although the magazine is not usually seen as a participant in the free-verse debate waged in *Poetry* magazine and elsewhere in the 1910s and early 1920s, Loy's "O Marcel"—which presented a new form of collagist poetry in that very "vers art" issue alongside experimental pieces by Robert Carlton Brown and Picabia—shows that *The Blind Man* was invested in free verse and was more than a prank magazine in the hands of Duchamp.

The innovative and provocative contributions and collaborations cannot hide the problematic representation of women elsewhere in little magazines.[44]

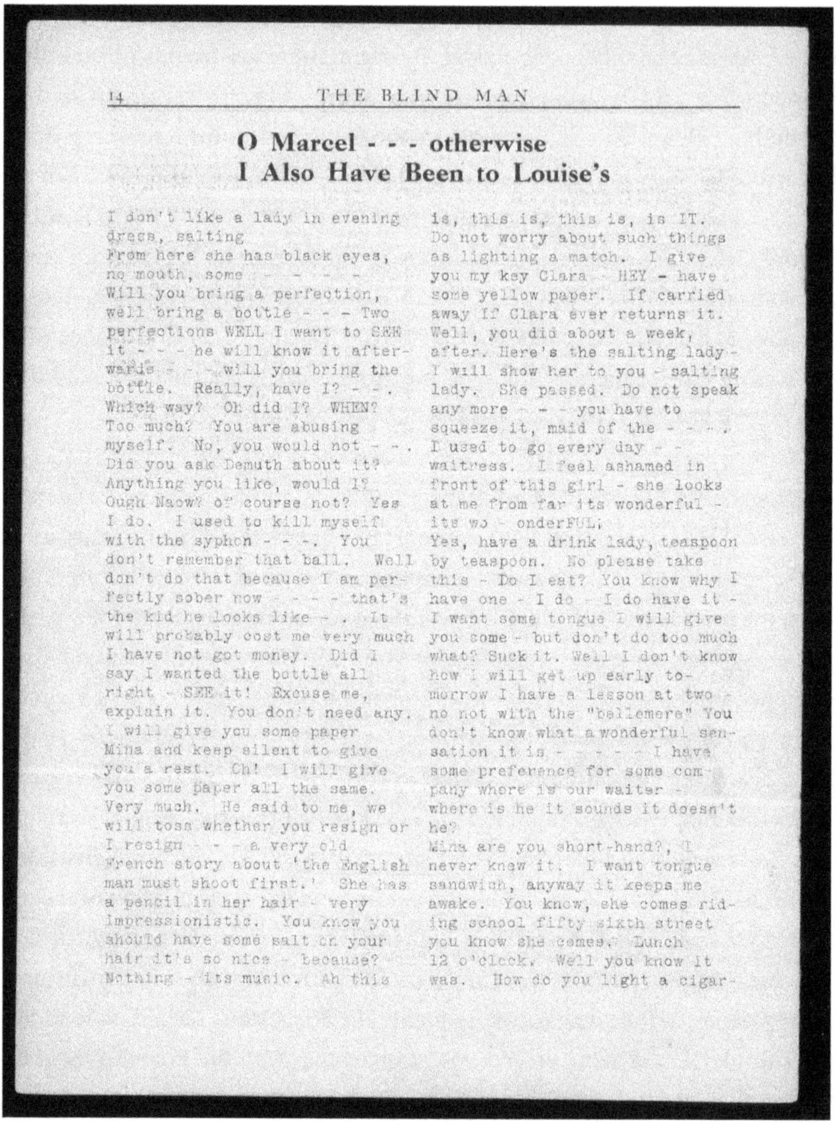

14 THE BLIND MAN

O Marcel - - - otherwise
I Also Have Been to Louise's

I don't like a lady in evening dress, salting
From here she has black eyes, no mouth, some - - - -
Will you bring a perfection, well bring a bottle - - - Two perfections WELL I want to SEE it - - - he will know it afterwards - - - will you bring the bottle. Really, have I? - - . Which way? Oh did I? WHEN? Too much? You are abusing myself. No, you would not - - . Did you ask Demuth about it? Anything you like, would I? Ough Naow? of course not? Yes I do. I used to kill myself with the syphon - - -. You don't remember that ball. Well don't do that because I am perfectly sober now - - - - that's the kid he looks like - . It will probably cost me very much I have not got money. Did I say I wanted the bottle all right - SEE it! Excuse me, explain it. You don't need any. I will give you some paper Mina and keep silent to give you a rest. Oh! I will give you some paper all the same. Very much. He said to me, we will toss whether you resign or I resign - - - a very old French story about 'the English man must shoot first.' She has a pencil in her hair - very impressionistic. You know you should have some salt on your hair it's so nice - because? Nothing - its music. Ah this is, this is, this is, is IT. Do not worry about such things as lighting a match. I give you my key Clara - HEY - have some yellow paper. If carried away If Clara ever returns it. Well, you did about a week, after. Here's the salting lady - I will show her to you - salting lady. She passed. Do not speak any more - - - you have to squeeze it, maid of the - - - . I used to go every day - - waitress. I feel ashamed in front of this girl - she looks at me from far its wonderful - its wo - onderFUL;
Yes, have a drink lady, teaspoon by teaspoon. No please take this - Do I eat? You know why I have one - I do - I do have it - I want some tongue I will give you some - but don't do too much what? Suck it. Well I don't know how I will get up early tomorrow I have a lesson at two - no not with the "bellemere" You don't know what a wonderful sensation it is - - - - - I have some preference for some company where is our waiter - where is he it sounds it doesn't he?
Mina are you short-hand?, I never knew it. I want tongue sandwich, anyway it keeps me awake. You know, she comes riding school fifty sixth street you know she comes. Lunch 12 o'clock. Well you know it was. How do you light a cigar-

Figure 4. Mina Loy, "O Marcel . . . Otherwise I Also Have Been to Louise's," *The Blind Man*, no. 2 (May 1917): 14–15, reproduced with permission of Roger Conover.

Misogyny is uncomfortably present in Picabia's eroticized machine drawings or, mixed with imperialism, in de Zayas's emphasis on discovery and fertilization in his description of New York's reception of modern art, which "like a circumspect young girl or a careful married woman . . . has taken all possible precautions against assimilating the spirit of modern art; rejecting a seed that would have found a most fertile soil."[45] Alongside a gender blindness in canonical Dadaism and Dada scholarship that persists today, misogyny often underlies the anti-institutional, anti-traditional language that many little magazines endorsed.[46] Duchamp, Picabia, Man Ray, and many others benefited from their male privilege, despite their much-praised critique of the institutions of art that they fed with works perfectly suited to them and that only worked as provocations inside a traditional museal framework. To elevate institutional critique as the avant-garde's characteristic par excellence—especially when applied ahistorically to the present—is problematic when it forgets the historical exclusivity pertaining to that very anti-institutionalism.

One poet who became crucial to a revision of that avant-garde paradigm, forcing institutional critique to include a critique of gender, is Loy. Loy's feminism and poetic innovation in striking imagery and paratactical syntax made her a model for many later poets. Her now famous lyric sequence "Songs to Joannes" was first published as "Love Songs" (sections 1–4) in the first issue of *Others* (1915) and in full in its April 1917 issue. Like "O Marcel," Loy's "Love Songs" echoes the *parole in libertà* of the Futurists in its scattering of nouns and non-linear syntax. Her editor, Alfred Kreymborg, recognized the resonance, arguing that Loy "transferred futurist theories to America, and in her subject-matter had gone about expressing herself freely—another continental influence."[47] Indeed, not "paced" to her lover's "clock-work mechanism," the speaker in "Love Songs" freely advocates a separation of love from sex.[48] This echoes her "Feminist Manifesto"—sent to Mabel Dodge in 1914 and not published until 1982 in the *Last Lunar Baedeker*—where she asserts that "*there is nothing impure in sex*."[49] In "Songs to Joannes" Loy did not shy away from explicitly erotic, yet also sometimes scientific, words like *spermatozoa*, *skin-sack*, *bird-like abortions*, and *irate pornographer*. She became herself what she had said of Gertrude Stein, a "Curie / of the Laboratory / of Vocabulary."

Despite Kreymborg's affirmation that no attempt was made to distribute the first issue of *Others* widely, after only a week "a small-scale riot ensued," protesting its profanity, earning the magazine a reputation for "infamy."[50] "Travesties" that ridiculed *Others*, particularly Loy's and Orrick Johns's poems, appeared in the *New-York Tribune* and *Evening Sun*.[51] It was not just Loy's subject matter that shocked readers but also, Kreymborg reported, "her elimination of punctuation marks and the audacious spacing of her lines."[52] For Carolyn Burke, the public reaction highlights the connections in Loy's poems between "the politics of the new woman and the principles of the new poetry," both of which *Others* seemed to promote.[53] The "New Woman"—a popular concept with antecedents in the 1890s and fueled by activists and social reformers such as Margaret Sanger and Emma Goldman (both contributors to *The Little Review*)—melded demands for greater personal freedom, suffrage, and sexual expression. The émigré Loy was regarded as a "new woman" because of her notoriety, her cosmopolitanism, and her writing about sexual self-realization. Her poetic innovations were read as inextricably linked to this persona, suggesting that a disrupted and abandoned syntax might signal a disruptive and abandoned woman, at least as far as mainstream critics were concerned. Second- and third-wave feminists, whom Loy inspired to integrate poetic innovation and sexual revolution, would soon explore this link further. They would ask whether female poets conformed to patriarchy if their syntax was not defamiliarized or if that defamiliarization was conditioned by its patriarchal practitioners.

The sexually explicit, radical semantic and syntactic innovations of Loy's poem positioned *Others* at the forefront of magazine experimentation. In the magazine, Loy's work is preceded by a coquettish love poem by Mary Carolyn Davies called "Songs of a Girl." Kreymborg remembered that he and Walter Arensberg (who provided the finances but remained in the background editorially) disagreed on contributors but eventually found their "mutual preferences among the poems of Mina Loy at one extreme and those of Mary Carolyn Davies at the other."[54] The editors embraced both extremes, a practice common in avant-garde magazines: not all contributions were modernist, innovative, or politically radical. Since the magazine laboratory is "a place for experiments" in which taste is developed and debated, the not-yet-canonical sits beside work that will be forgotten. This adjacency is part and parcel of the proto-forms of avant-gardes in which pure canonical forms of these groups simply did not exist.

The Blind Man Sees the Fountain

Proto-Dada magazines often discussed aesthetics through discourses of print, science, and gender and forged a critical language around their creative work. Manifestos, the most direct form of critical framing, have received extensive scholarly attention, not just as the theoretical outlet of avant-garde practice but as an art form in their own right. Martin Puchner's most instructive insight is that manifestos should not merely be judged by their efficacy but by their poetry, that is, by their *form*. Mary Ann Caws, somewhat conversely, calls the manifesto "a loud genre," "a document of an ideology, crafted to convince and convert."[55] But manifestos were not the only form of critical discourse within magazine communities. Margaret Anderson, William Carlos Williams, de Zayas, Meyer, Loy, and many others published statements about art, poetry, and the role of criticism in their magazines without calling them "manifestos." Sometimes these texts share the register of manifestos; at other times they strike a quieter note, without the glaring noise of Marinetti's Futurist or Tzara's Dadaist manifestos.

The avant-garde is often read through the supposed clarity of its manifestos rather than through its contradictory statements. Even when contradiction is acknowledged, it does not lead critics to reassess a particular avant-garde group.[56] A less reductive reading of a magazine community must therefore account for the contradictions, provisionality, and vagueness as more than Dada negativity or a feature of discourse and must serve as a corrective to programmatic readings. Although critical texts published in proto-Dada magazines made use of humorous and hyperbolic gestures familiar from the manifesto model, they did so for serious ends: to change the production and reception of avant-garde art and poetry. This modifies the conventional reading of Dada as attacking seriousness and taste-making outright, in particular Francis Naumann's proposal that "humor . . . is the most salient, consistent, and powerful operating factor behind the creation of all great Dada artifacts."[57] In fact, *291*, *The Blind Man*, *Others*, and *The Little Review* each tried to shape public taste in their creative, pedagogical, and historiographic endeavors—humor being only one among many qualities harnessed for that purpose.

Instead of positing a program in the form of a manifesto, *291* co-editor Paul Haviland wrote about *291* in the form of a fictional dialogue between a professor and "291." The caption reads: "*When I arrived at 291 the Spirit of 291 was manifesting itself at its best; 291 was at the height of an animated discussion with the Professor. 291 is a trinity; a place, a person and a symbol.*"[58] In humorous idolatry of 291 Gallery, the unusual gatefold of the first issue suddenly supports the parodic reading of the cover: the triptych is the material match for *291*'s trinity "spirit." While the cover shows *291* wearing Stieglitz's face, the professor asks *291* what it is. After all, the "sixty odd contributions" to *Camera Work*'s questionnaire about 291 Gallery only gave "the spirit of *291*" but not "what definite thing *291* represents"—surely a joke about the representational art the magazine and gallery rejected.[59] The reply from *291* hints at what could easily be called Dada negativity (à la "dada means nothing," as in Tzara's 1918 manifesto) but with a greater emphasis on provisionality and process: "It represents nothing definite; it is ever growing, constantly changing and developing."[60] The appearance of a magazine that, according to Pound's definition, "doesn't know what it thinks or where it is going," in fact, encapsulates *291*'s spirit. The editors championed provisionality as an adequate response to art through which conventional interpretative frameworks and the authority of the editors could be challenged.

That the piece was framed as an animated discussion hints at the lively exchange often ascribed to Stieglitz's 291 Gallery and *291*'s attempt to engage the public in dialogue.[61] In that it was not alone. *291*, *The Blind Man*, *The Little Review*, and *Others* railed against the bad taste of the American public, reluctant to please audiences, as *291* pointed out: "the efforts of '291' in placing its public in contact with the principal achievements of modern art has not had as its objective to amuse, but to further the progress of both the artist and the community through a commerce of ideas."[62] Experimentation was supposed to transform social life, at least in theory. Instead of a vague Bürgerian "sublation of art into the praxis of life," for proto-Dada editors and practitioners new art also necessitated a new language and focus of criticism through the magazine medium. Correspondingly, Agnes Meyer asserted in *291*'s first issue that contemporary art criticism "*IS OBSOLETE*. It measures a new product with old standards . . . and often befogs the mind of the public."[63] As an alternative, Meyer proposed an experimental attitude that would make criticism as modern as art, complementing the scientific discourse of *291* as laboratory: the critic must "*BECOME AN EXPERIMENTALIST*. . . . *HE MUST WELCOME ALL THE NEW SYSTEMS* in turn no matter how mad they seem," and then "carry his *EXPERIMENTALLY OBTAINED DEDUCTIONS* into the future."[64] The role of critical prose would be debated fervently in magazine communities from the 1970s onward, but the question applies equally to contemporary readers: are we measuring avant-gardes, historical and contemporary, "with old standards"?

In the critical literature, Meyer's statement goes unremarked, although it perfectly prefigures the establishment of an avant-garde tradition that values experiments and the role of the critic in defending the avant-garde. Meyer also articulated a methodology reminiscent of the typography and the imperative tone—the "must"—of the manifestos of the so-called historical avant-gardes. "*ART IS NOT DEAD*!" she exclaims. Like "a scientist," *291* "has resolutely devoted its energy to explaining the 'HOW' of art" ("its reasoned element") rather than the "WHY" ("its emotional side"). This new method of judging artworks does not "presume to establish permanent dogmatic rules for criticism" but is open to revision.[65] At this moment of self-definition the magazine espouses provisionality as progressiveness. The first issue of *291* demonstrates its place within an avant-garde that works through self-theorization, with recognizable Dada anger and exaggerated capitalization. Critical prose like Meyer's is normally understood to lay the foundation within which avant-garde practices are discussed. But perhaps because Meyer's account contradicts the irrationality canonically attributed to Dada, or because Meyer was largely forgotten, this example of self-theorization has not been considered a significant contribution to the formation of Dada.

Like many avant-garde magazines, *The Little Review* also promoted a discourse around experimental poems. To propel a reviewing culture, given that "criticism must be a blend of philosophy and poetry," the September 1914 issue introduced the "Reader Critic." In this section, Anderson (and soon Jane Heap, who became her co-editor and lover in 1916) provided commentaries on letters by readers and added humorous titles to contributions, thus harking back to the satirical bibelots and anticipating the shenanigans of Zurich Dada.[66] In an announcement opening the first issue in March of 1914, Anderson had already made the relationship between art and life the investigative focus of her magazine: "Its ambitious aim is to produce criticism of books, music, art, drama, and life that shall be fresh and constructive, and intelligent from the artist's point of view."[67] For her, "criticism is never a merely interpretative function; it *is* creation: it gives birth!" Anderson participated in an avant-garde discourse that used, as the art critic Rosalind Krauss rightly observes, an "organicist metaphor" to suggest that what united avant-gardists was their search for "a beginning from ground zero, a birth."[68] However mystical, for Anderson, this search for originality also applied to criticism. Just as Meyer had argued, criticism, too, had to be touched by the spirit of experimentalism.

In this way, *The Little Review* exemplified the manifesto-model associated with avant-gardism while embracing provisionality along the way. Assessing the magazine's first year, Anderson was surprised that readers (sensing a lack of a "transparent" program) repeatedly asked her "what we are really trying to do." Responding to the external demand to define her magazine, she countered that instead of offering rigid policies, she was "quite outlandishly anarchistic" and "uncritical, indiscriminate, juvenile, exuberant, chaotic, amateurish, emotional, tiresomely enthusiastic . . .—all the things that are usually said about faulty new undertakings." Turning readerly criticism into a flattering portrayal of herself, she even advertised limitations as her editorial vision: "I should much rather have the limitations of the visionary or the poet or the prophet than those of the pedant or the priest or the 'practical' person." To those looking for something definite, she replied that a magazine "should suggest, not conclude," and "stimulate to thinking rather than dictate thought." Having "none of the qualifications of the editor," she believed "*The Little Review* is in good hands."[69] In a characteristically anti-professional gesture, Anderson presented her project as improvised, even amateurish, and rejected "efficient editors and definite editorial policies" in favor of provisionality. The radical dilettantism that Anderson advocated is exactly what is now associated with the avant-garde's anti-institutional drive. But, like the process-oriented *291*, with its insistence on changing the art world for the better, *The Little Review* hoped to influence taste without appearing to do so.

Another short-lived proto-Dada magazine that hoped to shape public taste was *The Blind Man*. In April of 1917, the first issue opened with a statement of defiance—"The Blind Man celebrates to-day the birth of the Independence of Art in America"—and with a catalogue of promises:

> XI.
> The Blind Man's procedure shall be that of referendum.
> He will publish the questions and answers sent to him.
> He will print what the artists and the public have to say.
> He is very keen to receive suggestions and criticisms.
> So, don't spare him.
>
> XII.
> Here are his intentions:
> He will publish reproductions of the most talked-of works.
> He will give a chance to the leaders of any "school" to "explain."[70]

These promises drew their inspiration from the conviction that "Russia needed a political revolution. America needs an artistic one."[71] With such avant-garde fanfare, the editors—Beatrice Wood, Marcel Duchamp, and Henri-Pierre Roché—launched the so-called Independents Number to support the inaugural exhibition of the Society of Independent Artists, established by Katherine Dreier, Duchamp, Man Ray, Walter Arensberg, Joseph Stella, and others in New York in 1916. Seeking greater curatorial democracy than the 1913 Armory Show, the new society sponsored art under the tag line "No jury. No prizes," inspired by the French Société des Artistes Indépendants. For their magazine the editors adopted a similar jury-free, democratic editorial policy, modeled on a "referendum."

In its opening editorial, the personified "Blind Man" was fashioned as "the link between the pictures and the public—and even between the painters themselves," since it "realize[d] the need of the public and the artists educating each other."[72] For that, the public had to learn to appreciate new art, "like learning a new language," with a new vocabulary and a cultural openness to the unfamiliar.[73] The magazine functioned as an educational forum in which a dialogue between artists and their public could occur and where new seeing and reading (as in "O Marcel") could be practiced. But the public had "spectacles on wholesome eyes," as Mina Loy lamented in "In . . . Formation," one of her two polemical pieces in *The Blind Man*. Drawn to information rather than new art and writing, which were still in the process of formation, the public, for Loy, saw only "something that has been seen before," instead of "seeing IT for the first time," as artists do.[74] If the public did not practice "pure uneducated seeing"—free from traditional frameworks that were blind to new art—artist and public would never meet, Loy concluded caustically. Indeed, the public's blindness was further satirized in Alfred Frueh's cover drawing for the first issue, which portrays a guide dog leading a blind man past a painted and framed nude who is thumbing her nose at the blissfully unaware passerby.

The Blind Man adopted an eclectic editing policy geared toward irreverence and provocation but with serious aesthetics in mind. Critical essays in proto-Dada magazines sometimes served the purposes of satire, sometimes of pedagogy, and sometimes both. Duchamp, as co-editor, used *The Blind Man* to promote the first annual exhibition of the Society of Independent Artists, scheduled to open on April 10, 1917. That there was, in fact, an unofficial jury became clear when several committee members rejected the infamous *Fountain* (a urinal turned upside down, signed "R. Mutt") despite the society's proclaimed unrestricted submission policy. Duchamp and Arensberg consequently resigned from the society, and the second issue of *The Blind Man* defended *Fountain*, notably with most page space given to female contributors.

Since the original *Fountain* was never exhibited and only available for viewing to some invited guests at 291 Gallery, most audiences could only have seen it as a photograph in the magazine or as a replica in museums much later. As such a reproducible and repurposed object, *Fountain* certainly demonstrates how avant-gardes rejected the signature of genius and toyed with the institutional and receptive context of the museum (and, for that reason, Bürger, Rosalind Krauss, and Arthur Danto view it as one of the most significant avant-garde works in the twentieth century).[75] At the same time, Alfred Stieglitz's photograph of *Fountain* is highly aestheticized and cleverly staged. In a move that had his signature all over it, Stieglitz positioned the urinal on a pedestal in front of Marsden Hartley's *The Warriors* (with its veiled gay iconography) to create a portrait-like composition, thus turning *Fountain* not only into a work of art but also into a recognizable Stieglitz photograph. Importantly, it was through the collective effort of the magazine that ideas about troubling originality first gained public traction.

The Blind Man's second issue included a letter from Stieglitz, in which he praised the Independents' "desire to smash antiquated academic ideas."[76] In his letter to the editors, he advocated the noncommercial approach to judging art (not influenced by the reputation of an artist) that was also his own curatorial and publishing practice. He suggested that the following year's exhibition go a step further by eliminating names and numbering works instead, so that "the Society would not be playing into the hands of dealers and critics, nor even into the hands of the artists themselves. . . . Thus each bit of work would stand on its own merits."[77] *Fountain*, however, could not "stand on its own merits" judged merely by its aesthetic qualities; its appeal was and continues to be its contextual, institutional, and even biographical framing, even as such framing is entirely retroactive. Duchamp's name did not appear anywhere in the magazine in association with *Fountain*; the identity of its true "creator" was known only to a few friends, and Duchamp only claimed the work as his years later. Like Loy, Stieglitz considered anti-academicism a way for the public to "gradually see for itself," picking up the magazine's guiding conceit of the public as a blind man. *The Blind Man* thus positioned itself (through a gesture of inclusivity) against the exclusivity of art academies and exhibition spaces previously closed to the new art.

Little magazines like *The Blind Man* were sites of debate in which now-canonical works like *Fountain* were first framed in an art-historical context; in many cases, the editors and contributors self-consciously created that context. When read within their magazine context, we might understand how editors and contributors used their medium to refashion public taste. Like the more well-known and clamorous genre of the manifesto, essays and editorials served the purposes of satire and self-advertisement while also offering an implicit pedagogy for appreciating contemporary art. *The Blind Man*'s, *The Little Review*'s, and *291*'s criticisms of the public's bad taste (or lack of appreciation for modern art and writing) not only reveal their editorial strategies but also contribute to later generations' inheritance of the experimental as an avant-garde value. We need to look at these critical languages not because they are the key to important works but because they offer insights into group formation, self-definitions, the dialogues magazines invited or restricted, and the way their theory related to their avant-garde praxis. The answers such an approach makes possible are more complex and provisional than those offered through the manifesto model of avant-garde scholarship.

Modes of Sociality: Between Rudeness and Hospitality

The critical tendency to read manifestos, with their attributes of programmaticity, provocation, critique, and loudness, as metonyms for the avant-garde has led to the supremacy of the manifesto model of avant-gardism. That said, it is worth analyzing why so many little magazines are full of manifesto-like complaints about bad poems, bad editing, and bad readers, in a tone that often forgets civility. Raising the question of hospitality, largely absent from discussions of the provocations and agonistic rhetoric of avant-gardes, may reveal some strategical shifts in the way we read today and help us question our own elevation of the experimental as an avant-garde trademark.

Whether stridently or implicitly, little magazines frequently attempt to influence reception. In his editorials for the last issue of *Others*, which he guest-edited, William Carlos Williams published a diatribe against the poetry world: "Others is not enough. It has grown inevitably to be a lie, like everything else that has been a truth at one time. I object to its puling 4 × 6 dimension. I object to its yellow cover, its stale legend. Everything we have ever done or can do under these conditions is being done now by any number of other MAGAZINES OF POETRY! Others has been blasted out of existence."[78] Williams blasts his own magazine; even the innocent-enough design, dimensions, and color come under attack. For him, obsolescence is inevitable: truth turns to lies, innovation to stale legends. "Do we want to publish our own filth?" Williams continues. "What do I care if Carnevali has not written three poems I can thoroughly admire? . . . His poems are bad."[79] Perhaps surprisingly, the issue was dedicated to Emanuel Carnevali, an Italian émigré who had accused *Others* of becoming stale but who also represented "the promise and ambition that *Others* once championed."[80] Carnevali's poems are bad in a good way, Williams suggests, because they are not as stale as those of his fellow contributors, including himself. Whether one calls Williams's statement copycat Vorticist vitriol ("blasted out of existence" perhaps references the Vorticist magazine *BLAST*), Dada negativity, or the allegedly necessary anger we have come to expect from an avant-garde's revolutionary revulsion at tradition, there is a danger of getting caught up in a loop of scholarly clichés. Placed in the only issue with extensive editorials, Williams's piece could be said to have put a Dada spin on the magazine's character at the moment of its dissolution, but saying so would misrepresent the entire run. While his uncompromising language might be the model of critique we as critics tend to adore, the essay's tone cannot speak for *Others* or Dada, let alone the avant-garde.

While "Gloria!" announced the end of *Others* as a failure, Williams's second essay, "Belly Music" (in the same issue), rebuked conventional poetry criticism as a form of self-praise. Advancing on the avant-garde battlefield, Williams declared, "I am in the field against the stupidity of the critics writing in this country about poetry today."[81] Being "hipped on the question of 'good stuff' especially if it be 'lovely'" is "the disease of such criticism."[82] Like *291*'s call for carrying the insights of the experimental critic into the future, Williams found fault with other magazine editors because they took no risks: "Never is their criticism a new SIGHT of a SOURCE, a flash into the future of art. . . . They SEE nothing."[83] The exception: "Margaret Anderson is the only one of them all who gets up a magazine which is not a ragbag. I praise the Little Review."[84] Even this praise is a veiled insult—"She is limited ONLY by her own ignorance"—but at least "she does not select a poem because it is lovely."[85]

Indeed, *The Little Review* made a bane of loveliness. Attaching great importance to the value of critique and a vibrant reviewing culture, the editors Anderson and Heap engineered discord and heterogeneity as ways to build a community and enable the magazine to figure out, to invoke Pound again, "what it thinks or where it is going." For Anderson, the expectation that "Literary Criticism must be 'constructive'" is "an absurd notion"; instead, the critic's opinion has a right to "take first one form and then another."[86] Anderson even accused her contributors of failing to write adequate poems: "Helen Hoyt, you have a poem in this issue called *The Tree*. It is not Art; it is merely a rather good poem. You could have made it Art."[87] This insult was in line with Anderson's editorial project of irreverence toward decorum and compromise: "I loathe compromise, and yet I have been compromising in every issue by putting in things that were 'almost good' or 'interesting enough' or 'important.'"[88] Hoyt's bad poem suddenly acquires the status of exemplarity and what we'd now call Bourdieusian distinction; it's a roundabout way for Anderson to pat herself on the back. The logical consequence was the iconoclastic "blank issue." After announcing that "the September issue is offered as a Want Ad," eleven pages were left blank, followed by Heap's caricatures, "Light Occupations of the Editor While There Is Nothing to Edit."[89] Primarily humorous, the editors' proto-Dada stunt presents them as iconoclasts, which fits into our inherited model of the avant-gardist as untiring provocateur. Anderson, who "does not select a poem because it is lovely," turns the lack of good material into a problem for her magazine community.

And the community responded. One contributor, published in "The Reader Critic," complained, "*The Little Review* sickens me" because of its "sputtering trash, that colorless-degenerate edgarleemasters junk," and even gendered his reproach: "I see and feel *The Little Review* as a case of feminine callowism gone mad."[90] The editors labeled the letter "Freudian," and Heap replied: "You say *The Little Review* sickens you? With the above temperature and tongue? I should diagnose the case as autointoxication."[91] While these headings and commentaries are a way of "asserting control over their authors and correspondents," the fact of printing negative letters (if one can take them as authentic) could also be seen as loosening editorial control.[92] In no way second to Zurich or Berlin Dada, which deliberately enraged audiences, the editors provoked controversy, accepting the high political and financial stakes in such provocations. After all, they depended on subscribers, and a few years later they would be sued by the New York Society for the Suppression of Vice for publishing Joyce's "Nausicaa" episode. While the editors did not reflect (as later avant-gardes would) on the reasons for and effects of magazine sections like "The Reader Critic," Anderson and Heap operated under the conviction that when ideas were challenged, *The Little Review* would accomplish its aim to become "a magazine of Art and Revolution."[93]

To read *The Little Review*'s provocations as part of its pedagogical project to shape the public's taste and improve art and writing is reasonable and in line with avant-garde criticism's sympathy for its subjects. But as a pedagogical tool, learning by punishment is emphatically unjust. Whatever revolution a magazine community wishes for, can bad manners be good for it? Of course, rudeness or negativity dressed as discerning critique is often flattering to critics. So for Pound, "Bad art is merely an assertion of emotion, which intellect, commonsense, knocks into a cocked hat," a statement so uncannily close to home (i.e., to our own agendas as critics) it also risks becoming a default argument.[94] We must, of course, read such statements of blatant self-praise and grandiose belittlements while keeping in mind the vehement hostility with which avant-garde and feminist works were met by the mainstream press. But we should also read them as contemporary critics who can affect the tone of argument within our own scholarly and creative social worlds.

Through the discourse around "bad poems," we learn something from avant-garde magazine communities about poetic hospitality—namely, that provocation and dissent can sometimes foster dialogue and promote radical aesthetics and politics through exclusivity, hierarchy, and even hurtfulness. Provocation and dissent must not be seen as the only modes of sociality and engagement in magazines. The very periodicity of magazines facilitates ongoing dialogue, revision, and quick response; there is likely going to be another issue.[95] And unlike an anthology, the community remains, at least hypothetically, open. But as we have seen in *Others* and *The Little Review*, contributors are included in different ways and under different rubrics. Inclusion has its own internal topography. Not all guests are equal.

Little magazines were torn between this dichotomy: on the one hand, their snarky critical front (in some cases, just for show or with an awareness that their punitive approach was insufficient); on the other, their commitment to fostering talent and friendships, despite often dire financial situations. Reviews were one magazine feature in which these dual modes of sociality played out. Stieglitz's praise of anti-traditionalism and aesthetic independence in his letter to *The Blind Man* established a community of print between *The Blind Man* and *291* (then already defunct), one of the many examples of the inter-magazine exchanges of avant-gardes. Reviews or reader correspondence like Stieglitz's offer valuable insights into the history of magazine *reading*—a network often obscured for lack of historical records—and they often hint at a reviewer's agenda, which sometimes shapes the reception of the group and poets published in a magazine.

In a review of the *Others* anthology, Ezra Pound christened Loy's poetry "logopoeia" for his typology of poetry that distinguished melopoeia, imagism, and logopoeia—an example of Pound's self-fashioning through commentary on other poets.[96] For Pound, Loy's (and Marianne Moore's) poetry "is akin to nothing but language, which is a dance of the intelligence among words and ideas and modification of ideas and characters." For him, the writing lacks involvement of the senses; it is the "utterance of clever people in despair," but he claims that he "intend[s] this as praise," and these "girls" had managed to write "a distinctly national product."[97] This typology has had a curiously long afterlife. The phrase "dance of the intellect" would reappear in Charles Olson's influential "Projective Verse" essay, promoting a poetry less bound by traditional meter and more by breath, syllable, and line.[98] Pound's explanation of Loy's "intellectual" poetry would later become a guiding principle for some canonical Language writers who theorized themselves or were theorized by critics in terms of logopoeia. Marjorie Perloff resuscitates Pound's phrase in her book *Dance of the Intellect: Studies in the Poetry of the Pound Tradition* to establish a distinctly modernist lineage from Pound, through John Cage, to some Language poets, without acknowledging its origins in *The Little Review*, where it focused specifically on two female poets.[99] The adoption of the phrase "dance of the intellect" as a banner for a new poetics movement, following its usage in a little magazine (before being reused in Pound's better-known "How to Read" and *ABC of Reading*), is typical of the way in which such comments are sometimes edified in the hands of theorists of the avant-garde, particularly followers of the manifesto model.

In some cases, the editors themselves cleverly used reviews to reinforce the image they wanted to project. One issue of *Others* was prefaced with a quote from a review that had appeared in *Life*, in which J. B. Kerfoot concluded that "the new poetry *is* revolutionary. It is the expression of a democracy of feeling rebelling against an aristocracy of form."[100] To describe the liberties of poetic form in terms of social progress is a common avant-garde conjunction; here Kerfoot ties it explicitly to the collective effort of the magazine. Although happy for *Others* to be reviewed as a revolutionary project, Kreymborg resisted the description of the magazine as a coherent group: "It has been said in many places the contributors to Others (magazine and anthologies) are members of a group, a school. This is not true. Collectively or separately, they eschew everything which approximates ismism. Any one is free to come in or stay out of the magazine, subject of course to the none-too-infallible judgement of the editors."[101] In other words, everyone is welcome as long as the editors like them. Similar to the anti-authoritarian *Blind Man*, the *Others* editors declared they "do not sit on judicial or pedantic pedestals. . . . They are editors in name only."[102] The first issue of *Others* began with a demonstration of its declared otherness in verse; its simple but memorable slogan, "The old expressions are with us always, and there are always others," placed it squarely inside the modernist discourse of the new. *Others* aspired to hospitality and inclusivity: wanting to print solely "the new forms," "there was to be in no sense of the word a group," so both unknown poets and poets of repute were to be asked to submit.[103] Otherness, however, was largely restricted to aesthetics rather than the diversity of contributors (as only one poem by an African American poet, Fenton Johnson, was published throughout the whole run)—though outside of little magazines specifically dedicated to issues of race, like *The Crisis* or *Fire!!*, even token inclusionism was largely unheard of.[104]

Despite the protestation around groupness, Kreymborg himself had been introduced in *Rogue* in 1915 as "One of *Others*"—identified by his own magazine.[105] *Others* had also published two anthologies, a genre that often presents explicit community formations in print and can shape a group's institutionalization. The anthologies were reviewed as such.[106] It appears that Kreymborg did not reject collectivity per se, only the rigidifying of a group into an "ism," which several magazines embraced both ironically and playfully (e.g., *291*'s first issue, describing "simultaneism," "sincerism," "satirism or satyrism," and "idiotism").[107] Inspired by 291 Gallery's open doors, which enabled the crossover between the arts and the "extraordinary animation of the discussions," Kreymborg created a similar physical and textual "haunt" focused on literature with the hope of galvanizing a concerted movement.[108] Kreymborg's small house in Ridgefield, New Jersey (referred to as the Grantwood artist colony), provided a space for the Others group, just as 291 Gallery was a home to Stieglitz's circle. Mabel Dodge's salon, in turn, hosted suffragettes, feminists, anarchists, and socialists associated with *The Little Review*, and the Arensbergs' apartment at 33 West Sixty-Seventh Street was the headquarters of *The Blind Man*.

Proto-Dada magazines, like many little magazines, were often outlets for the editors' own work and that of their friends. Williams reminisced that "whenever I wrote at this time, the poems were written with *Others* in mind," and apart from a few poems sent to other magazines, "*Others* got them all and, of course, we—myself and my friends—owned it, so you see I wasn't really cutting much of a figure as a poet."[109] This is an extraordinary example of a retrospective historiography of Williams's engagements with magazines, which postulates a deliberate choice for his own magazine as an organ of friendship rather than careerism. Although an origin myth almost forty years after the fact, Williams's emphatic identification with *Others* accentuates that magazines were more than temporary containers for a poet's work; they were social venues that invited and perpetuated group-formations. It is therefore not surprising that a perceived magazine identity led people to infer an *Others* community based on sociality and aesthetics. This sense of identification also remains a prominent hallmark of avant-gardes up until the arrival of digital magazine communities.

The "Others Lecture Bureau," instigated by William Saphier, further strengthened a sense of community, the title already evoking a pedagogical and institutional setting. The bureau organized readings and talks by Conrad Aiken, Lola Ridge, Kreymborg, and Williams, among others, in Chicago in the spring of 1919.[110] Lola Ridge, for instance, gave a lecture titled "Woman and the Creative Will," and Williams talked about the role of poetry.[111] The lecture and reading series suggests that magazine contributors participated in a poetry performance scene with readings in New York and Chicago. These readings extended from the salons, a traditional performance context (particularly in Europe), to parties at Ridge's apartment or Kreymborg's shack in Grantwood.[112] But little documentation of such readings remains. The following announcement, collected by the important Dada patron Katherine Dreier, is an exception:

> CHANCE TO SEE LIVE POETS.
>
> Wooers of the Muse Read Their Own Verses at Art Exhibition.
>
> There is to be a convention of poets—those who are writing war verse and others—at the Independent Art Exhibition, Grand Central Palace, this afternoon. Classic poets, the cubist poets, futurists, vers librists and poets of other sorts will also read their own original verses.[113]

Not only are the reading poets advertised here as an attraction based on the rarity of the occasion; they are also described either by their style ("writing war verse") or by their supposed aesthetic school. The readers included Loy, Williams, Charles Duncan, Maxwell Bodenheim, Allen Norton, and others, and there was even a hint of the incipient tradition of an open mic reading: "After the readings those in the audience who are poets will be given the opportunity to read their poems."[114] Such public recitals and salon readings would soon be followed by university readings and increasingly frequent radio performances, and in the following decades readings would burgeon into the primary vortex of group affiliation and reception.

At a series of "lecture-readings" for the Others Lecture Bureau in Chicago, Ridge, Aiken, Kreymborg, and Williams "addressed hundreds of people, made a great many friends and sold a lot of their books."[115] If this estimate is accurate, the Others group had an audience the size of which later magazine communities could only dream. In the lecture series, the magazine became congruent with a group—hence the invitation of these four contributors to represent *Others* to a Chicago audience—which in turn strengthened their affiliation with each other and the magazine. But the Chicago lecture series was very likely the last reading of the group in association with the magazine. The last issue, edited by Williams, followed two months later. In his two editorials, the jaded Williams bemoaned the magazine's lack of a clear program, but it was a lack of funding and subscriptions that ultimately led to its demise.

Little magazines—*Others* was no exception—often promised projects that were never realized. *Others* announced, for instance, the introduction of a pamphlet series and special issues called a "Negro Number," "Fresh Winds," "Plays by Alfred Kreymborg," "A Lyric Number," and "A Cartoon Number"—none of which materialized.[116] These "speculative programmes" of magazines or issues that never happened show the reality of magazine publishing as provisional and dynamic but also how aesthetic and political plans are often hindered by practical concerns ranging from finances to a lack of enough good contributions.[117] Still, these unrealized promises are not incontrovertible evidence of the unavoidable aporia of the avant-garde. Bürger's and Hans Magnus Enzensberger's view of ingrained avant-garde failure assumes a teleology and a more complete formation of groups that is simply a retroactive fantasy. Instead, the projects that do not come to fruition, the intricate networks of affiliation, and indeed the conflicted views about group identity, emphasize the need to recognize provisionality at the heart of avant-gardes. Although David Lehman asserts, "If one were to list the necessary conditions for an avant-garde art movement, one would begin by postulating the existence of a group," such groups, in fact, have no concrete or permanent realities, and their boundaries are contestable.[118] Sometimes they affirm groupness; sometimes they reject it but appear "groupish" from the outside. Often, one print community is not clearly distinguishable from another, and the dialogues within or between magazines have to substitute for a wider readerly community.

Endings and Continuities

In October of 1915, *291* (issue 9) advertised the Modern Gallery, a new, commercially viable venue opened by the *291* editors that allowed them to distinguish themselves from Stieglitz's gallery. In an article published a year later in *Camera Work*, Stieglitz concluded coolly, "Mr De Zayas, after experimenting for three months on the lines contemplated, found that practical business in New York and

'291' were incompatible. In consequence he suggested that '291' and the Modern Gallery be separated. The suggestion automatically constituted a separation."[119]

In a letter to Meyer, possibly in response to one in which she urged a complete split from Stieglitz, de Zayas argued that for New York to become the world center of modern art, "the only thing for us to do, in my opinion, is to become an active and productive group" and thus "be useful to ourselves and to the general movement of modern art."[120] Meyer's and de Zayas's dissatisfaction with the group that Stieglitz represented, and their desire to become a more active group themselves, could easily be read as the point at which proto-Dada ossifies into an institutional form. But the "active and productive group" de Zayas called for never happened. Duchamp and Picabia left for France and became representative figures in the Dada and surrealist groupings there; Katharine Rhoades, whose abstract drawings in *291* were among the most innovative the magazine published, destroyed most of her work (because, according to Willard Bohn, she considered it amateurish),[121] retreated into obscurity, and later opened a religious library; Meyer became a philanthropist and journalist, and helped her husband after he acquired the *Washington Post* in 1933. Stieglitz, who was left with about eight thousand unsold *291* copies, sold them to a ragpicker for $5.80.[122] Ultimately, Katharine Rhoades's and Agnes Meyer's innovative contributions to *291* did not lead to a sustained practice and an artistic career. Meyer even belittled her own experiments in her autobiography and just fondly remembered "the pranks we played on the public."[123] Meyer's and Rhoades's exclusion from the Dada canon is also not helped by critics who see their work as derivative or anticipatory.[124] It is just such omissions and critical agendas that the provisionality of avant-gardes forces us to recognize.

Mina Loy offers another counterpoint to de Zayas's aspirational statement about active groups in her second version of "Love Songs":

> For the blind eyes
> That Nature knows us with
> And the most of Nature   is green
>
> ---
>
> What guaranty
> For the proto-form
> We fumble
> Our souvenir ethics to[125]

It is tempting to read "blind eyes" as a reference to *The Blind Man*, which was published that same month, and "souvenir ethics" as a metaphor for Loy's émigré status in the United States, as well as the international borrowings of avant-garde groups. Loy is both fascinated with and skeptical of the not-yet-formed or ideal forms of language and community; there is no "guaranty / For the proto-form"; it remains provisional. Likewise, one reason Loy was excluded from the canon until her literary rediscovery in the 1970s and 1980s might be that she did not belong to any one literary movement in a sustained fashion. She went on to publish in late-modernist magazines like *Accent*, *New Directions*, *Partisan Review*, and the surrealist *View* in the 1940s and 1950s; publications that substantiate both modernism's continuities beyond its core period and her own traversal of Dada, modernist, surrealist, and late-modernist circles throughout her writing life.

Despite its fervent group activity, *The Blind Man* ran for only two issues. Its bathetic end was determined by a chess game between Roché and Francis Picabia, supposedly to avoid competition with Picabia's *391* as another output for New York Dada. Given that Duchamp viewed chess games themselves as art and used them in his work, this game of competition and friendship suited his project of reimagining art's subjects. Picabia won and continued his magazine, *391*, while Duchamp, Roché, and Wood ended theirs. The moves of the match were printed in the single issue of the follow-up magazine *rongwrong* (a rather apt printing error for *wrongwrong*), also edited by Duchamp, Wood, and Roché, with the help of Man Ray. Compared to Duchamp, Man Ray, and the late-life novelist Roché, Beatrice Wood is now more or less forgotten because, instead of choosing the life of a painter, she dedicated herself to ceramics, an art form much less highly regarded in twentieth-century art criticism than the conceptual acrobatics of her male counterparts. Wood's trajectory exemplifies how the history of Dada and modernism has tended to occlude the work of female artists and writers, who are often remembered as wives or muses—or for interesting gossip—rather than for their own work.[126]

By the last issue of *The Little Review* in 1929, the editorship had firmly shifted from Anderson to Heap; more visual art and theater had entered the magazine's pages; and various co-editors and contributors had made the rounds, making the magazine an even more heterogeneous mix of genres, styles, and affiliations. Heap's preface bluntly praised the magazine as an organ of artistic revolution: "We have given space in the *Little Review* to 23 new systems of art (all now dead), representing 19 countries. In all of this we have not brought forward anything approaching a master-piece except the 'Ulysses' of Mr Joyce."[127] Yet, withdrawing from the magazine's premise that art could be equal to life, she continued more pessimistically: "Self-expression is not enough; experiment is not enough. . . . All of the arts have broken faith or lost connection with their origin and function."[128] *The Little Review*'s last issue also featured a questionnaire, similar to Stieglitz's questionnaire in *Camera Work*, which invited his readers and contributors to answer the question "What is 291?" However mediated, such interactive magazine features allow us to trace a history of magazine reading and thus function as magazine historiographies in miniature. Unlike Stieglitz's definitional attempt at a magazine community, *The Little Review*'s questionnaire teased, even ridiculed, its community, its trivial questions reminiscent of popular magazines: "What should you most like to do, to know, to be? (In case you are not satisfied)" or "What do you consider your weakest characteristics? Your strongest?" Only one question related to the arts: "What is your attitude toward art today?" Some declined; others replied in jest or in good faith.[129]

Heap's and Anderson's irreverence throughout the magazine's long run did not abate in propitiating final words, not even toward those contributors who answered the questionnaire and sent admiring praise. That the editors used the questionnaire acerbically, and not to generate inclusivity and agreement, illustrates their independence and, perhaps strangely, their seriousness about their project. Like Williams, the editors considered their battle against the public's small-mindedness unsuccessful. Anderson concluded, now seemingly in agreement with Pound, "As this number will show, even the artist doesn't know what he is talking about. And I can no longer go on publishing a magazine in which no one really knows what he is talking about."[130] The magazine's penchant for conversation had exhausted itself.

Others, in turn, made an attempt at a revival, almost as soon as it had ceased in 1919. Williams and Robert McAlmon discussed a follow-up project, called *Contact* in 1920, which, after its initial three-year run, was revived in 1932. Soliciting help from Stieglitz, Williams compiled a bibliography of "the American 'small magazine' since 1900, that is, magazines that have not been primarily commercial in their design."[131] Williams prefaced the bibliography (with additions in the next two issues) with an essay titled "The Advance Guard Magazine," further delimiting the kinds of magazines chosen for his bibliography.[132] At the height of the first period of avant-garde little magazines, Williams, alongside Pound's

"Small Magazines" essay, contributed to the historiography of little magazines as a medium, long before Hoffman, Allen, and Ulrich's seminal *The Little Magazine* in 1946. In a similar vein, Anderson introduced her readers in the second issue to the Pre-Raphaelite *Germ* as a predecessor to her own *Little Review*: "*The Germ* was published for four months, and then it died. Like all serious things it could find no immediate audience; like all revolutionary things it was called juvenile and regarded with shyness; and like all original and beautiful things it has managed to stay very much alive."[133] In the last issue, Heap also distributed metaphorical wreaths praising "Our Dead Contemporaries" to the *Seven Arts*, *Others*, *Broom*, *Contact*, *Secession*, and *The Dial*. In the first issue of *The Blind Man*, Henri-Pierre Roché—announcing America's artistic revolution—wrote momentously, "'291' and 'The Soil' have come."[134] That these avant-garde editors applauded other magazines as predecessors or fellow travelers evidences the exchange between magazines that energized practice and set a precedent for magazine publishing. It also demonstrates an awareness of the important role the magazine medium could perform in an artistic revolution. In the magazine laboratory, anti-traditionalism, anti-institutionalism, and new aesthetic forms were not abstract ideas but practical experiments, often with format and distribution, and always socially negotiated—among editors, contributors, and readers.

Despite the often-proclaimed ephemerality of Dada, writers like Williams and Katherine Dreier actively shaped a canon around these provisional magazine communities. Dreier did so through her Société Anonyme, an educational "museum of modern art" she founded with Duchamp and Man Ray, involving lectures, exhibitions, and publications, now archived at Yale. In 1921, the effects of Dada's emerging canonization were evident in Dreier's lecture "Do You Want to Know What a Dada Is?" for the Société Anonyme. But a so-called (and thus condemned) neo-avant-garde was not needed to establish Dada as an institution, stripping it of its authenticity, as Bürger waxed nostalgically. Many of Bürger's avant-garde poster children, in fact, happily inscribed themselves into that very institution. Ultimately, the 1936 MoMA exhibition "Fantastic Art, Dada, Surrealism," curated by Alfred H. Barr Jr., gave Dada its full entry into the museum. While MoMA was initially radical in its dedication to modern art, the concomitant changes of the museum industry toward a business model over the next decades have handed down to us an authoritative version of modernism and avant-gardism that firmly positioned Dada as an art rather than a literary or a magazine movement.

By reframing canonical and noncanonical authors in relation to the provisional magazine communities with which they were involved, we realize that within the avant-garde there are always counter-elements. In the process of becoming avant-garde, which in most cases means being recognized *as* avant-garde, a magazine community incorporates elements that will later be dropped or modified and includes work that contradicts the poetics of the group and magazine. More established magazines with greater financial backing and more continuity—such as *Poetry* (1912–today) and *The Dial* (1840–1929, intermittently)—institutionalized free verse after it had been tested in more radical little magazines, while manifesto-heavy magazines like *Dada* and *Cabaret Voltaire* became the emblems of canonical Dada. The elision of stylistic features and writers tallies with those reasons for noninclusion. Consequently, we can see the playfulness and humor associated with Dada as one experiment among many through which broader concerns about a magazine's relation to and within a public, the development of taste, and politics could be addressed.

The Blind Man, *291*, *Others*, and *The Little Review* exhibited to some extent the shock, revolutionary politics, collage techniques, and ready-mades around which Bürger based his theory of the avant-garde, which, tellingly, does not include little magazines—a medium that would have given Bürger ample evidence of writers expressing the wish for art and life to merge. At the same time, when Margaret Anderson demands "Life for Art's Sake," she is not talking about a Hegelian moment of sublation but something closer to the self-fashioning of a romantic, fin de siècle artist.[135] One of the problems with Bürger and critics who take up his terms ex negativo or as foil is that they apply non-little-magazine definitions of the avant-garde (i.e., consistent visions of artisthood and creative production without material attention to media history) to avant-garde material in a little-magazine world. We cannot boil down the projects of these magazines to consistent and lasting concepts. The magazines' insistent provisionality and the editors' contradictory statements therefore invite a revision of avant-garde theory by moving away from the terms that have come to dominate it.

2 The Page as Map in Proto-Conceptual Magazines

Against the Precious Poem

In 1967, Aram Saroyan, a contributor to *0 to 9* and the editor of *Lines*, wrote to Vito Acconci: "You and Bernadette are doing what nobody else is equal to doing. I mean this international breadth of the contents, and their consistent interest; I've never seen a magazine so rangey that could keep up any quality before."[1] What Saroyan colloquially refers to as "rangey" with regard to Acconci's and Bernadette Mayer's *0 to 9* is, I suggest, the crucial contribution of little magazines to the nascent conceptual art, which gained prominence between approximately 1965 and 1975. Mayer recently reflected on her affiliation with conceptual art and suggested that *0 to 9* moved away from the "precious" object, "from the idea, so promulgated, of the perfection of the poem with white space around it, set off from other things" by a luxurious margin.[2] In its place, Mayer and Acconci published works that did not look or sound like poetry but nonetheless, as Jerome Rothenberg described his and David Antin's magazine *some/thing*, had "the sound of a poetry . . . whether they were intended as poems or not."[3]

The two New York–based literary magazines *0 to 9* and *some/thing* exemplified a network of magazines that generated dialogue among poetry, performance, and what would soon become known as "conceptual art," challenging the form and content of the avant-garde little magazine. Lucy Lippard, one of the earliest scholars and curators of conceptual art, defined it as "work in which the idea is paramount and the material form is secondary, lightweight, ephemeral, cheap, unpretentious, and/or 'dematerialized.'"[4] The dematerialized art object was often supplemented or replaced by a text that outlined the purpose of the object or, in the absence of an object, of the project, and labeled it art. One could also say that conceptual art's "material is language."[5] Through its use of parodic supplementary texts or frameworks, conceptual art is often said to offer a model for institutional critique. Conceptualism's reputation as an information-based art owes much to statements by artists like Sol LeWitt, who argued in the proto-conceptual magazine *Aspen* that "the serial artist does not attempt to produce a beautiful or mysterious object but functions merely as a clerk cataloguing the results of his premise" in order "to give viewers information."[6] Indeed, many conceptual works catalogue, index, count, and plan as forms that display their own gathering and processing of information. Canonical conceptual art is therefore said to have promoted a discourse of the interesting, or the "'merely' interesting," as opposed to the beautiful or skillful.[7]

The interrogation of the print medium in *0 to 9* and *some/thing*, as well as in the other important little magazines of the period—including *Avalanche*, *Assembling*, *Extensions*, *Lines*, *Aspen*, *dé-coll/age*, *S.M.S.*, *Revue OU*, *Semina*, *Joglars*, the early issues of the UK-based *Spanner*, and various Fluxus publications, such as *cc V TRE* and *Something Else Newsletter*[8]—is part and parcel of the genre- and media-expanding conversations and design experiments in the art and poetry worlds of the 1960s. But even as they laid the groundwork for the conceptualism that followed, proto-conceptual magazines exceeded canonical conceptualism in their formal heterogeneity, with the inclusion of translation, modernist and non-Western reprints and ritualistic performance, and explicit anti–Vietnam War politics. While many conceptual artists critiqued the institution of the gallery and the visuality and object-focus of art, *0 to 9*, *some/thing*, and other proto-conceptual literary magazines critiqued the institution of commercial publishing and, in particular, the literariness of poetry.

Compared to other 1960s magazines, the six issues of Mayer's and Acconci's mimeographed *0 to 9* contained an unusual range of poetry, prose, and art. In addition to soon-to-be-celebrated conceptual and minimalist artists, they included what could be called late-Beat poetry, second-generation New York School poetry, French Tel Quel (Marcelin Pleynet), Oulipo (Raymond Queneau), land art (Robert Smithson), and Fluxus (Emmett Williams, Dick Higgins). There was also work by the dancer Yvonne Rainer, a documented collaboration between poetry and fashion (involving Hannah Weiner, John Perreault, Les Levine, Andy Warhol, and Claes Oldenburg), Native American songs, reprints of work by Gertrude Stein and Renaissance poets, and translations from the Brothers Grimm and Novalis. A special "Street Works" issue documented happenings and procedural performances. This heterogeneous pool of influences and practices troubles easy classification along the lines of a movement or style.

The offset-printed *some/thing* was edited by Jerome Rothenberg and David

Antin out of New York's Lower East Side, with issue 4/5 published in New York and San Diego. It promoted the emerging performance art and dramatic writing of Carolee Schneemann and Rochelle Owens, conceptual art by Andy Warhol and Robert Morris, Fluxus happenings (via George Brecht and Rothenberg), and procedural work by Antin and Jackson Mac Low. The magazine also published poetry associated with ethnopoetics, Deep Image, Beat (Allen Ginsberg), or with the San Francisco Renaissance or Black Mountain schools (Larry Eigner, Robert Duncan), and several female poets (Denise Levertov, Kathleen Fraser, Carol Bergé, Margaret Randall). Many contributors were influenced by Cagean aleatory procedures, and many even attended John Cage's experimental composition classes at the New School for Social Research.[9] Issue 3 of *some/thing*, titled "A Vietnam Assemblage," was dedicated to responses to the Vietnam War, with a cover by Andy Warhol. The magazine shared contributors with *0 to 9* (Mac Low, Rothenberg, Philip Corner, Dick Higgins, Warhol) and a keen interest in performance, ethnopoetics, concrete poetry, chance-generated work, and, crucially, in re-envisioning the literary-magazine genre.

There is no critical consensus on either of these magazines' avant-garde group affiliations. In the case of *some/thing*, this is because there has been no critical treatment whatsoever, apart from the occasional mention alongside other magazines, despite the fact that some of its contributors and editors (Rothenberg, Antin, Warhol, Schneemann) went on to become prominent writers, publishers, and artists. With *0 to 9*, however, the case is rather the opposite: critics have affiliated it with myriad aesthetics and movements: with "second-generation [New York School–]affiliated journals" or with "writing that began considering the formal concerns of Language writing."[10] For others, it presented "the textual counterpart" to conceptual art and was the "juncture between conceptual art and experimental poetry in lower Manhattan."[11] Particularly since the *0 to 9* reprint by Ugly Duckling Presse in 2006, the magazine has received renewed attention and still further attributions of group affiliation. Poet and musician Thurston Moore has even called *0 to 9* "punk."[12] Individual contributors, too, are seen to belong to disparate groups. Mayer is sometimes considered a member of the second-generation New York School alongside poets like Ted Berrigan, Ron Padgett, Anne Waldman, and Lewis Warsh.[13] At other times, Mayer and Hannah Weiner are regarded as the bridge between second-generation New York School writing and Language writing, whose experiments with an incoherent textual "I" these two already practiced.[14] But Mayer and Clark Coolidge have also been affiliated with conceptual and site-specific artists like Robert Smithson, who also appeared in *0 to 9*, and even with "early OULIPO-esque writing experiments."[15]

The formal heterogeneity and multiple affiliations of these magazines are, in fact, incumbent on their proto-conceptualism insofar as the emerging formation explicitly rejected medium-specificity and did not have a signature style.[16] But the canonical understanding of 1960s conceptual art, the vague neoconceptualism of the 1990s (meaning everything nonfigural and appropriative), as well as conceptual writing in the first decade of this century as represented in anthologies, critical studies, and exhibitions, has downplayed the formal and contextual multiplicity present in proto-forms of conceptualism. In addition to their play with media, *some/thing* and *0 to 9* are proto-conceptual in the sense that many of their contributors soon became well-known conceptual artists, such as Sol LeWitt, Robert Barry, Dan Graham, Robert Morris, Douglas Huebler, Lawrence Weiner, and Vito Acconci. Many of these artists began their career in little magazines. Acconci, for instance, came to New York as a writer, after attending the Iowa Writers' Workshop in 1964, but is now better known for his installations, videos, performance art, and sculptures. Others, like Adrian Piper, Eleanor Antin, Lee Lozano, and Arakawa, remained peripheral to canonical conceptual art (until recently in some cases) but played a crucial role in its emergence and in its little magazines. To read *some/thing* and *0 to 9* as proto-conceptual magazines means to acknowledge that they exhibit some features of canonical conceptual art but also to present them as part of a more diverse playing field than that given in retrospective accounts of conceptual art or the neo-avant-garde.

Despite the importance of proto-conceptual magazines and practitioners in the formation of conceptual art and for later generations, few retrospectives or anthologies select pieces previously published in magazines.[17] What they do include, primarily, are artist statements and other prose texts, which form only a small portion of the material found in the magazines themselves. This is not surprising, given that many anthologies, especially those that theorize conceptual art as a movement, tend to privilege work that foregrounds artistic intentionality and theorization. The recent anthologies focused on conceptual writing, *Against Expression* and *I'll Drown My Book*, in turn, focus on work that uses appropriative and procedural strategies, shifting the term's definition toward discernible formal features.[18] While appropriation and procedure were indeed common in proto-conceptual magazines, an overemphasis on these techniques or on paratextual framing alone eclipses the plural practices, documents, and influences that were crucial to the community's formation. Given that conceptualism's raison d'être is its contextual and institutional framing, the work has radically different meanings and effects within the context and medium of the magazine.

Magazine experiments with procedure, appropriation, and typography have varying origins and therefore varying meanings. The procedural work in *some/thing*, for instance, began as a serious engagement with non-Western poetry, while its special Vietnam issue exemplifies the potential political context for appropriation. By considering work that merges the personal and the found text, the canonical understanding of conceptualism's attempt to erase the personal is called into question. In *0 to 9*, innovations in and explicit reference to the magazine medium also complicate a reading of conceptualism as dematerialized. In addition to the visual performativity of the page, both magazines also published texts that document or envision a performance and require an active, and sometimes even interactive, reader. Taken together, this conversation between art and poetry, already begun in proto-Dada magazines, was extended into proto-conceptualism via a procedural turn, and again changed the form of the little magazine.

In her introduction to the recent Ugly Duckling Presse reprint of the magazine, Mayer finds an apt metaphor for her magazine's multimedia aesthetic: "The pages of *0 To 9* looked more like maps than literature and sometimes were maps or directions."[19] Mayer's self-reflexive image of the map is a useful framework for proto-conceptual magazines' questions about deixis, visuality, the place of text and language on the page, and that text's procedural forms. In another sense, I also "map" the landscape of proto-conceptual writers, artists, and magazines of this period. The formal heterogeneity evident in proto-conceptual magazines can then lead to an expanded understanding of the category of "poetry" and the literary magazine.

Formal and Material Heterogeneity

In a letter to Jerome Rothenberg, Dick Higgins identified a shared project of "dogmatic inconsistency" and "near-poetry" in *some/thing* and Higgins's own Fluxus-affiliated Something Else Press.[20] Looking back on the crossover between art and writing in the 1960s, Mayer suggests in an interview that "there was little reason to write poetry at the time and not do something else, like be what they called a conceptual artist."[21] This willingness to do something else (here directly associated with conceptual art), something other than perfecting a poem, produced a heterogeneity of forms in proto-conceptual magazines. Alongside various artist books, mail art, and Fluxus publications, the "near-poems" in *0 to 9* and *some/thing* demonstrate what it means for a magazine to encompass many media and materials, to evolve a hybrid visual and textual form, to become what Higgins called "intermedia," and to practice what could be called a poetics of the map.[22]

This poetics of the map, which no longer conceives of poetry and art as entirely separable categories, is especially evident in magazine covers. The magazine *0 to 9* was even known to have, as Clark Coolidge wrote to the editors, "The Best Covers in Town," each issue donning a different cover with the same rubber-stamped title.[23] The first issue's cover consisted of two layers: a printed title-page and an overlay of blue semitransparent uncut stencil paper. This not only gives the impression of a drawing pad for architectural sketches but also indicates the magazine's mimeograph origins. The cover's material and indexical doubleness reveals a medial and technological self-awareness that subsequent issues explored further. The second cover's US rainfall map foreshadowed the magazine's interest in such maps and maplike texts as Smithson's "Non-Site Map of Mono Lake, California" in issue 5 (fig. 10). The third cover printed the first lines of all texts in the issue. Issue 4 appropriated covers of books Mayer and Acconci had found at home and then glued onto the stapled magazine, with each printed copy thus indexing a different book (fig. 5). Issue 5 consisted of crumpled white paper, and issue 6 used six blank sheets of paper as multiply delayed and serialized covers, perhaps in a nod to Saroyan's untitled five hundred pages of empty paper, published by Lita Hornick's Kulchur Press in 1968.[24] While the "Street Works" issue contained a foldout, *0 to 9* overall maintained its codex form. Unlike proto-conceptual magazines that came in boxes, such as *Fluxus* no. 1 and *Aspen*, *0 to 9* exhibited a material and permutational excess on the level of the page. Inspired by Jasper Johns's series of works called *0 through 9*, in which numbered stencils were superimposed on the canvas, the magazine's title inscribes procedure and appropriation into its project. The magazine comes full circle in issue 6 by publishing Johns's notes for *0 through 9*, which wonder "whether to see the 2 parts as one thing or as two things."[25] The inclusion of Johns, whose early work also featured maps, encapsulates *0 to 9*'s concern for the visualization and spatialization of language in performance, innovative typography, and the materiality of its medium. A material encounter with the magazine makes tangible an experimentality and heterogeneity that its contents also display.

While much minimalist and conceptual work invited audiences to consider

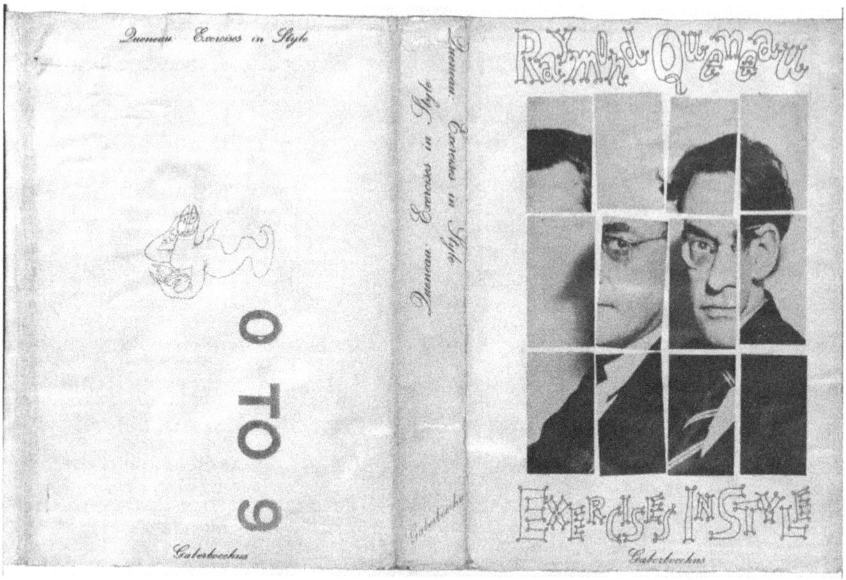

Figure 5. *0 to 9*, no. 4 (June 1968): cover. With permission of © ARS, NY, and DACS, London, 2018.

which elements were part of the artwork, music, or performance, the works featured in *0 to 9* asked their readers to consider what was part of the poem and what belonged to the magazine itself. Many contributions tested the limits of the magazine as a medium, questioning the conventions of having pages filled with original literary content or pages successively turned by readers, in which the material page usually vanishes into the background. For instance, Alan Sondheim's plates are described as "studies of abstracted machinery derived from investigations into music synthesizers, braille typewriters, violins, and analogue computers" (fig. 6), and Dan Graham contributes a faux-logical topological grid, registering the extension of time and distance (fig. 7).[26] Both draw on other fields of knowledge, troubling literary close reading and what one is supposed to *do* with these pages. Robert Barry's "The Space Between Pages 29 & 30" and "The Space Between Pages 74 & 75" only exist as titles in the table of contents and otherwise occupy the conceptual space "between" other pieces.[27] Adrian Piper's untitled, two-sentence piece similarly invokes an undefined void above the previous page, over which we're invited to imagine an "area measuring 2 1/8 × 2 3/4 inches."[28] Barry's and Piper's pieces, in particular, play with the magazine as a representational medium.

Treating the magazine performatively as a theater for serial reading, Acconci's "Act 3, Scene 4" distributes one line of a 350-line poem across 350 magazine copies, thus making each copy unique and a complete reading pretty much impossible.[29] Another piece by Acconci—"ON"—derives its material from the Coolidge text that precedes it and the Apollinaire poem that succeeds it, making the magazine context integral to the work.[30] Dworkin describes this merging of content and context as "crossing fore-edge and gutter to intextricably [*sic*] intertwine its text with the codex form of the journal itself."[31] The pun or fitting typo to in(t)extricably create text out of other contributions does not just treat language but the entire magazine as material. Most famously, such a contextual reading is written into Graham's "Schema," which consists of a formula to be filled in by the editor with information specific to the magazine in which the piece appeared, listing, for example, paper stock, the number of adjectives or lines, and the amount of white space. Graham published it in proto-conceptual magazines such as *Aspen*, *Extensions*, *Art-Language*, and *Studio International*, and sometimes even titled it "Poem."[32]

Likewise, *some/thing* showcased its combination of art, performance, poetry, or "near-poetry." Issue 1's cover was created by Amy Mendelson (later Goldin), an artist and art critic who had also designed a cover for the Deep Image magazine *Trobar* (edited by George Economou and Joan and Robert Kelly); issue 2 featured a photograph of a minimalist sculpture by Robert Morris; issue 3's cover was designed by Andy Warhol (fig. 8); and issue 4/5's cover showed three photographs of mouths by Fluxus artist George Maciunas (fig. 9). The magazine's logo—a Pima drawing of a labyrinth, which was reused in Rothenberg's next magazine *Alcheringa*—marks *some/thing*'s ethnographic affinities. The title's slash, in turn, calls attention to what the "thing" of the magazine itself is and highlights the materiality of writing technology: on a typewriter slashes indicated line breaks. Although *some/thing* was printed offset, the typewriter was by this point culturally engrained in alternative publishing, so much so that it almost spelled poetic innovation, as theorized and practiced by Charles Olson and Robert Creeley, whose slashes and spacing were employed to suggest poetic rhythm. Implicitly, *some/thing*'s title also pays homage to the radical typography of Dada. David Antin remembers that *some/thing* emerged out of his own and Rothenberg's study of international modernism, surrealism, Russian zaum poetry, and "tribal poetries" and that

Here are two more machines. The upper is an ideal power supply machine. Nothing is used up.

Large E: external environment.
Large small s: Lead Sphere.
PL: power loop.
o mistake 0°K (roughly): near absolute zero, where the machine functions best.
PL is a loop of wire with a current. A current properly set up in such a loop near absolute zero (say immersed in liquid helium) finds zero resistance to oppose it; it will travel indefinitely about the loop. If the loop is placed so that its plane is perpendicular to gravity and a lead sphere s be placed above it, it will induce eddy currents in s called persistant currents. These parallel the currents in PL. Parallel currents create parallel magnetic fields; because of the sophere's mistake sphere's placement, its field opposes that of PL and the sphere remains indefinitely suspended above p mistake PL, without any visible means of support.

The lower machine is an ideal feedback machine.

Large small i: input.
Large small o: output.
Large small x: unknown operation or maybe none at all.
Large E: external environment.
Small FL: feedback line.
FG: feedback gate.
FI: feedback input (or output depending on perspective.)

Two cases for the ideal feedback machine.

I: i and o are made identical in spite of x. o is returned to its original i state. NOTE: if x = absence of operation, this machine is an existence machine.

Example: the present theory of the oscillating universe.

II: o is fedback into i altering i; altered i becomes altered o which is fedback to doubly alter i until a perhaps explosive state (or state of equilibrium) is reached

Example: gravitational collapse of guitar.
Example: electric guitar rock feedback.

8

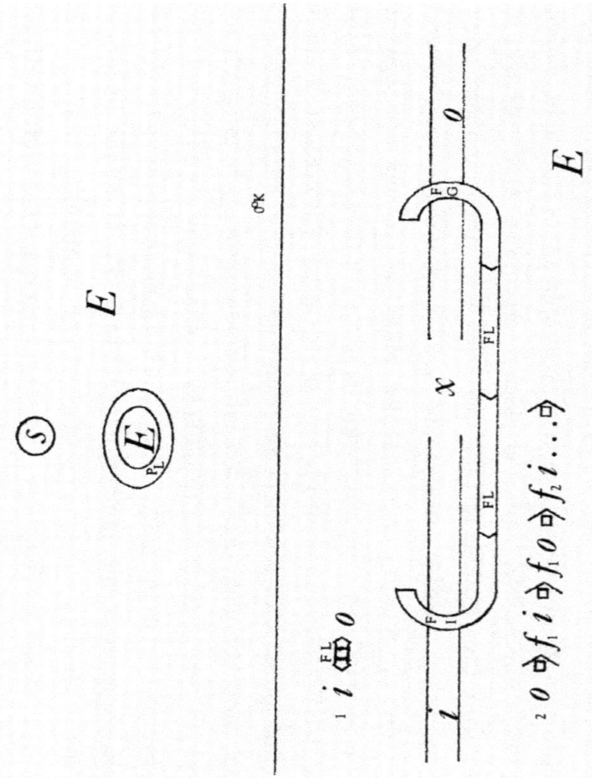

Figure 6. Alan Sondheim, “On Machines,” *o to 9*, no. 6 (July 1969): 8–9. Reproduced with permission of Alan Sondheim.

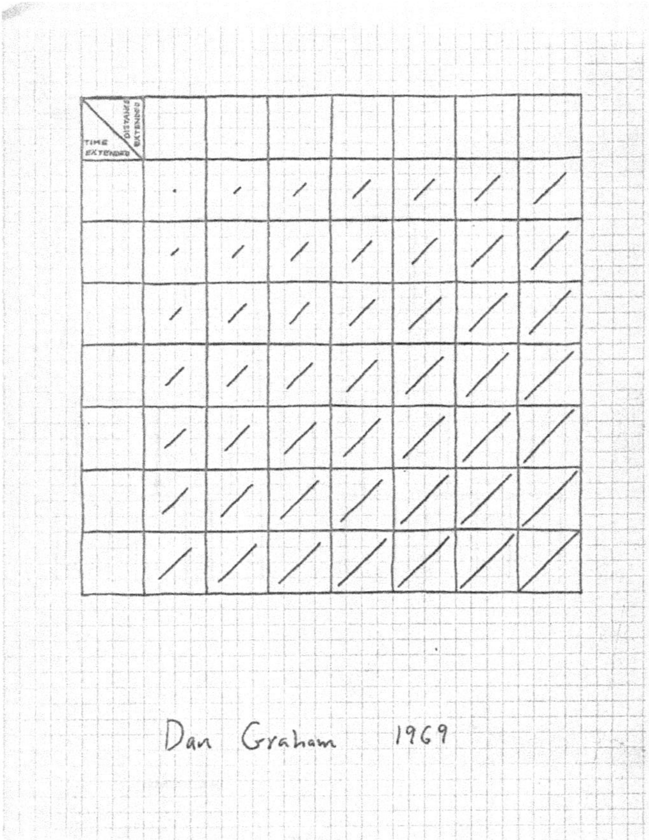

Bernadette Mayer X ON PAGE 50

half-inch inteRvals:

upper left corner to lower right corner: (in the margin), (at a line), (inside a photograph - at hair), (inside a photograph - at bridge of nose), (inside a photograph - at left jaw), (in an empty space above agonies), (in an empty space between been and not), (at Los), (at and), (in an empty space above will), (in an empty space between curious and Washington), (at inevitable), (at aside), (in an empty space between but and UN), (in an empty space between lunar and in), (in an empty space above seems), (in an empty space below can and at the center), (in an empty space), (in an empty space), (in an empty space), (in an empty space between Washington and Tom), (at matters), (at Dodd), (at be), (at explaining), (in an empty space above this), (in an empty space between two spaces), (in an empty space between two spaces), (at then), (in an empty space next to purposes), (in the margin)

upper right corner to lower left corner: (in the margin), (at a line), (in an empty space), (in an empty space), (in an empty space below waste), (in an empty space between Harriet and will), (in an empty space above astronauts), (in an empty space below we), (in an empty space above man), (at clever), (at bronzed), (in an empty space), (at a dot), (in an empty space below reminding), (at and), (in an empty space between have and will), (in an empty space between debate and U.S.), (in an empty space), (in an empty space below can and in the center), (in a photograph - at left side of forehead), (in a photograph - below left ear), (in an empty space), (at that), (at his), (in an empty space between be and an), (at the), (in an empty space between State and Senator), (at that), (at equal), (in an empty space between and and the), (in an empty space), (in an empty space above neighborhood), (in an empty space between not and then), (at self-governing), (in an empty space between -izing and of), (at disruptions), (in the margin)

next page: Sol LeWitt 113

Figure 7. Dan Graham, (untitled), and Bernadette Mayer, "X on Page 50," *0 to 9*, no. 6 (July 1969): 112–13. Reproduced with permission of Dan Graham and Bernadette Mayer.

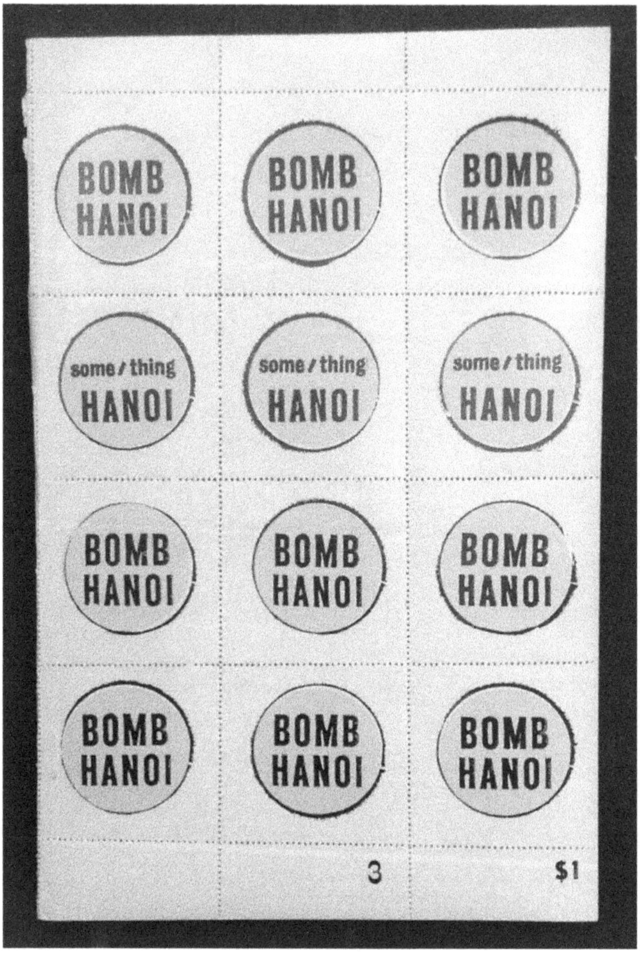

Figure 8. *some/thing*, no. 3 (Winter 1966): cover. Reproduced with permission of Jerome Rothenberg.

their contributions often "looked back to poets like Stein, . . . Kurt Schwitters, Hans Arp, [and] Tristan Tzara."[33] It continued the modernist interest in fragmentation and overcoming conventional linguistic representation through abstract language and found text.

In what Antin retroactively calls his manifesto for *some/thing*, a new kind of poetry could only emerge once the editors turned to "the foundations of language meaning-making" in earlier cultures "on a global scale."[34] This was necessary, he believed, because of the noise of contemporary life:

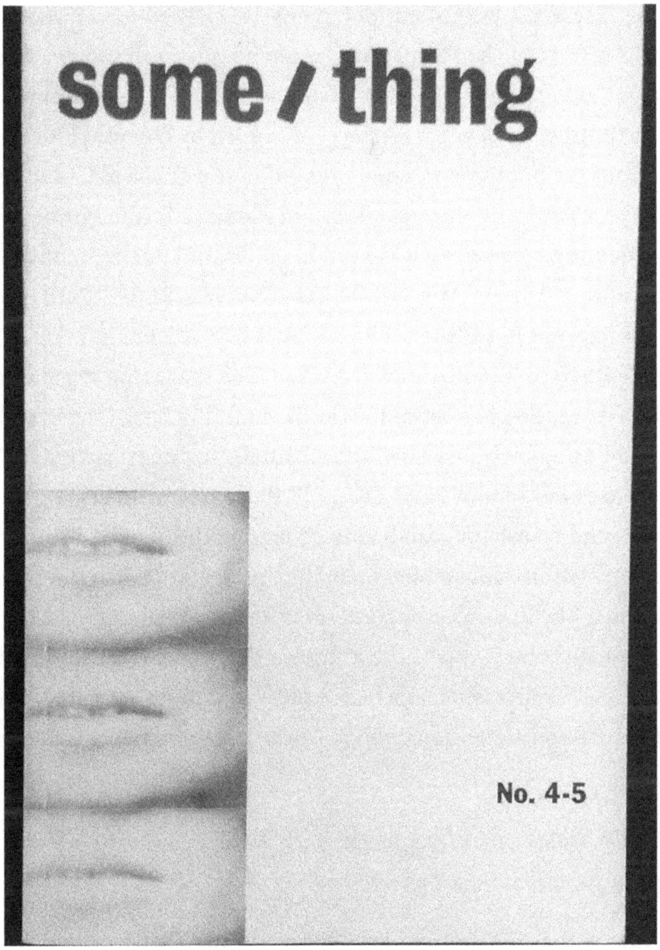

Figure 9. *some/thing*, no. 4/5 (Summer 1968): cover. Reproduced with permission of Jerome Rothenberg.

> THAT NOISE HAS USES IS FAIRLY OBVIOUS TO WHOEVER READS THE NEWS-PAPERS OR LISTENS TO PRESIDENTIAL ADDRESSES THEY CREATE A BARRIER THROUGH WHICH IT IS NEARLY IMPOSSIBLE TO HEAR OR SPEAK TO WRITE POETRY TODAY IS TO ATTEMPT TO COMMUNICATE OVER A VERY NOISY CHANNEL . . .[35]

For Antin, the task of editors and writers was to find forms that could be audible "against the torrents of cultural noise."[36] It is not far-fetched to hear the influence of Marshall McLuhan's work on new mass media here. Dick Higgins's

Something Else Press published McLuhan's *Verbi-Voco-Visual Explorations* in 1967, and *Aspen* published a special McLuhan issue in the spring of 1967 containing a poster version of McLuhan's famous dictum "The Medium Is the Massage" (substituting *massage* for *message*), designed by Quentin Fiore as a collage of pages from the book of the same title. In its search for meaning, *some/thing* was set up as a semiotic, ethnographic, and media-informed project.[37]

Consequently, *some/thing* was keen to go beyond poetry's conventional generic definition: "WHAT WE NEED TO KNOW ABOUT POETRY IS NOT WHAT MAKES IT DIFFERENT FROM PROSE IF WE DON'T THINK THERE IS A DIFFERENCE THERE ISN'T ANY."[38] The magazine expanded poetry's reach with George Brecht's definitions and events, Rochelle Owens's play scripts, and Jerome Rothenberg's translations of ritualistic poems such as "Notes on a Performance of the Seneca Eagle Dance."[39] Rothenberg, an ethnographer, poet, anthologist, and translator who had lived among the Seneca, brought to *some/thing* his interests in indigenous, shamanic, oral, and Jewish poetic traditions. The magazine, like its successor *Alcheringa* and Rothenberg's 1968 *Technicians of the Sacred* anthology, did not distinguish between indigenous and Western performances. The first issue, in which Antin's manifesto appeared, opened with translations of Aztec definitions, which Antin and Rothenberg treated as poetry:

> ELOCPULIN (a tree)
>
> Its foliage, its leaves, its fruit: broad, thick, fat, ball-like; each one ball-like, large, pulpy, breakable into small pieces, watery. . . .[40]

In introducing the translations, Rothenberg writes that we "can hear in these 'definitions' the sound of a poetry . . . whether they were intended as poems or not, for surely it should be clear by now that poetry is less literature than a process of thought & feeling & the arrangement of that into affective utterances. The conditions these definitions meet are the conditions of poetry."[41] Rothenberg's "Notes on a Performance of the Seneca Eagle Dance," *some/thing*'s Aztec definitions, and *0 to 9*'s Andamanese, Australian, Dama, Eskimo, and Semang Songs and Nehalem Tillamook Tales present non-Western work that canonical conceptualism is usually thought to exclude. One major innovation in both magazines was therefore to treat non-Western texts not only as poetry but as contemporary conceptual art. This hospitable embrace of oral traditions feeds the editors' proto-conceptual mission against aesthetic preciousness, because the oral and ritualistic are arguably less commodifiable than the precious poem or artwork, but it perhaps risks, like modernist orientalism before it, romanticizing and perpetuating the cultural appropriation the magazines so vehemently critiqued.

Arising from their fascination with Gertrude Stein and with Cage's lectures, Antin and Rothenberg chose the Aztec translations, as well as George Brecht's and Mac Low's work, because "their candidacy for membership in the genre of poetry appeared to us at the time as both questionable and desirable." What they published, then, was "a great family of texts generated from 'primitive' and modern performance and conceptual artworks."[42] Contributor Carolee Schneemann remembers that the editors "recognized the introductory texts to [her] *Meat Joy* performance as a poetic and literary breakthrough, and it was they who laid out and transposed the text for *some/thing*."[43] Her choice of the word *recognized* echoes the editors' desire to expand the candidacy for poetry. The questionable membership Antin speaks of is "a situation that calls for a kinship search perhaps involving possible affiliations with quite remote ancestors or merely peripheral relatives."[44] These genre-expanding works became "an opportunity for an extension of a practice" that allowed them to question Poetry (with a capital *P*) just as conceptual artists questioned Art, by making the magazine the family tree resulting from a "kinship search."[45] The first issue of *0 to 9* also began with work that was not contemporary: a Renaissance poem of uncertain authorship, "Her Face, Her Tongue, Her Wit," which scholarship sometimes attributes to Walter Raleigh, sometimes to his cousin Arthur Gorges.[46] Both the uncertain authorship and the poem's arrangement in three columns (as it is sometimes printed) must have appealed to Mayer's and Acconci's permutational sensibilities. In both magazines, the incorporation of historical and non-Western work maps a nonhierarchical community of print between past and present and makes the magazine determinedly unwieldy.

But the most visible result of publishing "near-poems" was that proto-conceptual magazines looked less like poetry, let alone literary, magazines. In their attention to maps and collective performance, the two magazines connect with another contemporaneous avant-garde across the Atlantic—the Situationist International—which, in turn, shared formal features with Happenings and Fluxus. Both situationist and conceptual artists were fascinated by maps because they "convey information in visual form," and sometimes even "delineate a utopian form of vision," "challenging the orthodoxies of power through an alternative cartography."[47] The administrative aspect of maps and their codes and legends appealed to the cataloguing logic of many proto-conceptual artists and writers, as did their signifying system of social interactions or physical inscriptions. Such mappings were featured in *0 to 9*'s rainfall-map cover for issue 2; Smithson's "Non-Site Map" in issue 4 (fig. 10) and "Urination Map" in issue 5; the "Street Works" issue, which traced real and imagined movements across New York City; the diagrammatic hand-drawn scribblings by LeWitt; Saroyan's geometrical lines comprising letters, words, or punctuation; and the many indices, numbers, spatial and performative descriptions published throughout the magazine's run. In *some/thing*, the numbering system and bullet points in Rothenberg's "Sightings" or George Brecht's "Dances, Events & Other Poems," Carolee Schneemann's *Meat Joy* performance instructions, and, most explicitly, Rothenberg's schema for a collective performance of the "Seneca Eagle Dance" establish spatial relations on the page but also indicate physical movement beyond it.

Maps, which many proto-conceptual works take as their model, are good examples of the often-theorized dematerialized conceptual work, in that they replace the object with its signifier and index that very object. Because maps and diagrams never give the exact shape of an object, situation, or location, but rather a schematic depiction, and because they tend to illustrate relations between parts and defy realism, they served artists as touchstones for questions about representation, typography, and models of reading. Maps can offer a set of directions for performance along unknown terrains, sketching out ideas and collapsing reality onto the flat two-dimensional plane of the page. For proto-conceptual magazines, to think of the page as a map draws attention to the visuality of the medium and the paper's status as an object. The magazine was not just a container for experimental work; its form was integral to a proto-conceptual vision of pushing the genre boundaries of poetry. For a magazine to reflect the multiple interests of 1960s proto-conceptual artists and poets, the page had to become a map of near-poems.

Procedural Poetics

In addition to testing the poetry candidacy of nonliterary, non-Western, and non-contemporary texts and to overhauling the look of the magazine page as substrate or material, proto-conceptual magazines probed the way texts were made. One way to avoid casting the poem as a precious object was to employ a procedure. Procedural poetics took the form of appropriations, permutations, algorithmic sequences, constraints, catalogues, scripts for performance, schemata, grids, and

Figure 10. Robert Smithson, "Non-Site Map," *0 to 9*, no. 5 (Jan. 1969): 9. Reproduced with permission of Holt-Smithson Foundation/VAGA at ARS, NY, and DACS, London, 2018. This is a detail from Robert Smithson's *Mono Lake Nonsite (Cinders Near Black Point)*, 1968.

lists. Proto-conceptual lists differed from the contemporaneous genre of the list poem, often considered a "much-copied New York School staple" that was part of a New York School "poetics of process," celebrating the quotidian and spontaneity.[48] Conversely, for LeWitt, who advised that "if the artist changes his mind midway through the execution of the piece he compromises the result and repeats past results," spontaneity distracted from procedural determination.[49] The processual writing of the New York School was content-based: a poem elaborated, for instance, the poet's daily life or writing process. Contrastingly, proto-conceptual magazine pieces not only recorded the processes of making (although some did) but used and foregrounded processual forms. This also affected the "I" (however fictional in any case), which became not the poem's coherence-giving principle but a ground for exploration as an indexical linguistic sign.

Rosalind Krauss famously detected a "logic of the index" (not a style but an approach) at the heart of much 1970s art, particularly in documentary forms such as photography, video, and earthworks.[50] Similar indexical experiments with print, typography, and language were explored in proto-conceptual magazines. Bernadette Mayer's poems in *0 to 9* are closer to this constraint-based indexical art than to the anecdotal poetry of some second-generation New York School poets that (however premeditated) often gives the appearance of spontaneity. Mayer's "One Thing" begins with a list:

> ONE THING
> (flowers, wind, oceans, crimes, stars, grounds, bridges, sentences,
> consonants, cars, accidents, plants, wonders)[51]

The following sentences present themselves as narrativized definitions of the listed "things" but without describing the word they are supposedly indexing, such as "plants":

> They were gray and sinking. We are sad now. That's the story. What was the outcome? We thought you were never coming. We were afraid it would never end. We told them that they were hurt. They followed us. We ran as fast as we could but we couldn't catch up. They were nice about it. It again. Plants?[52]

The question sets off a list of plant names—"death camas, poison ivy, opium poppy, horsetail"—that are complemented by endnotes with further, sometimes more abstruse, examples of their category. The plants are preceded and followed by definitions of the other named items such as crimes and consonants. Krauss defines the index as "the physical manifestation of a cause, of which traces, imprints, and clues are examples."[53] These traces then "produce the need for a supplemental discourse."[54] An experiment like Mayer's presents textual indices with deferred supplements in the poem's definitions and endnotes. It sets up a network of cross-references that catalogue things and stories without any immediate logic beyond a rigorously formal one.

One favored cross-referencing source for appropriative procedures across proto-conceptual magazines was the dictionary. Antin's "Definitions for Mendy," George Brecht's "Definitions," and the "Aztec Definitions" mentioned earlier either work with a dictionary or label themselves definitions.[55] Antin remembers that in the 1960s he availed himself of many sources, including "newspapers, detective novels, technical books, insurance manuals, grammars, dictionaries."[56]

The dictionary was also a popular source among conceptual artists, most notably used in Joseph Kosuth's series *Titled (Art as Idea as Idea)* [1966–68], which exhibited photostats of dictionary entries for words like *self*, *painting*, *theory*, and *meaning* on large panels. More than just an indexical format, a dictionary outlines a territory and creates a textual grid.

Mayer also documented her source materials in her poems directly. Her "Definitions at the Center of the Newspaper, June 13, 1969" does exactly that: it defines words or blanks found on different pages in that day's paper:

> 35—at *landmark*: any fixed object used to mark the boundary of a piece of
> land
> 36—at the empty space near a word[57]

Minimalism's and conceptual art's predilection for ordinary materials and objects and for anonymity again find their equivalent in Mayer's poem, where everyday words are accidentally discovered, just like the everyday names for winds and flowers in her poem "One Thing," constructing a textual reading map. There's an insistent leveling of aesthetic material that replaces the precious objectness of the poem by a procedural and serial representation, similar to the procedural "X on Page 50" (fig. 7). Unlike a cube or monochrome painting, however, there are hierarchies and irregularities. Mayer's serial method involves a great deal of variation; it is, as Judd put it, "one thing after another," but the repetition does not produce identical units. In both pieces Mayer might have been responding to Stefan Themerson's "Theatre of Semantic Poetry," which Acconci called "a manifesto we didn't have to write ourselves," in which Themerson describes his new method: "to replace some of the keywords of a poem by their definitions. But how to do it typographically? How to replace the one atomic element by the long ribbon of its spectrum? . . . Why shouldn't I write them as I would a musical chord one under another, instead of one after another?"[58] Such vertical layering also harkens back to Johns's *0 through 9* paintings, which likewise overlaid a numeric sequence that could be viewed both simultaneously and separately.

The proto-conceptual network was not the only avant-garde that focused on procedure. The French Oulipo group developed techniques based on constraints and permutations, some of which were mathematical, to generate new writing and explore subject matter within a set of formal parameters. Oulipo writers also drew attention to the rules and constraints governing any writing by nominating their own constraints. One Oulipo writer, Raymond Queneau, contributed a textual grid to *0 to 9*. In a series of rewritings of a micronarrative, these "Exercises in Style" (first published in English by Themerson's Gaberbocchus Press, whose cover was wrapped around one copy of issue 4; see fig. 5) follow the guidance of their different titles: "Notation" ("In the S bus, in the rush hour"), "Metaphorically" ("In the centre of the day, tossed among the shoal of travelling sardines in a coleopter"), "Hesitation" ("I don't really know where it happened . . ."), "Precision" ("In a bus of the S-line, 10 metres long, 3 wide, 6 high"), "Blurb" ("In this new novel, executed with his accustomed *brio*"), "Onomatopoeia" ("On the platform, pla pla pla, of a bus, chuff chuff chuff").[59] Thus, they create a strikingly different narrative each time. Queneau's contribution in this issue is significant in that it offers a model for a concept-based prose. Acconci would later even call it his and Mayer's "how-to book."[60]

Following Queneau's strategies, Mayer's first chapbook, *Story*, self-published by 0 to 9 Press in 1968, was written with formal constraints and concerned with numbers, pronominal relations, and things that fall. Through a series of poetic vignettes, the chapbook explores what makes a "Love Story," an "Anecdote," a "Lie," "Fiction," an "Article," a "Western," a "Narrative Poem," and "Myth." Mayer recalls *Story* as "a structure that is like a diamond shape where I accumulated other texts."[61] In line with Mayer's ethnopoetic interests, *Story* combined American Indian myths and other folktales with "some lists from the dictionary of other words for beginning, middle, and end. There's a recipe for a true sponge cake, there's a nineteenth-century letter about etiquette, a couple of quotes from Edgar Allan Poe, and an article by the biologist Louis Agassiz about coral reefs."[62] Although Mayer has not commented on the procedures she used in *0 to 9*, such procedural and appropriative techniques seem likely, given their similarity in style to *Story*—dense, descriptive, associative poetic prose—and the proximity of their publishing dates. Though connected to the conceptual staples of the grid and index, the typographical and stylistic constraints put forward by Themerson and Queneau present a new version of proto-conceptualism that *0 to 9* helped shape. In its proto-conceptual poetics of the map, the inclusion of Themerson, Queneau, and Johns shows that *0 to 9*'s experiments with typography, genre, and narrative are in many ways more excessive than the minimal linguistic gestures associated with canonical conceptualism.

Proto-conceptual magazine pieces sometimes accumulate pronouns, articles, deictics, conjunctions, and prepositions in ways that disrupt their normal syntactic functions, and many pieces play with seemingly intrinsic properties of a poem and its expected context and addressee. Their typographical and textual experiments often respond to both poetic tradition and the technological limitations of their chosen medium and resonate with developments in other fields, such as contemporaneous trends in type design that responded to the binary grid system of early desktop computers.[63] An emphatic, even excessive, repetitiveness of items and numbers tends to mark the administrative tasks, data management, and labor favored by proto-conceptualists, as well as later (post-)digital publishing projects they inspired. Counting is one such repetitive activity that highlights the passing of time and signals persistence and patience. But proto-conceptual magazines do not merely index the act of counting; they represent this work in typographically interesting ways. Rosemary Mayer's documentation of how many firecrackers could be heard per minute on July 4, 1968, for example, is printed as fourteen pages of *x*'s and black lines in seventeen rows per page.[64] Exemplifying *0 to 9*'s disregard for creating a pure conceptual gesture, Mayer's durational and visually arresting piece creates a minimalist grid that is excessive in its repetition and variation.

For Krauss, "the absolute stasis of the grid, its lack of hierarchy," is an exit point for affect and narrative because the overwhelming presence of repeated forms becomes the most important meaning-generating mechanism.[65] Applying such grids conceptually to poetic lines, however, does not necessarily undo narrative, hierarchy, and referentiality, as is clear from Queneau's and Mayer's pieces. The grid, Krauss suggests, also became "emblematic of the sheer disinterestedness of the work of art, its absolute purposelessness, from which it derived the promise of its autonomy."[66] For this reason, Alexander Alberro contends, audiences were no longer expected to read between the lines, "moving from surface to depth."[67] Indeed, such grid-like disinterestedness, "nearly evacuated of meaning or expression" (as Kotz remarked), was present in *0 to 9* issues even before LeWitt's famous "Sentences on Conceptual Art" in issue 5—for instance, in Aram Saroyan's one-word poems or blank pages, which represented an extreme reduction that questioned both the visuality of the page and the literariness of the poem.[68] The crucial difference to visual grids, however, is that the textual grids and maps of *0 to 9* and *some/thing*, while applying the disinterestedness of procedural techniques, retain certain narrative, referential, and expressive aspects. They can be looked at as an object and, at the same time, be read hermeneutically.

While the canonical features of conceptual art cannot be applied unreservedly to proto-conceptual magazines, the latter did publish some of the texts that allowed critics to form that canon. For instance, *0 to 9* printed what would soon be called one of the founding documents of conceptualism: Sol LeWitt's "Sentences on Conceptual Art." Together with his slightly earlier "Paragraphs on Conceptual Art," this essay has been taken as a theoretical formulation of conceptualism in its merging of art and aesthetics.[69] Anticipating the later purist conceptual discourse on the elimination of physical presence in the work of Robert Barry, Joseph Kosuth, Carl Andre, Lawrence Weiner, and others, LeWitt argues that "all ideas need not be made physical."[70] In a familiar avant-garde rejection of genius, LeWitt warns that "when an artist learns his craft too well he makes slick art."[71] This statement resembles Lucy Lippard's characterization of conceptual art as a "dismissal of the precious object or commodity."[72] If we recall Mayer's rejection of the precious poem, *0 to 9*'s self-conscious disdain for preciousness is its most overt marker of proto-conceptual discourse. LeWitt's "Sentences on Conceptual Art" accords with the magazine's overall aim not to publish precious and skillful texts. Instead, "successful art" for LeWitt "changes our understanding of the conventions by altering our perception" through, for example, "illogical judgments" that "lead to new experience," perhaps allying LeWitt with the situationists and Dada.[73] LeWitt's aim is to go beyond the limitations of a tradition in which one becomes enveloped by labeling something a "painting" or "sculpture," a rejection of tradition familiar from earlier avant-garde practice. LeWitt, in a Duchampian vein, goes a step further and demands that the "artist's will is secondary to the process he initiates," introducing the anti-expressivity paradigm that would later be associated with conceptual art.[74]

The overlaps between LeWitt's aesthetics and *0 to 9* are clear: a rejection of the merely beautiful object or phrase, an interest in procedure, and a critique of genre and media definitions. But "Sentences on Conceptual Art" was included in the magazine not because the piece was understood as a program but because it corresponded to one among many editorial interests. LeWitt's minimalist conceptualism, based on a mechanical execution of an idea, is not representative of the multiplicity of forms present in the magazine. As with Dada, naming or defining something might narrow its provisionality, but *0 to 9* does not cease to be proto-conceptual once LeWitt's "Sentences on Conceptual Art" appears in its pages. Having resisted any programmatic output in its first four issues, issue 5 seems to anticipate the crystallization of a style and program that readers had come to expect from avant-garde groups turning into movements; only in this case the implied program was the absence of a signature style.

Jolting the Reader

Conceptualism is often thought to exclude authorial presence and subjectivity, in line with LeWitt's contention that the task of the serial artist was to "follow his predetermined premise to its conclusion avoiding subjectivity."[75] Such suspicion of the uniqueness and authority of artistic vision as the source of creative production was widespread during the late 1960s. Many *0 to 9* and *some/thing* contributors would have been familiar with Marshall McLuhan's essays, some of which were published in his own magazine *Explorations*, on how new technologies were making self-expression less important. They would also have been familiar with Roland Barthes's "The Death of the Author," first published in the proto-conceptual magazine *Aspen* in 1967, and *Writing Degree Zero* (1953), which appeared in English that same year.[76] They might also have known Barthes's piece on the Nouveau Romancier Alain Robbe-Grillet, published in *The Evergreen Review* in 1958.[77] Barthes's notion that texts do not have a point of origin in an author finds its practical implementation in the forms of transcription, rewriting, and collaging in proto-conceptual magazines that challenge conventional authorial functions and readerly reactions.

Writing under the theoretical dispensations of McLuhan's media theory and Barthes's theory of the writerly text was not to everyone's liking. Contemporary reception of proto-conceptual magazines was divided. For those sympathetic to the new aesthetic direction, *0 to 9* presented an alternative to the predominant groups at the time familiar from the *New American Poetry* anthology, as well as first- and second-generation New York School poetry, and filled a gap for writers interested in, as Coolidge called it, "word-art."[78] In a letter to Acconci, Coolidge insisted that, of all the magazines to which he contributed, he found *0 to 9* "the most interesting since it's dedicated to really *new* attempts": "The guy who edits The San Francisco Earthquake (Jacob Herman) has asked me for some things but I really don't like the magazine: too . . . Burroughs cum Rimbaud for my taste. These guys out here [San Francisco] are *really* balmy & behind, it's almost unbelievable. So it's a sparse field at the moment."[79] Jerome Rothenberg also praised the magazine, especially because "the editors' work is strong, that's I guess the real touchstone."[80] In the absence of editorial statements, Rothenberg detected a strong editorial curation, implying a rigorous selection rather than one based on friendship. After praising Mayer for "doing very precise things with the language," Rothenberg established a link between *0 to 9* and his own magazine, *some/thing*, by asking Acconci and Mayer if he could get work from them for his next issue, concluding his letter, "'0 to 9' seems to me the most meaningful new constellation of works I've seen in recent years, & I'd like very much to maintain contact. I'm sending along some recent poems toward that end."[81]

Other readers were less enthusiastic. *Caterpillar* editor Clayton Eshleman (published in *some/thing*) expressed his dislike for the alleged "non-logical concerns of a lot of your material" and "the emotion, or feeling, that, in my sense of it, is intentionally lacking in 0–9."[82] Acconci responded to Eshleman's criticism by saying, "Yes, words have charge, they develop an orientation in the reader. Therefore, it is the work of the art situation to jolt the reader out of that orientation. That work cannot be accomplished by playing up to that orientation, by repeating that 'charge.'"[83] This jolting, a recognizably avant-garde gesture, was practiced in *0 to 9* by presenting readers with "near-poems" and with other typographical and procedural experiments that articulated the poetics of the map. Acconci depicted the difference between *Caterpillar* and *0 to 9* in a diagram:

private vs public, objects vs situation
| | | |
CAT. 0 to 9 CAT. 0 to 9[84]

Although simplistic in its binaries, Acconci's drawing proposes that the private, precious object is an idol to be smashed in favor of work that depended on a contextual reading, was public-facing and performance-based, and maintained the provisionality of situations. Eshleman's and Acconci's disagreement about the value of emotion throws into sharp relief the different magazine identities by which they had become known, quite literally standing out typographically. For both, *0 to 9* had a signature style, even though this style was only affirmed by some of its contributions.

The lack of overt emotion in *0 to 9*, however, was noted frequently. John Clellon Holmes—a Beat writer, friend of Kerouac's, and one of Acconci's professors at Iowa—considered the poetry in *0 to 9* to be "without joy, without feeling, without revelation,"[85] "a brave handfull [*sic*] of enigmatic fragments thrown into the wind."[86] The enigma that Holmes detected in *0 to 9*'s texts that lacked clear reference made it, he believed, both brave and stubborn: "most of the work has that *hard* quality, as of gems or certain new alloys, that will hold up even under an eye that does not always see the precise point of such stubborn toughness, unresiliency."[87] Compared to contemporaneous Beat or second-generation New York School magazines that embraced the poetic subject as vulnerable and insistently not indifferent, the proto-conceptual procedures of *0 to 9* could appear simply unfeeling, particularly as poetic emotional charge was an effect the magazine's editors sought to excise.

Holmes took aim at the apparent absence of a direct affective relation between poet and subject matter, because "arbitrariness that does not seem to be spontaneous, that seems to be always hinting at a system that is never disclosed, and sometimes [is] even denied, baffles me—like rather a lot of Robbe-Grillet."[88] The comparison with Robbe-Grillet is apt: be it Acconci, Mayer, the Nehalem Tillamook Tales, or Robert Viscusi's permutational lettrist poem "Dodecahedron," many contributions used third-person factual description and ambiguous declarative sentences, which undermined realist representation. Even the literariness of the contributions was doubtful. Like the Oulipo, the Nouveau Romanciers often employed formal constraints in their attempt to renovate the novel's conventions: "Who but a Frenchman could be so insanely logical to attempt to prove the novel-form . . . invalid by writing a novel? It seems hopeless, pointless, joyless—like reading a book-length conundrum," Holmes protested to Acconci.[89] Holmes's choice of the term *invalid* recalls the proto-conceptual inquiry into generic candidacy that *some/thing* championed. One could even say, as Holmes implies here, that *0 to 9* tried to prove poetry invalid by writing poetry.

Irrespective of a reader's preference for a poetic conundrum on the one hand, or emotional charge on the other, Holmes's critique was motivated by a hermeneutical desire for a disclosable meaning that—because it could not be fulfilled—was out of place in this writerly situation Acconci and other proto-conceptual editors wanted to create. The danger, to which Holmes alerted Acconci, was that such a conundrum leaves the reader wanting and makes the magazine an inhospitable place. As with responses to some modernist and proto-Dada work, formal experiment is often associated with absence rather than plenitude (emphasized here in Holmes's repetition of the suffix—"hopeless, pointless, joyless"): a lack of feeling, and consequently, a lack of concern for the reader. The perceived exclusion at the hand of the poet is thus often tied to the affective absence of the poet from the scene of writing.

The Politics of Appropriation

Proto-conceptual procedures did not simply eclipse the author or the text's expressive function. The author or artist's presence was still felt in a number of ways. In "Hannah Weiner Meets Hannah Weiner," in which Weiner traced all Hannah Weiners in the phone book, the artist is present nominally (or, one could say, indexically). In other instances, the author is present via evocation in the text's address to the reader. One of Adrian Piper's self-referential pieces in *0 to 9* asks readers to pay attention to their own reading speed, while another gives instructions on how to read a grid. Vito Acconci contributes a similarly self-reflexive text to another proto-conceptual magazine, *Extensions*, in which he addresses the reader in all caps: "READ THIS WORD THEN READ THIS WORD READ THIS WORD NEXT READ THIS WORD."[90] In a roundabout way, Piper's and Acconci's documents involve either the reader's body or an authorial presence, where expressivity is deferred or its responsibility is handed over to the reader. Compositional notes by Yvonne Rainer, Jackson Mac Low, Carolee Schneemann, and Jerome Rothenberg, in turn, involve the body of the performer or the audience.

The continued presence of the body is most clearly evidenced in *0 to 9*'s "Street Works," in *some/thing*'s Fluxus event scores, ritual performances (like the "Seneca Eagle Dance" mentioned earlier), and in Schneemann's *Meat Joy*, where focus on the body's messiness, on sensation, and the expressive form contradicts conceptual theory even as the emphasis on appropriation and procedure does not.[91] Schneemann used procedures such as appropriation from the dictionary for feminist purposes and specified at the beginning of "*Meat Joy* Notes as Prologue" that "the French text was made from a dictionary and a picture book, 'Look and Learn,' then collaged and superimposed on the English, along with the sound of a ticking clock."[92] This collage becomes a simultaneous, polyphonous, running commentary to Schneemann's embodied feminist performance. In a similar vein, in the transcribed tape recording "Lecture for a Group of Expectant People," Rainer shared her "categories to describe motion" and asks her audience to execute movements to create "an exercise situation" and, following her procedure, to "explore your own body."[93] Both artists insisted on the "persistence of feelings" in procedure.[94] Although LeWitt expressed many of the premises of *0 to 9*, his emphasis on ideas and the concomitant physical removal of the artist's body or personality is not generally reinforced in the magazine.

The authorial subject could also appear obliquely in proto-conceptual contributions but still generate radical consequences. Lee Lozano's "Dialogue Piece" in *0 to 9* called for readers to initiate a dialogue with "PEOPLE YOU MIGHT NOT OTHERWISE SEE," with the instruction that "THE PURPOSE OF THIS *PIECE* IS TO HAVE DIALOGUES, NOT TO MAKE A *PIECE*. NO RECORDINGS OR NOTES ARE MADE DURING DIALOGUES."[95] Likewise, "General Strike Piece," published in the same issue, declared "GRADUALLY BUT DETERMINEDLY AVOID BEING PRESENT AT OFFICIAL OR PUBLIC 'UPTOWN' FUNCTIONS . . . IN ORDER TO PURSUE INVESTIGATION OF *TOTAL PERSONAL & PUBLIC REVOLUTION*," encapsulating Lozano's radical critique of artists as commodities.[96] That refusal entailed Lozano's self-removal from—or we might say making-herself-minimal within—the art world, a decision taken to its logical conclusion in her *Dropout Piece*, where she defiantly, and eventually successfully, moved herself into obscurity. The rational, neutral, businesslike style of Judd, Kosuth, LeWitt, Morris, and Lawrence Weiner, who spent so much time "minimising personal decisions," thereby receives its feminist riposte, revealing the maximizing of the artist that such popular minimal work often produced.[97]

Just as Rothenberg described the Aztec definitions' "arrangement . . . into affective utterances," feeling can be procedurally produced. Proto-conceptual magazines often lack statements of intent, leaving readers instead with language-based works in which the "clarity of the concept" is made oblique.[98] In the absence of manifestos and editorial statements, contributors sometimes provide performance or composition notes. While manifestos are programmatic in their appeal to generality, notes are inherently "proto," preparatory, perhaps ad-hoc, and temporary. Mac Low's "Friendship Poems" are among the few texts in *some/thing* (and also *0 to 9*) that detail how they are intended to be read. The specifications turn the poem into a script for performance. But, as Mac Low writes elsewhere, they can be "notations for performance (if only by a silent reader)."[99] The magazine context is an ideal environment for silent reading, a medium-specific characteristic that Mac Low references knowingly.

In this performative, chance-generated text, procedure is executed not only mechanically but humorously:

1

mr/mp I have started again to write poems that say things
to people 1

r/mf I even wrote a chance poem that says & says &
says ½

[. . .]

7

m/mp The party was nothing but I like Walter Mullen
who'd invited both casts from the theatre 1
m/mf And when I saw Jamil, with whom I'd smoked a
couple of times 1/2
s/mp He looked at me close, saying, */vr/f/* "Man, are you
stoned out of your *mind*?" 5[100]

When read in the context of the magazine, Mac Low's "Friendship Poems" are ironic confessional, even New York School, poems, couched in and constrained by performative directions. Explained in the preface to the piece, the instructions for degrees of loudness, speed, and durations of silence in seconds and fractions of seconds frame the semantically easily legible text.[101] The expressivity demanded by the subtle and nuanced dynamic indications both lyricize the text and at the same time betray the lines' prosaic, even banal, quality; any attempt to speak or sing the lines according to Mac Low's parameters brings out their melodrama. These dynamics are applied somewhat mechanically (as called for by LeWitt), but they do not empty the poem of its poetic qualities (e.g., rhythm); they rather enhance them playfully. These instructions could also be read as the opposite of the connection linking breath, authenticity, and the body of the poet, established by Olson's "Projective Verse" (1950), where the typewriter is the miraculously authentic match for the poet's breath.[102] By directing the breath according to a procedure, Mac Low removes the poem from spontaneous voicing, using the body to create an oblique expressivity.

Similarly, appropriation and procedure were utilized for explicit politics beyond an examination of the politics of form. Political current affairs entered proto-conceptual discourse most overtly in *some/thing*'s "Vietnam Assemblage" issue (Winter 1966). Andy Warhol designed the cover with twelve detachable perforated yellow "Bomb Hanoi" stickers on offset lithographed wrappers. The stickers designated the magazine for use, suggesting that the cover was more than beautiful design. Eliot Weinberger, later editor of *Montemora* and contributing editor to *Sulfur*, recalled that the cover was "widely admired at the time" for its irony.[103] Weinberger counted *some/thing* and *Caterpillar* as two exemplary magazines that demonstrated the "deep sense of community among those against the war."[104] Warhol had initially planned to work with a Vietcong flag, but the editors asked him to use a "prowar slogan like 'BOMB HANOI!'" instead and "fuck it up any way you like," in the hope that—tricked by the familiar slogan of American warmongering—"any member of the American Legion could pick up a copy on a news stand and maybe read it."[105] The use of a Helvetica-like font for the stamps satirized the clean lines of official aesthetics. Helvetica had become "*the* establishment typeface" and for the designer Paula Scher was even "somehow responsible for the Vietnam War."[106] The satirical appropriation of a popular slogan and design showed the magazine's complex provocations and its use of found material for political ends. In a common twist of historical irony, the magazine issue fetches large sums at auctions today owing to Warhol's fame, but the issue remains a good example of the revolutionary potential that 1960s artists, designers, and editors attached to inexpensive design, print, and distribution.

Produced out of urgency, *some/thing*'s "Vietnam Assemblage" is the only issue with a clearly delineated political program and is its most aesthetically inclusive gathering of contributions. Although the majority of poetry contributions are traditional in layout, voice, and narrative, the magazine number as a whole might revise what we consider a poetry magazine to be, in its inclusion of cut-up newspaper clippings and government reports that intersperse the poetry pages and are presented as absurd facts in their appropriated displacement. As a collective work, the "Vietnam Assemblage" issue becomes the magazine's most explicit proto-conceptual project.

Part of this politically appropriative strategy, Mac Low's "Marines Defend Burning of Village," dated August 6, 1965, ridicules America's unjustified war actions by recycling official US propaganda into a lineated poem, undercutting any lyric or even pastoral expectation through deployment of line breaks: "Village was / Communist controlled."[107] Declarative statements become the fodder for the poem, almost elegiacally juxtaposed in facing columns:

Difficult	
to determine who should be clas- sified as Vietcong since they discover both young and old may be assisting the Com- munist forces.[108]	 Vietnamese civilians.

As if commenting on what was being done to Vietnamese bodies, Kotz notes that in some conceptual works "language has been reduced to a kind of object that has been isolated, broken apart, crossed out, and at times nearly evacuated of meaning or expression."[109] Although several pieces in *0 to 9* and *some/thing* show this reduction, just as many do not; others, like Mac Low's, present politicized models of reduced language. Kotz also identifies "the use of the recording mechanism, without apparent criteria of selection" as an extension of the Dadaist ready-made.[110] Mac Low's piece uses such a recording mechanism, but his transcription is carefully selected and arranged through a chance procedure. Like the many newspaper quotes strewn throughout issue 3 of *some/thing*, the poem serves as a political commentary. Importantly, though, Mac Low's arrangement claims to be poetry. Its neat lineation, repetitions, and alliterations highlight the text's artifice in stark contrast to the prosaic descriptions of the bombing of the villages as communist strongholds. If one follows Mac Low's instructions to read "with short breath pauses at the end of lines, longer ones at the end of stanzas," the seemingly rational arguments sound absurd.[111]

Mac Low's notes disclose that the poem was written "by means of systematic chance operations deriving from the letters of the title" of a *New York Times* article.[112] As with Mayer, the compositional method designates the text as a product of reading. In 2001, Mac Low remarked that by "us[ing] so-called non-intentional methods," he had made "an overtly political/didactic poem," which showed him "how an impersonally written poem can function as a strong political work."[113] The desire to comment on and reveal ideological content by cutting up official language is a technique shared with Russian Futurists, Dadaists, and Muriel Rukeyser's and Charles Reznikoff's documentary poetics, demonstrating a similar politics of form but in response to distinct cultural contexts. In *Poetics Journal*, Mac Low recalled that his experiments with chance procedures were influenced by the *I Ching* (an oracle accessed via chance operations) and by Cage's chance experiments in music (equally influenced by the *I Ching*).[114] When read in the context of *some/thing*, Mac Low's piece becomes further inflected by the ethnographic translations and ritual performances and thus joins *some/thing*'s project to look beyond the Western avant-garde to expand the category of poetry.

While conceptual artists themselves were often political in theory and in activism, their works differed from overt protest art in that their context and content were often too "oblique and neutral" to register beyond the artists' circle.[115] But magazine politics that had previously been oblique in *some/thing* became more explicit in the Vietnam issue, which asked what poetry could do to resist or leverage language's potential for persuasion, manipulation, and subversion. While Buchloh detects in conceptual art "a profound disenchantment with those political master-narratives that empowered most of '20s avant-garde art," *some/thing* joined other magazines in their endeavor to respond poetically to the Vietnam War. They did so by using appropriative techniques or by "dream[ing] (together) an end to the war" in Mayer's 1970s Poetry Project workshops—however oblique and indirect their politics and results may have been.[116]

Democratic Promises

The little magazine can serve as a proxy for a more or less coherent group. A provisional print community sometimes extends into or develops out of friendships and nonprint social interactions. Sometimes a community formation becomes more visible, as in *some/thing*'s Vietnam issue, which ends with the following editorial comment: "This issue of some/thing is not an anthology of individual & numbered pieces on a single theme. It was compiled with the help of many hands, & in a special sense it is a communal effort—an overall structure made up of words, a language trap to close-with a state, a process, a system—something afflicting & evading all of us."[117] The editors establish a distinction between an anthology (theme-based, professional, perhaps done by an authoritative editor) and a communal effort (explicitly political and collective), in which the magazine becomes "an overall structure made up of words" with which to confront the war. This communal work—however temporary its associational collectivity—established a more explicit community in print than previous issues had.

Proto-conceptual editors did not usually write sociability into the texture of their publications. They mostly published non-coterie magazines. A coterie is usually understood pejoratively to be a small group that does not "engage a wider, would-be democratic sphere."[118] When poet Lisa Jarnot asked Mayer about the role of New York School poetry during her time as editor of *0 to 9*, Mayer replied that she was much more influenced by the experimental music performances of John Cage and Yoko Ono, despite her personal connections with New York School poets like Ron Padgett and Ted Berrigan: "Ted and Ron would do these collaborations and send them to *0 to 9* and we would never publish them. . . . I guess it was because of their style or something."[119] Mayer did eventually publish them, but her reluctance reveals that she did not view *0 to 9* as an extension of a friendship or family.[120]

Friendship is precisely what scholars of New York School writing have emphasized: according to Andrew Epstein, for instance, for first-generation New York School poets Kenneth Koch and Frank O'Hara "friendship gets figured within the poetry itself."[121] Daniel Kane describes second-generation New York School poetry as "produced as and out of sociality" and urges us to consider "the poem as communal gesture."[122] Many magazines associated with Beat, Black Mountain, San Francisco Renaissance, and New York School circles dramatized friendship in their pages, either by dedicating poems to their friends or by disclosing intimate details of their lives. We find no such poems in *0 to 9* or *some/thing*—the exception being Mac Low's ironic chance-generated friendship poems discussed earlier. That *0 to 9* and *some/thing* solicited contributions outside their local circles and included non-Western and older texts speaks to an aesthetic rather than sociable magazine project, which, as the Vietnam issue demonstrated, could still be intensely social. The mimeograph revolution galvanized Lower East Side poetry communities and readers, with magazines "serving as [their] nucleus" and with "collating, stapling, and mailing parties" fostering such a collective spirit.[123] Yet friendship was not the inevitable means or end of avant-garde practice, and the printing technology did not automatically produce the same sociality, nor did it produce the same aesthetics among groups.

The aesthetic constraints of *0 to 9*, for example, find an equivalent in the material constraints of the magazine's production. Mimeographed magazines often used cheap inks and paper that was susceptible to deterioration. The mimeograph had limited flexibility, mistakes were difficult to correct, and complex design could often make the stencil too fragile. The imprecision of the stencils also gave mimeographed magazines their distinctive look: ink smudges, incomplete letters, or letter bowls filled with ink after several copies were printed. Since the machines could not print large areas in color particularly well, *0 to 9* and many other publications used colored paper instead.

Despite its shortcomings, the mimeograph was easy to use: stencils were typed on a typewriter, which were then wrapped around a rotating, inked drum. Like tabletop platen presses before it, mimeography allowed the quick production and distribution of work, suited to independent projects geared toward a small-press community. The mimeograph was readily available and familiar to writers through their office work or educational institutions, which strengthened its association as an everyday machine. It also lowered the barrier to entry into print, which in turn enabled more publishing of the "proto" and "rangey." Editors did not need a financial backer who understood their programmatic place in the literary scene in order to break through. Taking the production process into their own hands gave relative financial and ideological independence for marginalized literary communities including Black Arts groups, feminist organizations, and poetry-oriented publications like *0 to 9*. Although it is often said that mimeography produced ephemeral writing projects that invited spontaneity,[124] neither the mimeographed *0 to 9*, *Lines*, or *Joglars*, nor the offset *some/thing*, *Aspen*, or the various Fluxus *ccV TRE* newsletters, read like quickly produced magazines, designed to get their writing into the world.

Whereas the mimeograph was most often found in business offices, offset printing was more commonly found in industrial settings. Both printing methods "call[ed] into question the terms of finite production, especially the limited edition so central to [the fine art] tradition."[125] Commercial printing companies used offset lithography or photo-offset as they produced cleaner and more reliable results geared toward larger print runs than the mimeograph or letterpress. While offset required a skilled printer, it likewise appealed to conceptual artists because it was associated with deindividualized mass production and did not bear the mark of the perhaps nostalgic veneration of letterpress or woodcuts, and in this "industrial mode," as Drucker argues, it was related to video, another medium explored by proto-conceptual artists at the time.[126] In this way, offset "counter[ed] the premises and claims of the auratic original" and was therefore arguably allied with the mimeograph's democratic promise.[127]

Proto-conceptual magazines emerged in the context of visual art's turn to language in the 1960s and 1970s, and many visual artists wrote specifically for the magazine context. Piper's, Acconci's, Graham's, and Barry's *0 to 9* pieces, for example, did not have so-called originals outside the magazine. Many artists were aware of the usefulness of printed matter, such as the write-up or other forms of documentation and ephemera, which can be seen as "the defining media of Conceptual art in the 1960s."[128] Yet for many proto-conceptual artists and writers the gallery was not "still discursively located even within journals as the primary context" for reception, nor was the work distributed or sponsored by a gallery.[129] Certain conceptual works that were printed in the glossy *Avalanche* (1970–76) presented a version of conceptual art that was geared toward galleries. Sprinkled with interviews, artist statements, and advertisements for galleries and exhibitions, *Avalanche* resembles commercial magazines like *Artforum* (which also turned to conceptual and minimal art around 1971) and the later *October*.

Proto-conceptual magazines, by contrast, present far more haphazard, noncommercial, and poetry-focused projects.

Compared to the subsequent generation's proto-Language poetry publications, neither the politics of small-press publishing nor the inclusion of modernist or non-Western poets were theorized extensively in proto-conceptual magazines. The paucity of paratexts in *some/thing* and *0 to 9* is in line with the anti-academicism of the poetry and art worlds of the 1960s. One exception is Mayer's paean for the mimeograph, published years later in the *Poetry Project Newsletter*. In "Mimeo Argument," Mayer writes that it is better "to blend [poems] in to a long series or a longer work, better to superimpose them, better to keep them forever in your back pocket!"[130] Superimposed poems become serial pieces, like Johns's numbers, Themerson's poetic "chord," and Queneau's excessive exercises in style. Since governments and sponsors "prefer the glossy and the bound," mimeographing and noncommercial self-publishing are political acts: "To prefer glossiness to modesty, for its own sake, is a step in the direction of condemning plagiarism, and its friends, obscenity and political freedom."[131] Along those lines, the perfect-bound book represents "bourgeoisie value"; wanting "lasting precious books" is for "jobbers." Here, Mayer echoes Walter Benjamin, a writer highly alert to the power of provisional publishing formats, who suggested in 1928 that "significant literary effectiveness . . . must nurture the inconspicuous forms . . . in leaflets, brochures, articles, and placards," since they serve "active communities" better than the "pretentious, universal gesture of the book."[132] While the "mimeograph has a traditional reputation for being for beatniks and desperate Russian writers," Mayer continues, "this momentary and urgent dissemination of poetry, which is also full of pleasure, is not the marketplace but a kind of cupbearing for the knowledge and pleasure of poetry."[133] In her equation of the "ephemeral" with freedom and permanence with capitalism, Mayer applies a classic avant-garde argument about the politics of form to the mode of printing and distribution.

The proto-conceptual magazine *Assembling*, sharing this democratic promise, handed over editorial power to its contributors. Those contributors, by "becoming [their] own printer," sent one thousand copies of their pieces (printed in any manner they wished) to be assembled by the editors, producing a rich mix of materials.[134] Such assembling can be seen in terms of literary politics that attempted to make publishing more accessible and inclusive. Proto-conceptual magazines promoted a democracy of participation similar to that of Fluxus or pop art in that they were, in certain ways, very accessible (most of the participatory Street

Works experiments and visual magazine pieces deliberately abhorred skill and craft, used cheap materials, and were presented for free or inexpensively). In other ways, they were, of course, considered inaccessible and difficult, as the aforementioned reader responses made clear.

Proto-conceptual magazines must be read with the idea of the democratic multiple in mind—a notion that was popularized in the 1960s among artists who believed that the distribution of artworks via cheap printing or books as everyday, mass-produced objects would be more democratic than the elitist gallery system.[135] A distribution service such as Printed Matter, started by Lucy Lippard and Sol LeWitt in 1976 and dedicated to artists' books, was crucial in helping art circulate outside the traditional gallery system. Responding to Benjamin's well-known argument about the loss of aura resulting from reproducibility, Andreas Huyssen notes that technology was instrumental in achieving the avant-garde's desired "transformation of everyday life," in practices like collage or montage and in media like film and photography, which "are in fact designed for mechanical reproducibility."[136] At the same time, it is not the technology itself that produces an avant-garde effect. Reproducibility was used commercially by pop art and, indeed, other consumable art criticized by Benjamin. Proto-conceptual magazines used reproducibility to demolish the precious work, but that effect was the result of the conscious manipulation of aesthetic elements rather than the automatic output of available technology.

Like the antiprofessional gestures and cleverly mass-marketed and institutional strategies employed by some proto-Dada magazines, 1960s artists' books were supposed to create the likeness of an antiprofessional work in their simple or offhand design, an effect that was, of course, also calculated to an extent.[137] Certainly, this "Myth of the Democratic Multiple," as Drucker calls it, while not ultimately successful in democratizing art, did produce intelligent works that engaged with the print medium as suitable to art production. The mimeograph, cheap offset, and DIY publishing more broadly constituted one strand of the practical pedagogy embraced by these little magazines. As Lippard and Chandler argued in contradistinction to McLuhan, "the medium need not be the message, and some ultra-conceptual art seems to declare that the conventional art media are no longer adequate as media to be messages in themselves."[138] Proto-conceptual magazines complicate that picture by engaging with the magazine medium itself as a conceptual object. While the idea in many contributions is indeed paramount, the material is in no way secondary. The magazine as an atlas for various maplike documents gestures to real, imagined, and textual performances, but the very fact that they are intended to be read on the page rather than on a gallery wall—indeed, the fact they are meant to be read at all—not only makes them literary but broadens the concept of writing. The dematerialized works are, after all, printed in the material object of the magazine.

Moving into the Gallery

The little magazine was an ideal place to test ideas-based works because it did not necessitate large spaces or high material costs—a crucial factor for emerging artists and poets. Some proto-Dadaists also bridged the gap between poetry, performance, and visual art in their typographic experiments, but the sheer proliferation of these intermedia developments in 1960s proto-conceptual magazines further reduced the boundaries between one art form and another. Innovations in the materiality of the text and the magazine as exemplified in *0 to 9* and *some/thing* foregrounded creative reading strategies through a visible engagement with a wide range of texts, which are quoted, appropriated, or even wrapped around a magazine's copy.

Proto-conceptual magazines practiced an institutional critique of the literary magazine as a medium that shapes reception. Both *some/thing* and *0 to 9* asked readers to rethink their definitions of art, shifting the location from the gallery wall to the page; they also asked them to recognize poetry as a document or script for performance and to consider its visuality, distribution, and maplike qualities. One way to defamiliarize poetry was to incorporate historically or ethnographically distant works that challenged the "candidacy for membership in the genre of poetry."[139] These non-Western and historical pieces, alongside pieces that involved the body and subjectivity, have been eclipsed by canonical conceptualism. What's more, conceptualism's popularity in the art world has led to the devaluation and oversimplification of its poetic origins. It is not the case that high-profile conceptual artists like Andre, Acconci, Warhol, and Weiner eventually "follow through on the implication of [their specifically poetic] experiments"; rather, critics and curated retrospectives reduce proto-conceptual magazines to mere stepping stones to success.[140] But the heterogeneity, inclusivity, and mixtures of procedure and subjectivity that marked proto-conceptual magazines were important values in their own right. These magazines questioned poetic convention *and* remained legible as poetry, precisely through their capacity to broaden the genre of poetry itself.

Making poetry by other means, in other media and spaces, canceled out the precious poem and precious magazine, resulting in a formal heterogeneity that makes such works harder to classify.[141] If canonical conceptual art questioned the art object's materiality and relationship to the site within which it was exhibited, proto-conceptual magazines attacked literariness and the medium of the page but not at the exclusion of literature. Ultimately, some of the proto-conceptual or proto-minimalist work published in experimental 1960s magazines would find a permanent home on the gallery wall. Although *0 to 9* had resisted the well-crafted poem with white space around it and poetry's and visual art's traditionally formal and emotional preciousness, much conceptual and minimalist art did, indeed, look precious once surrounded by white gallery walls and the cushioned thickness of an anthology's covers, driving home the magazines' original critique of how much the reception context matters for the aesthetic and political meaning of a work.

But, of course, not everyone was ultimately embraced by the art world. Despite her early affiliation with proto-conceptualism, Bernadette Mayer did not become a canonical conceptual artist. In 1973, her work *Memory* (consisting of eleven hundred film stills and six hours of tape recordings) was condensed and included as a three-ring binder in Lucy Lippard's all-female exhibition *c. 7,500*. Lippard's "only explicitly Conceptual project" attempted "a narrative of a feminist Conceptual language" and featured, among many others, *some/thing* and *0 to 9* contributors Eleanor Antin and Adrian Piper.[142] Mayer's project was supported by Holly Solomon, a patron, collector, and gallery owner, and first exhibited at her gallery 98 Greene Street.[143] Despite Lippard's important work of connecting feminism and conceptualism in her criticism, as well as in her involvement in the feminist collective and magazine *Heresies*, the history of conceptual art has been mostly masculinist to date, an exclusion that critics like Eve Meltzer, and younger scholars like Rachel Warriner and Amy Tobin, have begun to rectify.[144] Several female magazine contributors, such as Antin, Madeline Gins, Alison Knowles, Mayer, Lozano, Piper, and Schneemann, have not or only belatedly entered the (conceptual art) canon, though a number of recent retrospectives are bringing them greater recognition.[145]

During and shortly after editing *0 to 9*, Mayer tried to figure out her next steps: "I wasn't sure what I wanted to do. So then when we stopped publishing the magazine I began to think about it and I inadvertently started to write *Moving*. And after I finished *Moving* I realized I really still wanted to write, and not try to be an artist."[146] Because Mayer's changing practice did not have a signature style, she is often grouped with different schools but not acknowledged as having played a crucial role in any of them. In this slipperiness of categorization, Mayer resembles Carolee Schneemann, who "has never pursued a slick, stylistic approach to materials" and was therefore largely omitted from the canon, which favors work that is "stylistically coherent and accessible."[147] But exclusions from the avant-garde canon also happen for reasons having to do with gender, money, institutional backing, the types of jobs available, and the artist's degree of willingness to pursue cultural capital. In the face of such considerations, Mayer posited in *L=A=N=G=U=A=G=E* in 1978, "Work your ass off to change the language & dont [*sic*] ever get famous."[148]

Some proto-conceptual magazine contributors did, of course, get famous. LeWitt is often presented as the programmer for conceptual art, as his "Paragraphs on Conceptual Art" (the twin piece to "Sentences on Conceptual Art") is frequently called "the first manifesto of conceptual art"; his "Sentences," in turn, is celebrated as a "cool-headed manifesto" or one of his "two manifesto-like pronouncements."[149] "Sentences on Conceptual Art" was also reprinted in the first issue of the important *Art-Language* magazine in 1969, which bore the subtitle *The Journal of Conceptual Art*. Why have LeWitt's "Sentences" and "Paragraphs" attained the status of manifestos, while other artist statements published in *0 to 9* have been neglected? Had Stefan Themerson's "Theatre of Semantic Poetry" or Raymond Queneau's "Exercises in Style" been given the same attention, *0 to 9*'s typographical, musical, performative bent, on the one hand, and its Oulipian and narrative influence, on the other, would have been regarded quite differently today. One possible answer lies in the convenience of categorical statements. Unlike Queneau's or Themerson's statements, LeWitt's sentences follow the instructional form and imperative tone of a manifesto. By authoritatively positioning "Sentences on Conceptual Art" at the beginning of the penultimate issue of *0 to 9*, the subsequent pieces are inevitably inflected by it. But LeWitt's manifesto is not a manifesto for the magazine; it is simply another example of the plurality endorsed in its pages.

In his introduction to the Ugly Duckling reprint, Acconci describes the fifth issue of *0 to 9* as showing the first signs of the two editors parting ways. LeWitt's "Sentences on Conceptual Art" is stamp-approved by Acconci, who signs most pieces in the issue in the bottom right corner with his initials and the word *moving* plus the last word of the contribution in question. LeWitt's piece thus concludes with "moving art—V.H.A." Though the product of a chance procedure, it is an ironically apt comment on LeWitt's argument, seemingly so opposed to emotional art. Acconci's signature makes readers aware of discourses of authority and of institutional recognition—whether we classify or expect something to be moving (touching) or moving forward in avant-garde progressiveness. Very literally, Acconci performs an act of moving by moving the last word of a contribution to the corner of the page, chiming with the magazine's fascination with self-referentiality and the architecture of the page. It is also an editorial attempt to steer the magazine in a particular direction, toward a more emphatically conceptual, ironic, and overtly curatorial style.

That Acconci signs off on all contributions without Mayer speaks to a shift in the editorial process, a moment of aesthetic solidification. Prior to this issue, editorial power appeared equally distributed, although some traditional roles persisted (Mayer recalls typing all the stencils whereas Acconci sought out most contributions).[150] But through the appropriation of his contributors' words, Acconci now surfaces as an editorial voice in the magazine. Acconci even practices LeWitt's call for the mechanical execution of a piece, down to the last item on LeWitt's list: "These sentences comment on art but are not art."[151] But Acconci's sentences go beyond commentary in their appropriation, bringing his editorial work closer to that demanded by the conceptual magazine *Art-Language*, which treated the editorial essay itself as "a work of conceptual art."[152]

Conceptual art, Joseph Kosuth claimed provocatively in the same magazine, "both annexes the function of the critic, and makes a middleman unnecessary."[153] Those artist-critics, who used supplementary text in conjunction with or as a replacement for their performance, photography, or other work, have dominated the discourse around conceptualism. Proto-conceptual little magazines offer an alternative history of conceptual avant-garde practice and anticipate, in their demand for the active role of the reader, the collective challenges to the ontology of poetry, criticism, and the magazine represented by the disparate communities, that, approximately ten years later, would become known for publishing and theorizing "Language Poetry."

3 Proto-Language and New Narrative Magazines as Theoretical Implements

About Language

If you leaf through editorial statements in the 1970s, you notice a distinct trend: the little magazine has become a critical-theoretical apparatus. *Là-bas*, for instance, according to its editor, published not only poetry but also "revisions and reactions," theory, and reviews.[1] *Roof* located a discourse about poetry inside the poetry itself. Magazine contributors frequently engaged in theoretical discussions and critiques of their own social, institutional, and print communities, and Rae Armantrout's question, "What does language-oriented mean?" in the first issue of *L=A=N=G=U=A=G=E* in 1978, exemplifies the self-examination and theorization that became integral to many little magazines and their developing aesthetic and political positions at the time.[2] In the views of many scholars, Language writing—as the period's preeminent avant-garde poetic community eventually came to be known—therefore appeared to fulfill, through its publications, Joseph Kosuth's call for the artist to "annex the function of the critic."[3]

In the 1970s and 1980s, the definition and membership of then-nascent Language writing was subject to dissent from both inside and outside the group's tentative borders. In 1988, nearly two decades after the first publications subsequently regarded as part of the Language network, the feminist poet-critic Rachel Blau DuPlessis argued in the little magazine *Sulfur* for Language poetry as a "set of related groups" rather than any singular entity.[4] *Sulfur*'s contributing editor Eliot Weinberger had objected to the inclusion of Clark Coolidge, Susan Howe, Michael Palmer, Jackson Mac Low, Bernadette Mayer, Lydia Davis, and Robert Glück in Language anthologies because "their presence is surely the product of personal and not group affinities"; once such presences are separated out, he argued, "what's left is an extraordinarily cohesive set of practices and concerns."[5] But by eliminating those voices and practices that did not quite fit, Weinberger manufactured coherence out of a disparate assemblage of practices. By looking at peripheral figures and at how such critical and theoretical debates as DuPlessis and Weinberger's influenced the perception of the group, we can situate the emergence of particular features and the dialogue around them firmly in little magazines. Through such investigations, the proto-forms of Language writing show a more divided and diverse network than is acknowledged in canonical accounts.

To trace the development of proto-Language magazines' engagement with poetics and critical theory requires not only examining the group's poems, prefaces, editorial statements, correspondence, and reviews but also viewing them alongside contemporaneous developments in the New Narrative group, Language writing's West Coast–based fellow traveler. For New Narrative magazines like *Soup* and *Poetry Flash*, theory was mixed with queer activism and embodied writing. As editor Steve Abbott put it in *Soup*, thereby coining the term for the group: "New Narrative marks an emotional moving forward. . . . New Narrative explodes, speaking to and creating community."[6] Kathy Acker, a writer who traversed various communities, exposes the false opposition between supposedly anti-theoretical autobiographical writing and the purportedly anti-affective, anti-embodied Language writing. Theorization, self-theorization, and sexuality affected the formats of magazines and their dynamic communities. As James Sherry explained in his introduction to the so-called Legend collaboration of Bruce Andrews, Charles Bernstein, Steve McCaffery, Ray DiPalma, and Ron Silliman in Sherry's magazine *Roof*, "The best way to understand what these poems are about is to read them, since they are continually talking about themselves."[7]

While self-theorizing was also utilized in New Narrative texts to repurpose narrative and queer content, the appeal made by magazines to bring poetry and criticism into proximal contact—an avant-garde aspiration since at least the proto-Dada magazines—aided Language writing's successful canonization and contributed to its perceived academicism. But within the proto-Language network, the little magazine served as a theoretical implement for a publishing pedagogy through which new poetry criticism and theoretically informed poetry could be practiced, very much as an alternative to the academy. Xeroxed reprints of modernist and other out-of-print poetry, available through a number of DIY distribution services advertised in little magazines, similarly established the magazine as a network through which a genealogy of small-press experimental poetry could be accessed.

Since *L=A=N=G=U=A=G=E* was and is considered one of the Language group's most important outlets, it is not surprising that its major contributors—Charles Bernstein and Bruce Andrews (the editors), Lyn Hejinian, Ron Silliman, Bob Perelman, Barrett Watten, and Steve McCaffery—have been discussed and anthologized as the canonical group.[8] Other writers who published prolifically in proto-Language little magazines—for example, Kathy Acker, the lesbian editor Barbara Baracks, and the gay writer Steve Abbott—have largely been omitted from canonical accounts of Language poetry or demoted to the status of influences, fellow travelers, or early practitioners.[9] To re-encounter those figures, we must study the little magazines published before, during, and after the run of *L=A=N=G=U=A=G=E* that included a range of writers associated with the group and that can, for social and aesthetic reasons, be considered proto-Language magazines, such as *4 3 2 Review* (edited by Simon Schuchat), *A Hundred Posters* (Alan Davies), *Big Deal* (Barbara Baracks), *Gnome Baker* (Madeleine Burnside and Andrew Kelly), *Hills* (Bob Perelman), *L Magazine* (Curtis Faville), *Là-bas* (Douglas Messerli), *MIAM* (Tom Mandel), *Open Letter* (Frank Davey; Steve McCaffery was a contributing editor), *Paper Air* (Gil Ott), *Personal Injury* (Michael Sappol), *Poetics Journal* (Lyn Hejinian and Barrett Watten), *Primary Writing* (Phyllis Rosenzweig and Diane Ward), *QU* (Carla Harryman), *Roof* (James Sherry), *Slit Wrist* (Paul Brown and Terry Swanson), *Sun & Moon* (Messerli), *Temblor* (Leland Hickman), *The Difficulties* (Tom Beckett), *The Figures* (Laura Chester), *This* (Barrett Watten and Robert Grenier), *Tottel's* (Ron Silliman), and *Unmuzzled OX* (Michael Andre and Erika Rothenberg). Some of these magazines published writers later identified or anthologized as Language-affiliated or who moved within the same friendship circles and shared influences, such as modernist and proto-Dada poets or teachers like Bernadette Mayer, Jackson Mac Low, and David Antin. Other magazines published work that showed features associated with canonical Language writing, such as the exploration of nonnarrative, nonreferentiality, and metatextuality, a distaste for confessional poetry, and an interest in contemporary continental philosophy and New Left politics.

Most critical studies of Language writing tend to focus on a narrow range of authors, and even when they analyze magazines, they often discuss *L=A=N=G=U=A=G=E* exclusively.[10] No thorough contextual and comparative reading of several contemporaneous little magazines of the period has yet been published.[11] To correct this oversight, after a brief analysis of the reception and institutionalization of canonical Language writing, I will turn to specific magazine communities and assess how they use or refuse theory or self-theorization and to what end and effect. Such assessments not only allow for an understanding of the development of Language writing within the larger context of avant-garde little magazines of the period but also reveal which rhetorical strategies and personal and social affiliations appear to have aided or prevented canonical incorporation during the formalization of a poetic tendency.

From Tendency to Movement

The scope of criticism on Language poetry is vast, ranging from early reviews by Marjorie Perloff and Jerome McGann in scholarly journals to essays, monographs, dissertations, and critical books by the poets themselves.[12] "Language writing" is often anthologized as a movement emerging in the 1970s and 1980s in New York City, the Bay Area, and Washington, DC. Though the group's work is occasionally labeled "*L=A=N=G=U=A=G=E* writing,"[13] the little magazine *L=A=N=G=U=A=G=E* (1978–81) was not the origin of the group but rather identified an existing practice that was then subsumed under its name.

Critics have contributed to the perception of Language writing as a unified practice by repeating characteristics common to some of the group's texts: discursive framing, belief in the readers' co-production of meaning, the poem's construction from language itself rather than from the writer's experience, absence of a single coherent voice, nonnarrative or disruption of narrative, disjunction, and increased use of parataxis, as well as a grounding in Marxist and poststructuralist theories of language, by which those experimental formal features can serve as ideological critique.[14] Practitioners themselves often referred to "an aesthetic tendency whose definition is not a matter of doctrine but of overlapping affinities," differentiating themselves from the less provisional associations of movements and schools.[15] The so-called Language "tendency" began with *This* (1971–82, especially issue 7 in 1976), *Tottel's* (1970–81), and *Roof*'s summer 1977 issue; and became self-aware in the phrase "language-centered" in 1975 in the *Alcheringa* issue "The Dwelling Place: 9 Poets" and in Ron Silliman's commentary on his own work "from 'Language Writing'" in *L=A=N=G=U=A=G=E* in 1978.[16] It was popularized in 1979, when the Bay Area's *Poetry Flash* newsletter dedicated a special issue to "Language poets," with essays by Alan Soldofsky and Steve Abbott.[17] Further critical responses appeared in *Parnassus* and *Sulfur*, and special issues appeared in the United Kingdom in *Reality Studios* and *fragmente*.[18] The special *Alcheringa* issue also marked the beginning of "Language-oriented" or "Language-centered" compilations in primarily non-Language magazines, such as those edited by Charles Bernstein for *The Paris Review* and *boundary 2* and Silliman's *Ironwood* issue, all of which presented a broad range of authors.[19]

Another stage in Language writing's development from tendency to movement comprised issues dedicated to individual poets, as in Tom Beckett's *Difficulties* issues for Bernstein, Silliman, David Bromige, and Susan Howe, or Tom Mandel's *MIAM* single-author issues by Stephen Rodefer, Silliman, Bob Perelman, and Steve Benson. Language poetry reached a wider audience through contemporaneous reviews, public talks, readings, inclusion in major critical collections such as the Norton Anthology and anthologies such as Bernstein's and Andrews's *The L=A=N=G=U=A=G=E Book: Poetics of the New* (1984), Silliman's *In the American Tree* (1986), and Messerli's *"Language" Poetries* (1987).[20] Taken together, these publications and events established the name and the group. Prominent academic critics such as Fredric Jameson and especially Marjorie Perloff, and academic journals like *Critical Inquiry*, helped to inscribe Language writing in the canon by highlighting specific poetic elements and specific poets.[21] Lastly, negative reviews of proto-Language writing also provided a coherent image of the group, albeit a simplified one.[22]

Although the definition of Language writing continues to be disputed, the group's early critics generally agreed that it rejected the "expressive self" of the so-called romantic lyric and marked a "shift of emphasis away from subjectivity."[23] Perloff's first essay on the group, "The Word as Such," a title that looks back to the Russian Futurist manifesto, consolidated nonreferentiality and the materiality of the sign within the Language project, while also associating it with political revolution. In *Dance of the Intellect: Studies in the Poetry of the Pound Tradition* (1985), Perloff set Language writers, other "postmodernists" like Cage and Antin, and modernists like Zukofsky, Pound, and Stein against mainstream confessional poems and the romantic lyric, away from the "cry of the heart" and toward "the play of the mind."[24] Perloff argues that these writers transformed the romantic lyric into a multiplicity of voices and fragments through collage, or by leveling distinctions between poetry and prose, taking poetry "closer to the language of philosophy than to psychological self-projection."[25] But the languages of philosophy and psychological self-projection in practice often rubbed shoulders from one magazine contribution to the next or even within a single text.

Though antilyricism, reader participation, and parataxis were indeed frequent strategies for some proto-Language poets, they were not characteristic of all proto-Language magazines. The distortions in the critical representations of the romantic lyric (distortions that just as often derive from poets themselves) were duly criticized, in particular by feminists, and many critics and writers have detailed the importance of lyric to Language-affiliated compositional practices, so I will not repeat their arguments here.[26] Despite such recent reassessments, scholarship on and negative criticism of Language poetry as a movement have tended to establish a monolithic narrative over the years—whether of group belonging or of style—with only a few exceptions.[27] The notion that Language writing is a consistent object with identifiable characteristics or core members holds strong, even as writers identified with the movement have questioned the accuracy or usefulness of such assumptions.[28] To elucidate the development of Language writing, then, debates about labels, group membership, the language of philosophy, and the role of the reader must be analyzed not in relation to the group's canonizers and critics but in relation to where the debates first materialized: in little magazines, emerging from and addressed to a small-press audience. In such a context, the contested labels and generalizations, as well as the now-canonical writers, occupy a less privileged position among a plethora of practices and opinions.

Many proto-Language magazines were full of disquiet about the labels "Language Poetry" and "language-centered" and their implied group identity. Several magazines and individual poets described their practices by making direct reference to "language," often via semiotics, Marxian theories of language, and Steinian considerations of language as material, but as a common appellation "Language poetry" was at first more frequently used by critics than by practitioners. In *L=A=N=G=U=A=G=E*, Jackson Mac Low critiqued the term *language-centered* because it assumed some works were more "centered in language" than others.[29] In a footnote to Mac Low's essay, the editors endorsed his criticism of "terms which we also feel tend to inhibit understanding of the work they attempt to characterize. We hope that this reiteration will underscore the fact that these are not our terms."[30] As an alternative, Mac Low proposed the term *perceiver-centered*, while McCaffery offered *counter-communicative* and *cipheral* as descriptors.[31] None of these suggestions stuck.

Similarly, in the "Politics of the Referent" symposium edited by McCaffery for *Open Letter* and reprinted in *L=A=N=G=U=A=G=E*, the editors prefaced McCaffery's essay by distancing themselves from the label "language-centered" and its implied "entrapments of stylistic fixation": "our project, if it can be summarized at all, has had to do with exploring the numerous ways meanings can be (& are) realized. . . . The idea that writing could be stripped of reference is as troubling and confusing a view as the assumption that the primary function of words is to refer, one-on-one, to an already constituted world of 'things.'"[32] As the preface demonstrated, the group and individuals within it displayed a strong anti-institutional impulse from the start. In a letter to Tom Beckett, for a *Difficulties* special issue on Bernstein's work, Bernstein expressed his "ambivalent feelings about the expression 'language writing' 'as a compositional mode,'" but he recognized that the term might be a "fait accompli."[33] Despite "certain shared views about reading, . . . this is not a movement," he wrote, but rather "the social project of writers committed to a transformation of the society . . . , of which writing can be an important arena in terms of its investigation of the nature of meaning."[34] Bernstein's view of his writing community as potentially transformational is familiar from avant-garde discourse, but, unlike other avant-gardes, he expresses wariness over identifying that "social project" as a "movement."[35]

Unlike some earlier twentieth-century avant-gardes who were keen to present themselves as a soi-disant school or movement, poets were now increasingly suspicious of avant-garde institutionalization. This self-awareness may have been partly driven by the newly published English translations of theories of the avant-garde by Poggioli (1962/trans. 1968) and Bürger (1974/trans. 1984), which had inscribed the failure of the historical avant-garde.[36] The emerging identity of the proto-Language group was therefore at first based on its rejection of a labeled group identity. Ironically, the poets' habit of "talking about themselves," even to deny their collective cohesion, contributed to the formation of a group identity ascribed to them by readers and critics.

Conversely, attempts to discursively foster a print community did not ensure canonical presence, and some magazines have been excluded from the history of little magazines and the Language group in particular. *Unmuzzled OX* (1971–2001), edited by Michael Andre, sometimes with Erika Rothenberg, participated temporarily in the discourse of proto-Language poetry. Its first editorial, however, emphasized the inclusive masthead: "*Unmuzzled Ox* is not a neighborhood magazine. . . . We will print the best writing we can. Some of the writers we print, if we met them, we would dislike; some, we suspect, may dislike us; and some clearly dislike one another. None of which matters."[37] Presenting an image of inclusivity, the editorial policy purports to be based on quality, not sociality. But it also gestures to real problems of hostility among poetic avant-gardes and indicates that magazines can be the ground on which these conflicts are fought or avoided. In other ways, the editorial lines up with 1960s counterculture, and the magazine's humorous title is not used for programmatic and professional self-presentation but for entertainment.

The special issue of *Unmuzzled OX* titled "The Poets' Encyclopedia" maintains the magazine's humor, but it adopts the discourse of proto-Language writing, with two later-identified Language poets framing the issue. It announces that "much of the writing in the *Encyclopedia* is language-oriented; that is, the language is used not only as a tool of description but as the object of that description as well. The first entry is 'About' by James Sherry, the last is 'Zyxt' by Ron Silliman."[38] The year the *Encyclopedia* was published—1979—was also the year "Language writing" entered the critical vocabulary more widely through *Poetry Flash*. A year later, another magazine, *The Difficulties*, also announced: "We are starting a new journal of the arts which is to be devoted to process-oriented, language-centered work."[39] For *Unmuzzled OX* (and *The Difficulties*) to use a term that was on everyone's lips is a clear signal of attempted allegiance. *Unmuzzled OX*, however, did not make it into the canon: neither Andre nor the magazine is anthologized alongside other Language poets, despite Andre's adoption of the term *language-oriented*. The magazine's eclecticism and prankster humor, which align it with some 1960s mimeograph magazines of the New York downtown scene, and the absence of a consistent project and affiliations, do not make it a likely candidate for inclusion.

But even greater visibility does not guarantee canonical longevity. In Ron Silliman's "Dwelling Place" section of *Alcheringa*, group belonging was initially rather broad: "9 poets out of the present, average age 28, whose work might be said to 'cluster' around such magazines as *This*, *Big Deal*, *Tottel's*, the recent *Doones* supplements, the Andrews-edited issue of *Toothpick*, etc. Called variously 'language centered,' 'minimal,' 'non-referential formalism,' 'diminished referentiality,' 'structuralist.' Not a *group* but a *tendency* in the work of many."[40] Group identification is here emphatically based on magazines. "The Dwelling Place" featured Bruce Andrews, Barbara Baracks, Clark Coolidge, Lee DeJasu, Ray DiPalma, Robert Grenier, David Melnick, Ron Silliman, and Barrett Watten. Silliman's afterword also mentioned Charles Hine, Alan Sondheim, Charles Bernstein, The Black Tarantula [Kathy Acker], Lynne Dreyer, and Keith and Rosmarie Waldrop, all of whom had "moved into this area" since the gathering of the issue and had formed "a community of concern for language as the center of whatever activity poems might be."[41]

Baracks's and Acker's appearance in Silliman's afterword reveals a great deal about proto-Language poetry's self-fashioning in little magazines. Baracks was consistently included in early reports on Language poetry, and her chapbook *No Sleep* was published by Lyn Hejinian's Language-affiliated Tuumba Press in 1977. The above-mentioned *Toothpick* issue contained Baracks's "Thousands" (fig. 11), which in turn was quoted by McCaffery in "The Death of the Subject" and by Perloff (via McCaffery) in *Differentials*.[42]

For McCaffery, Baracks's poem exemplifies the rewards of nonreferentiality: syntax is broken down to the level of single words, forming a grid of aleatory possibilities. The poem asks readers to focus on the internal relations between words and their letters, word length, how letters recombine to form new words, and on words thus somewhat "removed from function" and "experienced as event per se."[43] In the magazine, an actual grid follows the poem; it is a crossword puzzle with answers and no questions. Both pieces are reminiscent of proto-conceptual work by Aram Saroyan and Clark Coolidge, as well as McCaffery's own visual poetics. *Toothpick*'s special issue was even modeled on *0 to 9*'s poetic maps and its experiment in design: halfway through, the issue had to be flipped when the printed text appeared upside-down.[44] It is easy to see why such an early poem by Baracks lent itself to an argument about nonreferentiality, cipherality, soundplay, and the supposed interpretative freedom of ambiguity. But it was atypical of Baracks's work as a whole. The poem from 1973 was more disjunctive and minimal than the prose poems included in her own magazine *Big Deal* and in *4 3 2 Review*, *Roof*, and *Alcheringa*. McCaffery selected a rather uncharacteristic poem to illustrate an extreme form of referential reduction, which Baracks very soon chose to abandon but which McCaffery felt to be at the heart of the budding Language group. Baracks would shortly thereafter be reduced to an influence only, her name relegated to the introduction of *In the American Tree*, the first Language anthology proper. Eleven years later, the same editor (Silliman) did not consider her work important enough to be included in the anthology, perhaps because by that point Baracks had disappeared from the writing scene completely, or partly because of what Baracks regarded as the scene's misogyny.[45] Her last published poetic works were xeroxed manuscripts distributed by the *L=A=N=G=U=A=G=E* Distribution Service in 1978, although she continued to write feminist criticism into the 1980s.

Any reconsideration of Language writing's emergence must include figures like Barbara Baracks, whose writing exemplifies the features of Language writing in its early stages, as identified by McCaffery. The fact that Baracks is not typically

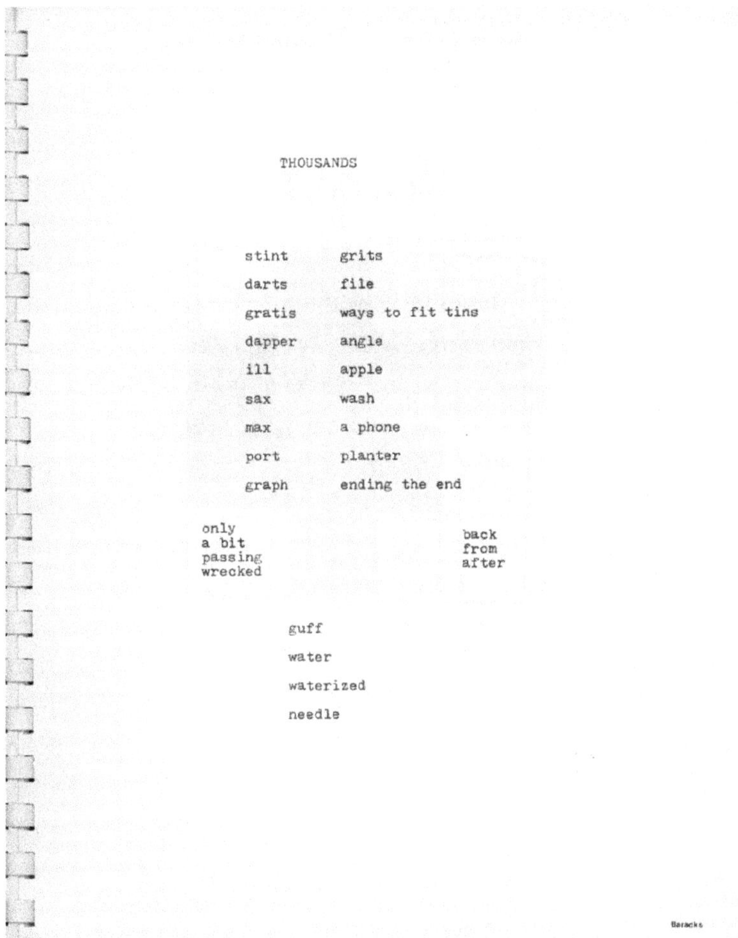

THOUSANDS

stint grits

darts file

gratis ways to fit tins

dapper angle

ill apple

sax wash

max a phone

port planter

graph ending the end

only
a bit
passing
wrecked

back
from
after

guff

water

waterized

needle

Baracks

Figure 11. Barbara Baracks, “Thousands,” *Toothpick, Lisbon, and the Orcas Islands* 3, no. 1 (Fall 1973), unpaginated. Used with permission of Barbara Baracks.

included in the Language canon speaks to the centrality of theorization and high visibility to installation in the avant-garde hall of fame, and to the contingency of group formation. The example of Baracks raises an interesting conundrum: because extreme disjunction and reduced referentiality in poems cannot achieve the political emancipation of their readers by themselves, a discourse supplementary to those poems is required if the goal is to extend beyond the literary. Baracks did not theorize herself, so her work was theorized for her. McCaffery and other self-theorizers would carry the flag from then on.

The Poem and Magazine as Theory

The theorization of Language poetry by critics was preceded and accompanied by the writers' own statements on poetics, often taken up verbatim by their critics. These discursive writings, which began in little magazines and were further developed in academic books, foregrounded a discourse inspired by French theory, Russian Formalism, Ludwig Wittgenstein's language games, and modernist predecessors. Such theorizing ultimately played a major part in circumscribing the group's identity, while magazines became the vehicle where poetry and theory (or literary criticism) could merge. If the page functioned as a map in proto-conceptual magazines, it often became blocks of prose, a lineated essay, or a typographic explosion of ciphers in proto-Language magazines.

The perception of Language writing's antilyricism was perhaps instigated by Robert Grenier's declaration "I HATE SPEECH," in the first issue of *This*, which advocated a poetry that avoided "formal habit" by diverging from the rhythmic flow and normal syntax of American speech but did not exclude "feeling" per se.[46] What critics often identified as Language poetry's outright dismissal of the lyric genre was in many cases simply a disavowal of "the primacy of the individual voice" or of an unquestioning "natural mode."[47] In an essay in *L=A=N=G=U=A=G=E*, Charles Bernstein argued that the "person" and the appearance of "naturalness" in, for instance, Frank O'Hara, Jack Kerouac, or Bernadette Mayer (especially in *Memory*) are used to great effect in their respective works because they are "completely intended, complex," and "dense, embedded."[48] Proto-Language magazines also published several lyric poems alongside poetry of non-lyric abstraction and fragmentation. They combined a critique of the voice- and speech-based poetry of many associated with New American and Black Mountain poetry, which privileged authenticity, with a critique of the subject that was inspired by poststructuralist thinkers and perhaps familiar from the proto-conceptual magazines of the previous decade. Proto-Language magazines continued conceptualism's investigation of literariness and a rejection of preciousness—normalized qualities in which, as Silliman argued, "the line is the cheapest signifier of The Poetic."[49]

Unlike their proto-conceptual predecessors, who published little critical prose, proto-Language magazines often theorized their interrogation of "the literary" in essays or poetry that accentuated their theoretical grounding. When *L=A=N=G=U=A=G=E* dedicated an entire issue to Roland Barthes, it not only paid tribute to a major influence; it also offered a poetic and editorial model of what a Barthesian exploration of "texts," rather than "works," could look like. It did so by taking inspiration from Barthes's own performative and playful style, by questioning authorship and taking the word as "dwelling place" (rather than narrative) and, as Peter Middleton argues, by creating a palimpsest of quotes, extracts from letters, paraphrased theory, and creative commentary.[50] Barthes's *Writing Degree Zero* (1953/English trans. 1967), *S/Z* (1970/English trans. 1975), and *Image, Music, Text* (1961–73/English trans. 1977) proved influential in replacing the closed work with the open text, the readerly with the writerly text. We find similar formulations in proto-Language magazines. If a poem is "open," "generative," and "rejects . . . authority," as Lyn Hejinian posits, more power is allotted to the reader—an aim many proto-Language magazines advance.[51]

The group's attempt to empower the reader was often integrated into a Marxist critique of the commodification of language. Difficult poetry, understood as uncommodifiable, could change a reader's political consciousness. Bruce Andrews, for example, maintained that one had to avoid the capitalist belief that meaning is transparent.[52] Instead, with echoes of Benjamin's "author as producer," Andrews proposed that "altering textual roles might bring us closer to altering the larger social roles of which textual ones are a feature. READING: not the glazed gaze of the consumer, but the careful attention of a producer, or co-producer."[53] The consumer-producer paradigm is of course a sticky one: production is not inherently anti-capitalist, nor is consumption entirely avoidable or particular to capitalism. The ideology of reader empowerment was also visible in a paratextual remark by Tom Savage that prefaced his "Kits" in *Roof*. The poems, he claims, "invite the reader to participate in their meaning" by adding to or subtracting words from them or by "simply read[ing] them as finished poems."[54]

Sometimes the line between theoretical discourse and poetry became formally blurred in proto-Language magazines: poems "talk[ed] about themselves," as James Sherry had presciently remarked in *Roof*. Bernstein's essay-poem "Artifice of Absorption"—first published as a special issue of *Paper Air* and later reprinted by Harvard University Press in Bernstein's collection *A Poetics*—engages with Veronica Forrest-Thomson's *Poetic Artifice* to argue against readerly "absorption," which is understood as "engrossing, engulfing / completely, engaging, arresting attention" and in favor of "impermeability," "artifice, boredom, / exaggeration, attention scattering, distraction."[55] At the same time, however, it also acknowledges the paradoxes and benefits of absorption, which does not automatically entail getting lost in ideology, and notes that absorptive and anti-absorptive modes of reading usually co-exist. Printed as a poem with line breaks, but written in prose, Bernstein's piece is effectively an essay about how typography shapes meaning. While easily dismissed as a gimmick, it embodies the ambition of some proto-Language magazines to merge poetry and prose or poetry and theory. It was fitting that the piece was published by Gil Ott's *Paper Air*, the insistently and outspokenly political magazine that focused on "social engagement," poetry, art, and criticism.[56] It also displayed an openness to a number of practices and ars poetica and published, for instance, British experimental poets Wendy Mulford, Tom Raworth, Ken Edwards, John James, and Ulli Freer, as well as special sections on Japanese, Palestinian, and French poetry.

Ironically, the essay's attempt at anti-absorption produced just such absorption in one particular reader, who wrote in a letter to the editor that "the essay was easier to digest because of its typography."[57] Bernstein dismisses the "self-glossing" of much mainstream writing as producing an absorptive reading experience, yet his own essays have provided a gloss for his poetry and have helped make the difficult poem very teachable today.[58] Such theorizations reinscribe the author into the text. Poet-critics are both author and reader of their own text, and the binaries of writing and reception, or poetry and criticism, collapse. While espousing a liberatory readerly practice, self-theorizing poets might also appear more controlling over the way their texts should be read, and critics who only engage with the poets on their own theoretical terms can compound the sense that the poems are intended for directed or authorized reading practices.[59]

What does poetic engagement with theory do to the format of the magazine? There are three distinct kinds of proto-Language magazines: those that reference theory directly, often in critical essays; those that publish primarily poetry and creative prose; and those that do not contain any critical prose. *Poetics Journal* and *L=A=N=G=U=A=G=E* devoted themselves exclusively to prose, while *Paper Air*, *The Difficulties*, *This*, and *Hills* published both poetry and criticism. *Big Deal*, *Roof*, *4 3 2 Review*, *L Magazine*, *Slit Wrist*, and *Personal Injury* contained theoretically explicit texts but did not foreground or isolate them from surrounding poems. The publication of critical essays proposed poetics as an important extension of, or alternative expression for, poetry rather than a mere accoutrement of poetry. The magazines that mixed poetry and theoretical prose presented the magazine as a venue for theoretical argument and dialogue, diminishing differences between so-called academic writing and creative practice. While emphatically more ludic than the criticism published in academic journals, theoretical engagement also inscribed the little magazine into a tradition of learning, linking back to the self-edifying historiography of some proto-Dada magazines and the democratic promises attached to the mimeograph and cheap offset for proto-conceptual writers.

A Xerox Mentality

Proto-Language magazines that explicitly engaged with theory often did so via a reappraisal of modernist texts, as an expression of their magazine pedagogy. *L=A=N=G=U=A=G=E* was determined to reclaim radical modernists such as Gertrude Stein, Louis Zukofsky, George Oppen, and Laura (Riding) Jackson and defended them as part of its attack on mainstream confessional poetry. Dedicated to Stein, the sixth issue of *L=A=N=G=U=A=G=E* asked several writers to respond to *Tender Buttons* in ways that "might seem relevant to their own concerns in writing."[60] Many responses were rewritings through *Tender Buttons* that played with repetition, sound-play, and wit. The emphasis was on reading as a creative practice. While Michael Davidson read Stein as a poststructuralist avant la lettre, Robert Grenier added parenthetically that "it's at best a 'creative misreading' of Stein to take her work as an instance of 'language-oriented writing'" because all her works "show her thinking language not as object-in-itself but as composition functioning in the composition of the world."[61] To take *Tender Buttons* "as a variously interesting arrangement of words, alone," Grenier warned, "is to perpetuate the initial journalist-parody response to the work as 'nonsense.'"[62] The magazine was full of such disagreements, and it is important to remember that it did not present a unified view.

In the 1960s, avant-garde magazines and small presses had already curated a lineage in reprinting Stein but without explicit theoretical deliberation. In the 1970s, magazine discussions of modernism morphed into critical evaluation.[63] In 1967, Stein appeared in *0 to 9*, adjacent to Native American songs, a map by Robert Smithson, and translations from Novalis. The nonhierarchical editorial policy at *0 to 9* resulted in an assemblage where the relation between contributions was left for the reader to discover. In a proto-Language magazine, by contrast, this championing of modernist texts was more argumentative and was used for exercising a poet's critical faculty in prose writing.

Proto-Language magazines did not just reprint modernists; some also (re)printed texts by theorists and linguists. *L=A=N=G=U=A=G=E* excerpted Barthes, Fredric Jameson, and Stanley Cavell, while *Poetics Journal* published the linguist George Lakoff, the literary theorist Viktor Shklovsky, and the philosopher and psychotherapist Félix Guattari. Peter Middleton therefore argues that *L=A=N=G=U=A=G=E* "became an agony/advice column for discussing authorship under many names," aided by the editors' "directorial style of authorship through excerpting and anthologizing."[64] In *L=A=N=G=U=A=G=E*, excerpts and other contributions appeared side by side, with contributors' names at the bottom of a piece, "to the point where the editors can seem to be speaking through the choice of words and passages in these carefully framed contributions, as if those contributions were quotations in an editorial argument."[65] The magazine could indeed give the impression of a collective editing process, aided by the layout, in which contributions—in Courier typeface—were not visually distinguished. Middleton's suggestive discussion of the challenge to authorship through excerpting can be strengthened by considering the increasingly widespread technology of the photocopier and its influence on a new mentality of working with text and language as material.[66]

If we recall Bernadette Mayer's fond memories of the mimeograph and its social element of collaboration, the photocopier, the quintessential modern office instrument, might not immediately invite comparable fondness. But Xerox, too, promised "a potential element of self-making," as Lisa Gitelman has shown, and "suggest[ed] the potential fluidity of print publication—its fixity melted by selection, excerption, collection, versioning, and reproduction."[67] Although photocopying did not fully erase human labor—editors still had to type a master copy on a typewriter or early computer or handwrite or collage a piece—it certainly made reproduction easier than typing mimeograph stencils or setting letterpress type. Exceptions to this include Susan Howe's typewriter/Xerox poems and Steve McCaffery's Xerox series *Carnival: The Second Panel, 1971–75*, which created laborious and playful manipulations of the page after the composition and at the level of printing. Howe produced poems by cutting and pasting text, xeroxing it, then cutting and pasting the photocopy again; McCaffery smudged, overprinted, and blurred his text.

Disassociated from its office setting, the Xerox changed artistic sociality. Artists and poets would photocopy a draft of their new work and share it with friends. This form of private and fairly haphazard distribution was extended by the photocopy networks of the Segue and *L=A=N=G=U=A=G=E* distribution services. *L=A=N=G=U=A=G=E*, for example, made available photocopies of out-of-print books, zines, and unpublished manuscripts "at the cost of the photocopying and packaging plus a twenty-five-cent royalty to the author."[68] This practice, like self-publishing, print-on-demand, and small-press publishing more broadly, allowed editors and poets to sidestep conventional channels of approval and finance. Since the unavailability of many works was "closing off a dialogue," *L=A=N=G=U=A=G=E*'s reprints promised to instead "sustain" and "expand" that dialogue.[69] Reprints included two manuscripts by Baracks; Mayer's first pamphlet from 0 to 9 Books, *Story*; Hannah Weiner's work; and books and magazines edited by *L=A=N=G=U=A=G=E* contributors, such as *Big Deal* and *Toothpick*.

In addition to the distribution service, some proto-Language and New Narrative magazines were photocopied by the editors themselves, such as Silliman's *Tottel's* and Dodie Bellamy and Kevin Killian's *Mirage #4 / Period[ical]*. *L=A=N=G=U=A=G=E* was first composed on a typewriter, then offset printed, and additional copies were later photocopied.[70] The characteristics of photocopying lauded by Gitelman are strikingly similar to those that proto-Language poets claimed for their poems and magazines, namely, the expansion of what was considered a text or document. Kate Eichhorn similarly suggests that xerography instantiated "an entirely new paradigm of document reproduction" that allowed an individual to copy independently an entire book, magazine, or text, or mix and match them, very quickly and often secretly.[71] This secrecy suited politically radical texts like "militant manifestos, [and] smutty gay fiction" because they easily bypassed "the censors and gatekeepers."[72] For New Narrative magazines, like *Mirage #4 / Period[ical]*, which emerged within a context of queer subculture, this ability to avoid heteronormative censorship was appealing. For proto-Language magazines, the ability to circumvent institutional control over language and monetary resources suited their Marxist critique of poetry. Photocopying not only enabled the agile mustering and recirculating of poetic materials appropriate for supporting editorial directives; it also required little skill, and poets were able to access photocopiers through work or cheap copy shops, which facilitated rapid responses and interventions. By photocopying their own works or those of others, proto-Language magazines and small presses could easily extend their avant-garde family tree. The Xerox machine served as an essential tool in this inexpensive revival of print works and as a speedy, practical medium for the development and circulation of proto-Language small-press politics of dialogue.

Dialogue as Pedagogical Implement

Another way for proto-Language writers to socialize in print and develop in relation to other writing communities was to recommend and contribute to like-minded magazines. Several magazines, such as *Paper Air*, *Poetry Flash*, *L=A=N=G=U=A=G=E*, and *The Difficulties*, published lists of other magazines and recent chapbooks, thereby establishing links among magazines and publicizing their shared interests. This encouraged their own contributors to submit to or read these other periodicals and to extend their network beyond a friendship-based circle of readers. *L=A=N=G=U=A=G=E*, for example, dedicated a whole issue to small-press UK experimental poetry, guest-edited by cris cheek. The magazines that *The Difficulties* or *L=A=N=G=U=A=G=E* recommended were not all in the spirit of the nascent Language writing and thus provide further evidence of the initial inclusivity of the proto-Language network.

This dialogic engagement was also attempted formally, as contributors debated the tone and form of theoretical essays and poems. Whereas anthologies and critical monographs imply cohesion, the magazines themselves embraced creative differences and fostered discussion by inviting responses from readers or hosting so-called symposia in print. Like the championing of modernist texts, symposia gave poets the opportunity to practice a new critical prose style. A special symposium titled "The Politics of Poetry" (see fig. 12) appeared in *L=A=N=G=U=A=G=E* in 1979, with respondents discussing "what qualities writing has or could have that contribute to an understanding or critique of society, seen as a capitalist system."[73] Some contributors referenced Fredric Jameson, Gilles Deleuze and Félix Guattari, Viktor Shklovsky, or Marx's respective views on the political potential inherent in aesthetic expression; others asked if writing had to address capitalism directly in order to critique it. Bernstein's "The Dollar Value of Poetry," for example, argued that poetry could resist serving capitalism or having an exchange value by making itself "unparaphrasable."[74]

Bruce Boone, a Bay Area writer affiliated with the nascent New Narrative group, responded to Bernstein by proposing that to probe the politics of writing—a practice he viewed as on the rise in poetry circles—means to ask "how writing can relate to revolution."[75] Boone believed that the contemporary writing featured in *L=A=N=G=U=A=G=E*, which he identified as formalist and modernist, needed to ask, "[Is] it possible to imagine a modernism that doesn't assimilate itself into the project of symptomatic reading?"[76] Boone

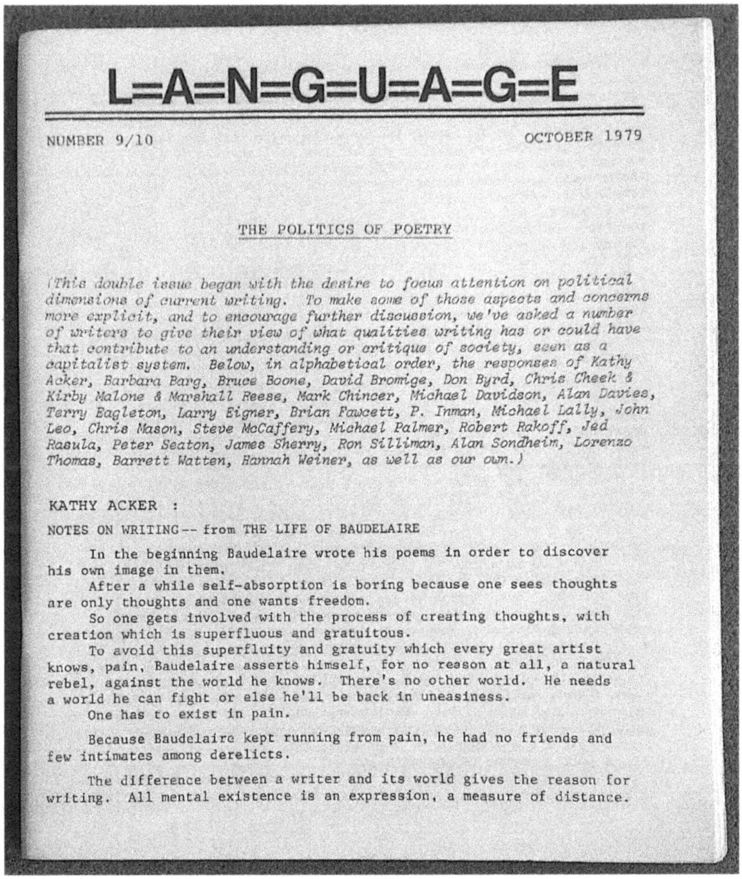

L=A=N=G=U=A=G=E

NUMBER 9/10 OCTOBER 1979

THE POLITICS OF POETRY

(This double issue began with the desire to focus attention on political dimensions of current writing. To make some of those aspects and concerns more explicit, and to encourage further discussion, we've asked a number of writers to give their view of what qualities writing has or could have that contribute to an understanding or critique of society, seen as a capitalist system. Below, in alphabetical order, the responses of Kathy Acker, Barbara Barg, Bruce Boone, David Bromige, Don Byrd, Chris Cheek & Kirby Malone & Marshall Reese, Mark Chincer, Michael Davidson, Alan Davies, Terry Eagleton, Larry Eigner, Brian Fawcett, P. Inman, Michael Lally, John Leo, Chris Mason, Steve McCaffery, Michael Palmer, Robert Rakoff, Jed Rasula, Peter Seaton, James Sherry, Ron Silliman, Alan Sondheim, Lorenzo Thomas, Barrett Watten, Hannah Weiner, as well as our own.)

KATHY ACKER :

NOTES ON WRITING-- from THE LIFE OF BAUDELAIRE

In the beginning Baudelaire wrote his poems in order to discover his own image in them.

After a while self-absorption is boring because one sees thoughts are only thoughts and one wants freedom.

So one gets involved with the process of creating thoughts, with creation which is superfluous and gratuitous.

To avoid this superfluity and gratuity which every great artist knows, pain, Baudelaire asserts himself, for no reason at all, a natural rebel, against the world he knows. There's no other world. He needs a world he can fight or else he'll be back in uneasiness.

One has to exist in pain.

Because Baudelaire kept running from pain, he had no friends and few intimates among derelicts.

The difference between a writer and its world gives the reason for writing. All mental existence is an expression, a measure of distance.

Figure 12. *L=A=N=G=U=A=G=E*, no. 9/10 (Oct. 1979): cover. Used with permission of Charles Bernstein.

criticized Language writing's putative aesthetic autonomy, with its ostensible absence of self-expression and more direct community work. He believed that it was not enough for writing to be "a political absence validated by the notion of a critique of power in an autonomous writing area"; writers, for him, "are simply people engaged in reaching, political organization, community work and liberation groups"; and writing is a means of "self-expression, and a group practice," which is "the opposite of modernism and écriture."[77] The symposia allowed *L=A=N=G=U=A=G=E* to include dissenting voices, such as Boone's, in its own pages, without necessarily changing its practice. Boone's criticism in the journal also ultimately proved crucial in establishing his own group with New Narrative.

Not all responses fit conveniently into the supposedly academic profile of *L=A=N=G=U=A=G=E*. Kathy Acker opened the symposium with an autobiographical essay about Baudelaire that never directly answered the topic question (fig. 12). Different also was Barbara Barg's contribution of a questionnaire; it included multiple-choice statements, such as

> 11. When writers converse in public they
> a) defend Melville against his critics b) show that Kerouac wrote well
> c) describe Rimbaud's growth as a literary artist d) should listen to themselves talk
>
> 12. Women writers
> a) are only concerned with content b) don't have happy marriages
> c) should always have men edit their works d) are naturally gullible
> e) are always referred to as "women writers."[78]

Here, Barg offers a clever feminist critique of a male-dominated public literary discourse that privileges male writers. Barg's intervention responds to complacency in male poets' self-representation by pointing out that they make their critiques of society from a position of sanctity. A magazine like *L=A=N=G=U=A=G=E* is not exempt from complicity merely because it interrogates the politics of poetry, Barg suggests, especially when its interrogation excludes the gender politics of poetry.[79]

Contrary to the programmatic coherence subsequently ascribed to *L=A=N=G=U=A=G=E* and its community, there was in the symposium no consensus of style and argument. That said, the more overtly programmatic statements by Bernstein, Andrews, McCaffery, Davidson, Jed Rasula, and the excerpt from Terry Eagleton, which outweigh in length and number the more creative responses, proved more easily quotable and contributed to *L=A=N=G=U=A=G=E*'s appearance as academic. For some readers, however, these critical writings were still too playful and obscure to function as poetic theory or analysis. John Taggart sent in a letter in which he complained about the magazine's reviews: "As I remember, the main thing was information. . . . Most of it (the reviews) is just too self-conscious, too cute to be of use. Many of the reviewers seem to feel an obligation to turn the review into a performance as near an 'original work' as possible." In Taggart's opinion, the role of a review was to establish "the basic identity of the text," after which "there may be a place for Barthes' choreography du text," but "it is a disservice to the writers involved. & if you say after all everybody knows everybody else, well I ask you!"[80] Taggart's indignant exclamation reveals an outsider's perspective on proto-Language writing, according to which everyone inside had easier access to the writings' difficulty and in which the magazine represented a closed social club, despite protestations that it was not.

Loris Essary responded to Taggart's objection in the subsequent issue, stating that rejecting "reviews that are anything other than hard 'information' strikes me as parochial as it is misguided." The inherent ability of a piece "to evoke further creative acts in its readers/perceivers" is, he wrote, its "evidence of success." For Essary, "to review a work in the usual academic terms of 'hard' information, those of 'influences,' 'style' and so on, tells us less about the work under consideration than it does about 'influences,' 'style,' 'criticism' itself." Instead, he advised, "Taggart would also do well to recall what Merleau-Ponty says about criticism itself": that traditional criticism is an exercise of a "secondary order."[81] Essary articulated the growing interest among poets, critics, and readers in new forms of criticism that blended literature and theory—forms for which Language poetry has become retrospectively known. Citing Merleau-Ponty in abbreviated form assumed at least some familiarity with the latter's argument on behalf of Essary's readers: that familiarity with theory indeed characterized many contributors and readers but also created divisions among them as a consequence. Preceding Essary's letter was a piece by Hejinian, which highlighted the magazine's curating of dialogue as if it commented on the letter that followed: "All theory is safest ascribed in retrospect. . . . The critic is a performer, good or bad."[82] Essary's and Taggart's contributions also revealed an avant-garde paradox with regard to accessibility and dialogue: reviews that were found to be useful to readers could potentially violate the ethics of reader-as-producer espoused by some proto-Language writers. As in some proto-Dada magazines, even a well-intentioned magazine pedagogy based on dialogue was not always received as hospitable.

The Rise of Theory

Retrospective anthologies often neglect the magazines' heterogeneity and contradictory theoretical positions in favor of the morsels most easily savored by the canonically trained palate: extracts that conform to prevalent cultural discourses at the time of the group's solidification, such as poststructuralism, and the expected self-explanation of avant-gardes following their historical models, as put forward in prominent avant-garde scholarship. Language writing's critique of the subject, for example, which was a reaction against the emerging Master of Fine Arts (MFA) industry and voice-centered New American Poetry, made it very "assimilable" to postmodern theory and the academy.[83] Scholarship on Language writing often repeats the self-theorizing statements made by poets themselves or uses the same theory with which poets also engage in their poetry or critical writing. In both cases, since "the theory and the poetry already seem to be 'speaking' to one another," as Sianne Ngai astutely observes, there is "a certain redundancy or obviousness when the two discourses are placed in dialogue with one another now."[84] The blame for the institutionalization of the Language group cannot be laid entirely at its own door; it is partly due to its readers' familiarity with and receptivity to theory. After all, the reader that Language poetry addresses had generally been made conscious "of the conventions that the writing subverts" through institutional training: this was "a reader with a high tolerance for opacity and somewhat informed about the poststructuralist views of language that the poetry itself embodies."[85]

The self-theorizing statements of proto-Language poets emerged in a social context in which the playful criticism offered by poststructuralism interested a wider readership than did previous developments in philosophy. Literary journalism and para-academic publications such as those by Semiotext(e) became popular venues for poet-critics, academics, and philosophers alike. Graphic design, too, was influenced by deconstruction's interest in ambiguity and illegibility. Derrida's *Glas*, for example, performed autodeconstructive commentary on typography in its arrangement in columns and different typefaces, a print-based experiment that interested Derrida because of the "constraints of paper—its hardness, its limits, its resistance."[86] The equals signs in *L=A=N=G=U=A=G=E*, in a logo designed by Susan Bee (fig. 12), gesture similarly to the instability and materiality of language. With the rise of poststructuralism in public discourse, universities, and museums from the late 1960s onward, theory became a significant stimulant for creative production and justification for difficult poetry. Gerald Graff establishes a connection between the rise of theory in the 1960s and academics' rejection of New Critical premises as a political move. Tired of having "to hunt for 'hidden meanings,'" Graff writes, scholars soon developed "stylish polemics 'against interpretation,'" based on the conviction that "interpretive techniques were not innocent but part of a larger technology of control."[87]

Dedicated theory and poetics journals, often explicitly political, proliferated in the 1970s and expanded their audiences. These included the art magazine

October, established in New York in 1976 by Rosalind Krauss; the American left journals *Telos* (1968), *New Left Review* (1960), the *Partisan Review* (1934), and the French *Tel Quel* (1960), which published many poststructuralists; and many other American journals like *Yale French Studies* (1948), *Diacritics* (1971), *SubStance* (1971), *boundary 2* (1972), *Semiotext(e)* (1974), *Glyph* (1976), *Social Text* (1979), and *Differences* (1989), which introduced Americans to French theory in the 1960s and 1970s. These journals, like proto-Language magazines, fostered radical critical thinking, and combined theory, Marxist politics, and art—a connection welcomed by poets, some of whom even listed these theory journals in their magazines. The 1970s American campus journals were united, François Cusset argues, by a "critique of the subject in its various modalities" and "a ludic relation to the translated concepts" of French theory.[88] Since the student movement of the late 1960s had failed, the presentation of French theory via these journals was an attempt at the "(purely discursive) subversion of the university institution."[89] An institutional environment such as the English department, in which knowledge became increasingly specialized and rarefied, was predisposed to welcome a poetry requiring such knowledge for adequate reception.

Many poets were cognizant of this problem of address and access. Silliman, for instance, commented on "the class origin of [Language poetry's] practitioners" and "the educational level of the audience," often the result of their own class positions.[90] But as feminist poet and editor Juliana Spahr pointed out in response to a discussion on the Buffalo Poetics List, Silliman's "investigation of privilege" largely neglected questions of race and gender.[91] One critique often leveled against Language poets is that they used the academy for self-promotion. Alan Golding, by contrast, sees this as taking "effect for intention." He argues that writers criticized the institution and its powers through a "provisionally complicit resistance" from within that very institution.[92]

Canonical Language writing's problematic relation to the academy is symptomatic of the perils of avant-gardes: institutional critique does not preclude, but can in fact further, one's entry into that institution. This affected the cohesiveness of groups and their chosen poetic and editorial pedagogy. Canonical Language poetry succeeded in part because it tapped into that enthusiasm for institutional critique and poststructuralism, at the same time as it was a product of it. In the public discourse surrounding postmodernism, a form such as a hermeneutically decodable lyric was also under attack for its alleged adherence to capitalist logic. The predilection of some proto-Language writers for an academic analysis of capital was thus flatteringly recuperable to the academy. But many poet-critics associated with Language writing also considered themselves to be making an overtly political intervention in poststructuralist discussions of language by way of parody, critique, and poetry, to counter the dogmatisms of the American synthesis of French theory they perceived in the academy. This poetic response to theories of language must be seen as an attempted counter-canon to the powerful sway academic institutions held over pedagogy and the reception of poetry, particularly contemporary poetry. To return, then, to the magazine networks in which these experiments in theoretical writing were initially conducted cannot undo that institutional trajectory but can offer a more complex historical understanding of Language writing's engagement with theory.

While many proto-Language essays were "understood or misunderstood [as] elitist"[93] or full of "intellectual *argot*"[94] by some readers, they would not have made it through the peer-review process of an academic journal. Claims about an avant-garde's elitism are not new: recall the outrage over Mina Loy's free verse or Pound's claim that Loy's and Marianne Moore's work was the "utterance of clever people in despair," or complaints that *0 to 9* was "without joy, without feeling." Indeed, responses to avant-garde magazines frequently revolve around issues of accessibility, autonomy, and, quite simply, feelings.

Theory with Feelings

Proto-Language writers were not the only group concerned with self-commentary and theory. New Narrative explored theory through subjective story-based prose that often blended fiction and autobiography, emphasized the body, and sometimes appropriated material from pornography, gossip, popular culture, and canonical literature. In Kevin Killian's *Bedrooms Have Windows*, a memoir about the narrator's teenage years and sex life that is enmeshed with fictional elements, the narrator, who is sometimes an "I," sometimes "Kevin Killian," describes sexual encounters poetically, theoretically, and explicitly ("His cock was hot and pulsed in my hand like a trapped skinned animal"); mentions "unsatisfactory fumbles toward 'safe sex' with a writer I used to admire, Dennis A.," which takes place in the New Narrative writer Aaron [Shurin]'s kitchen; imagines co-writing a book called *Bedrooms Have Windows* with his lover, George; and jokes in another passage that "it was as taboo as anything in Levi-Strauss."[95] In one chapter, the character Travis asks Carey to "Undo me," leading the narrator to reflect on this as "a sexual deconstruction. What our bodies do, not for love or pleasure, but towards a more highly qualified social structure."[96] Reviewing the book for *OutWeek* in 1989, Sarah Schulman wrote that Killian belonged to "an evolving literary movement that has yet to be named" and "consists of gay and lesbian writers who are informed by the last 30 years of the avant-garde but show feelings, don't think they're better than other people and put words together in a way that everyone can understand, even while using unusual rhythms and word orders. It's like a kinder, gentler avant-garde."[97] Although the literary movement had, in fact, been named New Narrative by 1981 (in *Soup*, no. 2), the fact that it was perceived as still evolving in 1989 contrasts with Language Poetry's currency as a label and style by 1979.

Like Language writing, New Narrative emerged in the 1970s and produced more explicit theoretical articulations in the 1980s. But unlike Language poetry, New Narrative has a greater claim toward contemporaneity. Robert Glück, Gail Scott, Mary Burger, and Camille Roy founded the short-lived online journal *Narrativity* in 2000. Bellamy's and Killian's *Mirage #4 / Period[ical]*, itself a follow-up magazine of Killian's New Narrative *Mirage*, ran from 1992 until 2009 (with new issues in 2018 and 2019). The recent anthology *Writers Who Love Too Much: New Narrative Writing, 1977–1997* (New York: Nightboat, 2017), also edited by Bellamy and Killian, gives 1977 and 1997 as bracket dates for the first generation of New Narrative writers, a second generation of which could extend to writers published in Bay Area magazines, such as the xeroxed *TRY!* (Sara Larsen, David Brazil, 2008–11) and *Digital Artifact* (Chana Morgenstern, Ren Evans, Amanda Davidson, 2007–9), which keep the New Narrative lineage alive or even deliberately present themselves as contemporary New Narrative writers through their interest in collaging and queering texts. This contemporaneity is made explicit in the title of yet another anthology, *From Our Hearts to Yours: New Narrative as Contemporary Practice* (2017), out through the publishing project *ON: Contemporary Practice* (discussed in Chapter 5). Maggie Nelson's *Argonauts*, Chris Kraus's *I Love Dick*, and even shows like Amazon's *Transparent* are hard to imagine without New Narrative.

At first glance, proto-Language writing's promotion of disjunctive syntax and reduced referentiality would seem to put it at odds with New Narrative. Practitioners were suspicious of "narrative in the conventional sense"—that is, "creating and resolving tension, introducing material, motivating sequence."[98] They sought literary alternatives to what they perceived to be the "the deep slumber of chronology, causality, and false unity (totalization)" at a time when teleological historical narratives were also under attack in the writings of Jean Baudrillard and Jean-François Lyotard.[99] In various disciplines, scholars like Hayden White, Jacques Derrida, Clifford Geertz, and Richard Rorty rejected both positivism and the notion that meaning was transparent. An elimination of narrative and a proliferation of abstraction was seen by many Language writers as politicizing the text and facilitating the reader's participation in the meaning-making process. New Narrative writers, in contrast, considered narrative a stylistic aid to this readerly emancipation in its capacity for expressing politics and engaging with their larger community. In the wake of the gay liberation movement, the AIDS crisis, and Reaganism's homophobic violence, queer writers found themselves confronted with the inescapability of and compulsion to return to the body and its vulnerability. They asked themselves, if we are part of this community in which many of our friends are dying of AIDS, how ought that to change our writing practice?[100]

Writers associated with New Narrative and Language differed, therefore, in their approach to form, but both integrated critiques of representation, realism, and ideology into their poetics. Kaplan Page Harris and Rob Halpern have recently argued that the two groups represented related responses to New Left politics in America, energized by many personal friendships across groups.[101] Halpern states that the "poetry wars" in the Bay Area retrospectively produced "reductive arguments" and a "caricature" of Language writing, ignoring the "generative dynamism" that had been at the heart of both literary communities.[102] Indeed, it is by such reductions that avant-garde "movements" usually become known; looking at their little magazines offers an opportunity to correct these caricatures. *L=A=N=G=U=A=G=E*, *The Difficulties*, *Poetry Flash*, *Soup*, *Mirage*, *Hills*, and *Poetics Journal*, for example, published writers from both scenes, and many contributors participated in the same reading series. Some proto-Language magazines even featured special issues on non/narrative, like *Poetics Journal* (1985), and Carla Harryman's newsletter-like *QU* experimented with poetic prose.

Some New Narrative writers, like Robert Glück and Bruce Boone, saw the Language group as overwhelmingly straight, white, and male and considered their "formalist fireworks" attractively rigorous though also indicative of "luxurious idealism" and "professionalism."[103] One of the reasons for New Narrative's emergence, Glück writes, was the feeling that some questions "were only partly addressed by Language poetry," which New Narrative writers saw "as an aesthetics built on an examination (by subtraction: of voice, of continuity) of the ways language generates meaning. The same could also be said of other experimental work, especially minimalisms, but Language Poetry was our proximate example."[104] Nevertheless, in its earliest incarnations New Narrative recognized many points of commonality with Language writing. *Soup* (San Francisco, 1980–85), edited by Steve Abbott, began its four-issue run with a clear statement of admiration and affiliation with proto-Language magazines such as *This*, *Paper Air*, and *L=A=N=G=U=A=G=E*, which "provide[d] a context of dialogue & dialectic with which most SOUP contributors are familiar."[105] Similarly, under Abbott's editorship, *Poetry Flash* published "Language Poets: An Introduction" in 1979 and continued to advertise and discuss Language-affiliated magazines such as *L=A=N=G=U=A=G=E*, *Poetics Journal*, and *The Difficulties*. Abbott himself maintained a correspondence with *Difficulties* editor Tom Beckett.

While the first issue presented *Soup* as a Language magazine, the second moved toward New Narrative. In his editorial, Abbott provided his own definition: "New Narrative is language conscious but arises out of specific social and political concerns of specific communities."[106] While distinguishing New Narrative from Language writing, he also acknowledged that "it is too early to close dialogue on these matters. Ron Silliman's review [of poetic autobiographies] offers a divergent viewpoint."[107] Bruce Boone, in turn, argued that Language writing "succeed[s] on its own terms," in its focus on "abstraction, [and] language experimentation," but remains too "distant from life."[108] Despite such misgivings, Boone reviewed Perelman's "China" favorably. Reading it for affect, he found it "aware of social dimensions in things" and "history as a problem." Boone's reading, juxtaposed with the poem itself on facing pages in the journal, leads Rob Halpern to argue rightly for a "productive tension" between Language poetry and New Narrative, a "dynamic" that *Soup* stimulated.[109] Its last issue, guest-edited by Boone and designed by Dodie Bellamy, inscribed the magazine more firmly into a New Narrative project. In the publisher's note, Abbott maintained that the two main purposes of the magazine had been "to combine an avant garde or High Art sense of craft with a community based sense of energy and to feature a writing of the 80s such as New Narrative poetry, fiction, translation and criticism."[110]

Abbott shifted the focus of his magazine away from Language writing, because, as he later wrote to Tom Beckett, he "distrust[ed] overemphasis on 'system,'" and saw "too much introverted self-seriousness in the project," though he admitted that he still "like[d] the West Coast L=A=N=G=U=A=G=E writers better than the East Coast crew & wld rather read Alice Notley than any of them (well, I flip abt alot [*sic*]—sometimes Bernadette Mayer, often Cheri Fein, etc.—and certainly Kathy Acker."[111] The general trajectory toward New Narrative was evidenced further in *Soup*'s announcement of Kevin Killian's new magazine, *Mirage* (1985–89), which in many ways became *Soup*'s successor. Perhaps unsurprisingly, Steve Abbott is generally omitted from the Language canon, partly because of his decision not to be included and because of his early death in 1992 from AIDS-related complications. In a 1990 letter to Dennis Cooper, whose magazine *Little Caesar* was itself a precursor to New Narrative, Abbott reflected on his promotion of New Narrative as "an avant garde project countering Language formalism because grounded in community concerns."[112] Abbott's case demonstrates that neither social affiliation nor shared practices automatically guarantee group belonging. Groups often require sustained textual or physical presence, repeated inclusion in critical accounts, or visible ties of friendship strong enough to outlast divergent aesthetic and political changes. Abbott's refusal of a "Language writing" identity shows that by *Soup*'s last issue, in 1985, Abbott's practice and social affiliations had changed, because distinctions between Language writing and New Narrative had become sufficiently sharp that they could be referred to as categorical or generic differences.

The New York–based *Big Deal* (fig. 13) had provided a home for the emerging New Narrative and Language groups ten years earlier. Edited by Barbara Baracks, it published Kathy Acker, Ron Silliman, Ray DiPalma, Bruce Andrews, Lyn Hejinian, Bernadette Mayer, Lucy Lippard, Alison Knowles, David Antin, John Cage, Jerome Rothenberg, Robert Smithson, and many others from a wide variety of aesthetic communities. In his *Alcheringa* section (1975), Silliman aligned *Big Deal*, alongside *Tottel's*, *This*, *Doones*, and *Toothpick*, with a project of "diminished referentiality." In issue 3 of *Big Deal*, published in the same year as Silliman's assessment, however, Baracks saw her magazine within a different framework: "I've recently become interested in narration, and put BIG DEAL 3 together with that in mind. Some of this issue's contributors may claim no interest in the subject themselves. But my own fascination with evidence, causality, continuity did shape the gist of the matter (the magazine)."[113] "Evidence, causality, continuity," and narration are not usually associated with Language poetry, except by their pointed absence. But in this proto-Language magazine, narrative and nonnarrative writing lived side by side.

In *Big Deal*'s narration issue, Kathy Acker appeared in the table of contents

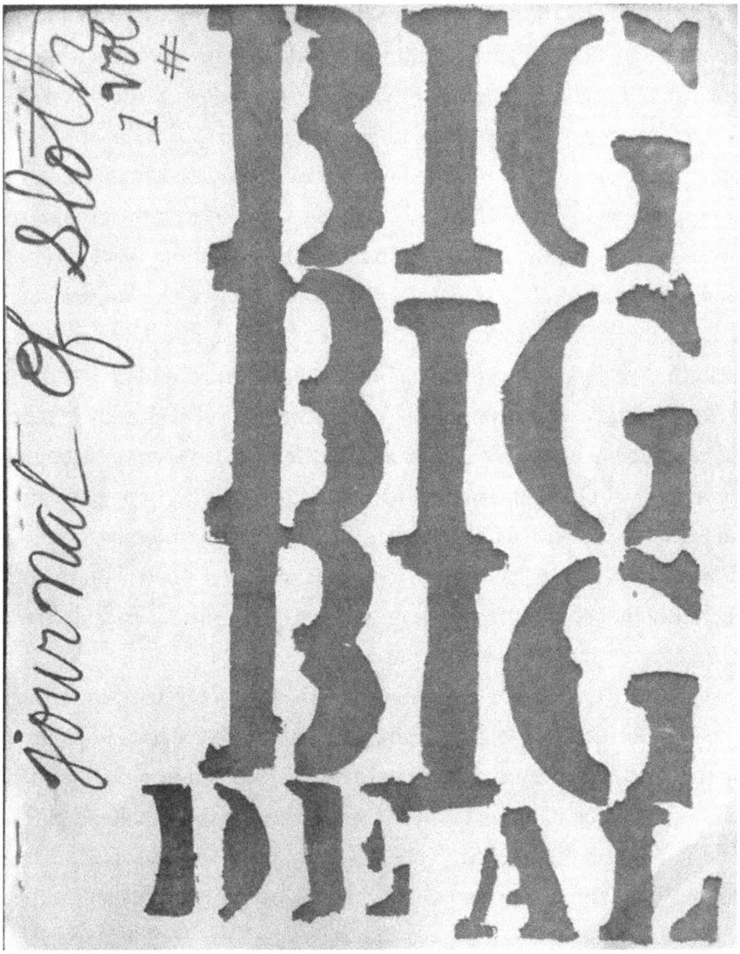

Figure 13. *Big Deal*, no. 1 (Spring 1973): cover. Used with permission of Barbara Baracks.

as "Ripoff Red" with her real name in brackets, as was standard practice for her, problematizing the relation between the author's voice and her fictional personas. When Red states, "Narratives you know are purely for shit. Here's the information go fuck yourself," Acker's critique resembles what has been identified as Language poetry practice: a rejection of a narration based on authorial experience or information.[114] Acker would later call straightforward narration "the bourgeois story-line" because she viewed such modes as related to ownership and manipulation and therefore believed that they required subversion.[115] To be sure, neither a rejection of narrative (Language writing), its implementation (New Narrative), nor its hybrid modification (Acker) has (yet) been effective in overthrowing bourgeois society, but these claims demonstrate how avant-gardes often attach utopian political ideals to particular forms.

Acker's inclusion in proto-Language and New Narrative magazines, both of which expressed admiration for her, can help us in assessing the groups' respective boundaries. Acker is mentioned in Silliman's "Dwelling Place" section and was published in *L=A=N=G=U=A=G=E* and other New York Language-affiliated journals, like *Big Deal*, *Personal Injury*, *4 3 2 Review*, and *Unmuzzled OX*, as well as in the West Coast magazines *Hills*, *Poetics Journal*, and *QU*, and the UK-based *Reality Studios*, which published many writers subsequently identified as Language writers. During that same period, she was also seen to belong to New Narrative or was regarded as a major influence on it. Acker appeared in *Soup*'s second issue (1981), with a characteristically erotic faux-autobiographical piece called "First Days of Life," alongside Silliman's review of poetic autobiographies by Lyn Hejinian, David Bromige, and Ted Berrigan, and was included in *Biting the Error: Writers Explore Narrative* (2004).[116]

Acker's affiliation with proto-Language writing was not accidental: her interest in disjunction, Ludwig Wittgenstein, poststructuralism, and self-examination during the writing process drew her to the same publishing venues, and editors and fellow poets took notice of her work, strengthening the link. Reflecting on her early work, Acker remembered, "I came out of a poetry tradition . . .—the Black Mountain poets, the Language poets."[117] Acker not only published in the same magazines and read at the same reading series in New York and the Bay Area (Segue, New Langton Arts, Grand Piano), but she was also, like many Language-affiliated poets, influenced by the appropriative techniques of proto-conceptual art. For her Tarantula stories in particular, excerpted in proto-Language magazines, she was influenced by the work of female conceptual artists, such as her mentor and friend Eleanor Antin, who played with "exchanging identities and doing performance work with identity."[118] Acker's Tarantula series was initially distributed privately as mailed Xeroxes using the same mailing list Antin had used for her *100 Boots* photographic series.[119] It was then picked up by TVRT, a press associated with Sol LeWitt, whom Acker mentioned in a conversation with Bernstein as an influence, alongside Joseph Kosuth and Dan Graham.[120] Bernstein and Acker, in turn, met at Bernadette Mayer's Poetry Project workshop in 1974 or 1975, where Acker gave a talk.[121] Acker's aesthetic and social ties make her an excellent example of the provisionality, receptivity, and heterodoxy of the proto-Language network.

In issue 2 of *Big Deal*, Acker's Tarantula reflects on her use of language and the relation between experience and writing, but she does not yet directly quote or reference French theory, as she would in her later novels:

> I use language, as a prediction system, prediction of every event since all events I know of are mediated through my consciousness (thus using time, space) to change this world. . . . All abstractions therefore are tools I use and can use consciously to perceive therefore to change. . . . I'm not a mirror, there's no such thing as a mirror; I'm not objective. . . .
>
> (1) Physical acts: . . . I liked to stick my finger in my cunt, and smell my finger. Physical non-controlled acts are therefore not physical but sensual acts, and are "mental" pleasures. My body is pleasure.[122]

This embrace of the "not objective" and the investigation of embodied writing are characteristic of Acker's pieces in proto-Language and New Narrative magazines alike. Acker's work blends Language writing's radical critique of a consistent monovocal subjectivity with attention to the body and identity more closely aligned with feminist and queer movement writing, New Narrative, or New York School poetry. Acker's pseudo-autobiographical fiction subverts the avant-garde objectivity and nonreferentiality paraded by some proto-Language poets and their critics, but it also distorts bodily or subjective presence and affronts a reader's desire for them. She explains in an essay in *L=A=N=G=U=A=G=E* that she "write[s] as [she] masturbate[s]," combining a "savage text" with a "learned text" of research, and then "mechanically insert[s] one text into another text," echoing proto-conceptual proceduralism.[123] Where canonical Language poetry objected to the seemingly reactionary element of writing from bodily experience, Acker restored it in perverse forms in a way that turned her work into a powerful critique of patriarchal and bourgeois norms.

In Acker's contributions to proto-Language and New Narrative magazines, plot and character development were backgrounded, with characters and author adopting multiple identities. For someone like Acker, the photocopier, which had shattered "the sanctity of print, . . . copyright and authorship," was the technological match for her autobiographical poetics of copying.[124] By leveling heterogeneous sources, Acker's fake autobiographies disrupted the genre's conventions of truth and referentiality: "Obviously I can be anyone I want to be since 'anyone' is an identity, a particular set of images."[125] To plagiarize desire and fantasy is to displace authenticity and biography as markers of identity. Such interrogations of narrative and referential instability were negotiated in little magazines: "I was interested in how if you wrote based on other texts you had a sort of ambience, rather than a centralized meaning. Later on, the Language poets came along, and they were interested in the same thing. That's how I got in with the Language poets."[126] Feminist poet and editor Kathleen Fraser identified Steve Benson's "use of shifting pronouns, . . . how we 'try on' other people and are never consistently one 'I,'" as characteristic of Language writing—but that description could equally apply to Acker's work in both proto-Language and New Narrative magazines.[127]

Acker's magazine works also present a model for what Language poetry is said to have avoided: autobiography, pleasure, and explicit personal details. Her novels *Rip-Off Red* (1973), *The Childlike Life of the Black Tarantula by the Black Tarantula* (1973), and *I Dreamt I Was a Nymphomaniac, Imagining* (1974)—all first published in proto-Language and other prose magazines like *Periodics* and *Top Stories*—ostensibly describe childhood memories of rape, incest, being a "toilet birth," murder, Acker's actual birthdate (April 18, 1947), pelvic inflammatory disease, bisexuality, absent fathers, suicidal mothers, go-go dancing, and some physical features like tattoos: "I put autobiographical material next to material that couldn't be autobiographical."[128] Such practices confuse distinctions between the real and the imaginary. The declarative grammatical mood combined with a confident first-person pronoun pretends to provide referential footholds, but these are as unreliable as the disjunctive poetic line favored by proto-Language poets. Acker's magazine pieces show attempts to reconfigure an embodied subject within a disjunctive narrative. Narrative, for Acker, is necessary to reveal violent acts such as rape and state violence, because it allows for a greater degree of identification and immersion that can, in turn, be used politically. In this regard, her aesthetic aligns with New Narrative.

Acker's syntax is disjunctive in ways that appealed to proto-Language magazines, but her disjunction exploits the "expository logic and speech derived syntax" that Bernstein had rejected, sometimes in the form of disconnected sentences and story lines or a subject position that shifts continually, either through outright plagiarism or through the imagined adoption of another identity for the speaking subject.[129] Instead of ambiguity within words or phrases, Acker's texts see ambiguity arise across sentences and paragraphs. It is a cumulative experience of reading sentences that often contradict or qualify previous statements. In this sense, her work is related to that of Hejinian in *My Life*, Ron Silliman's long sentences, or the works of Carla Harryman, Barbara Baracks, and Alan Davies, while diverging from them in its extremity of content, its emphatic use of personal pronouns, and its abrupt change of tone and discourse. Acker's transgressions against autobiography in little magazines are politically charged, especially through her background as a sex worker, which she wrote about in her fiction and talked about in interviews.

Another feature Acker shares with both New Narrative and Language writing is self-commentary. Proto-Language writers, for example, emphasized process over a workshop-poem perfectibility, reminiscent of proto-conceptual magazines' revolt against precious poems. In *Big Deal*, Acker's author-character Tarantula writes, "I'm becoming depressed: this book can't be interesting to anybody."[130] This direct commentary on her writing process intervenes in the narrative and would be called "text-metatext" in New Narrative, a technique that, as Glück describes in *Soup* issue 4, "cuts naturalistic illusion making. It includes the reader" and "asks for critical response, makes claims on the reader, [and] elicits commitments."[131] Glück's comments resemble Bernstein's writing on artifice and anti-absorption, highlighting the proximity of their interests in engaging the reader as a co-producer of the text. Both Language and New Narrative groups engaged intensely with theory, metanarrative, and self-theorization—philosophers and theorists appeared by name, and theoretical ideas were discussed at length. Acker's later writing, too, is theoretically explicit, especially her novels of the 1980s, such as *Great Expectations* (1983), *My Death, My Life by Pier Paolo Pasolini* (1984), and *Don Quixote* (1986). In 1976 Acker met Sylvère Lotringer, who introduced her to French theory, like Deleuze, Guattari, and Foucault.[132] Although Acker already referred to her writing of the 1970s as "de-narrative," theory gave her an academic vocabulary to describe *Tarantula* and *Nymphomaniac* as an attempt "to escape that male, centralized meaning."[133]

Elements of Acker's writing appealed to Language-oriented poets: its interrogation of meaning-making, the unstable epistemic basis of its speakers, its references to the writing process, its quotations from other writers (and, later on, philosophers), and its reluctance to "control" readers or turn them into consumers. New Narrative writers, in turn, fêted the writing's focus on desire, the body, messiness, excess, and sex-positivity. Acker is now associated more frequently with New Narrative because of her influence on writers published in *Soup*, *Mirage*, and other New Narrative magazines and because of her gender politics and the queering of her writing. Critics and practitioners themselves ultimately tended to separate New Narrative and Language writing along the lines of gender and sexuality, despite the fact that several writers associated with Language writing even today are women and/or queer.

Acker moved to San Francisco in 1981, and her physical presence there strengthened her bonds with New Narrative in the Bay Area. Although she incorporated poststructuralist theory more explicitly in her work in the 1980s, she also became increasingly interested in myth and storytelling in the 1990s. Coming out of poetry and performance art scenes on the East and West Coasts, Acker began to affiliate with novelists as her work became more popular. Language writing solidified as a label around the same time that Acker left the East Coast scene, which was when the first major anthologies appeared, in 1984 and 1986. Despite her early mention in the first "language-centered" *Alcheringa* section, Acker was not included in those later anthologies. In 1997, at the height of her career, she died of breast cancer.

Acker's and New Narrative's embodied poetics in proto-Language magazines did not have the effect on inherited notions of Language poetry that they could have had, despite individual poets acknowledging Acker's and New Narrative's influence. Silliman remembers Acker as one among three significant influences on his work *Ketjak*, stating in 2000, "I was hardly attempting anything half as radical" as Acker.[134] Kaplan Harris, too, argues that some canonical Language poets, such as Hejinian and Harryman in their collaborative *Wide Road*, "assimilated [New Narrative's] lessons" of gender politics, eroticism, and autobiography.[135] But New Narrative gained little traction until recently, because it lacked major academic support. The conference "Communal Presence: New Narrative Writing Today" (October 2017, UC Berkeley) and two 2017 anthologies—*From Our Hearts to Yours* and *Writers Who Love Too Much*—are likely to change this. AIDS had also tragically decimated the group's practitioners and readers, which makes a contemporary recuperation even more politically urgent. Furthermore, the associations of embodied poetics with identity politics, often contrasted with purely "aesthetic" work, as well as its explicitly "indecent" nature, made New Narrative harder to teach to undergraduates until fairly recently.

A group and its formation can be better understood by its edge cases because they present the group's actual dynamism and provisionality, proving the retrospective canonized image to be only one version among many possibilities. Acker is such an edge case, peripheral but crucial to both Language and New Narrative groups, neither of which can claim her as theirs alone. Other writers also never made it into the inner circle of a group but were facilitators, such as the editors Rosmarie and Keith Waldrop (Burning Deck Press), Madeleine Burnside (*Gnome Baker*), Tom Beckett (*The Difficulties*), Phyllis Rosenzweig and Diane Ward (*Primary Writing*), Laura Chester (The Figures), and Michael Andre (*Unmuzzled OX*). None of the above insights may change our notion of what Language writing has become or is now, but they do offer an alternative view of what Language writing was and could have become. Such resistant, loose affiliations do not mold into avant-garde representations that are easily legible, yet they tell us more about a group's internal conflicts and emergent interests than might be gleaned from any survey of its avant-garde features, its purported theoretical identifiers, or its official histories alone. The place where this necessary provisionality is most clearly visible is, again, the little magazine.

That said, there is a correlation between canonical success and a magazine's discursive presentation. Literary networks often become more visible to the academy through self-theorizing texts. In a 1981 *Poetry Flash* survey about readers' favorite magazines, *L=A=N=G=U=A=G=E* was the most frequently named.[136] *Poetics Journal* was recently reprinted and partially digitized with an extensive critical guide by Wesleyan University Press. The University of New Mexico Press is currently preparing three volumes of letters around *L=A=N=G=U=A=G=E*, slated to appear in 2019. In recent years, digital databases and listservs like the Buffalo Poetics List, the EPC (Electronic Poetry Center), PennSound, *Jacket2*, Eclipse, and UbuWeb—many of which are set up by writers associated with Language—present a direct digital extension of the Xerox mentality and have enabled global access to marginalized small-press practices. But such inclusive gestures often facilitate institutional acceptance of particular poets, because academics are trained in the same languages of theory and explication, and because universities often host most of these projects.[137]

The use of theory as pedagogy can be a benefit and a liability: it has the potential to empower and distribute knowledge freely, but it is often perceived as a display of the writer's education and erudition. In this respect, pedagogy vis-à-vis theory becomes entangled with issues of education, class, race, sexuality, and gender. Contributors unhappy with Language writing's particular version of theory began to ask how magazines could negotiate forms of rhetoric, pedagogy, and theory that avoided being authoritarian and exclusive yet remained confident and rigorous. What would an alternative rhetoric grounded in, for example, the values of equality, hospitality, and active listening look like? These contributors would eventually found their own magazine communities, dedicated to questions of experimental form, editorial conduct, and the politics of inclusion from an explicitly feminist angle.

4 Feminist Avant-Garde Magazines and Hospitality After 1980

Mrs. Avant-Garde

In 1992 and 1994, the feminist avant-garde magazine *Raddle Moon* hosted a roundtable, "Women/Writing/Theory," and published the contributions in two of its issues. This forum, in its discussion of feminist politics, avant-garde poetics, and critical theory, would become a litmus test for the cohesiveness of *Raddle Moon*'s community. The filmmaker and poet Abigail Child asked her forum collaborators, "Are we trapped in a politics of struggle where the representation of social antagonism and historical contradictions can take no other form than a binarism of theory versus politics or theory versus poetry?"[1] In doing so, she identified a critical cul-de-sac in her feminist avant-garde community. How could feminist poets confront patriarchy in forms outside conventional binaries in which identity politics and theory were believed to be opposites? Little magazines and magazine forums offered hospitable venues in which the supposed oppositions between questions of theory and questions of identity, between politics and poetry, and between avant-gardism and feminism could be debated and given a politics of form. In other words, magazines and forums came to be considered political forms rather than mere receptacles for politics.

The artist Mira Schor, for example, asked in the 1994 forum "On Creativity and Community" published in *M/E/A/N/I/N/G*, a feminist journal dedicated to the visual arts and art criticism that she co-edited with Susan Bee, how an avant-garde magazine could constitute an "enduring and trustworthy community" that would also be hospitable to newcomers and to diverse opinions.[2] Feminists like Schor and Child used the magazine medium and the forum in print and online as experiments in collaboration and nonhierarchical dialogue that tested their community's hospitality. Magazines and forums also allowed them to forge a feminist avant-garde identity that drew on theory and formal experimentation, as well as gender and self-expression, bringing theory and identity politics into a productive relation.

In their poem for a collaboration issue of *Black Bread*, Jennifer Moxley and Beth Anderson melded experimentalism and identity politics to argue for the necessity of their conjunction:

let us form around form and
command: here we will
move closer to it
conform as an act of generosity
speak only within and to no counterpart
and what allows survival on uneven ground
that unbound lever to follow
will undo all that is maintained
But if maintenance is our breaking train
asseverate
pertinence
careful, careful,
some germane posture will inquire
as follow to fallow
have we become but the shadows of gesture[3]

Motivated by a desire for radical autonomy ("speak only within and to no counterpart"), the poem envisions maintenance as a disruptive force (a "breaking train"), an aporia that lies in the association of "maintenance" with everything but radical breaks. The poets "will undo all that is maintained," but, in doing so, they risk becoming only "follow[ers]" of the avant-garde's conventional conception, left over from previous movements, as a reactive agent. The poem's insistence on maintenance as discontinuation ("maintenance is our breaking train") recalls Mierle Laderman Ukeles's 1969 "Maintenance Art Manifesto," in which she challenged the denigration of domestic and affective labor often performed by women.[4] Ukeles's maintenance art positioned itself squarely against the expected avant-garde drive toward innovation, in favor of care. Anderson's and Moxley's poem analogously negotiates the labor of feminist magazines: following the marriage of avant-gardism and feminism, how might the feminist avant-garde avoid becoming the "shadow" of the avant-garde's infamous "gesture"? How could it do more than take the surname of the avant-garde, metaphorically speaking? What strands of avant-garde continuity would be useful to their project and what strands would have to be "undo[ne]"?

The feminist avant-garde surveyed in this chapter emerged in and around little magazines in the 1980s, 1990s, and early 2000s. I focus on five magazines whose overlapping contributors have often been described as trailblazers for American, Canadian, and British avant-garde writing and art by women: *HOW(ever)* (edited by Kathleen Fraser, with various associate editors, 1983–92), *HOW2* (Kathleen Fraser et al., 1999–2009), *Raddle Moon* (Susan Clark, later with co-editors, 1983–2003), *M/E/A/N/I/N/G* (Susan Bee and Mira Schor, 1986–96; online 2002–16), and *Chain* (Jena Osman and Juliana Spahr, 1994–2005).[5] *HOW(ever)* stands as perhaps the seminal magazine for the concerted efforts of the literary feminist group formations that would follow: a magazine with exclusively female editors and contributors, it published experimental poetry and criticism that became reference points for subsequent feminist literary magazines and poets.[6] Alongside other feminist poetry magazines, *HOW(ever)* signals the advent of late second-wave and early third-wave feminism in avant-garde poetry, coinciding with a wider shift in both feminist and avant-garde discourse.[7] Together, these five magazines form an important avant-garde cluster whose publishing history has not yet been given the level of critical attention it merits, partly because twentieth-century poetry anthologies and criticism habitually distinguished between identity- and theory-driven poetics, a scheme in which experimental feminist communities find no place and the very problem Abigail Child articulated. Feminist avant-garde writers helped to soften the border between identity politics and theory even if they did not, in the end, manage to open it completely. That division remains pressing to avant-garde criticism today.

Unlike other avant-gardes, the feminist avant-garde as a literary network has been defined inconsistently, partly because feminism is too broad and multifarious an ideological position to fit neatly into conventional models of literary avant-garde movements and partly because it is not identifiable as a poetic style. Such broadness, however, must be incorporated into our notion of avant-gardism. Indeed, the provisional avant-garde network around *HOW(ever)*, *HOW2*, *Raddle Moon*, *M/E/A/N/I/N/G*, and *Chain* announced its own provisionality as a welcoming broad church through participatory formats particularly suited to its feminist politics, such as forums, chain letters, and other collaborative pieces. Acting as feminist newsagents and educators, feminist avant-garde magazines created inclusive publishing communities for writers, critics, and readers and advocated renewed attention to female modernists. Influenced by recent feminist theorizations of hospitality and pedagogy based on "identity, inclusiveness, reciprocity, forgiveness, and embodiment," I consider hospitality a useful metaphor for the complex negotiations around the inclusiveness, hierarchies, and gift-exchange of magazine communities.[8]

What I call a feminist "politics of the forum," which aimed for hospitality and nonhierarchical dialogue in avant-garde communities as a pedagogy and an editorial model, sometimes materialized in the genre of the magazine forum. The forum, a written dialogue among multiple participants, realized formally the implicitly hospitable politics of experimental feminist magazines. But hospitable forms, because they were cast as hospitable, sometimes ended up highlighting the failings of solidarity and producing unease. The desire for greater inclusivity was often accompanied by anxiety, even paranoia, about seemingly ineluctable complicity and privilege. In calling these feminist projects "paranoid," I draw on Sianne Ngai's argument about the connection between paranoia and feminist theory, which she views as a useful lens through which to read feminist experimental poetry from the 1990s onward. Similarly, I've been inspired by Eve Kosofsky Sedgwick's distinction between paranoid and reparative reading; the former is based on demystification and distance, the latter on surprise and reconciliation.[9] Though influenced by psychoanalysis, neither Sedgwick nor Ngai understand this paranoia as pathological but rather as a pattern of feminist and queer thinking.[10] Such an analysis of the politics of the forum can contribute to a new understanding of avant-gardism based on the concepts of hospitality and provisionality, even though these magazines and forums remained imperfect examples of communal solidarity and inclusiveness.

The feminist magazines discussed in this chapter function as critics of the avant-garde in varying degrees of explicitness. In previous chapters, I demonstrated the methodology of studying avant-garde proto-forms by focusing on provisional communities of practice as opposed to the accounts of monolithic avant-gardes still dominating scholarship today. Without a canonical version against which to compare the proto-form, the feminist avant-garde manifests the proto-form model and turns it into a pedagogy of its own. Such a pedagogy of the proto-form critiques previous, traditionally male-dominated avant-gardes by attending to what has been excluded and what must remain provisional and by proposing a new model of avant-garde community based on greater hospitality. In this view, the allegedly anti-identity, theory-driven, hierarchical, and manifesto-heavy avant-garde is only one among many other possible manifestations of avant-gardeness rather than the measure of all others.

Rae Armantrout's response to the question "Why Don't Women Do Language-Oriented Writing?" in the first issue of *L=A=N=G=U=A=G=E* (1978) discredited the assumption that women prefer representational modes over the "analytical tendencies of modernist or 'post-modernist' art."[11] Armantrout argued that style is not gender-specific. She proposed that the real question worth asking would be why critics and practitioners have excluded women from discussions of "language-oriented" writing.[12] In this example, Armantrout positioned herself as a critic of the avant-garde, with which she was involved but to which she also remained peripheral. This position of the avant-garde critic who speaks out against exclusions and proposes new questions from within (though on the margins) also describes many of the feminist magazines under discussion. Rather than portraying a rigid separatism, since many feminists continued to publish in other venues and many feminist magazines included men, the conversations in which feminist poets engaged and the heterogeneous materials their magazines featured suggest an alternative mode of forming literary communities that was deliberately more provisional than in traditionally defined avant-garde groups. In some feminist literary avant-gardes the "proto" in my concept of the "protoform" was already built in.

Theories of the Feminist Avant-Garde

The hospitable pedagogy of feminist avant-garde magazines needs to be considered within the wider recuperative project of feminists who recovered forgotten female voices and developed hospitable venues for experimental women writers. Because a comprehensive overview of feminist scholarship and theory is beyond the scope of this study, I will limit the following discussion to how the feminist poetic avant-garde was theorized from the 1980s onward, with particular attention to how this affected magazines, as this period was in many ways a crucial turning point for the group dynamics and popularization of long-developing feminist avant-garde practices.

The relation between the identifiers *woman* and *experimental*, or between *écriture féminine* and *aesthetic experimentation*, was very much discussed in feminist little magazines and feminist literary criticism in the 1980s and early 1990s. In 1994, *HOW(ever)* and *Chain* contributor Joan Retallack, for instance, called for women to use the "feminine" forms outlined by Julia Kristeva and Hélène

Cixous, such as multiplicity, discontinuity, marginality, transgression, fluidity, openness, subversion, and absence of hierarchy, to forge an avant-garde literary feminism.[13] Poet, critic, and later *HOW(ever)* co-editor Rachel Blau DuPlessis also explored what she called "female aesthetic, but not *a* female aesthetic, not one single constellation of strategies."[14] DuPlessis deployed a historical metaphor: much as the Etruscan language was superseded and occluded by Latin, so had women's writing been suppressed in the male-dominated avant-gardes. This view was part of the radical revisionist project in feminist avant-garde magazines: an aesthetics and politics through which women chose their own lineage and revived occluded historical and literary records.[15] Because DuPlessis considered both traditional and innovative poetic forms "male-gendered," she believed that a female writer "must consciously address the social and formal imbeddings [*sic*] of gender," and not just include female experience as the content of poems.[16]

Not all feminists were on board with the project of defending a female aesthetic or woman's distinctiveness as put forward by such writers and theorists as Cixous, Kristeva, Audre Lorde, Carol Gilligan, and Adrienne Rich (who advocated "writ[ing] directly and overtly as a woman, out of a woman's body and experience").[17] Experimental novelist and critic Christine Brooke-Rose noted wryly that "for a woman to be genuinely welcomed and attended to as an 'experimental' writer," and not as an "experimental woman writer," and to gain recognition during her lifetime or during the height of an avant-garde's activity, was "peculiarly more difficult" than it was for men because the tradition of literary innovation remained gendered male.[18] To circumvent what Brooke-Rose aptly called "fluttering around a canon," beginning in the 1970s an increasing number of self-identified feminist collectives and publications dedicated to issues of gender, sexuality, and race instituted their own canons or attempted to do away with canonicity altogether.[19] These included literary magazines with special issues about women, anthologies or magazine issues by and for lesbians or women of color, and "mainstream," nonliterary, or consciousness-raising feminist magazines.[20] But in practice, there were few points of contact among prominent feminist publications such as *Chrysalis*, *Heresies*, *Azalea*, *CALYX*, and *Conditions* and the self-consciously experimental literary magazines.[21]

The efforts of explicitly avant-garde magazines to generate hospitality and provide opportunities for innovative female writers were matched by feminist small presses such as Kelsey Street Press, O Books, Tuumba Press, and (later) Belladonna* in the US and Street Editions in the UK, some of which did not exclusively publish women or label themselves feminist. In the 1980s and 1990s, there was also an increase in anthologies of feminist avant-garde poetries and academic work focusing on women's small-press publications and a growing acknowledgment of community as an important hinge for poetry.[22] Several conference panels were dedicated to women's writing, often connecting contemporary with modernist writers; some, such as DuPlessis's seminar for Workshop 9 or Kathleen Fraser's "Feminist Poetics" seminar at San Francisco State University in 1982, were organized by magazine editors or contributors.[23]

Despite these important and influential efforts, Juliana Spahr and Stephanie Young argued that as of 2007 "numbers trouble"—that is, lack of gender parity—still existed in Anglo-American literary publishing. This was especially true for anthologies and small-press catalogues, where women made up only 27 percent of contributors, and in periodicals, where women made up around 37 percent of contributors between 1990 and 2005.[24] Spahr's own magazine *Chain* had already presented a countertrend: its last issue began with "facts" about itself, detailing *Chain*'s concerted effort to publish women—especially women outside the editors' friendship circles—poetry in translation and work across media, and to invite numerous guest-editors.[25] Such an expansive magazine community was possible thanks to the capaciousness of the magazine medium and the popularity of *Chain*'s big annual issues, but it still constituted a relatively small exception to the overall male-gendered rule of literary publishing.

By the 1990s, the label *avant-garde* had even become suspect and was frequently replaced with *emergent* in contemporary anthologies. Marjorie Perloff saw the development of the feminist and other minority publishing collectives leading this reconsideration of tradition as evidence that a "new avant-garde thus seems to be in the making—indeed, oxymoronic as it may sound, a new avant-garde consensus."[26] For Perloff, who previously theorized the avant-garde by means of its "language of rupture," an avant-garde defined by agreement was an oxymoron. Ron Silliman, too, in a post on the Buffalo Poetics List responding to the publication of *Writing from the New Coast*, an anthology edited by Juliana Spahr, Peter Gizzi, and Connell McGrath, implied that the anthologized poets were "apolitical" or "modest." Spahr responded to Silliman in an essay by proposing that the anthology's critics should instead "read this 'modesty' as a communal reinvention."[27] To abjure "the aesthetic separations of various schools and to deliberately create an aesthetic of joining" became important to a younger generation of poets who published in magazines like *Chain*. Spahr's proposed "aesthetic of joining" contrasted with an avant-garde tradition that "assume[d] that literary movements are breaches" and "denie[d] relationship[s]."[28] This "aesthetic of joining" registered a desire for a "connective poetics" that Ann Vickery, Redell Olsen, and Kaplan Page Harris identify as common among feminist and queer literary communities of the last three decades.

By the new millennium, despite the previous two decades' feminist reconsiderations of avant-garde tradition, poet Harryette Mullen stressed that "the assumption remains, however unexamined, that 'avant-garde' poetry is not 'black' and that 'black' poetry, however singular its 'voice,' is not 'formally innovative,'"[29] an assumption evident from Perloff's quip that the "perhaps excessively diverse 1990s" could no longer just uphold the old "make it new" catchphrase.[30] No matter how inclusive feminist avant-garde poets were among themselves, Anglo-American avant-garde scenes remained splintered, with only nominal awareness of the problems of the rigid divisions that persisted. Although female poets by now appeared firmly positioned on the poetic and academic map, with the help of magazines, anthologies, and conferences, many remained skeptical that solutions like name-dropping or token inclusions of female and minority writers would change the canon or prevailing attitudes toward women and minority groups in publishing.

To achieve substantial change in publishing, we need a workable theory of the feminist avant-garde in experimental art and writing. In an attempt to construct an alternative canon, several recent anthologies and critical studies have continued the crucial work begun in the 1980s and 1990s, and feminist critics have offered helpful models for reading feminist poetry, theory, and avant-gardism in conjunction.[31] But there is still very little research available on the feminist avant-garde magazines of the last thirty years, apart from pioneering work by Linda Kinnahan, Ann Vickery, and Elisabeth Frost. Moreover, critical writings about experimental women writers have tended to overemphasize the writers' commonalities and to underemphasize the unique goals and achievements of specific groups. While the feminist literary avant-garde that emerged in and after the 1980s has often been defined by critics and defined itself in relation to previous male avant-gardes, like Language writing or a genealogy of female modernists, it must also be seen as an avant-garde in its own right.[32]

The feminist poets discussed in this chapter were not avant-garde merely because they "play[ed] with words and syntax" to "alter conceptions of rigid gender and racial division" but because they worked within a community of practice in and around magazines that engaged with social, political, and aesthetic questions and, in the process, debated and disagreed on what *avant-garde* meant to them.[33] Elisabeth A. Frost states correctly that "the feminist avant-garde . . . collectively . . . expose[s] the gendered nature of cultural inheritance."[34] But to probe what exactly its collective work entails, we need to look at magazines and magazine forums and take into account their sophisticated attempts at carrying out the project of theorizing a feminist avant-garde identity themselves.

Newsagents and Critics of the Avant-Garde

In her contribution to *Chain*'s "Gender and Editing" forum, the poet and founding editor of *HOW(ever)*, Kathleen Fraser, recalled being asked by readers about her magazine's affiliations and aesthetics, and she noted that she resented "such insistent need for codification . . . [with] the casual assumption of a static absolute," because the queries "assum[ed] that literary decisions of consequence were . . . initiated, articulated and canonized by Male Editors, Critics, Anthologists."[35] Fraser, as a critic of the avant-garde, disapproved of unquestioned authority and hoped instead to present an "able female counterpart" that participated in canon-forming in a way that maintained provisionality (no "static absolute").[36] The reluctance of female poet-critics like Fraser to theorize a monolithic and codified feminist avant-garde for poetry is a direct reaction against a perceived male tradition of discursively constructing avant-garde groupings with rigid boundaries. Instead, feminists constructed an avant-garde identity and canon based on hospitality, for which the medium of the little magazine and the format of the forum were essential.

In twenty-four issues, published between 1983 and 1992 with various associate and guest editors, *HOW(ever)* enacted a revision of the avant-garde by recuperating female modernist poets and publishing both new experimental writing and recent scholarly work by women. The magazine emerged from a feminist reading group for women, as many of that group's participants joined *HOW(ever)*'s editorial board. Similar in format to magazines like *QU* and *L=A=N=G=U=A=G=E*, the off-white, 8.5″ × 11″ magazine was folded for mailing, almost like a newsletter. As "a kind of news that transcends the present," as one reader observed, the magazine served as the hub of a welcoming community in which feminist writers could converse and where readers would find new writing, reviews, announcements of new books and readings and conference reports.[37] The label *HOW(ever)*, Vickery notes, "is often used to denote a specific group of poets (such as Fraser, Dahlen, [Frances] Jaffer, [Susan] Gevirtz, and DuPlessis)."[38] While the perceived groupness of the women and the label certainly have not caught on in the way other avant-garde labels have, *HOW(ever)*'s historical importance is corroborated by the fact that critics like Vickery and Eliot Weinberger, who calls the *HOW(ever)* group one of four movements "in America since 1960," insist on the journal's cohesiveness and its equivalence to a group.[39]

Starting the magazine "out of isolation and the shared frustration of editorial powerlessness," Fraser's decision to "claim sixteen pages every four months [was] a modest proposal with which to assert our choices."[40] The magazine's "aesthetic credo" was to "resist hardening into a certain 'aesthetic position,'" publishing writing "unaffiliated with particular aesthetic or political ideologies."[41] Fraser's desire for aesthetic, social, and editorial independence arose from her experience of impermeable group boundaries during her time in New York in the 1960s. She had published in second-generation New York School magazines, such as Anne Waldman's *The World* and Jim Brodey's *Clothesline*, appeared in *some/thing*'s Vietnam issue and Rothenberg's *New Wilderness Newsletter*, and read alongside Deep Image poets at Les Deux Mégots and Le Metro. Being on the periphery of the New York School and the younger Black Mountain group, Fraser found it distressing that "no one was interested in reading work outside their own proposed aesthetic parameters."[42]

In an interview for the Bay Area newsletter *Poetry Flash*, Fraser described how she "consciously chose not to align [her]self exclusively with any one clique or aesthetically defined group, though there were many opportunities to 'sign on.'"[43] Instead, *HOW(ever)* identified with what Fraser saw as a "developing feminist poetics," which might have shared formal strategies similar to those of earlier avant-gardes, but showed "an understandable wariness in simply following [their] diagrams."[44] This led the editors to search out methods and formats somewhat different from previous avant-gardes or even their own mentors, who were often "male-dominant in their theoretical documents."[45] *HOW(ever)* thus allowed Fraser and her co-editors to bypass "male editorial approval" and to produce a magazine that was "absolutely based in the dilemma of and attunement to gender."[46]

Similarly, Marianne DeKoven, a *HOW(ever)* contributor and modernist scholar, argued in 1989 that "feminist critics, [and] women experimental writers," needed to establish themselves "as an 'ambiguously nonhegemonic group' *in relation to male avant-garde hegemony*, simultaneously within it and subversive of it." Picking up DuPlessis's phrase from her influential essay "For the Etruscans," DeKoven conceded that ambiguity "did not materially alter patriarchy's essential subordination of women."[47] Still, like DuPlessis and Fraser, DeKoven recognized the need to establish a group and poetics based on arguably shared feminisms, but "ambiguously" and provisionally so, as an inserted "however" in the syntax of avant-garde hegemony.

The magazine's title itself pronounced its new direction within an avant-garde tradition, both linguistically and politically: the conjunctive adverb *however* signals a contrast, a qualification of what was said before, epitomizing the magazine's corrections of modernism and the avant-garde. When Frances Jaffer stated in her first editorial, "We want to publish an exception, however," this exception referred to both the group's contribution to the avant-garde paradigm of the "new" and the magazine's specific critique of that paradigm. *HOW(ever)* set out to be the exception to experimental and new publications that ignored women and the exception to feminist magazines that ignored experimentalism.[48] Even typographically, through Dodie Bellamy's logo (fig. 14), the magazine signaled its intervention in literary history and showed its allegiance with other feminist publications, many of which were also influenced by deconstructive design.[49]

Although *HOW(ever)* shared with proto-Language magazines an interest in deconstruction and theory more broadly, it targeted a different audience than the Language poets and other avant-gardes reached, one that did not presume knowledge of theory or familiarity with a particular style.[50] That said, many feminist poets were familiar with theory, discussed it in their critical writings and in reading groups, taught it, or incorporated it in their own work. Several essays and poems published in feminist avant-garde magazines demonstrate their debt to the authors' readings of feminist poststructuralist writers like Hélène Cixous, Julia Kristeva, and Luce Irigaray, and Fraser mentions these theorists as having influenced the development of her own work as well as *HOW(ever)*'s formation.[51] The magazine was in dialogue with emerging scholarly feminist journals such as *Signs*, *Frontiers*, and *Feminist Studies*, which, as Vickery argues, "provided [Fraser] with an example of how effectively a journal could change the intellectual climate" but against which she "was also competing" because peer-reviewed journals were preferable outlets for "career academics."[52] Though the removal of academic standards in *HOW(ever)* was liberating and certainly appealed to some poet-critics like Rachel Blau DuPlessis, Fraser admits that forgoing peer review made it difficult to find scholars who were willing to take "the jump" into a more creative format.[53]

As part of this creative-critical format, *HOW(ever)*'s editors selected quotations from scholars and writers to match the theme of each issue and featured them on the back covers (fig. 14); the themes themselves were never predetermined but "always emerged from the works chosen."[54] In one issue, Mary Jacobus is cited as proposing that "the transgression of literary boundaries" reveals "what it would be like to revolutionise them," the quote itself typographically bordered and highlighted as in a school textbook.[55] Jacobus's statement that "a refusal of mastery" in women's writing is "a challenge to the literary structures it must necessarily inhabit"[56] recalls the unavoidable complicity in patriarchy DeKoven viewed as a condition for revolution in her call for an "ambiguously nonhegemonic" group and "subversion from within."

The issue in which Jacobus's quote appears, "Transgression/Digression: The Politics of Form," published Susan Howe's discussion of Emily Dickinson's textual variants, compositional intentions, and poetic forms; Hannah Weiner's typographically rich text "*from* WEEKS" with underlined words, diagonals, and generous spacing between words, linking back to her experiments in proto-conceptual and proto-Language magazines; and Susan Gevirtz's poem "Who Can Speak, Cough or Breathe," which she called a "vigil on aphonia," and which reflected on the metaphorical and physical choking of women. In the endnotes, the editors took Jacobus's politics of form as a guiding principle. They proposed that to be "politically engaged as poets" means to "re-structur[e]" experience and form: "Resistance surely flexes itself linguistically."[57] Such linguistic flexing, which engaged critically with traditional poetic or avant-garde tropes and real hierarchies of power, would continue to characterize *HOW(ever)*'s project well beyond this issue. As critics of the avant-garde, *HOW(ever)*'s editors became historians who looked for those who had been excluded from various canons.

Readers, too, recognized *HOW(ever)*'s mission to act as critics and newsagents of the avant-garde. Having announced that the magazine would end with volume 5, no. 4, the editors received letters of praise, "begging urgent reconsideration."[58] One reader—Karen Kelley—described *HOW(ever)* as an educator and facilitator through which "all these mysteriously disparate writers are suddenly IN CONTEXT . . . those overlooked by The Canon."[59] Moreover, *HOW(ever)* gave readers "not only news about small small [*sic*] presses, but addresses—what a treat!" It established a network of readers and writers—a community of print—irrespective of geographic location, for whom news and poems were a "gift," as another reader put it.[60] This network for news and gifts included both

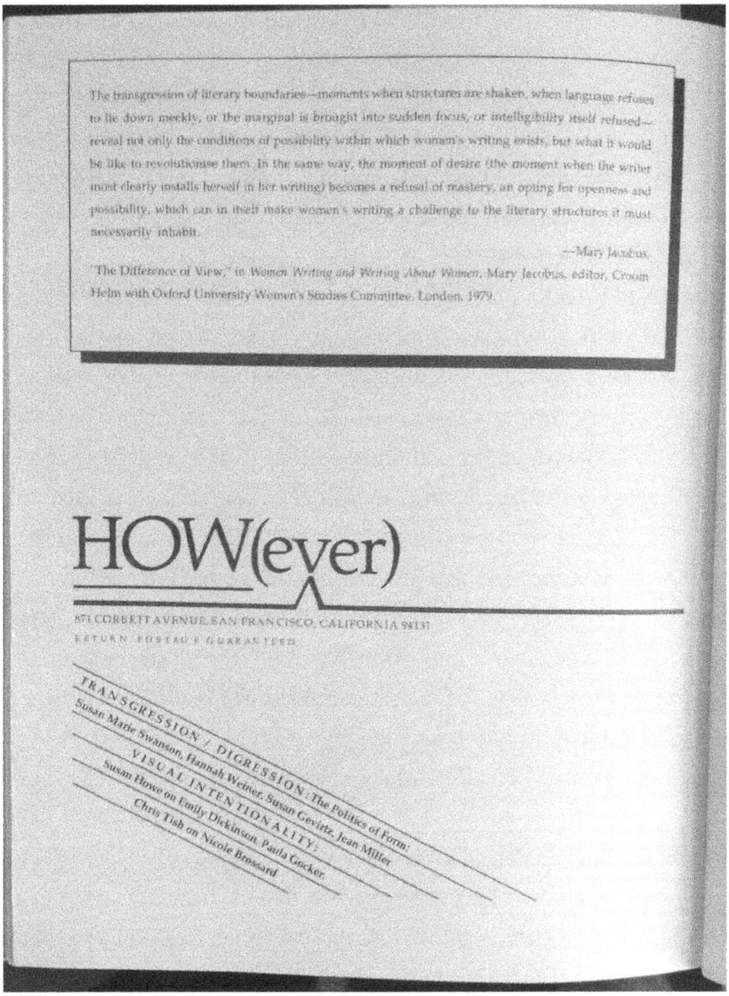

The transgression of literary boundaries—moments when structures are shaken, when language refuses to lie down meekly, or the marginal is brought into sudden focus, or intelligibility itself *refused*—reveal not only the conditions of possibility within which women's writing exists, but what it would be like to revolutionise them. In the same way, the moment of desire (the moment when the writer most clearly installs herself in her writing) becomes a refusal of mastery, an opting for openness and possibility, which can in itself make women's writing a challenge to the literary structures it must necessarily inhabit.

—Mary Jacobus,

"The Difference of View," in *Women Writing and Writing About Women*, Mary Jacobus, editor, Croom Helm with Oxford University Women's Studies Committee, London, 1979.

HOW(ever)

871 CORBETT AVENUE, SAN FRANCISCO, CALIFORNIA 94131

RETURN POSTAGE GUARANTEED

TRANSGRESSION / DIGRESSION: The Politics of Form:

Susan Marie Swanson, Hannah Weiner, Susan Gevirtz, Jean Miller

VISUAL INTENTIONALITY:

Susan Howe on Emily Dickinson, Paula Gocker,

Chris Tish on Nicole Brossard

Figure 14. *HOW(ever)* 3, no. 4 (Jan. 1987): back cover. Used with permission of Kathleen Fraser.

older work and contemporary writing that showed the "varieties of female experience previewed in the works of modernist women innovators."[61] Fraser's choice of the word *preview* proposed a continuity of experience but also revealed the avant-garde position of the magazine: it previewed new work "in advance" and acted as the avant-garde's scholar by reviewing forgotten work for critical appraisal. Some of those "previewed" by feminist avant-garde magazines became major contemporary authors, having written what are now considered feminist "classics" within experimental poetry circles and even on university syllabi: Lisa

Robertson's *XEclogue* (first published in *Raddle Moon*, no. 12); Theresa Hak Kyung Cha's *Dictee* (*HOW(ever)* 5, no. 1); Alice Notley's *The Descent of Alette* (*HOW(ever)* 5, no. 4); Hejinian and Harryman's *The Wide Road* (*Big Allis*, no. 2); Caroline Bergvall's *VIA* (48 Dante Variations) (*Chain*, no. 10); and M. NourbeSe Philip's "Discourse on the Logic of Language" (*(f.)Lip* 1, no. 2 and *Chain*, no. 3, pt. 2). For Fraser, the editors' "task was to attend" and care for the contributors, not to prescribe directions.[62]

What could be called *HOW(ever)*'s feminist literary attention blended the aesthetic and political in its selection of what was read, as Fraser explained. This attention was pedagogical in intention and aimed to obtain examples of feminist literary activity formerly subsumed within male-dominated avant-gardes. *HOW(ever)* acknowledged the activities of other women publishers living and dead, dedicating, for example, an issue to Kelsey Street Press publisher Karen Brodine. The Diego Rivera painting reproduced on the cover of that issue (fig. 15) shows women at the assembly line, their hands tied to the machine, watched by a male supervisor. That image, along with the title "telegrammatic" (promoting *HOW(ever)*'s urgent communications) and the caption celebrating Brodine's repurposing of work time, offers a neat parallel to the feminist adoption of machines of economic production for their own cultural production. Publishing a magazine thus became constitutive of constructing an alternative avant-garde identity.

Susan Bee, who had designed the logo and layout of *L=A=N=G=U=A=G=E*, ultimately started her own feminist magazine, *M/E/A/N/I/N/G*, with Mira Schor to invest her labor in her own publishing independence. In her response to *Chain*'s forum "Gender and Editing," Schor "recommend[ed] small publications as a feminist arena and strategy"[63] because they "made for a kind of intimacy within the project, and with our readers and contributors," and allowed them "to trust in the political efficacy of small cells."[64] Evoking the guerrilla tactics of activist groups like their contemporaries the Guerrilla Girls, the editors fashioned themselves as a revolutionary publishing nucleus. To make various exclusions visible, *M/E/A/N/I/N/G* published eight participatory forums, one of which asked its contributors, "Do you feel that contemporary art discourse has neglected or repressed any art issues, aesthetic, political issues, ways of working, or specific bodies of work of particular concern to you?"[65] In response, the magazine forums addressed precisely those neglected issues, from sexuality, motherhood, recent political art, and the state of art criticism to the invisibility of female and

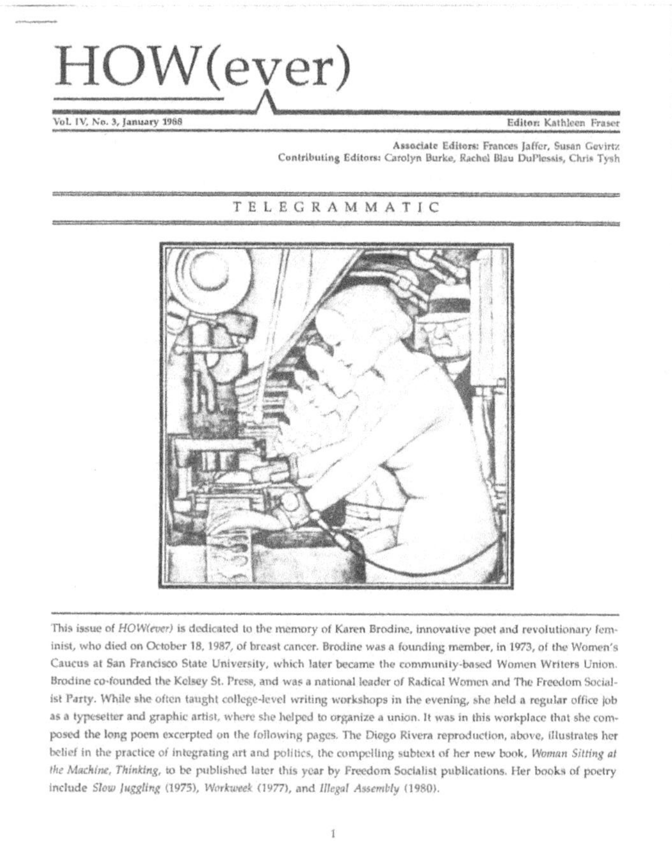

HOW(ever)

Vol. IV, No. 3, January 1988 — Editor: Kathleen Fraser

Associate Editors: Frances Jaffer, Susan Gevirtz
Contributing Editors: Carolyn Burke, Rachel Blau DuPlessis, Chris Tysh

TELEGRAMMATIC

This issue of *HOW(ever)* is dedicated to the memory of Karen Brodine, innovative poet and revolutionary feminist, who died on October 18, 1987, of breast cancer. Brodine was a founding member, in 1973, of the Women's Caucus at San Francisco State University, which later became the community-based Women Writers Union. Brodine co-founded the Kelsey St. Press, and was a national leader of Radical Women and The Freedom Socialist Party. While she often taught college-level writing workshops in the evening, she held a regular office job as a typesetter and graphic artist, where she helped to organize a union. It was in this workplace that she composed the long poem excerpted on the following pages. The Diego Rivera reproduction, above, illustrates her belief in the practice of integrating art and politics, the compelling subtext of her new book, *Woman Sitting at the Machine, Thinking*, to be published later this year by Freedom Socialist publications. Her books of poetry include *Slow Juggling* (1975), *Workweek* (1977), and *Illegal Assembly* (1980).

1

Figure 15. *HOW(ever)* 4, no. 3 (Jan. 1988): cover. Used with permission of Kathleen Fraser.

nonwhite artists. As one of many "participatory media" that shaped feminist history, the feminist avant-garde little magazine enabled such attention as essential to its hospitable politics.[66]

Reinventing the Archive

Called upon to uncover what was excised from the historical record, the communities of print established by avant-garde feminist magazines revised the avant-garde canon by "thinking back through our [literary] mothers if we are women," as Virginia Woolf famously put it.[67] This "thinking back," a well-established, perhaps overcited, feminist critical dictum, was often employed in the 1980s and 1990s through the language of familial links, the child looking up to the parent, or the student to the teacher, as in Sandra M. Gilbert and Susan Gubar's "female affiliation complex," Alice Notley's "Doctor Williams' Heiresses," or Linda Kinnahan's genealogical metaphor of female modernists as Williams's "poetic daughters."[68] Conversely, to avoid what Moxley and Anderson called the "shadows of gesture," feminist film scholar Linda Williams rightly asks of the "generational" thinking of feminism, "Why should we need recourse to family structures to legitimize our work?"[69] Besides, Clare Hemmings highlights that it is often unclear where "a generation begin[s] and another one end[s] when we are describing communities of practice."[70] Even with its acknowledged limitations, this language of genealogy served an important purpose in the 1980s across a number of experimental poetry magazines. Often, older or modernist writers, like Loy, H.D., Marianne Moore, Laura (Riding) Jackson, and Gertrude Stein, were taken as aesthetic and political role models, and feminist magazines documented and taught this self-chosen lineage. By publishing the work of modernist and contemporary writers and scholars side by side, the feminist avant-garde magazine as a diachronic medium of transmission makes both kinds of work contemporary.

HOW(ever)'s follow-up digital project, *HOW2*, ran from 1999 to 2009, with rotating editors. It continued *HOW(ever)*'s dedication, as critics of the avant-garde, to revising the canon for earlier and contemporary feminist experimental poets. In the opening editorial to *HOW2*, Fraser wrote that *HOW(ever)* "filled an original need for identifying and publishing a hybrid group of women poets" who were formally experimental and "claim[ed] the modernist women writers—mostly erased from active canon approval and availability—as their foremost family of choice."[71] *HOW2*, like its predecessor, became a platform for feminist writers' elective affinities, a nexus of exchange between and beyond generations, a revisionary and hospitable reading of the past, and an active transformation of the present. It was also noticeably more diverse than its predecessor, publishing a greater number of nonwhite Anglophone writers, as well as special sections for translations of experimental female writers from Singapore, India, Japan, and other regions.

Modernism's refashioned presence in little magazines, and especially those associated with feminism, is the expression and instrument of a deliberate pedagogy. If a particular canon establishes the principles that govern a subject, such as modernism or the avant-garde, feminist avant-garde magazines after 1980 often adjusted those principles. Modernist poems and publication practices were treated as pedagogical theory, with the hope of changing a poetic education system previously dominated by straight white men toward nonauthoritarian and inclusive modes that accounted for a number of different subjectivities. To advance this pedagogical cause, Fraser edited a guide for teachers in the disciplines of creative writing and women's studies. *Feminist Poetics: A Consideration of the Female Construction of Language* included American female modernists and nineteen contemporary women poets.[72] Analogously, *HOW(ever)* devised the magazine as an alternative syllabus that had been denied to Fraser and her peers in their school and university curricula.[73]

As reprints of modernist poets and critical discussions of their work increased in magazines from the 1960s and 1970s onward, they offered models for formal experimentation to a number of print communities.[74] They justified, for instance, proto-conceptual writers' interest in repetition, seriality, and the visuality of the page, and proto-Language poetry's turn to abstraction and difficulty as ideology critique. Within the attentive project of feminist poets, contemporary extensions of modernism in *HOW(ever)* and *HOW2* had a markedly different intent. They allowed feminist avant-garde magazines to fashion a revisionist literary history. Even the byline of *HOW2* proclaimed that it was "extending *HOW(ever)*'s original spirit of inquiry into modernist and contemporary innovative writing practices by women," so engrained was this revisionist praxis in its publishing project. For both proto-Language magazines and feminist magazines, modernist poets, especially Stein, Loy, and Riding, helped their community's formation and indicated the magazines' selective history. For *HOW(ever)*, *HOW2*, and other feminist magazines, the recovery of female modernists was accompanied by a critique of gender-based canonical exclusions and gendered uses of inherited aesthetics. Male modernists like Ezra Pound, T. S. Eliot, William Carlos Williams, and Louis Zukofsky remained important models for many poets, but they were not discussed as frequently and insistently in feminist magazines as were female modernists.

The difference between a proto-Language and feminist reception of modernism will become clear from an examination of critical responses in two specific little magazines. In 1983, Jed Rasula reviewed several republished volumes by female poets in *Sulfur*. With regard to Laura (Riding) Jackson's *Anarchism Is Not Enough*, Rasula established a clear link to his contemporaries: "Riding's suggestion that 'if you must write yourself, write *writing-matter*, not *reading-matter*,' has as its proper climate the Seventies more than the Twenties."[75] For Rasula,

Riding's *writing-matter* exemplified Barthes's writerly text. In Rasula's estimation, Riding reached into "the philosopher's domain," through her "rigorous enquiry within the scope of her own poetry into questions of being and truth" and her "relentless and aggressive intellect."[76] Rasula was likely drawn to Riding because the proximity of poetry and philosophy in her work was also theorized in the poetics magazines with which he was involved. Kathleen Fraser and Beverly Dahlen responded to Rasula in *HOW(ever)*, refuting his claim that "feminists have ignored the modernist women writers as blissfully as the men have." Fraser's riposte was this: "If he is truly interested in encouraging further critical study of women modernists, it seems a rather shop-worn and ultimately diversionary tack for him to trot out the traditional 'j'accuse,' chiding feminists for ignoring their own—especially given his limited research. From whom does he think the sudden demand for reprints and critical studies of modernist women has come?"[77] Well, Fraser hints, the demand for reassessment of modernist women came from feminists like her, and what was needed was an assessment of the "concrete esthetic criteria [that] decide what work is significant enough to *sustain* in print."[78]

To examine those "esthetic criteria" and "power structures underpinning the making of a canon," two "reappreciations" of Gertrude Stein appeared in *HOW(ever)* in 1986.[79] Stein's playfully condensed texts and meandering repetitions that foreground liberating and nonteleological experimentalism often served as a formal exemplar for *HOW(ever)* contributors. For Marianne DeKoven, Stein became a model for a new syntax: "Any of us can adapt her 'semi-grammaticalness,' her disruptions of the sentence which abrogate but do not demolish syntactical convention."[80] While this resembles concerns raised in proto-Language magazines, Stein's work was endorsed in *HOW(ever)* for its democratic adaptability for "any of us," in which the *us* has an implied female gender. *HOW2* also dedicated a section to Stein, bringing together scholars and writers whose work "develops a Steinian poetic."[81] Carla Harryman discussed Stein's libretto "The Mother of Us All" as a work that invites reflection on "the markedly gendered sites of interrogation and conflict [that] are the basis for a challenge to conventions of the genre" of opera or performance.[82] In all the contributions, Stein's experimentalism was linked to her gender and to questions of "authority, [and] authorship"—a connection that was absent in the "Reading Stein" section in *L=A=N=G=U=A=G=E* published twenty-six years earlier.[83]

HOW2 also published a special Mina Loy symposium in 2001. Alex Goody praised in Loy what Harryman appreciated about Stein: the performativity of the text and its rethinking of subject and voice. Goody saw in Loy's work the "empowering employment of a multiple, duplicitous voice" and described it as "a subject-in-process," applying Kristeva's then-fashionable literary critical term to align Loy with contemporary poetic practice.[84] In her reading of *Insel*, Hilda Bronstein argued that Loy's "use of quirky vocabulary and polysyllabic words . . . combined in convoluted or only partially punctuated sentences, and in illogical or paradoxical juxtapositions," and that her puns "make persistent demands on her readers."[85] In another issue, Elizabeth Savage drew on Joan Retallack's coinage "poethical practice" to invoke Laura Riding and Retallack as teachers of reading: "poethics, or ethics as poetry, extends an invitation to the reader to create the poem's meaning. Taking the 'poethical wager' includes also a responsibility—and opportunity—to consider the aesthetic, political, and personal directions my reading process takes."[86] Repeatedly, the feminist reader is invited to learn through her process of reading and to choose her own learning material. *HOW2*'s and *HOW(ever)*'s "praxis of feminist reading"[87] needed *practice*, for which the pages of the magazine provided the pedagogical implements.

Loy, Stein, and Riding's critical and creative work, which often originally appeared in little magazines as well, informed late-modernist feminist politics and aesthetics. To theorize one's own practice as modernism disputes the canonized periodicity of modernism and frames the canon as a body of work subject to feminist intervention.[88] But it also involves questioning the politics of such a lineage: in a culture that values patrimony, what forms of learning do women-edited magazines establish?[89] Lynn Keller and Cristanne Miller's *HOW2* essay "Gender and Avant-Garde Editing: Comparing the 1920s with the 1990s" is an early example of scholarly interest in the contributions of modernist female editors to the founding, running, and financing of little magazines and small presses. By providing a detailed history of female networks and editors' self-reliance, Keller and Miller situated the project of their own contemporaries within a legitimate and valuable tradition. The recognition of their modernist "legacies" revised the avant-garde critic's role: we "need to record the complicated networks of recent publishing" and be "vigilant" to give female editors "the credit due them."[90] In line with *HOW(ever)* and *HOW2*'s objectives, Keller and Miller proposed that the study of female modernist communities would yield a new pedagogy for writers and critics through precisely such little magazines and small presses. *HOW2* and *HOW(ever)* served as the source for this information and as venues for other magazines to see their own projects as part of a long tradition of women-edited magazines. Specifically, the magazines' pedagogy of the proto-form is realized in their editorial, literary-historical, and poetic attempts to circumvent a hierarchy between teacher and student, a pedagogy that often questions the very premises of the acquisition of knowledge and the construction of a canon on a fundamental level.

Growing interest in alternative canon formation via little magazines also naturally involved greater interest in archival practice. Many contributors to *HOW(ever)* and *HOW2* reported their visits to the Emily Dickinson, Mina Loy, and Muriel Rukeyser archives. Hannah Möckel-Rieke even saw *HOW(ever)* itself as "an archival space": "I was just reading what Derrida has to say about archives and patriarchal power and that reminded me how important it is to disturb, disperse and distribute this control. *HOW(ever)* has been—among other things—a wonderful archive of women's experimental writing."[91] After all, the archive creates, Derrida noted, a fraught situation of hospitality. Derived from the Greek "*arkheion* [home of the archon, the ruler]," the archive is embedded in power structures; it is a place "of which we are the guests, *in* which we speak, *from* which we speak. *To* which we speak." It thus holds an authority that *HOW(ever)* tried to subvert.[92] Again, a theoretical text (by Derrida) and historical research (on, for instance, Dickinson) were mobilized for *HOW(ever)* and *HOW2*'s project of dispersing power though attentive pedagogy. This "*mak[ing] present*" in the avant-garde's provisional archive, it was hoped, would pave the way for a different future reception.[93] Feminist "outrage," as media scholar Kate Eichhorn writes, is put "in order" in the archive, not in an attempt to objectify but to present knowledge and taste as subjective and political and to make that knowledge and aesthetic choice widely available and usable.

HOW(ever)'s "working notes," which accompanied new writing in the journal as "formal problems" and "stimuli," were another way to forge a contemporary archive and enact an attentive pedagogy and politics of the forum, which connected readers and contributors via the format of the little magazine.[94] As pedagogical devices, the notes proposed reading routes for the magazine audience, sometimes by offering creatively fragmentary summaries, at other times by referencing a poem's source texts (as in Rosmarie Waldrop's use of Wittgenstein) or by noting a poem's place within a larger project. For Fraser, the working notes, provided by the featured author, were meant to open difficult texts to mainstream feminists and feminist literary scholars "afraid of *un*common language," to encourage them to join forces with the feminist avant-garde.[95] Despite this attempt at accessibility, the notes do not explain the poems they accompany, nor do they follow what Fraser identified as "a male style of logic and argument with its confident and enlightened pressures."[96] Rather, the working notes offered brief and provisional thoughts as an invitation for dialogue. In this way, the hospitable and provisional pedagogy of feminist magazines appealed to those who felt unable to contribute to more exclusive and potentially intimidating magazines that required fully developed scholarly essays. For others, however, such a fragmentary and improvisatory style would come to be regarded as a concession to feminine stereotypes.

HOW2 explicitly encompassed its educational purpose in its title—a "how-to manual" for editing an experimental feminist magazine. The turn to the digital format facilitated access to the forgotten and contemporary women it published to an even greater degree than its predecessor, *HOW(ever)*, but it was, of course, selective nonetheless. In *HOW2*'s first issue, in 1999, Meredith Stricker explained the need for *HOW2* as a "navigator" because "there is no way I can count on Microsoft or AOL to open to the sites of new writing I need to encounter. *HOW2*, then, can be envisioned as a site that confronts the chaos of free-market hyperbole—where being gender-specific is a device that enables us to select, direct, pay attention—toward inclusion."[97] For Stricker, *HOW2*, with its capacity for attention and inclusion, became the necessarily selective filter in the confusing inundation of Internet data. *HOW2* not only extended its predecessor's promotion of contemporary and past modernist texts but also continued to explore the magazine format as part of its hospitable feminist pedagogy. *HOW2* imaginatively built on *HOW(ever)*'s sections of working notes, conference alerts, and postcards. To blend theory and poetic practice, it added "POST(ed)," which annotated recommended publications; "In'Print," which listed recently published books of interest; and "reading/s," dedicated to extensive commentary on modernist or contemporary women writers. It also introduced a regular forum, which crystalized its desire for inclusive conversation.

Feminist Forums

Feminist avant-garde writers disagreed about the existence of a specifically female aesthetic and often upheld an ideal of provisional identities. One magazine feature, the forum, uniquely suited this emphasis on differing views under the umbrella of multiple feminisms. The forum became increasingly popular in feminist little magazines as an ideal format in which to test the possibilities of hospitality that were crucial to an avant-garde project based on inclusivity. *Chain*,

HOW2, *M/E/A/N/I/N/G*, and *Raddle Moon* offered so-called forums as "a gesture toward conversation" that mitigated editorial authority.[98] The forum posited a communicative situation different from, but related to, the community expressed in letters to the editor, reviews, or other dialogic magazine features, in that it suggested hospitable community building and aimed to counteract the perceived fragmentation of feminists across a range of otherwise disparate communities.

Historically, dialogue and collaboration are not unique to the forum; they structure many magazines and, according to Walter Benjamin, they arguably constitute the medium's radical political potential by turning readers into authors through reader contributions.[99] While some avant-gardes fashioned an exclusive dialogue dominated by white male voices, feminists tried to activate the democratic potential inherent in the magazine medium through the forum. Joan Retallack, Tina Darragh, Lynne Dreyer, and Phyllis Rosenzweig, for example, met regularly over two years at Retallack's home in Washington, DC, composing what they called "a collaborative round-robin interview."[100] The participants had "clear political feelings" about the form, Retallack wrote in a letter to Tom Beckett, in whose magazine, *The Difficulties*, the four-way interview was supposed to appear; "the way we chose to do it," she noted, "was very feminine in a Kristeva/Gilligan sense."[101] Although it was never published, their "round-robin interview" exemplifies the nexus of feminism and forums in this period, through which Julia Kristeva's formal indeterminacy ("woman can never be defined") and Carol Gilligan's "ethics of care" were implemented directly.[102] In mentioning the names of these feminist theorists, Retallack also suggested that the forum constituted important feminist theoretical work.

One way to theorize how the forum functioned in this specific feminist avant-garde community is to see it as a variation of the questionnaire frequently found in modernist magazines, which Lori Cole considers a genre as crucial as the manifesto. Highly "self-reflexive," modernist manifestos, questionnaires, and forums helped to define artistic identity and "perform a community-building function," or, in the case of questionnaires and forums, to point out divergent views and the problems within a community.[103] Unlike questionnaires, however, the roles of questioner and respondent, or even questions altogether, are often less clearly defined in forums. Although they share the pedagogical intent of the manifesto, feminist forums tend to be more ambiguous about positing a movement and its attendant stylistic characteristics. The forum took on a special significance in feminist avant-garde magazines because it offered a form suitable to their politics of hospitality, attention, and diversity. In their nonprogrammatic experiment in provisional collectivity, feminist avant-garde forums diverged from questionnaires and manifestos by challenging inherited literary norms through a questioning of even a collective's own authority.

To challenge its authority in constructing a new community, the magazine *Chain* opened its first issue with the forum "Gender and Editing." *Chain*'s forum participants reflected on practical as well as aesthetic and political editorial decisions, considering issues of race, gender, sexuality, and class. Lee Ann Brown, for example, wrote about her Tender Buttons Press; Susan Clark, Catriona Strang, and Lisa Robertson about *Raddle Moon*; Susan Bee and Mira Schor about *M/E/A/N/I/N/G*; Avis Lang about *Heresies*; and Fraser about *HOW(ever)*. In that first issue of *Chain*, Spahr and Osman sought to create "a forum that takes that invitation [toward conversation] seriously, that is not just going through the motions of what it means to instigate response; it *requires* continuation."[104] Spahr, in her own critical work, has called for a practice of "connective reading," which views reading as "reciprocal, as shareable" and is related to a political practice of "consciousness-raising."[105] *Chain* promoted such connective, participatory reading through its editorial model.

Similar to the distributive pattern of the forum, the "chain" section in *Chain*'s first issue broke down editorial hierarchies. To avoid installing the "editor as autocrat," Spahr and Osman sent invitations to a number of women to build a collaborative poetic chain with other female poets.[106] Chain poems presented a different model of textual circulation: instead of books going from producer to reader, poems passed between readers as co-producers—an ideal strategy for a project that championed "non-hierarchical development."[107] While the magazine's chain letters and forum extended to poets beyond the editors' immediate community, the issue was still, as one "interjection" in Osman's and Spahr's editorial admitted, limited to writers and friends of friends. This notwithstanding, because the "chains" depended on the contributors' willingness to collaborate, *Chain*'s first issue was immediately legible as a coherent political statement. By inviting their feminist community to participate in a dialogue in print, the editors publicized their belief that not only a select few should have the cultural capital to discuss gender and editing but that feminist concerns needed to be addressed in collective solidarity, however idealized that collectivity transpired to be. The forum and chain letter, with their participatory politics, thus became the signature of *Chain*'s feminist avant-garde hospitality and a prototype for editorial accountability.

Drawing attention to the politics of form became a major characteristic of the feminist avant-garde forum. Like questionnaires and manifestos, feminist forums not only fostered communities but frequently incorporated self-conscious and self-critical reflection on such formations. Osman and Spahr acknowledged that "it is impossible to make a frameless frame" in editing *Chain*, but by asking contributors in their "Gender and Editing" forum "how and why journals are created and in what ways questions of gender have informed those decisions" and how "current feminist theory influenced [their] editorial practice," they illuminated those frames as "a way of creating a body that shows its own skeleton."[108] In their attempt to create "an editorial equivalent of the [Brechtian] half-curtain," *Chain* revealed its editorial processes so readers could "see the scene being changed," a desire for editorial transparency also evident in the alphabetical arrangement of each issue's contributions.[109] This editorial "half-curtain" was commonly used in feminist publishing more broadly: by the 1970s, many American mainstream and politically oriented feminist journals, 65 percent of which were collectively run, devoted their editorials to explaining their process in an attempt to "replace what appeared to be either the hierarchical organization of the mainstream press or the haphazard workings of the underground press."[110] Feminist journals across the board, then—irrespective of their emphasis on poetry, theory, or consciousness-raising—espoused a more egalitarian and responsible publishing ethos than previous, less explicitly feminist publications.

The collectively edited *HOW2* described its new forum feature as "an ongoing discussion site" in which guest editors selected topics, correspondents, and reader responses "with an eye for introducing varying points-of-view."[111] The topical range of *HOW2*'s digital forums—which covered gender specificity, cyberspace, public intellectual debate, taking risks in critical writing and its relation to university tenure, transnational communities of experimental women writers, and *HOW2*'s potential complicity in Anglo-American publishing dominance—counteracted the unifying programmatic intent we have come to expect of avant-garde magazine communities. In a forum on small-press publishing, *HOW2* guest editor Jane Sprague explained that the purpose was

> a true public Forum in the spirit of Juliana Spahr and Jena Osman's Call for Work for their forthcoming pamphlet series *Chain Links*:
>
> *Think of these books as a conference panel for the page, a panel that is being held at an unusually interdisciplinary conference of leftists, environmentalists, inventors, freethinkers.*

> Think of this Forum as a kind of virtual panel, one which might be added to over time. Think of this Forum as a variation on the idea of aperture, a Forum which might continually expand, open and allow more in.[112]

The metaphor of the aperture epitomizes the hospitable setting of feminist avant-garde magazines. While the conception of the forum was potentially less open when viewed as a site of academic activity requiring access to the codes and practices of conference panels, *HOW2*'s revolving editorship and the forum's numerous respondents demonstrated an inclusivity greater than that of coeval nonfeminist poetry magazines, aided by the digital format's hypothetically unlimited space.[113]

In its lo-fi, early Internet aesthetic, *HOW2*'s first issue was fundamentally a print magazine put online, in which even innovative formats like the forum were presented in a conventionally linear, hierarchical layout. Finding the issue difficult to browse, Linda Russo suggested in the forum that the "'official' entry to sections to which the table of contents is a 'master plan'" reminded her "that we live in a 'man-made' world, that the 'journal' itself is a 'man-made' form. Does it need to be re-imagined?"[114] Russo's question encapsulates the feminist avant-garde's self-conscious concerns about its chosen medium and an anxiety about the extent to which *HOW2* challenged literary patriarchy. *HOW2*'s focus on widening access and the geographical range of its contributors initially came at the expense of rethinking the magazine's very layout, with its hierarchal reading order. *HOW2* certainly welcomed such doubts as crucial to its inclusive editorial policy.

If the forum presented experimental collaborations that afforded inclusivity, then hospitality in avant-garde feminist magazines was especially tested when it broached the old divide between academia and poetry, a subject particularly contested since the emergence of poststructuralism on the public and academic stage. In reviewing the magazine, Sheila E. Murphy praised *HOW2*'s capacity for "integrating difficult, conceptual works with a human dimension—i.e., personal experience."[115] Murphy's comment echoes a widespread presumption that feminist avant-garde work had to be both difficult or theoretical *and* "personal," a position that many contributors debated passionately in precisely such magazine features as the forum, and this debate proved to be the most contentious in the development of this feminist avant-garde community.

Johanna Drucker organized the roundtable "Women/Writing/Theory" between 1990 and 1994 with a group of women, some of whom were friends—Susan

Clark (*Raddle Moon*'s editor), Abigail Child, Laura Moriarty, Jessica Grim, Chris Tysh, Kathryn MacLeod, Jean Day, and Julia Steele. The participants circulated their work among themselves prior to publication in *Raddle Moon*, with work by Norma Cole and Juliana Spahr sent in response to the first installment in 1992.[116] Drucker began the exchange by asking her correspondents about their relationship to theory, whether they regarded it as "inherently masculinist" and how the nexus of gender, writing, and theory played out in their own praxis.[117] The unpublished correspondence preceding the roundtable proper showed much concern for inclusivity and equality among participants. In her first letter addressed to everyone, Drucker emphasized that "this project should be as *non*exclusive as possible"; the invited respondents were "merely the result of conversations and contacts rather than any selective criteria."[118] While her wish for inclusivity elides the fact that magazines often require a socially connected editor with significant cultural capital in order to launch successful projects and that "conversations and contacts" are often highly selective, Drucker's reassuring address to her friends practiced the politics of the forum and the hospitable pedagogy of the proto-form characteristic of feminist magazines.

In the published *Raddle Moon* exchange, the worry over inclusivity was attached to theory itself. One major disagreement arose between those who rejected theory outright and those who saw it as an important part of their practice. Jean Day, for instance, expressed a "disinclination to think of [theory] as more than a tool."[119] Citing her collaborators in parentheses, Chris Tysh responded by pointing out the danger in wrongly identifying all theory with masculinity: "The conventional beef about theory's HAR(D)NESS, 'overly systematic' (Day), 'mastery' (Steele) regrettably . . . can only profit the patriarchal status quo." In fact, Tysh posited, the participants (herself included) were complicit in a system that already involved theory: "Far from a self-marginalized topos inside which we survey theory as DE BIG BAD WOLF hungry to swallow our differences, we remain absorbed within. I am saying that we trash 'the towering constructs' (Grim) and confiscate 'theory's lordly function' (Clark) because we are, as Spivak argues, part of the structure, living *inside* the space from which we de facto speak, work and write."[120] The spatial metaphors of *inside* and *within*, the elusive personal pronoun *we*, and the reference to Gayatri Chakravorty Spivak suggested that feminists, writers, and readers were inescapably implicated in the theoretical culture they hoped to critique or from which they claimed to dissociate themselves. Abigail Child, in turn, wanted to "enact" theory rather than for her writing to "be *about*" theory, because "WOMEN ARE ALWAYS TALKING THEORY ONLY THEY DON'T NAME IT AS SUCH."[121] One way to "talk theory" in practice was through the forum, which implemented feminist theories of hospitable collectivity.

What sounded like an opportunity for an inspiring exchange was also "fraught with problems," as Drucker remembers in *Chain*'s "Gender and Editing" forum: "The project started with great optimism and enthusiasm on my part," but after a while, "instead of sisterhoodly exchange, there was only paranoia, jealousy, and weirdness." For Drucker, the fact that they were women set up the second-wave feminist expectation that they could all identify with one another, implying "less capacity for distance/difference." Consequently, the project ended prematurely: "we never got to the 'editing' stage. Communications broke down and Susan Clark took the project to completion so that I didn't, ultimately, participate in giving it a final shape in any editorial sense."[122] Behind the scenes a disagreement over Drucker's second-round contribution had offended many participants. Drucker's letter acknowledged that in that contribution "there is some degree of sharpness, but not meant as negative confrontation, rather, as a means of clarifying my own position," and while "this will no doubt pique a number of you, . . . it was probably impossible to imagine we could invite each other to response [*sic*] without risk of accentuating differences."[123] Drucker carefully critiqued the other contributions but also pointed out that some women, herself included, had a stake in theory, because it was "essential to our survival" in the academy.[124] Since the difficulties were "very real" and not "comfortable," Drucker did not "feel tolerant of the condemnation of theory when that rejection proceeds from defensiveness and ignorance, or claims that somehow theory is 'other' than writing. For me," she wrote, "the two are intimately bound up in my intellectual life, professional life, daily life."[125]

While the title "roundtable" evokes a chain letter (like *The Difficulties*' intended "round-robin interview"), a round in a musical canon or a boxing match, or the equality of the Knights of the Round Table, it also suggests the authority of academic roundtables. Drucker's "Response" is an example of a potential academic paper that engages critically with the other contributions and identifies what would be considered incoherent thinking in an academic context. Of course, that resemblance also reveals the exclusivity of the institutions of theory and academia, and the kinds of conversations they produce—and *cui bono*? An academic would receive institutional credit from a theoretical engagement with the avant-garde through such a magazine roundtable; nonacademic participants would not. Moreover, the alleged exclusivity of theory was often identified with a particular argumentative tone and style and contrasted with the fragmented, nonlinear forms with which some *Raddle Moon* responses experimented. Expressing doubts about a supposedly "feminine" style, Drucker wrote in her letter that she "do[es] not want to condemn women writers to a theory position which necessarily requires that they be *diffuse*, *plural*, and *polysemous* just because the idea of clear articulation and assertive, reductive statements has a tradition of coming from male writers."[126] Drucker deemed such a notion unhelpfully anxious.

Not having heard back from any participants in three months, Drucker sent another letter, worried that the "dynamics of exchange" were now skewed: "I have a feeling (and, without wanting to sound *paranoid*, have heard rumors) that in fact you have responded and that you simply have not responded to me. I was intentionally polemical, hoping that we would all push each other toward greater clarity, definition, and exchange."[127] The rumors Drucker alluded to indicated that her co-editor, Susan Clark, had asked the other participants about their willingness to continue the project. The silence and the subsequent offended responses imply that the project inadvertently ended up perpetuating the exclusionary politics it sought to overcome. Drucker, for her part, felt that "you are all projecting your own issues about authority onto me and working them out emotionally" and that she was suddenly "the object of hostility which is orchestrated as a group dynamic."[128] Hospitality turned into hostility, with Drucker, one of the two academics participating in the forum (as she was then an assistant professor in the Columbia University art history department), being viewed as an authority figure. Owing to this rift, two participants withdrew their pieces, and Drucker resigned as the forum organizer. Feeling "under attack," Drucker pinpointed the problem they encountered in their attempt at group conversation: "it seems that you all have problems with the 'tone' of my response. Well, my tone is one which assumes authority. I want it to be. . . . Yet, I do not vaunt it as the only position."[129] Often, feminist magazine forums, like *Raddle Moon*'s, operated on the premise of kindness and accord, in opposition to what was understood to be masculine agonistic rhetoric. Not only theory but disagreement itself was identified with masculinity, posing the challenge of how to tolerate discord *within* feminist collectives.

As the fronts between the participants softened and two further responses were circulated, Clark published the first round of contributions and a delayed second round with an edited version of Drucker's letter that toned down her criticisms. For Day, their "problem of finishing this project [was] one of vocabulary"; "it was never clear *what* theory we were talking about."[130] Another problem was "how we address each other": "Then came Johanna's response, invoking much I find troubling in traditional intellectual debate. I felt unwilling to take up its terms."[131] Day, who preferred more "speculative" modes, did not find Drucker's rhetoric "productive," a position she has since revised.[132] Drucker, conversely, saw "programmatic assertion" as the only viable feminist "real politik."[133] Drucker seems to have anticipated critique from outside their circle—she wrote, "I don't want to see my theory turn all deferential, lady-like, and polite"[134]—and such critique was indeed forthcoming. Marjorie Perloff dismissed *Raddle Moon*'s roundtable, the "Poetics and Exposition" section of Mary Margaret Sloan's feminist anthology *Moving Borders*, as well as other "postlanguage" tendencies "especially true of women poets" as examples of the "good bit of 'soft' theorizing" that followed the "foundational" (and by implication harder) theory of the male Language poets.[135] Perloff's dismissal shows what is at stake in a feminist engagement with theory: question a particular mode of theory and you are considered "soft"; engage with it and you can "found" an avant-garde movement. Feminist avant-garde magazines like *Raddle Moon* negotiated this conundrum of how to "talk theory" without mimicking potentially anti-feminist models and how to be inclusive without disallowing disagreement.

More incisively, Sianne Ngai sees *Raddle Moon*'s roundtable as operating under a paranoid logic. Some participants judged theory to be patriarchal and wanted to resist being complicit in it, while others considered gendering style a form of complicity. If modernist questionnaires, as Cole argues, signaled anxiety about their self-definition, the feminist avant-garde's call for a new magazine hospitality resulted from a feeling of complicity and paranoia—negative affects Ngai identifies as crucial for feminist poetics.[136] According to Ngai, this philosophical or political paranoia about complicity exemplifies the feminist avant-garde's dilemma: "In these works, fear of unintended collusion with a system in which one is already inscribed . . . becomes the primary focus of investigations."[137] Little magazine forums offered a form to this necessary self-criticism in the service of feminist solidarity. Paranoid about continuing the exclusionary history of the avant-garde, the feminist avant-garde realized its complicity with and its inability to be entirely outside of patriarchal and hierarchical structures and compensated by dispersing editorial authority into the hands of the contributors. But therein lay also its strength.

In *HOW(ever)*, Drucker posited that the task of a contemporary avant-garde "has got to be the undoing of that mythic autonomy in recognition of the complicity of (still male dominated) power relations as they structure the ongoing production of literature as its own critical history."[138] Quoting Spivak in her last *Raddle Moon* response, Tysh accurately summed up the roundtable and a wider problem encountered in feminist experimental poetry communities: "in order to intervene one must negotiate. . . . You must intervene even as you inhabit those structures."[139] Forming an "ambiguously nonhegemonic group," as DuPlessis and DeKoven envisioned, came with strings attached. The *Raddle Moon* exchange revealed what is perhaps the forum's characteristic undercurrent: the desire of female editors to "do it right" and increase inclusivity, and the paranoia that can be the underside of poetic hospitality. Worried about falling into patriarchal patterns with which they were entangled, feminist poets were anxious to interrogate their own positions and choices in order to instantiate ethical editorship.[140] The weight of centuries of patriarchal editing failures rested heavily on the shoulders of feminist editors and contributors. There was a desire to explain, motivated by the wish not to alienate possible allies. Always offering the possibility of another response was the paranoid, but necessary, rejoinder to the shutting down of dialogue many of these poets experienced in nonfeminist publishing ventures. It was a cautionary act fundamental to their politics and pedagogy.

While often idealized and unrealized, feminist forums experimented with a model of hospitality that was not conditional—in other words, not a one-way invitation or guest–host hierarchy—but one that promoted reciprocity and mutual learning. Feminist avant-garde magazines involved more writers from different social, gendered, generational, and racial backgrounds and bridged a greater number of topics than previous, nonfeminist little magazines; thus, they presented a greater concerted effort toward inclusivity. That said, the realms of academia and even feminist theory, within which many of these avant-garde magazines moved, often reprised class and racial privilege. Feminist writers attempted to instantiate a theory and practice of hospitality within the medium of the magazine, for which the forum feature, and a politics of the forum more broadly, served as tools. But in many cases, as in the breakdown of the *Raddle Moon* exchange, the forum failed to instantiate a hospitable community. Nevertheless, the forum did materialize a pragmatic feminist position that gave magazines the opportunity to avoid being "autocratic" and to increase the multivocality of their contributions. The forum allowed feminists to explore an alternative feminist and avant-garde identity, for which an awareness of gender-based exclusion and the necessity of hospitality were constitutive. Set up as a space for learning and discussion, the feminist forum and the magazines within which it appeared mimicked a pedagogical situation, though with the goal of eliminating conventional teacher–student roles. As an exercise in community building, collective articulation, and attentive listening, the magazine forum admitted to saying "we don't have the answer to this, we want to hear from you." It allowed feminists instead, as Anderson and Moxley wrote, to "form around form."[141]

The hospitable community building visible in forums and other participatory magazine features was part and parcel of the wider feminist project to interrogate avant-garde traditions associated with institutional and rhetorical exclusions. If feminist magazines sought to use hospitality as a utopian corrective, then the limits of hospitality—what Derrida called its "conditional" and "de-termining" function that maintains the inequality between guest and host—problematized the idea of utopian inclusivity.[142] The contribution made by experimental feminist writers to the concept of magazine hospitality, which always depends on an editor granting that hospitality, was to redefine editorial hospitality with an understanding of the concept's inherent contradiction and to view "this necessary impossibility as [a] condition of possibility."[143] It is therefore understandable that the very aim of their pedagogy and poetics—hospitality—could become the object of paranoia about complicity, or even generate that paranoia. Offering hospitality is also, as Derrida highlights, an act of language.[144] Jean Day's insistent query about "how we address each other" was manifested in the complex negotiations among *Raddle Moon*'s forum participants, but it is also directed at us. In which language do we address each other as editors, writers, critics, and readers? The provisionality of any possible answer may be the condition under which hospitality must be invited. Feminist avant-garde magazines posit precisely those possible/impossible hospitable spaces, where criticism of the avant-garde does not mean there should not or cannot be one, but where a pedagogy and poetics based on provisionality has to be relearned repeatedly.

5 Communities of Print in the Digital Age

Movable Contemporaneity

When Ezra Pound titled his twenty-part review series of magazines in the British weekly *The New Age* "Studies in Contemporary Mentality," he made a connection between periodical publishing and contemporaneity still apposite today.[1] Regardless of whether critics can make good on Pound's promise to understand contemporary mentality, the medium of the little magazine remains, long after modernism, particularly conducive to describing "the contemporary" of any historical episode, including the present moment. As ever, through their chosen publishing medium avant-gardes may be recognized as provisional and diachronic communities that offer, as magazine editors Michael Cross and Thom Donovan put it, "glimpse[s] into the emergent." In *ON: Contemporary Practice* (2008–), a print and digital magazine of discursive writing about "one's contemporaries," Cross and Donovan state that they are "motivated by desire, friendship, sociopolitical commitment, and discourse among one's communities and peers."[2] It is these commitments and contemporaneities for which the little magazine acted as a barometer throughout the twentieth century and has continued to do so into the twenty-first. What is new is that digital formats and print that is informed by the digital are shaping avant-garde communities and writing, publishing, and reading today. Critical attention to these contemporary developments might, in turn, come to play an active, even transformative, part in the avant-garde and its reception.

But what is "the contemporary," and is "the Period Formerly Known as the Contemporary," as Amy Hungerford quips, even a period? While grouping creative works under "post-1945" or even "long modernism" might situate them more neatly, the label *contemporary* remains useful as avant-garde terminology because its boundaries are rather nicely undefined.[3] Tired of proclamations that contemporary writing is lacking in the more radical forms of the historical avant-gardes, I have argued throughout this book that we need to instantiate avant-gardism as a contemporary concept, beyond the simple model of the original and its lesser copy. Avant-garde reprints in later magazines already raised questions of temporality and futurity: whether any "historical" object or text can become contemporary simply because it is selected for contemplation today or only when it is presented as instructive for or akin to contemporary practice. The editors of *ON: Contemporary Practice* aptly ask, how "can we observe a present while it is still occurring; that is, before it has ossified into events consigned to a representative past," or, conversely, how can we observe what is supposedly ossified as something contemporary?[4] Because our sense of the past and present is always shifting, the avant-gardes in this book sometimes appear more and sometimes less contemporary, more or less of one period. Contemporary publishing communities also follow the logic of a movable contemporaneity and often even make "nowness" rather than "newness" a thematic and technological focus of their work.

Traditionally, critics have declared the avant-garde to be ahead of its time based on an assumption that, as Bruno Latour recognizes, "modernizing progress is thinkable only on condition that all the elements that are contemporary according to the calendar belong to the same time. For this to be the case, these elements have to form a complete and recognizable cohort."[5] The contemporary avant-garde might in some instances form a recognizable though certainly not a coherent and homogeneous "cohort." But when "different periods, ontologies or genres" are "mix[ed] up," "a historical period will give the impression of a great hotchpotch. Instead of a fine laminary flow, we will most often get a turbulent flow of whirlpools and rapids."[6] While Latour excludes the avant-garde (as traditionally defined) from such an assessment, this very "hotchpotch" and the "whirlpools" have characterized magazine communities, past and present, and heterogeneity and cross-group influence remain vital models for the contemporary avant-garde.

How are critics to write about the contemporary hotchpotch, then? A contemporary avant-garde can be theorized, like avant-gardes before it, as a provisional model of necessarily heterogeneous and dynamic practices. Contemporary avant-gardes in the making are to be found in little magazines, many of which address self-reflexively the politics and hospitality of small-press publishing. Yet scholars of contemporary literature tend to focus not on magazines but on the novel. For the Post45 website, Sarah Chihaya, Joshua Kotin, and Kinohi Nishikawa survey the proposed topics they received for a conference on contemporary literature at Princeton University in 2016.[7] A total of 43 percent of all submissions focused on fiction, 7.4 percent on poetry, another 7.4 percent on digital media. Across all submissions, the majority chose well-known authors and theorists. That fiction would top this (admittedly very small) list of conference topics is not surprising, as it matches the novel's dominance in the contemporary marketplace. When contemporary critics discuss magazines, they often focus on mainstream or at least widely popular periodicals, like *Timothy McSweeney's Quarterly Concern*, edited by Dave Eggers (author of the best-selling memoir *A Heartbreaking Work of Staggering Genius*).[8]

One exception to this dearth of scholarly attention to contemporary magazines is Ian Morris and Joanne Diaz's recently edited collection *The Little Magazine in Contemporary America*, which includes chapters on *Bomb*, *n+1*, *Callaloo*, *Fence*, *L=A=N=G=U=A=G=E* (which is no longer running), *Poetry*, *McSweeney's*, and other similarly established, well-known, or not exactly "little" magazines. As with many avant-gardes, scholarship often lags behind the more immediate responses generated within a poetry community itself. Contemporary criticism by poets themselves increasingly finds expression via the responsive interfaces of blogs, Facebook, Instagram, and Twitter, of which the latter two are usually limited to short commentaries, quotes, photographs, or the sharing of a text, photograph, or link. The effects and longevity of these sometimes semipublic forms of reception and taste-making are hard to assess, but they point toward an almost entirely unexplored reservoir for future criticism.

The next few decades will clarify the changes in small-press and avant-garde publishing today, in what media scholars call the "late age of print." But to speak of the book or print as an anachronism is to forget that "there are no anachronisms, only ways of seeing things as anachronisms."[9] That print is anything but anachronistic is evident in the sheer quantity of newly produced printed matter and the symbolic value attributed to it; writers are still routinely asked if they are a "published author" (meaning print publishing), and readers still proudly display their bookshelves to visitors. During the process of "mediamorphosis," or "remediation," a new medium is often conceived and explained in relation to a previous one.[10] Online publications, for example, are often produced and read as if they were print, and specifically as if they were made for a codex. Design features, too, are often skeuomorphic: that is, they look like an analogue version of a different medium (such as paper) but no longer function the same way. Despite ominous remarks by critics that "the period between 1980 and 2015 will be seen as the end of the ascendency of print periodicals," a focus on digital media need not imply a belief in the supersession of the supposedly obsolescent medium of print.[11] *Intermediation* is a better description of contemporary creative engagement with materials and techniques than *post-print*, because it accepts the ongoing coexistence and mutual transformation of print and digital technologies.[12] *Post-digital*, in turn, might refer to print within a digital media environment. Indeed, digitality now informs nearly all the processes of production, distribution, and reception, whether a work is printed or not.

In a digital publishing space in which magazines are easier and cheaper to launch and to maintain, in which the "now" is often published faster, have the politics of inclusion shifted toward greater diversity and hospitality? How does the virtually infinite expanse of the digital commons with its overabundance of data affect contemporary modes of reading? Since digitization and availability tackle the scarcity attached to avant-garde materials, approaches to distribution and reception of little magazines need to be revised. This does not mean that avant-garde publishing communities are now only to be found in digital form or in digitally inspired print forms. Many avant-garde print magazines continue either the DIY cheap-print and photocopy mentality or, conversely, the letterpress tradition. This chapter therefore examines what it means for an avant-garde to engage inventively with the digital medium today and how that engagement affects avant-garde socialities and identities.

Thinking the Unprintable

In a 2013 interview, poet and publisher J. Gordon Faylor jokingly remarked that the American publishing collective *Troll Thread*, which publishes PDF files and print-on-demand (POD) versions of those PDFs, "exploit[s] [the print-on-demand platform] Lulu's bookmaking technology in more diversely insidious ways" than his own *Gauss PDF*, another Tumblr-based project that publishes PDFs and multimedia works.[13] These contemporary uses of online or POD publishing are so "diversely insidious" not because they bypass carefully calculated and often handmade print runs, or because these presses publish work that might not otherwise appear elsewhere (which has become an avant-garde truism in itself over the last century); rather, the artful exploitation lies in *Troll Thread*'s and *Gauss PDF*'s publication of works that seem out of place in a codex, that cannot or should not be printed, but that insist on printedness, even if only imagined, all the same.

What I would like to call the "imagined printedness" in the digital and POD publishing projects of *Troll Thread*, *Gauss PDF*, and *Triple Canopy* allows these publishers to escalate definitions of "poetry," the "magazine," the "book," and "publishing" within their overlapping contemporary small-press and avant-garde communities.[14] Born-digital publishing and what Lisa Gitelman terms the "near print" technology of the PDF enable new experiments with the production, distribution, and reception of avant-garde work.[15] An online Tumblr that publishes PDFs and/or other file formats, often single-author works but also collaborations, might not immediately look like a magazine, but *Troll Thread* and *Gauss PDF* can be considered metaphorical extensions of avant-garde little magazine communities. One reason is that they display their contributions in ways that resemble the table of contents of a magazine issue, with content added and distributed periodically. Aesthetically, too, there is a clear sense of seriality. In this way, these digital publishers follow the practice of some earlier magazines, such as the proto-Language magazines *QU* or *A Hundred Posters*, in their publication of generally one author per "issue." Moreover, like avant-garde magazines in the twentieth century, *Troll Thread* and *Gauss PDF* have established a small community around their publications with several contributors in common.

Historically, many little magazines also doubled as a small press. *Others* had an imprint for books by its contributors, as did *0 to 9*; *Roof* began as a magazine and continued as a press; *Chain* was a magazine and had the spin-off book series Chain Links. But for the avant-garde in the digital age, the distinction between individual work, book, small press, and magazine becomes even less clear-cut, changing how avant-garde communities and their publishing projects work inside and outside of this differently networked online environment. So what does it mean to think printedness in digital avant-garde publishing? The following publications often highlight their medium of composition and distribution (each with a specific materiality) and make processes of mediation their investigative focus. We are invited to read these digital materials as akin to print even when analogue printedness is only imagined or simply impossible. If, as Jerome McGann writes, "literary documents bear within themselves the evidence of their own making," the remainders of print in a never-printed document complicate that trajectory: they show traces they can never quite have.[16] I will now turn to these imagined remainders.

Holly Melgard's *Black Friday* was released by *Troll Thread*, the publishing collective she co-edits, on Black Friday, November 2012, as an 8.5″ × 11″ print-on-demand book. Of its 740 pages, 734 are entirely black except for their white page numbers. As the poem's dedication page specifies, it is a book "for BLACK INK ON WHITE PAPER." Though couched in the language of the printed book, a PDF like *Black Friday* also invokes the antecedent of the codex: the scroll, a form that lends itself to compendious and sequential reading, bringing it closer to oratory and time-based media. *Troll Thread* was started in part, as co-editor Chris Sylvester puts it, "to make massive quantities of text or data or whatever available all at once and in the same place . . . as 'one thing.'"[17] This generically indefinable "or whatever" is an apt rallying cry for a publishing project intent on troubling literariness and on differentiating the book from the codex. Melgard similarly describes *Black Friday* as an experiment with her medium: "poems can exploit what it is in books that makes texts appear as 'text'; how their distributions and multiple frameworks of production may play a material role in their composition, their poetics."[18] These "material" frameworks include Melgard's computer, her word processing and publishing software, and the specifications of Lulu's book-making facilities, as well as the project's monetary value, or lack thereof. Indeed, *Black Friday* probes its existence within a small-press print economy that in monetary terms often costs more than it returns, and its entirely digital circulation invites readers to reflect on the circulation of money. Ostensibly an attempt to "break an industrial printer," Melgard literalizes the conventionalized avant-garde trope of rupture, testing if or how poetry could actually, and not just metaphorically, break things.[19] But, judging from the error messages the author receives from the POD platform Lulu whenever someone attempts to purchase a copy, the breaking remains only a thought experiment. Rather than a demonstration of the end of printed matter, *Black Friday* demonstrates the specific possibilities of POD publishing: since Lulu charges a publisher the same for blank or black pages, at least hypothetically, and since 740 is the maximum number of pages Lulu allows for a perfect-bound book, *Black Friday* attempts, like its inadvertent twin Jean Keller's *The Black Book* (2010/2013), "the lowest cost and maximum value for the artist."[20]

Other *Troll Thread* titles likewise thematize the economics of poetry publishing and the long history of avant-garde unprofitability. Melgard's *REIMBUR$EMENT* (2013), subtitled on its dedication page "For Work," features images of lottery and scratch-off tickets, the cost of the book amounting to the money Melgard lost to gambling during graduate school to make up for her unpaid labor, thus turning the avant-garde gift economy on its head ("A Gift Economy is a Debt Economy in my book").[21] *MONEY* (2012) by "Maker" publishes cutouts of hundred-dollar bills, avouching cheekily that the responsibility concerning counterfeit law lies with "the document's printer," who is the work's "maker."[22] Joey Yearous-Algozin's recent *HOW TO STOP WORRYING ABT THE STATE OF PUBLISHING WHEN THE WORLD'S BURNING AND EVERYBODY'S BROKE ANYWAYS AND ALL YOU REALLY CARE ABT IS IF ANYONE IS EVEN READING YR WORK* (July 2016) is a half-serious, half-ironic instruction manual in the form of a two-page lineated "poem" in large type that practices the cheap DIY and POD publishing it preaches.[23] What could be called *Troll Thread*'s POD manifesto, *HOW TO STOP WORRYING* demystifies the publishing business by showing how easy it is to self-publish and start a small press, reminiscent of the many paeans for the small press put forth by earlier avant-gardes. But Yearous-Algozin's "how-to" document lacks the utopian tinge associated with that genre of avant-garde writing and is in fact quite pragmatic:

> don't worry about making it look good, gutters,
> paratext, etc.
> that's all just marketing
> leave that to "editors" who can pay "designers", i.e.
> bosses
> or until you learn more about laying out books, which
> you never need to learn
> save yr cover as a .jpg & upload it in the cover
> designer or use the default settings
> whatever
> set the price at zero revenue
> that way you can buy more copies when lulu has coupons
> for free shipping
> also, this is poetry, you shouldn't be making a profit
> don't be an asshole[24]

That poets do not usually make a profit—there are, for instance, far fewer "professional" poets than novelists—is a realistic assessment, but it also ironizes the widespread avant-garde imperative for poets to position themselves outside capital. Although *Troll Thread* borrows its house format and approach to media from *0 to 9*, 8.5″ × 11″ is also simply one of the default sizes available in Lulu's bookmaking facilities. It is worth noting that several *Troll Thread* authors work with such default settings as constraints for creative production, letting the default determine the work. Within a history of print publishing dominated by an esteem for craft, manual skill, the intricacies of typographical design, and the time and expense required for the production process, *Troll Thread*'s labor and rationale for publishing the "books" in their catalogue (or in Melgard's case, the labor of "composing" *Black Friday*) is much harder to determine, and deliberately so.[25] The form and content of *Black Friday* and *HOW TO STOP WORRYING* think of "the book" as a (failed) commodity and as a (failed) material object.

That said, *Black Friday* in particular is also a self-consciously literary work. While *Tristram Shandy*'s famous black page (which is an explicit reference point for Melgard) shows its own self-awareness as a mechanically produced book rather than as a manuscript copied by scribes, *Black Friday*'s black pages show it no longer needs to be mechanically produced in order to be a book: it can exist as a digitally imagined book, even an unprintable one.[26] In *Tristram Shandy*, the black page is a mimetic attempt at mourning the character Yorick's death via the medium of the book. *Black Friday*, which commemorates "BLACK INK ON WHITE PAPER" in the form of a serialized tombstone in pages, humorously mourns not the end of books but rather the readers' attachment to a particular understanding of the printed page. Black ink on white paper as print is thought but unrealized; the one exception to the work's unrealizability involved a librarian who snatched a meager thirty pages from the critic Brian Reed, resulting in "a failed partial printout [that] will now be archived as a paper form of a digital artefact."[27] Perhaps such an incomplete and imperfect print reproduction is the ideal in-between condition for *Black Friday*: instead of a slick perfect-bound book with high production values, the loose pages with their cheap and streaked black ink flaunt, or taunt us with, the idea of the unprintable, even if or precisely when they are printed. In a stroke of bibliographic irony, Melgard has recently been able to order a hardbound copy of *Black Friday*, and in its failed dematerialization one could therefore say, as Melgard put it in conversation with me, "I guess the project is over."[28]

Troll Thread's awareness of printedness, publishing technology, and (supposedly) unprintable content and forms aligns it with the many formal and generic experiments of earlier avant-gardes. Whereas avant-garde publications across the twentieth century often mixed genres, digital platforms enable a mixing of media that was impossible to the same extent in previous print technologies. As "a publication suited to any type of media file," J. Gordon Faylor's *Gauss PDF* (which ceased publication in 2018) features PDFs as well as numerous other file types, such as .mov, .rtf, .jpg, .mp4, .mp3, and .zip, in addition to YouTube playlists, image collections, and poems in Word documents.[29] It shares this multiplicity of file formats with the largely digital publishing project *Badlands Unlimited*, whose series "Files" publishes artists' editions as collectors' items to download.[30] But *Gauss PDF* operates primarily in a (conceptual) writing context, even though the majority of pieces would be difficult to categorize as poems or even as literary texts; they are simply works fascinated with digital materiality, medium specificity, and genre. Tonya St. Clair's *Cloud Storage for Everyone* (GPDF048, 2012), for example, is a PDF consisting of a link to a Dropbox folder containing all previously published *Gauss* PDFs, the link itself blown up into large type with line breaks. Feliz Lucia Molina's *A Letter to Kim Jong-il Looking at Things* (GPDF045, 2012), in turn, repeats a letter addressed to Kim Jong-il (then already deceased) in 143 Microsoft Word fonts, alongside various pictures of the dictator looking at toilet paper, a tractor, "people starving, etc.," and other images trawled from a Tumblr called "Kim Jong-il Looking at Things."[31] In both publications, digital storage, navigation, and the customizability of personal computers become part of the pieces' meaning-generating mechanisms.

The variety of genre and media references notwithstanding, *Gauss* PDFs are unified in the way they are displayed on the *Gauss* Tumblr. The consecutive numbering of each publication as GPDF + number in its "catalog" section evokes bibliographic standards and archival practices usually associated with print, though in this case the bibliographic reference also constitutes part of a Tumblr URL. In 2013, *Gauss PDF* began publishing Gauss Editions using the POD service Lulu, and Faylor describes the editions as appearing "somehow a priori digitized; the books all have that same look and feel. It's as though the publishing wizard is somehow inscribed behind the text, like a watermark."[32] Through Lulu's layout templates, *Gauss PDF* publications look like they were always meant to remain digital. Nevertheless, Faylor uses a print historical term—*watermark*—to explain a phenomenon rooted in digitality. Historically, a watermark indicates to readers that the paper of a book is handmade and therefore more valuable, while the watermark's specific shape functions as a papermaker's signature. No longer handmade, *Gauss PDF*'s digital watermark imbues the digital object with the promise of a signature and with a materiality specific to its publishing technology and screen-based reading environment.

That printedness can be realized digitally is the design conceit of a recent *Gauss PDF* piece by Daniel Wilson (figs. 16 and 17). *Files I Have Known: Data Reminiscences* (GPDF199, 2016) is an autobiographical account of the author's memories of files that no longer exist. The imagined "book" traces Wilson's encounters with ephemeral files on his computer. Both visually and conceptually, the project exploits the disjunction between a file and its description in another medium, as Wilson explains in the foreword: "Can the original essence of a data file be recreated purely by words?"[33] Unlike other publications by *Gauss PDF* or *Troll Thread* that complicate close reading owing to the sheer quantity or illegibility of the material, *Files I Have Known* rewards sequential story-based reading. In narrativizing digital materiality, Wilson's specifications of file types, file sizes, file names ("amb1.wav," "fafda.rtf," "!A19TOP!.S3M"), and creation dates (from the 1990s to 2015) are offset by the old-fashioned look of the decaying page, which, readers are invited to imagine, is weathered by age and bad archival conditions. The whitish, fungi-induced patches on a cover with crumbling edges and a yellowed dedication page with brownish stains that are usually the result of light exposure and age-related deterioration ("foxing") contradict the title's and the contents' utter contemporaneity. Or rather, the files' decomposition is represented visually by a process that is not local to their digital environment.

Wilson does not just mirror the skeuomorphism of digital-design inventions; he exploits it poetically. Although the cover's decorative border matches the paper, the title's retro-art-nouveau font and the interior text look tagged on, unblended with the supposedly aged page. Of course, the PDF "pages" are not the deteriorated paper of a book called *Files I Have Known*; they are either modified scans of an extant printed book or photoshopped pages with a "vintage" effect applied. Given the range of design possibilities today, including apps that create a letterpress look, Wilson is less interested in a perfect copy of print than in a media-specific originality. *Files I Have Known* fakes printedness, but fakes it badly, in order to create its own uniquely digital printedness.[34]

While Melgard's and Wilson's tongue-in-cheek simulations of printedness cleverly explore distinctions and overlaps between print and digital, e-readers and software that displays digitized material simulate print without irony or media-specific awareness. Not every digital project that publishes avant-garde work or circulates within an avant-garde community is automatically avant-garde in the way it engages with its publishing medium. The online archive of Ugly Duckling Presse (UDP), a New York–based independent publisher of historical

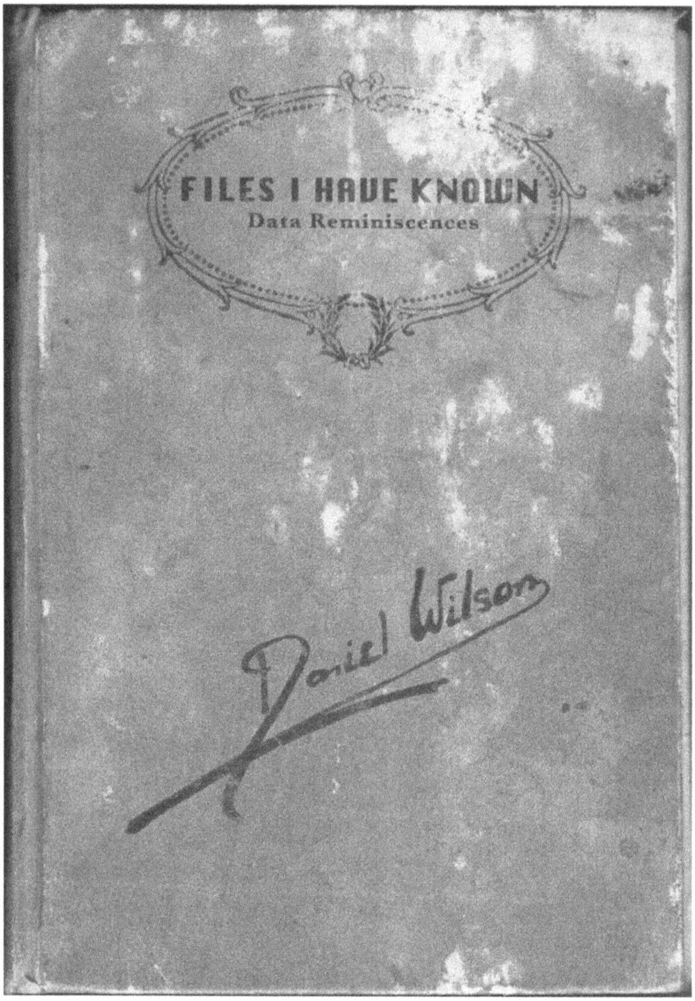

Figure 16. Daniel Wilson, *Files I Have Known: Data Reminiscences* (*Gauss PDF*, 2016), cover. Courtesy *Gauss PDF*, © 2016.

and contemporary avant-garde writing, art, translation, and performance, as well as less experimental materials, hosts scans of out-of-print publications in an animated Flash-based reader that enables the comparative reading across page spreads that readers are accustomed to in books and magazines. These documents include the scan of a damaged copy of UDP's magazine *6×6* (fig. 18).[35] The burnt edges might immediately call up associations of censorship and book burning, to which underground presses have been subject in the past, while its off-center and slightly diagonal title, set in wood type, alludes to the

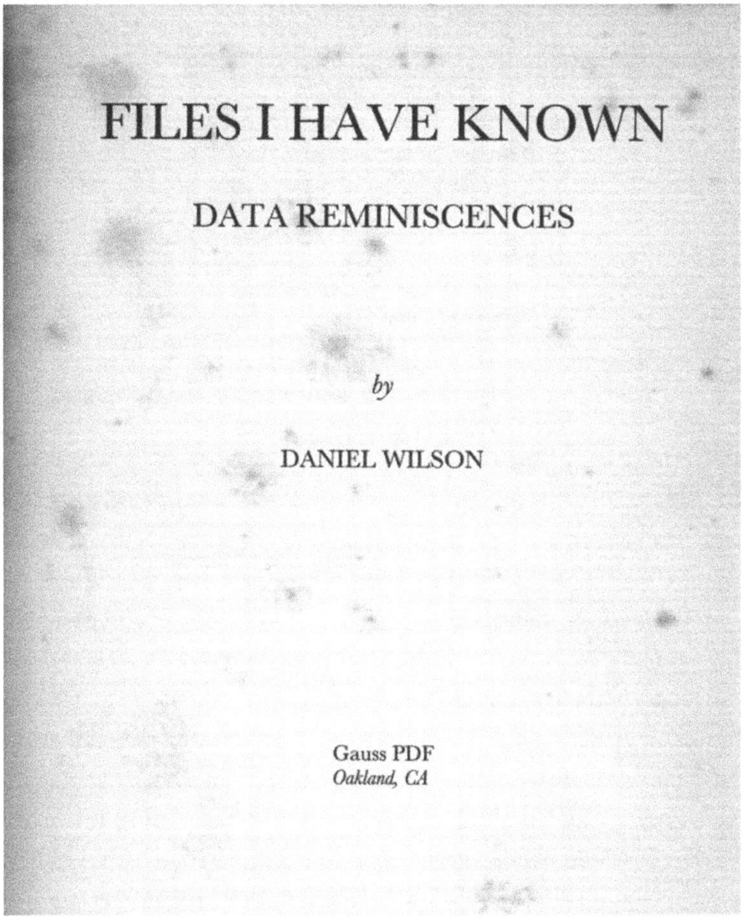

FILES I HAVE KNOWN

DATA REMINISCENCES

by

DANIEL WILSON

Gauss PDF
Oakland, CA

Figure 17. Daniel Wilson, *Files I Have Known: Data Reminiscences* (*Gauss PDF*, 2016): 3. Courtesy *Gauss PDF*, © 2016.

typographical experiments of Dada. But unlike the knowing irony of the material traces in *Files I Have Known*, these are "real" stains and the result of a fire in the press's old storage facility, a fact unknown to readers except by word of mouth. These burn marks might grant the magazine a deceptively palpable materiality, but in the online viewer the materials have been rendered digital, a process carried further by the mediation of the flip-book software in its simulation of paper reading. I can hover my cursor over a corner, which will then curl its dog-ear toward me, as if I had touched it after lightly wetting my fingers to mark my place. And when I turn the page—that is, when I "click to read" (fig.

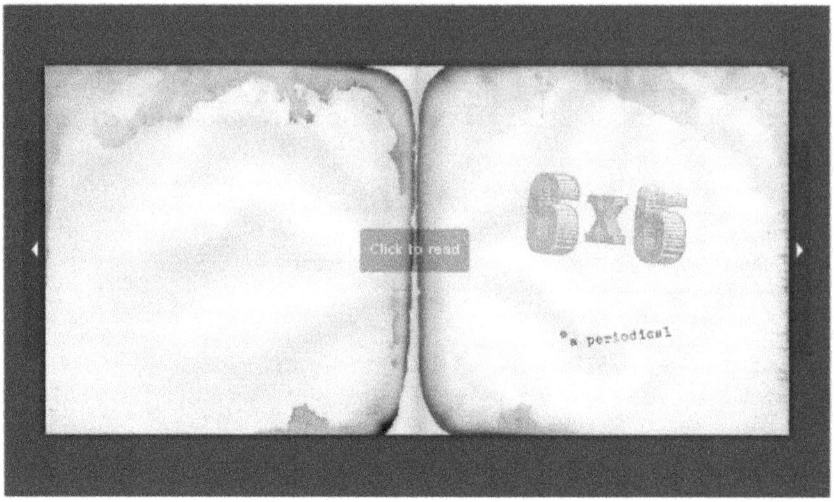

Figure 18. *6×6*, no. 5 (Dec. 2001), Ugly Duckling Presse Online Chapbook Archive.

18)—I hear a swoosh sound, like the movement of paper, as if in pursuit of the tangibly authentic in the digital realm. This software gimmick seems simultaneously adequate and ludicrous for a magazine that highlights its materiality and small-press credentials.[36] The pristine display of the software creates a mismatch, making the magazine appear more precious, even kitschier, than its print version. The issue's cover text, "its autobiography of touch," taken from the first poem in the issue, suddenly reads like a remark on the object's material journey: as if it knew it would be "touched" by fire but not, in its digital iteration, by my readerly cursor-hand.

While UDP's online archive uses Flash, a publishing technology well-suited to multimedia projects, it is not surprising that *Gauss PDF*, *Troll Thread*, and peer projects such as *SOd*, *Hysterically Real*, and *Badlands Unlimited* use PDFs. Such a capacious file format—it is either an index of a once-printed object or a digital object that is only imagined to be printed—appeals to projects that explore alternative models and scales of printedness and the codex. The PDF is "framed by the genre of the document" or "gray literature," such as government reports or product manuals—in other words, nonliterary texts.[37] PDFs also can, since Adobe's introduction of Acrobat X in 2010, embed audio and video files; and the introduction of that new functionality indeed coincided with the founding of *Troll Thread* and *Gauss PDF*. For Lisa Gitelman, PDFs are "documents that may be said to conjure themselves"; they are both text and an image of that text.[38]

Following Derrida's remarks about screen-based writing, one could argue that Melgard's *Black Friday*, Wilson's *Files I Have Known*, and, most explicitly, UDP's burnt *6×6* issue "retain the memory of what has disappeared: the paper, the page of the codex."[39] The PDF's "look of printedness" has nevertheless been "separated from paper and mobilized online,"[40] and there is no sense of anachronism or nostalgia attached to these experiments, at least not for *Troll Thread* or *Gauss PDF*.

Although *Troll Thread* still designs its PDFs in recto/verso pages for printing a codex, it does not necessarily "expect people to actually purchase the physical copies," and it views Lulu primarily as "a means to host the PDFs, something Tumblr's platform doesn't accommodate, without having to pay for our own domain."[41] For this reason, Hannes Bajohr suggests that *Troll Thread*, *Gauss PDF*, and his own *oxoa* are treating "POD as [an] artistic practice."[42] For critics of such writing this might mean that, as Nick Thurston urges, "we have to find new ways of *reading* publishing," namely, by "re-conceptualiz[ing] reproduction as a form of production."[43] More broadly, to understand "publishing as artistic practice," as a recent title by the avant-garde publisher Sternberg Press suggests, might offer a conceptual category for such media-blending and indeterminate work. Focusing on distribution, the *Troll Thread* editors argue, is part of their project's avant-garde appeal: "in flattening out the text and making it more easily distributed, it loses an important part of its aesthetic, i.e. exceptional, status."[44] In some ways, this is an avant-garde gesture familiar from *The Blind Man*, *0 to 9*, and 1970s xeroxed magazines and is at heart a Benjaminian argument about the nature of reproducibility simply hiked up to a new scale. But in the mundane context of the web, more so than in other media, a reader's reverence for the digitized object might be lessened. Perhaps the avant-garde's aura will "wither," and we will remove it from the pedestal it has occupied in our political and cultural imagination, and that could prove to be a healthy turn of events.[45]

It is apt that the platform that hosts *Gauss PDF* and *Troll Thread* is the multimedia-based Tumblr. Although both publishers use a template that evokes a minimalist Swiss design, Tumblr is not a static website and does not usually have the look of other more literary and professional blogs or websites: as a hosting site for sharing, it foregrounds its blogging aspect, and one of its default designs presents the dashboard as a true hotchpotch of images and notes. While the printed book is a discrete unit with a starting and ending point, the borders of the sometimes multimedia, sometimes nonliterary, and sometimes long and sprawling work published by *Gauss PDF* are less clearly defined. Similarly, the born-digital magazine *Triple Canopy* (2007–) veers inquisitively toward print, digital, and something else entirely. It expands the traditional magazine issue generically, temporally, and spatially by defining it as "includ[ing] digital works of art and literature, public conversations, books, editions, performances, and exhibitions . . . published over the course of several months, often concurrently."[46] In this multimedia approach, *Triple Canopy* resembles and deliberately evokes earlier media-spanning magazines such as *Aspen*, the magazine-in-a-box, with its flexi-disks, flip-books, and foldouts, but *Triple Canopy*'s temporally unbounded nature is a particular affordance of its online environment.[47] While *Aspen* featured a variety of media as separate items in a box, *Triple Canopy*, like *Gauss PDF* and other digital publishers, can blend these media and undo the hierarchies among them. To include public events in the definition of an "issue" (or a "book," as UDP did with its performance-based "paperless books") is then only the logical extension of a field already broadened by the distributive and material multiplicity of the web.[48]

Displaying its links to the print tradition, *Triple Canopy* experiments with its online environment by tilting the scroll model of websites to a sideways click or swipe, akin to flip-books or flip-book software. It does so in the hope that such an experiment provides "subtle cues that a proper reading experience is under way," but its design also invokes the smooth elegance of Apple products.[49] While there were indeed earlier, often commercial, websites with clickable content that proceeded frame by frame, the design remains unusual for a contemporary literary magazine. Reminiscent of such websites but also of turning pages in a print magazine, *Triple Canopy* combines an imagined resemblance to each of the technologies it intermediates, which the editors relish in referring to the page as a "metaphor."[50] *Triple Canopy* is a highly self-conscious enterprise precisely in this regard: its slogan is to "slow down the internet."[51] The editors also remain aware of the built-in "obsolescence" at the heart of their new media project.[52] This obsolescence is less philosophical than practical: display formats are not accessible forever; links break, and browsers update. Between 2011 and 2013, the editors therefore published three volumes of *Invalid Format: An Anthology of Triple Canopy*—a selective gathering of materials published in the magazine's first four issues, documentation for their public events, and some editorial correspondence.

In its self-archiving, the magazine reversed the practice of using the digital as a means of preservation, and instead considered "printable PDFs," "curat[ing] shows in galleries," or "publishing books . . . as a form of 'artful archiving.'"[53] Specifically, the editors asked themselves how the magazine's digital material could be "degraded elegantly, without disappearing entirely, in print."[54] The anthology's design paid equal homage to older print technologies: all fonts were digital renderings of earlier fonts, including an eighteenth-century Dutch typeface, a 1903 Gothic typeface, the typewriter font Courier New, and Helvetica, one of the most popular design fonts to this day.

As with any change in print technology, digital publishing has specific affordances and a specific bibliographic code. Matthew Kirschenbaum, N. Katherine Hayles, and Jerome McGann have long insisted on the materiality of electronic texts and on reading them as cultural and historical forms in ways similar to how printed texts are analyzed.[55] Such attention to digital literary materials benefits from knowledge of print history and traditional textual scholarship and must also include the writing implements that are integral to any textual or artistic production. Given that many authors now type their work, without ever copying from a handwritten draft, notions of authorship and composition processes naturally require adjustment. An author can write, produce, and distribute a work in a single day; the chain of production, reception, and distribution, or what Robert Darnton famously called the "communications circuit," is thus radically reduced.[56] Digital media also lend themselves to revision in ways the letterpress, mimeograph, and photocopier did not: revision can be more invisible than the manual corrections in letter-pressed text or photocopies or the correction fluid used for mimeographed mistakes.[57] In this way, new publishing technologies adjust the labor—or at least the outward appearance of labor—involved in publishing.

Throughout the history of small-press publishing, editors have frequently commented on the labor of typing mimeograph stencils or setting letterpress type.[58] Today, knowing which digital program poets and editors used, and knowing the affordances of InDesign, Lulu, or Tumblr, might offer a new understanding of a piece or an author's mode of working. Unlike the letterpress or mimeograph, our computers are not purely technologies for printing. We use them for other things, too: drafting a poem, listening to music, scheduling meetings. Although some texts do become more fragmented when digitized, digital reading is not exclusively or automatically "segmented, fragmented, discontinuous."[59] Nor is it necessarily matched by the interactivity, intertextuality, and nonlinear readings that are said to be built into the magazine format, because some works and magazines, despite their fragmented structure, demand a linear reading.[60] The medium does not affect objects and reading experiences always in the same way.

The aforementioned publishing projects each participate in the contemporary trend toward what Jessica Pressman calls an "aesthetic of bookishness," which is not "merely another move of postmodern reflexivity" but rather "a serious reflection on the book—and the literary book in particular—through experimentation with the media-specific properties of print illuminated by the light of the digital."[61] Unlike the novels Pressman studies, the projects considered here do not experiment with bookishness or printedness for fear of the "death of the book" or magazine; their aim is not to inject "vigor" into the print medium in order to "remain innovative."[62] Instead, these works incorporate print technology and its concomitant materiality, reading habits, and literariness into the digital to create printedness digitally without attachment to paper. The printed book, as Kirschenbaum has recently argued, is only one possible outcome that shares the distributive and receptive infrastructure of other media while equally functioning as a "book." For projects that display such qualities, Kirschenbaum has coined the phrase "bookish media," where the adjectival *bookish* can be a quality that applies to digital forms as well.[63] Bookish media exhibit a "secondary materiality," something that is "both remarkably like and remarkably unlike materiality."[64]

The situation is similar for what I call the "magazine-ish" media published by *Troll Thread*, *Gauss PDF*, UDP's "paperless book department," and *Triple Canopy*, which are all "printish": they invite a redefinition of print as the inscription and impression on a surface that need not be paper.[65] Whether it is the sound effect of rustling paper and the burnt pages in UDP's online archive, or the little white hand in PDF readers mimicking a tactile material interaction, or Daniel Wilson's handwritten signature and faded paper imitation, or the economic and symbolic value of print in various *Troll Thread* titles, this imagined printedness, or what Derrida refers to as the "paper-form of thinking" and the "order of the page," reconceives digital publishing.[66] These works look like print or pretend they work like print; thus, they uphold for readers "the spectral model of the book" at the same time as they transform that model.[67] In other words, they think print even if they remain or must remain unprinted. They are thought experiments in contemporaneity, where innovation is no longer the primary motivating factor for an avant-garde. As the Poetic Research Bureau puts it in its contribution to *Triple Canopy*'s *Invalid Format* anthology, "'make new' is of less import than make now."[68]

People You May Know

"A bad day on the Internet is a bad day forever," says Ian Heames, a poet and small-press editor based in Cambridge and Oxford, who refuses to publish his work online. When I told Ian that I would quote him in my chapter, he told me he adopted this *bon mot* from the American poet Peter Gizzi, who was a visiting poet at Cambridge in 2011; another Cambridge-based poet, Drew Milne, apparently used it as a line in a song. This anecdote stresses the now-familiar *ressentiment* for our digital futures, but it also reminds us that gossip can often be a good indicator for a poetic network—in this case, of a nonvirtual but also transatlantic poetry community at Cambridge. Heames's refusal to play the digital game is possibly nostalgic or possibly simply a matter of taste and may or may not affect the contemporary and future reception of his work. In other words, being "good at" social media may in some cases significantly increase someone's contemporary cultural capital. How poets spend their days on the Internet will, in turn, affect the kinds of communities they can build.

The digital medium, whether used for the production, distribution, or reception of avant-garde work, establishes new connections among material, technology, genre, and sociality. To the extent that *Triple Canopy* engages inventively with its publishing medium, it certainly fulfills the criteria for avant-gardes established by earlier magazines. Its awareness of the pedagogical possibilities of magazine publishing, too—as evident in its annual "Publication Intensive," a two-week summer workshop on print and digital materiality and new media's "politics of access and identity"—is common among avant-garde communities.[69] But *Triple Canopy* does not self-identify as an avant-garde publication, nor does it construct a discourse of experimentalism around itself, unlike many earlier magazine communities.

In an email chain later published in the first volume of the *Invalid Format* anthology, the soon-to-be editors disagreed on the aims and aesthetics of the new magazine, thinking through the tradition of avant-garde self-fashioning. Sarah Kessler, for one, did not want "anything insider-ish"; Emily Witt, too, wrote that "excessive analysis of New York cultural minutiae makes me tired," because it is politically insufficient in such "harrowing, complicated days" when what is needed is "to either report something seriously or look for ways to reveal humor or absurdity or societal insanity beyond employing irony or sarcasm."[70] The founding editor, Alexander Provan, suggested in response that "clearly, we won't be providing something our society is in serious need of at the current moment, unless we think society would benefit from more [of] our words floating around the Internet." As a consequence, he noted, "too much effort spent distinguishing this magazine from the legions of other publications that bear some similarity to it is an unnecessarily self-reflexive exercise. . . . There's something to be said for not defining ourselves too narrowly."[71] Despite this caveat, a proposed letter sent out to potential contributors initially mentioned all the magazines the editors previously worked for. Differing from the deliberate lineage embraced by many avant-gardes, Kessler wondered if displaying "our 'credentials' . . . conveys the validity of this project[.] It makes the magazine seem totally homogenous—just another mag started by people who already work for other mags." How, she asked, could it be more than "the younger brother of a list of already respected and admired (by a certain milieu) publications"?[72]

Both *Triple Canopy*'s disagreements and Heames and Gizzi's reservations about digital publishing seem symptomatic of the difficulties contemporary literary and artistic communities face: does it still make sense to align with the avant-garde, past or present, and deliberately aim for a limited audience, ideologically or technologically? While reflections on ideal readership and nontextual politics are widespread among a range of magazines during their emergence, *Triple Canopy* signals a change in the way many contemporary magazine communities think of themselves. Some are suspicious of claims about their social efficacy or the need to set themselves apart from other publications in a gesture of radical novelty. They no longer seek to "make new" but to "make now," to recall the Poetic Research Bureau's objective.

The contemporary online environment and its shift toward "nowness" also affects the sociality of avant-garde communities and the reception of new work. Compared to earlier magazines, readers praise contemporary publishing projects less frequently for their ability to forge a community, or are doubtful about the value of explicit group-formation, as in *Triple Canopy*'s founding email exchange. One might conclude, therefore, that magazines no longer generate the sense of community that they did in earlier avant-gardes. But since correspondence has almost completely moved online—email, Facebook, Twitter—it may simply be the case that contributors and editors express solidarity and affiliation over private channels that may or may not ultimately become available to researchers. Most contemporary magazines and presses do not yet have archives in university libraries; *Triple Canopy* is a notable exception, as it is in the process of establishing a collection at New York University's Fales Library. That said, if the trend is for poets and editors no longer to identify with one publication or, like W. C. Williams, to reserve all the best poems for one magazine ("*Others* got them all"), then avant-garde publishing communities may be more difficult to form in the digital era.[73]

In print magazines, textual evidence of sociality is often obscured. On social networks, affiliations already *seem* to be on the surface: Facebook labels everyone a "friend" and, based on various algorithms, suggests "people you may know." This mode of digital connection is deceptive, as the nature of an online friendship remains as opaque as affiliations in print media. Nevertheless, readers' views of interactions among contemporary practitioners have changed markedly. It is now clear, owing to social media, who attends the readings for which they accepted invitations, who is more than merely "interested," and who "likes" or comments on a post, how often, and in what context. That said, a "like" in 2007, say, meant something different from a "like" in 2017. Currently, its function is closer to registering awareness of a post than offering an expression of taste, for which there are by now other emoticons added to the emotional palette. In other words, though likes or retweets look quantifiable on the surface, beneath each user's digital response lies a hinterland of complex motivations, and this complexity problematizes the usefulness of social media for literary analysis of contemporary communities. Researchers and readers only seem to know more about their contemporary objects of study than ever before, particularly as information that might previously have been confined to print, private correspondence, or gossip is now publicly shared online.

One work that cannily exploits the networked structure of digital publishing and sociality is Josef Kaplan's long poem *Kill List*, published in October of 2013 as a free PDF by the Baltimore-based *CARS ARE REAL*, that was shared primarily over Facebook and Twitter.[74] It consists of an alphabetized list, divided into stanzas of four lines each, following the formula "X is a rich poet" or "Y is comfortable." The selection of poets was fairly arbitrary: Kaplan, a writer based in New York who moves within avant-garde digital-publishing circles, asked his friends to label a number of fellow poets as either rich or comfortable. The piece is thus based on gossip, speculation, and an ironic premise, since hardly any contemporary poet could be characterized as truly "rich," and since avant-garde poets would undoubtedly prefer not to be described as socially and culturally "comfortable" given that an avant-garde identity has so long depended on passionate discomfort. Wasn't social inequality, and sometimes even poverty, the very condition for the avant-garde's call to arms, the justification for its political outrage?

Compared to the notoriety of Duchamp's *Fountain*, discussed in the pages of *The Blind Man* in 1917, or the reaction to *The Little Review*'s "blank issue" in 1916, such provocations can now reach a nonlocal audience more easily and quickly, and Kaplan's piece duly ruffled more than a few feathers. For some, the very form and title of the poem made it an unethical project in its evocation of McCarthyism and, more recently, the US government's kill list for suspected enemies. Others saw the appropriation of that discourse as constitutive of its politics. In either case, *Kill List* effectively questions the value poets and audiences still grant the figure of the poet, in particular the avant-garde poet. It underlines how the class anxieties and class realities of contemporary poetry circles, along with the digital visibility of communications of taste, come to shape an avant-garde's self-understanding.

A few days after a social media outburst of disgruntlements and defenses following the publication of Kaplan's poem, Joey Yearous-Algozin published *Real Kill List*, for which he lifted a Facebook thread that discussed Kaplan's piece, pasted it into InDesign, and uploaded the resulting PDF to the *Troll Thread* Tumblr. Sophia Le Fraga, in turn, published a "Chill List" as a Facebook status, replacing "rich" and "comfortable" with "X could afford to chill," "Y is pretty chill," and "Z is chill."[75] The adaptation of the formula by two of Kaplan's friends and the earlier responses by the poetry community highlight all three pieces' knowingness about their media-specific reception online. Like Xerox, online publishing has made sharing, appropriation, and distribution increasingly easy and rapid. But unlike the (often clandestine) reproduction and distribution of xeroxes, the hyperimmediacy and visibility of social media's networked and hyperlinked sociality can produce an often-proclaimed "echo chamber," reverberating ideas and feelings unchallenged, or, conversely, it can propel digitally amplified indignation at the click of a mouse.

Since much contemporary and historical poetry is published, republished, consumed, and debated online, social media and digital interfaces are crucial to our understanding of how a contemporary avant-garde works and views itself. Whereas Facebook and Twitter are only incidentally resources for the study of contemporary communities, other platforms deliberately present themselves as pedagogical projects. Archives of audio recordings like PennSound and Archive of the Now are pedagogical in intent and "magazine-ish" in format. They are repositories for individual works (often added serially) and media through which communities form or become visible. A digital audio file is also a form of publication, and several online audio projects call themselves magazines, gesturing back to analogue magazines like *Black Box*, whose issues consisted of two cassettes per box.[76] Danny Snelson therefore argues that readers can indeed understand what he terms "little databases" like PennSound and other digital distribution platforms through a combination of close textual, media-specific, and quantitative analyses.[77] In their new engagements with community and pedagogy, the magazine-ish projects of today display and sometimes actively shape contemporary practices and their paths to institutionalization.

As with print publications, there are institutional differences between self-funded and university-funded digital projects, the latter having benefited greatly from digital-humanities funding over the last decade. Likewise, as in earlier print communities, self-theorization and self-conscious pedagogy are criticized by those who uphold the notion of avant-garde anti-institutionalism. Poet and publisher Richard Owens, for example, is less open to the self-declared contemporary avant-garde called "conceptual writing" (much of which takes its data-driven maximalism—or minimalism—from the Internet and is often distributed online), stating in a piece in *ON: Contemporary Practice* that "what publicly announces itself as avant-garde through market and state funded megaphones scarcely ever is. Their daring lies in doing what others have done with the blessing of the market." For Owens, today "any identification with an avant-garde or commitment to innovation paves the way for a promising career in the culture industry."[78] Though literary careerism is no doubt less predictable or easy than Owens makes it sound, his use of the Adornian term *culture industry* highlights that for some practitioners and critics today's avant-garde ought to avoid becoming a commodity or seeking institutional acceptance.

Publication and archiving are indeed sometimes strategic, but they are also often accidental mechanisms in the institutionalization of avant-garde groups. Though online magazines typically consist of persistent traces that can be recalled by keywords or hyperlinks—I can search or quantify phrases, titles, authors—their digital functionality might distort nonvirtual practices and affiliations. Just as Meredith Stricker complained in *HOW2* in 1999 that she could not rely on AOL to show her the content she needed, today's search engines and social media might play an increasing role in conditioning access.[79] Online publishers encode their decisions and influence their search-engine discoverability by codifying their metadata in textual markup, thereby determining how a digital object may be found and, in turn, influencing the corpus available to researchers today and in the future. Google has its own "PageRank" algorithm to privilege what it considers the most relevant websites—a black-box index that depends on a proprietary amalgam of signals of importance. The supposed wilderness of the avant-garde thus remains intact, despite its supposedly high visibility jacket in the digital landscape.

Echoing Owens, poet and magazine editor David Lau regrets the "avant-garde co-optation" of conceptual writers and their digital curatorial practices in PennSound, Eclipse, and UbuWeb, and other online archives, because they "create . . . neutralized and depoliticized archives of avant-garde literature."[80] But it is debatable if any archive can be truly neutral. Lau offers a somewhat technologically deterministic view, in which digital remediation defangs the avant-garde: "the politics, historical openings, and possibilities that gave rise to [the earlier 'movements'] are largely left offstage," and they "can't be easily digitized and animated on screen."[81] Lau's distinction between what could be called a merely aesthetic avant-garde and a political avant-garde resembles dismissals of the so-called neo-avant-garde of the 1950s and 1960s.[82] Namely, both avant-gardes were dismissed as merely a "conservatory"—in the case of the digital avant-garde as a result of "the contemporary mode of conceptualist appropriation."[83] While one might disagree on the political valences of these projects, Lau does raise a fascinating point about media: what exactly happens to the politics and possibilities of earlier works once they are "digitized and animated on screen"? Any process of transmediation produces new frames and negotiations, and no medium makes a work more or less political on its own. Poet and critic Tyrone Williams rightly states that "to assume that the avant-garde of the late 20th and early 21st centuries must resemble the 'historical avant-garde' of the early 20th century in its forms and practices is to freeze history and thus [nullify] the avant-garde."[84] Rather than dismiss the effects of the digital environment, whether on the production, distribution, and reception of work or on social forms of interaction, readers must ask what this publishing reality means for their own modes of reading, a question avant-garde communities have already begun exploring in their own magazines.

The Digital Magazine as Vivarium

The potential of avant-garde literature has not ceased to bother and excite writers and editors in the contemporary, digital moment. In the winter of 2014, *Lana*

Turner: A Journal of Poetry and Opinion—a print and digital magazine of cultural critique that draws self-consciously on the revolutionary understanding of the avant-garde—published a special "Avant-Garde Forum" on contemporary writers, from which the aforementioned comments by Lau (one of *Lana Turner*'s editors) and Williams were excerpted. Other contributors included scholars Brian Reed, Jed Rasula, McKenzie Wark, Robert von Hallberg, translator and poet Joyelle McSweeney, and poets Cathy Park Hong and Cathy Wagner. Alongside the expected characterizations of the avant-garde's innovative aesthetics and/or radical politics, the forum included discussions of the avant-garde's inclusiveness or lack thereof—discussions that feminist magazines from the 1980s onward have firmly installed in avant-garde debates. Hospitality requires continuous work, and writers rightly continue to question the contemporary avant-garde's claims to progressiveness when it proceeds to exclude so-called minority writers.

Hong's much-discussed forum essay "Delusions of Whiteness in the Avant-Garde" dismisses the avant-garde's assumptions that an eradication of expression, voice, and subject is anti-authoritarian, suggesting instead that the notion of "post-identity" is wishful thinking possible only from a standpoint of privilege.[85] Hong refers mainly to contemporary conceptual writing, but such critiques and counter-critiques of identity, voice, and subject have been leveled at or by avant-gardists repeatedly; as in this forum, they often appear at charged historical moments and coincide with larger political and social movements. This particular forum was published several months after the Black Lives Matter protests in Ferguson, Missouri, instigated by the police shooting of Michael Brown, and followed a summer in which allegations of sexual assault were made within various Anglophone poetry communities. Within these communities, increasing dissatisfaction with societal and institutional racism led to greater participation in political activism and protest. Furthermore, rejection of persistent misogyny and what Spahr and Young in a 2015 essay called "the white room" in experimental magazines, presses, and reading series led to several meetings in New York, the Bay Area, London, and elsewhere. Alternative reading series and projects were also proposed, some of which were published or mentioned in a special 2015 *Chicago Review* issue featuring "A Forum—On Recent Actions in Response to Sexism, Misogyny, and Sexual Assault in Literary Communities."[86]

While the critiques themselves were not new, digital publishing and call-out culture enabled faster communications across broader networks. The seeming limitlessness of the digital space and the sheer availability of materials make it easier, at least hypothetically, for readers and editors to educate themselves and learn about previously less accessible materials and unknown writers. In theory, such access to information makes claims like "there just aren't as many experimental women and/or minority writers" moot. At the same time, the barrage of daily, nonliterary information and the overabundance of writers all sharing the same virtual space does undoubtedly make it more difficult to adequately read the contemporary literary landscape.

If avant-gardeness is indeed constructed by a community of practitioners, readers, critics, and other less visible participants over time, and if the avant-garde is what is called avant-garde, then we as contemporaries can shape the contemporary avant-garde through our habits of reading. We could, for instance, become avant-garde readers through reading work in different languages and in translation, countering monolingualism and the cultural monopoly of English (it is notable that in *Lana Turner*'s avant-garde forum three contributors—Sandra Simonds, Cathy Wagner, and Joyelle McSweeney—discuss the avant-garde in the context of translation). Poets and translators Jen Hofer and Sawako Nakayasu argue idealistically in a printed conversation in *ON: Contemporary Practice* that "translation also intervenes in typical forms of canonization" and is "potentially even counter to it."[87] Translation, which is a "peculiarly intensive mode of reading," might be instructive for what Derek Attridge (via Derrida) calls "hospitable reading." For critics and readers, this could mean upholding "the unlimited, unpredictable force of unconditional openness to whatever might arrive" in a literary work.[88] Derrida even saw a connection between hospitality and paper, which we could extend metaphorically to digital paper: "Credit or discredit, legitimation or delegitimation, have long been signified by the body of paper."[89]

This legitimizing function of print also applies to digital small-press publishing. Although not being published has none of the serious consequences Derrida describes for someone being denied immigration papers, editors act as symbolic gatekeepers who bestow the identity of "published writer," an act of legitimation that certainly affects a writer's cultural capital and sometimes even their livelihood. Contemporary critics can also grant hospitality and shape the future of the canon and simply choose not to participate in a trend. This chapter's focus on more modest and simultaneously more ambitious projects by a number of younger poets and editors, for instance, "selectively refus[es] to participate" in canonizing more prominent writers or groups, opening the possibility that aesthetic attention can also be political.[90] In such a way, the contemporary scholar might, to slightly rephrase Amy Hungerford's formulation, stop being "the servant of the culture she studies" and rather serve the culture she is helping to create.[91]

Avant-garde magazines themselves often develop sophisticated modes of reading their contemporaries. *ON: Contemporary Practice* was a perfect-bound magazine that appeared for two issues in 2008 and 2010, edited by Michael Cross, Thom Donovan, and Kyle Schlesinger; after a hiatus it was relaunched in 2013 as a PDF archive and a new PDF-and-monograph series run by Cross and Donovan. *ON* prefaced its first issue in 2008 with a quote from Philip Whalen's "Scenes of Life at the Capital":

> There is a wonderful kind of writing
> Which is never written NOW
> About this moment. It's always done later
> And redone until it is perfect.

To belatedly fulfill Whalen's wishes, *ON*'s editors offered such writing "written NOW / About this moment" by dedicating an entire magazine to reviews of contemporary writing by fellow writers. The more than one hundred pages of reviews in each issue covered a wide range of approaches and topics, from reviews of individual poets (sometimes reflecting on the reviewer's relationship with a poet, such as Dale Smith's review of his partner Hoa Nguyen's poetry), to assessments of older "contemporaries" like Beverly Dahlen, co-editor of *HOW(ever)*, to recently added online-only essays on trends in contemporary writing, such as Jeanine Webb's work on "weak intimacy" in contemporary Bay Area poetics or the public's mediated consumption of celebrity culture. Some reviews took the form of extended commentaries, such as Kyle Schlesinger's essay on the book artist Emily McVarish via her San Francisco fine-press predecessors, such as Gelett Burgess, Ernest Peixotto, Bruce Porter, and Porter Garnett's *Le petit journal des refusées* (1896) or Wallace Berman's *Semina*, and small presses like Auerhahn, Poltroon, and Zephyrus Image, paying close attention to the materiality and design of these projects. This attention to the hotchpotch of the contemporary, rather than an attempt to forge one particularly cohesive group or aesthetics, constitutes *ON*'s hospitable approach.

The two print issues have since been digitized and uploaded as full PDFs, alongside individual contributions indexed as alphabetized PDFs. Formally, the PDF archive becomes its own magazine, with a rolling contributor list that print magazines would not be able to accommodate. The PDF series is both an archive and a periodically cumulative table of contents for the magazine. Since in the new format most PDFs no longer contain publication dates and are simply arranged alphabetically, the distinction between older and more recent publications is deliberately indistinct. *ON* issue 1, for instance, contains barely any bibliographic information: no colophon, no date, no editors' names. Both the print and PDF reviews are relatively short and dive right into the work without initial biographical or contextual details that might ground the work in a particular time, though some essays in issue 2 do end with a more academic "Works Cited" section. Intended as an intervention in the present, *ON* dispenses with reviews that are written with an eye to being legible in the future archive and thus at least appears to be unconcerned with how someone might write about the magazine in the future.

ON's recent print-based monograph series, by contrast, offers sustained critical writings by contemporary voices that the editors consider to have been overlooked. The series, so far, consists of *Visceral Poetics*, by Eleni Stecopoulos; *Supple Science*, by Robert Kocik; and *From Our Hearts to Yours: New Narrative as Contemporary Practice*, by Rob Halpern and Robin Tremblay-McGaw. The editors want the series, like the magazine, "to generate discourse around problems and conversations that we feel are vital for an understanding of contemporary writing and aesthetics."[92] The magazine's second issue detailed their belief in a reviewing culture that is more than merely supplementary to creative work: "Critical writings about one's contemporaries," the editors note, "should not be consigned to the back pages of magazines and journals of record; nor should we approach them without a sense of consequence." Instead, they propose that reviews must be seen as "of the utmost importance to grounding an activist function of poetry."[93]

ON is rare as a contemporary magazine focused entirely on reviews; it shares this distinction with the UK-based *Hix Eros* (founded in 2013), which is published as a PDF at irregular intervals. But in its attention to discursive writing, *ON* joins the ranks of older avant-garde magazines like *L=A=N=G=U=A=G=E*, *Paper Air*, *HOW(ever)*, and *HOW2*, which put reviews and critical prose on a par with poetry. For *ON*, as for those earlier communities, the magazine can thus "serve as a space for dialogue" but specifically "for the acknowledgement of unrecognized subjects," asking itself how the magazine can enable the "otherwise submerged, suppressed, or invisible . . . to emerge so that we might read and address it." In a utopian avant-garde spirit, *ON* "would like to create a possible world."[94] In order to do so, the magazine "seeks understanding rather than critique per se."[95]

In this, *ON* represents a distinct move away from the rhetoric of critique in some contemporary avant-garde praxis and scholarship; such critique has traditionally been a common framework for discussions of the avant-garde following Brecht, Adorno, Bürger, and Frankfurt School dialectics. One contingent continues to insist on critique as a valuable dialectical tool, whilst the other considers it limiting. Following recent calls for surface, distant, descriptive, or more phenomenological reading, critique is now increasingly perceived as only one among many scholarly modes of reading.[96] I will return to the questions these trends raise in my epilogue, but I want to conclude this chapter by briefly connecting them to the issue of hospitality in (post-)digital publishing. Many practitioners argue that critique continues a legacy of white, male, and straight privilege; they instead propose more inclusive models of criticism and of the "avant-garde" label.[97] In the past, while flag-waving anti-institutionalism suited many (often male-dominated) avant-gardes and in fact facilitated their entry into the canon, for feminist and other "minority" avant-gardists the need to take canon-making into their own hands often required throwing some accepted avant-garde paradigms overboard.

The same need for definitional capsizing holds for the contemporary avant-garde. Sometimes, those who can afford an aggressive anti-institutional attitude already have the monetary or cultural capital or other privileges (based on ability, gender, race, or sexuality) to be able to do so; at other times, belligerence is simply a preferred rhetorical style. One alternative model of contemporary criticism "would be through the Hippocratic oath of the poet, designer, and architect Robert Kocik: *at least do not do harm*," a proposal that led poet and editor Thom Donovan to ask, "How can critique be in the interest of the world one would want? Too often 'negative' criticism makes claims about what is 'wrong' with something/someone before saying what it would want from poetry/art/cultural phenomena."[98] While the notion of the avant-garde as an agent of change is the ideal by which the avant-garde is traditionally known, that poets and critics frame not just avant-garde practice but also readerly habits and literary criticism explicitly within the metaphoric discourse of hospitality is a contemporary development prepared for by the many intersectional avant-garde projects preceding it.

The question of hospitality and what readers ought to pay attention to arises partially because contemporary writers are, as Holly Melgard claims, experiencing a "crisis of the physical page."[99] Avant-garde magazine-ish projects in the digital age become multimedia containers, "filemakers," data generators, distributors, and consumers—sometimes simultaneously.[100] Unlike earlier changes in publishing, the digital instantiates a medial shift, making paper only one possible medium for publishing and reading text. The availability of both historical and contemporary data, because of digitization or new digital production, requires rethinking what it means to make literature "now," where the imperative to make "new" might be more of an encumbrance than the liberating battle cry it once was.[101] Little magazines, both print and digital, come out faster than poetry collections or exhibitions, so they are usually much closer than other publishing formats to the current discussions and feelings within a poetry community, friendship circle, or a particular development within a poet's or artist's career. This is not to valorize the more immediate over the supposedly belated, as the collection can construct its own timeliness, dialogue, and intervention in a field; nevertheless, the magazine shows a nowness and interconnectedness that becomes visible through the very same aesthetic object. Poetry readings are similar in that regard, in that poets often perform new work, sometimes drafts, or work that will remain unpublished for years or forever. Digital magazines and other magazine-ish publishing projects make this nowness—which is technologically possible to an even greater degree—the probe for their experiments and poetics.

The little magazine today, as it was for the proto-Dada community, remains a laboratory, but the experiments in, and realities of, form, politics, and sociality are available for much larger networks to see and participate in. The avant-garde magazine has become a vivarium: the reader, or "user," can observe a small ecosystem as it takes place. It is all about visibility. As noted in earlier chapters, if the same names keep appearing together, they are often read as related, but we must be careful not to mistake the map for the territory. Juliana Spahr's insight or aspiration that in the early 2000s, "contemporary poetry [wa]s impossible to map finally" is instructive for other historical and contemporary moments as well: a description of an avant-garde is a provisional model, not a representative map.[102] By describing in detail the trends, patterns, shortcomings, and promises and, more importantly, by reading this hotchpotch of materials from the early twentieth century into the present day, I hope to have upset some of the conventional and persistent ideas about what it means to be avant-garde and, more broadly, what it means to form a literary community. Instead, a focus on the provisional and diachronic networks of multiple participants, on their media of publication and reception, and on an avant-garde's own discourses has led to a more hospitable and flexible theory of the avant-garde that we can carry into the future.

EPILOGUE
Avant-Garde Fever

How do we get the world we want? The crisis of the physical page that contemporary magazines have encountered and debated is, after all, also a crisis of what we are looking at and what we are looking for. To read avant-gardes through their failed political transformations misses the point. Ironically, to insist on political efficacy as the only criterion of the avant-garde is to devalue all avant-gardes by closing down the imaginative possibilities for community and aesthetics they developed and might develop today. It's necessary to look beyond the search for effectiveness and instead look toward the network of participants who debate such effectiveness in small communities of practice, such as little magazines, and ask whether effectiveness is even a useful measure for success. Rather than forever lament the revolutionary failure of avant-garde writing, we need to ask when, in which contexts, and for what purpose particular aesthetics or politics were rallied and how magazines participated in and often shaped those discourses—across the twentieth- and into the twenty-first century.

For Sianne Ngai, the aesthetic category of the "cute" shares with the avant-garde "its lack of political consequentiality" and the "short or limited range of its actual address."[1] Robert Scholes and Clifford Wulfman likewise mention in passing that the *little* in "little magazines" implies cuteness.[2] Because "the cute object seems to insist on *getting something* from us (care, affection, intimacy) that we in turn feel compelled to give," and because of its comparative weakness, Ngai detects a sadistic element inside the tender protectiveness we feel toward the cute object, which might lead us to reject that very object.[3] Poet and editor Cid Corman remarked about his magazine *Origin* that, for the magazine reader, "the cost is one of care and attention."[4] The avant-garde little magazine demands we pay attention, with care; it is an object that we might wish to be politically stronger at the same time that we believe we can no longer reject it because it is too intimately ours.

But when avant-gardism is separated from political efficacy, the little magazine does not lose its teeth and become a fetish object that gives us the sweet distraction we craved all along. Moving away from political efficacy in this case means rejecting the idea that a poem or artwork has a predictable, consistent, or easily describable effect in the world. It is not meant to deny that magazine editors and contributors very much want(ed) their work to have an effect. The magazine format is frequently evoked by editors and contributors as not only an important vehicle for politics, formal innovations, and social interaction but as political in and of itself. The medium's specific production, distribution, and reception can indeed make up its politics rather than the content of poems or artworks per se. Similarly, aesthetic form has often been seen as a strategy for an individual's or a group's avant-garde intentions. But not every magazine feature is monovalent, not every forum is democratic, and not every editorial is a manifesto. Readers need to pay attention to the contexts in which these features appear.

A new model of avant-garde criticism based on diachronic reading and provisionality allows us to interrogate why a particular notion of avant-gardism as unique, exclusionary, or programmatic remains so popular. Avant-garde vocabulary that simply no longer matches artistic practices hinders the reception of contemporary experimentation. To avoid dogmatism and ossification, critics must acknowledge that preservation for the future at the same time shapes that future. The archive and the archivist always produce more traces: as Derrida puts it, "the archive is never closed," and, in fact, ought not to be.[5] Readers might therefore want to embrace the provisionality of avant-garde work and the equally provisional subjective and institutional position of the critic. However much one might applaud an avant-garde's anti-institutionalism, all studies of the avant-garde institutionalize it according to their own logic, and some readers might resent this as complicity.

The idea of the "never enough" and the unavoidable embeddedness in patriarchal or capitalist structures was a particularly feminist, queer, and intersectional paranoia. Editors believed they could never ask enough questions and thought that there was always an inadequacy of definition and inclusion. There is perhaps also a paranoia of avant-garde critics, though of a different kind. Paranoid about their complicity in institutionalizing the avant-garde and institutionalizing the very notion of anti-institutionalization, avant-garde scholars adopt the avant-garde's language of transformative promise, using avant-garde writing as a reiteration of the validity and timeliness of their inquiry. There is a fear, but also a celebration, of the ephemeral, that which does not leave traces. The critic's (not necessarily the avant-garde's) greatest apprehension is inefficacy.

So contemporary critics are torn: "tormented by the fear of not being critical enough" and aware of their own complicity, they still want to defend the possibility of change.[6] Given that critics have fashioned the avant-garde as the ultimate agent of critique, it is not surprising that their expectations of creative and critical practice are matched. Avant-garde scholars and practitioners therefore need to move beyond exposure, opposition, contradiction, and radical breaks as default answers that often simply produce a scholarly and creative cul-de-sac. But in a practical sense, exposing the still dominant forms of privilege and prejudice in institutions of the avant-garde and contemporary writing more broadly remains necessary—in publishing, reading series, reviews, and on syllabi and committees. The feminist avant-garde's imperative was and continues to be to expose the sexism and racism in avant-garde publishing. In this way, it matches the scholarly practice of critique, or what Sedgwick called "paranoid reading," which "places its faith in *exposure*."[7] At the same time, the politics of the forum in avant-garde feminist magazines has both paranoid and reparative motives and effects: to highlight systemic oppression but also to promise pleasure and amelioration, which Sedgwick groups under reparative modes of knowing. While Sedgwick correctly surmises that exposure is "not a mere hop, skip, and jump away from getting it solved," in the case of small-press publishing, such exposures have, over the last few years, successfully led to changes in practice.[8] But such changes are unpredictable.

Avant-garde magazines with a feminist, queer, and intersectional agenda, then and now, can teach "the many ways selves and communities succeed in extracting sustenance from the objects of a culture . . . whose avowed desire has often been not to sustain them."[9] And it is a reparative reading that their paranoid project invites from contemporary critics. If these communities offer new pedagogical models of what Attridge calls "hospitable reading," we, too, can ask ourselves how we might become more hospitable in our attention and writing and address our own complicities productively.[10] Along those lines, experimenting with other forms of avant-garde criticism and practice is not a form of political acquiescence by any measure—opposition to the status quo, oppression, and inequality is as pressing as it ever was. But getting rid of the "protocols of professional pessimism"—or, conversely, an optimism that is only imaginable for the future—often tied to "a logic of perfectionism or absolutism" with regard to the avant-garde would go a long way toward engaging hospitably with contemporary avant-garde writing.[11] Avant-gardes do not have to be perfect, nor could they be.

Given that critique "is conspicuously silent . . . on the many other reasons why we are drawn to works of art: aesthetic pleasure, increased self-understanding, moral reflection, perceptual reinvigoration, ecstatic self-loss, emotional consolation, or heightened sensation,"[12] how could we read avant-gardes differently, and across time? In the *Arcades Project*, Walter Benjamin describes the collector as someone who dreams of a world "in which things are freed from the drudgery of being useful."[13] The possibility of noninstrumentality could energize contemporary avant-gardes and their readers. One way to talk about the pleasure of avant-garde work is to be led, in what Anne Anlin Cheng calls a "hermeneutics of susceptibility," by the subject or work in question.[14] Another might be to not always look for an overarching argument, in a practice akin to glossing.[15] The latter resonates with the descriptive reading promoted by Sharon Marcus, Heather Love, and Stephen Best, who note that "description might become a noninstrumental accumulation of particulars with no immediately clear purpose," in no "particular rush to make a broader claim."[16] Such noninstrumental descriptive reading might help create a hospitable contemporary writing community. Marcus, Love, and Best's proposal that "better describers attend to what eludes easy categorization and understanding" and "the world's messy profusion of stray details that cannot be assimilated to an already existing theory" accords with the complex nature of avant-garde practice.[17] Critics need to make that "messy profusion" the core of a contemporary theory of the avant-garde.

At the same time, a political and historicist commitment on the part of the critic is crucial to revise the canon's exclusions. In that spirit, I hope that this book has introduced some new names, new work, and new perspectives, while remaining fully aware that a simple expansion of the categories of conceptual art or feminism, say, is not yet enough. What is called for is a real renegotiation of the language and concepts by which artistic careers and literary history are measured. A critic's politics lie partly in her choice and mode of reading: by spending time with avant-garde communities; paying attention to their textual, material, and social forms; reading them hospitably; and accepting their "mediating effectiveness,"[18] a critic can extend avant-garde commitments into the present.

To accept provisionality at the center of avant-garde print communities across time means to accept a multiplicity of definitions. My term *proto-form* aims to capture this. Following the insight from genetic criticism and book history that there are multiple versions of a single poem, book, or magazine—in editions, anthologies, revised reprints, and digital facsimiles—we must also acknowledge the same multiplicity within avant-garde groups and the concept of the avant-garde itself. A new set of critical tools is needed to analyze avant-garde proto-forms as "groupings" that are "subject to repeated redefinitions or abandonment" and to account for the editorial, distributive, and readerly structures within which magazines and avant-garde communities are produced and read.[19] My suggestion that "to be avant-garde is to be read as avant-garde" finds its match in Ralph Cohen's argument that genres "are groupings of texts by critics to fulfill certain ends"—groupings that exist in relation to others.[20] Cohen's claim of a genre's historical embeddedness and interrelatedness and Jerome McGann's insight about textual editing—that no text can be "correct"—must function as guides for a contemporary avant-garde theory as well.[21]

Rather than asking if a contemporary avant-garde poet is "merely a copy," critics would do well to remember, as Bruno Latour and Adam Lowe point out, that *copy* is etymologically related to *copious* "and thus designates a source of abundance. A copy, then, is simply a proof of fecundity."[22] There are several versions of avant-gardism, not one true original, and the appearance of modernist and proto-Dada authors and artists in proto-conceptual, proto-Language, and feminist magazines continued *and* transformed the avant-garde project. Sometimes these earlier voices lent credence to a magazine's present venture or opened new dialogues in print. At other times, earlier poets and/or magazines rejuvenated the later magazines' gender politics or served as an aesthetic model for a present requirement. But taking earlier poets and theorists as authorities has also been problematic for a poetic culture intent on the overturning of concepts of authority, especially from the 1960s onward.

Ideally, then, late modernist and contemporary little magazines offered and continue to offer spaces for collaboration and friendship with what the poet Christian Hawkey aptly terms "between-voices": "to read the deceased is to reanimate their words; the between-voice is a ghost, a host."[23] To host such conversations with between-voices in little magazines allows critics, writers, and readers to collapse period-bound conceptions of avant-gardism. Reading avant-gardists alongside their predecessors, their successors, and their contemporaries, and understanding their poetics and politics within their original historical context, their new magazine interactions, and the present moment might be a way of starting to theorize a diachronic and dynamic model of avant-gardism and a hospitable model of criticism.

Both print and online magazines circulate in gift economies, but framing them as "free" (if they're digital) or outside of capital (in print) obfuscates the real economic and cultural capital involved. Especially online archives need substantial institutional funding, technological support, and often volunteer labor for their upkeep. *Triple Canopy*, for instance, frequently updates its website to remain compatible with different web browsers and mobile devices and, like many magazines, depends on funding, even more so because it is free for readers. But there is, of course, a promised reward for those involved in unpaid labor: if we do not quite want to call it a half-paid ticket to the canon party, it certainly foments group identities and exchanges. But there is no guaranteed return, only the prospect of one.

Hannah Arendt avowed that "the remedy for unpredictability, for the chaotic uncertainty of the future, is contained in the faculty to make and keep promises."[24] Arendt might help writers and readers understand their desire for avant-garde promises but also to see the possibilities in embracing uncertainty when studying avant-gardes. "Binding oneself through promises," she writes, "serves to set up in the ocean of uncertainty, which the future is by definition, islands of security without which not even continuity, let alone durability of any kind, would be possible in the relationships between men."[25] Promises for Arendt are connected to community. They "depend on plurality, on the presence and acting of others."[26] This "binding power" of the promise of an avant-garde magazine community and its various forms of labor is central to the avant-garde's continuing significance—not for some deferral to a better future but because it leaves the unpredictability and provisionality of avant-garde communities and practices intact.

What promises does this book uphold? What does it mean to "do" criticism on practice when you are also a practitioner? Toward the end of the project, I increasingly felt that I owed it to my fellow poets to write about them. Having studied the exclusions of artists, writers, editors, and organizers, and thus also the pitfalls and pressures of institutionality, I realized that resisting or shaping the canon was now up to me! So I could end this epilogue with an O'Hara-esque homage by referring to my friends, or to writers and artists I love, who have inspired me, whose work I wish would make it into the history books; I could refer to them by their first names or first letters (as Kathy Acker, Bernadette Mayer, and Hannah Weiner were wont to do in their magazine contributions) and establish my own little coterie in writing. But I would still be conditioned by the matrix of imperfect inclusion. Perhaps—and this is my own utopian nugget, cherished as a promise to hold on to—the historical and theoretical perspectives in my project can offer a rigorously provisional and generous model for criticism, artistic practice, and editing and curation today.

"The way of periodicals is strange," Morton Dauwen Zabel remarked in 1929, writing an elegy for *The Little Review* and *The Dial*.[27] Laura Riding, too, introduced the first issue of her own little magazine *Epilogue* with the acknowledgment that "it is awkward to appear in periodical form."[28] To hospitably embrace the strangeness of the medium and the impossibility of fully knowing an avant-garde group, as this book set out to do, is to adjust the parameters necessary for reassessing avant-gardes for the twenty-first century.

Notes

Introduction

1. Mónica de la Torre, "Response to Race and the Poetic Avant-Garde," *Boston Review*, March 10, 2015, https://bostonreview.net/poetry/monica-de-la-torre-forum-response-race-avant-garde.

2. My concept of provisional avant-gardes is also applicable to other print communities (say, Surrealism, Black Mountain, the New York School, the Black Arts Movement) that appear here only when they intersect with my chosen magazine networks.

3. Mina Loy, "Songs to Joannes," *Others* 3, no. 6 (April 1917): 19.

4. For feminist discussions of hospitality see Maurice Hamington, ed., *Feminism and Hospitality: Gender in the Host/Guest Relationship* (Lanham, MD: Lexington Books, 2010); and Maurice Hamington, "Toward a Theory of Feminist Hospitality," *Feminist Formations* 22, no. 1 (Spring 2010): 21–38.

5. Virginia Woolf, *Three Guineas* (London: Hogarth Press, 1938/1986): 112–13.

6. Susan Gevirtz, "Postcards," *HOW(ever)* 6, no. 4 (Jan. 1992): 14.

7. William Carlos Williams, "The Advance Guard Magazine," *Contact*, n.s. 1, no. 1 (Feb. 1932): 86–90, 89–90.

8. Morton Dauwen Zabel, "The Way of Periodicals," *Poetry* 34, no. 6 (Sept. 1929): 330–34, 332.

9. See Peter Bürger, *Theory of the Avant-Garde*, trans. Michael Shaw (Minneapolis: University of Minnesota Press, 1984); Renato Poggioli, *The Theory of the Avant-Garde*, trans. Gerald Fitzgerald (Cambridge, MA: Belknap Press of Harvard University Press, 1968); Benjamin Buchloh, "Theorizing the Avant-Garde," *Art in America*, Nov. 1984, 19–21; Hal Foster, *The Return of the Real: The Avant-Garde at the End of the Century* (Cambridge, MA: MIT Press, 1996); Matei Calinescu, *Five Faces of Modernity: Modernism, Avant-Garde, Decadence, Kitsch, Postmodernism* (Durham, NC: Duke University Press, 1987); Clement Greenberg, "Avant-Garde and Kitsch," *Partisan Review* 6, no. 5 (1939): 34–49; Marjorie Perloff, *The Futurist Moment: Avant-Garde, Avant Guerre, and the Language of Rupture* (Chicago: University of Chicago Press, 1986); Paul Mann, *The Theory-Death of the Avant-Garde* (Bloomington: Indiana University Press, 1991); and Richard Murphy, *Theorizing the Avant-Garde: Modernism, Expressionism, and the Problem of Postmodernity* (Cambridge: Cambridge University Press, 1999).

10. Alan Golding's *From Outlaw to Classic: Canons in American Poetry* (Madison: University of Wisconsin Press, 1995) distinguishes between the "poet-based" and the "institutional" canon (41).

11. Jerome McGann, *The Textual Condition* (Princeton, NJ: Princeton University Press, 1991), 56, 13. See also Jerome McGann, *Radiant Textuality: Literary Studies After the World Wide Web* (New York: Palgrave, 2001).

12. The "material turn" in the humanities focuses on culturally produced objects or materials in history, society, and literature.

13. See Douglas Mao and Rebecca L. Walkowitz, "The New Modernist Studies," *PMLA* 123, no. 3 (May 2008): 737–48.

14. David Antin, *Radical Coherency: Selected Essays on Art and Literature, 1966 to 2005* (Chicago: University of Chicago Press, 2011), 252.

15. See Margaret Anderson, "The Germ," *The Little Review*, 1, no. 2 (April 1914), 1–2.

16. "Survey of Contemporary Art Magazines," *Studio International* 193, no. 983 (Sept./Oct. 1976): 145–86. The "Art Magazines in Reprint" ad appeared on the inside back cover of the same issue of *Studio International.*

17. Bürger, *Theory of the Avant-Garde*, 26.

18. See, e.g., James M. Harding, *The Ghosts of the Avant-Garde(s): Exorcising Experimental Theater and Performance* (Ann Arbor: University of Michigan Press, 2013); and Gabriel Rockhill, *Radical History and the Politics of Art* (New York: Columbia University Press, 2014).

19. Bürger, *Theory of the Avant-Garde*, 49.

20. Andreas Huyssen, *After the Great Divide: Modernism, Mass Culture, Postmodernism* (Bloomington: Indiana University Press, 1986), 158.

21. See Poggioli, *The Theory of the Avant-Garde*; Greenberg, "Avant-Garde and Kitsch"; Calinescu, *Five Faces of Modernity*; John Weightman, *The Concept of the Avant-Garde: Explorations in Modernism* (LaSalle, IL: Library Press, 1973); Jürgen Habermas, "Modernity Versus Postmodernity," *New German Critique* 22 (Winter 1981): 3–14; and Huyssen, *After the Great Divide.*

22. Greenberg, "Avant-Garde and Kitsch," 40.

23. Max Horkheimer and Theodor W. Adorno, *Dialectic of Enlightenment: Philosophical Fragments*, trans. Edmund Jephcott, ed. Gunzelin Schmid Noerr (Stanford: Stanford University Press, 2002), 116.

24. See Huyssen, *After the Great Divide*; and Walter Benjamin, "Der Autor als Produzent," in *Gesammelte Schriften*, ed. Rolf Tiedemann and Hermann Schweppenhäuser (Frankfurt: Suhrkamp, 1977), 2:2, 683–701.

25. Peter Bürger, "The Significance of the Avant-Garde for Contemporary Aesthetics: A Reply to Jürgen Habermas," trans. Andreas Huyssen and Jack Zipes, *New German Critique* 22 (Winter 1981): 19–22, 20; and Walter L. Adamson, *Embattled Avant-Gardes: Modernism's Resistance to Commodity Culture in Europe* (Berkeley: University of California Press, 2007).

26. Huyssen, *After the Great Divide*, 32. Theodor Adorno, *Aesthetic Theory*, ed. Gretel Adorno and Rolf Tiedemann, trans. Robert Hullot-Kentor, new ed. (London: Continuum, 2004), 26, 203.

27. See Perloff, *The Futurist Moment.*

28. Rosalind E. Krauss, *The Originality of the Avant-Garde and Other Modernist Myths* (Cambridge, MA: MIT Press, 1985), 157.

29. In "'Avant-Garde': Some Terminological Considerations," in *Literarische Avantgarden*, ed. Manfred Hardt (Darmstadt: Wissenschaftliche Buchgesellschaft, 1989), 90–112, 92, Matei Calinescu points out that the term acquired political connotations during the French Revolution, becoming associated with the aim of revolution.

30. Martin Puchner, *Poetry of the Revolution: Marx, Manifestos, and the Avant-Gardes* (Princeton, NJ: Princeton University Press, 2006), 25.

31. Bürger, *Theory of the Avant-Garde*, passim.

32. See Benjamin H. D. Buchloh, *Neo-Avantgarde and Culture Industry: Essays on European and American Art from 1955 to 1975* (Cambridge, MA: MIT Press, 2000); Foster, *The Return of the Real*; Elisabeth Frost, *The Feminist Avant-Garde in American Poetry* (Iowa City: University of Iowa Press, 2003); Krauss, *The Originality of the Avant-Garde*; Marc James Léger, *Brave New Avant Garde: Essays on Contemporary Art and Politics* (Winchester: Zero Books, 2012); David Lehman, *The Last Avant-Garde: The Making of the New York School of Poets* (New York: Doubleday, 1998); Puchner, *Poetry of the Revolution*; Mark Silverberg, *The New York School Poets and the Neo-Avant-Garde: Between Radical Art and Radical Chic* (Farnham, Surrey: Ashgate, 2010); and Timothy Yu, *Race and the Avant-Garde: Experimental and Asian American Poetry Since 1965* (Stanford: Stanford University Press, 2009).

33. Murphy, *Theorizing the Avant-Garde*, 290.

34. Hans Magnus Enzensberger, "Die Aporien der Avantgarde," in *Einzelheiten* (Frankfurt: Suhrkamp, 1962), 290–315; Donald Kuspit, *The Cult of the Avant-Garde Artist* (Cambridge: Cambridge University Press, 1993); Leslie Fiedler, "The Death of Avant-Garde Literature," in *The Collected Essays of Leslie Fiedler* (New York: Stein and Day, 1971), 2:454–60; and Greenberg, "Avant-Garde and Kitsch," 38.

35. Ben Hickman, *Crisis and the US Avant-Garde: Poetry and Real Politics* (Edinburgh: Edinburgh University Press, 2015), 157.

36. Lawrence Rainey, *Institutions of Modernism: Literary Elites and Public Culture* (New Haven, CT: Yale University Press, 1998), 11. Rainey describes the economic entanglements and savviness of modernist artists, collectors, and publishers.

37. Charles Bernstein, "Provisional Institutions: Alternative Presses and Poetic Innovation," *Arizona Quarterly* 51, no. 1 (Spring 1995): 133–46; Jeremy Braddock, *Collecting as Modernist Practice* (Baltimore: Johns Hopkins University Press, 2012), 2, 6, and passim.

38. For a discussion of the careers of anti-establishment poets and their institutional strategies see Libbie Rifkin, *Career Moves: Olson, Creeley, Zukofsky, Berrigan, and the American Avant-Garde* (Madison: University of Wisconsin Press, 2000).

39. Foster, *The Return of the Real*, 8.

40. Bürger, *Theory of the Avant-Garde*, 58, 91.

41. Rockhill, *Radical History and the Politics of Art*, 227, 7.

42. Rita Felski, *The Uses of Literature* (Oxford: Blackwell, 2008), 108, 114.

43. Felski, 120.

44. The Modernist Journals Project, http://modjourn.org.

45. See Ann L. Ardis and Patrick Collier, eds., *Transatlantic Print Culture, 1880–1940: Emerging Media, Emerging Modernisms* (Basingstoke, UK: Palgrave Macmillan, 2008); George Bornstein, *Material Modernism: The Politics of the Page* (Cambridge: Cambridge University Press, 2001); Braddock, *Collecting as Modernist Practice*; Peter Brooker and Andrew Thacker, eds., *The Oxford Critical and Cultural History of Modernist Magazines*, 3 vols. (Oxford: Oxford University Press, 2009/2012/2013); Suzanne W. Churchill and Adam McKible, eds., *Little Magazines and Modernism: New Approaches* (Burlington, VT: Ashgate, 2007); Patrick Collier, "What Is Modern Periodical Studies?" *Journal of Modern Periodical Studies* 6, no. 2 (2015): 92–111; Sean Latham and Robert Scholes, "The Rise of Periodical Studies," *PMLA* 121, no. 2 (March 2005): 517–31; Mark S. Morrisson, *The Public Face of Modernism: Little Magazines, Audiences, and Reception, 1905–1920* (Madison: University of Wisconsin Press, 2001); Robert Scholes and Clifford Wulfman, *Modernism in the Magazines: An Introduction* (New Haven, CT: Yale University Press, 2010); Eric B. White, *Transatlantic Avant-Gardes: Little Magazines and Localist Modernism* (Edinburgh: Edinburgh University Press, 2013).

46. Eric Bulson, *Little Magazine, World Form* (New York: Columbia University Press, 2016). See also Brooker and Thacker, *Oxford Critical and Cultural History of Modernist Magazines*.

47. See Margaret Beetham, "Open and Closed: The Periodical as a Publishing Genre," *Victorian Periodicals Review* 22, no. 3 (Fall 1989): 96–100; and Laurel Brake and Anne Humphreys, "Critical Theory and Periodical Research," *Victorian Periodicals Review* 22, no. 3 (1989): 94–95.

48. See David Bennett, "Periodical Fragments and Organic Culture: Modernism, the Avant-Garde, and the Little Magazine," *Contemporary Literature* 30, no. 4 (1989): 480–502; and Stephen Voyce, *Poetic Community: Avant-Garde Activism and Cold War Culture* (Toronto: University of Toronto Press, 2013), 15.

49. Frederick J. Hoffman, Charles Allen, and Carolyn F. Ulrich, eds., *The Little Magazine: A History and a Bibliography* (Princeton, NJ: Princeton University Press, 1946), 1. For an extensive follow-up for the years 1960 to 1992 see Loss Pequeño Glazier, *Small Press: An Annotated Guide* (Westport, CT: Greenwood, 1992).

50. Elliott Anderson and Mary Kinzie, "Prefatory Note," in *The Little Magazine in America: A Modern Documentary History*, ed. Elliott Anderson and Mary Kinzie, *TriQuarterly* 43 (Fall 1978): 3–5, 3.

51. Suzanne W. Churchill and Adam McKible, introduction to *Little Magazines and Modernism: New Approaches*, ed. Suzanne W. Churchill and Adam McKible (Burlington, VT: Ashgate, 2007), 3–18, 6.

52. See D. F. McKenzie, *Bibliography and the Sociology of Texts* (Cambridge: Cambridge University Press, 1999); Rainey, *Institutions of Modernism*, passim; and Morrisson, *The Public Face of Modernism*, passim.

53. Scholes and Wulfman, *Modernism in the Magazines*, 60.

54. Voyce, *Poetic Community*; Christopher Beach, *Poetic Culture: Contemporary American Poetry Between Community and Institution* (Evanston, IL: Northwestern University Press, 1999); Michael Davidson, *The San Francisco Renaissance: Poetics and Community at Mid-Century* (Cambridge: Cambridge University Press, 1989); Daniel Kane, *All Poets Welcome: The Lower East Side Poetry Scene in the 1960s* (Berkeley: University of California Press, 2003); Andrew Epstein, *Beautiful Enemies: Friendship and Postwar American Poetry* (Oxford: Oxford University Press, 2006); Anne Dewey and Libbie Rifkin, introduction to *Among Friends: Engendering the Social Site of Poetry*, ed. Anne Dewey and Libbie Rifkin (Iowa City: University of Iowa Press, 2013), 1–18; Ross Hair, *Avant-Folk: Small Press Poetry Networks from 1950 to the Present* (Liverpool: Liverpool University Press, 2016); Loren Glass, *Counterculture Colophon: Grove Press, the Evergreen Review, and the Incorporation of the Avant-Garde* (Stanford: Stanford University Press, 2013); Alan Golding, "*The New American Poetry* Revisited, Again," *Contemporary Literature* 39, no. 2 (Summer 1998): 180–211; Martin Duberman, *Black Mountain: An Exploration in Community* (New York: Dutton, 1972); and Rifkin, *Career Moves*.

55. Benedict Anderson, *Imagined Communities: Reflections on the Origin and Spread of Nationalism* (London: Verso, 1991).

56. Ruth Stone, "Postcard," *HOW(ever)* 1, no. 3 (Feb. 1984): 15.

57. Kathleen Fraser, "Dear Daphne," *HOW(ever)* 5, no. 2 (Jan. 1989): 14.

58. Janice Radway, "Interpretive Communities and Variable Literacies: The Functions of Romance Reading," *Daedalus* 113, no. 3 (Summer 1984): 49–73, 53.

59. Michael Davidson, *Guys like Us: Citing Masculinity in Cold War Poetics* (Chicago: University of Chicago Press, 2004), 28.

60. Yu, *Race and the Avant-Garde*, 1. Dorothy J. Wang, *Thinking Its Presence: Form, Race, and Subjectivity in Contemporary Asian American Poetry* (Stanford: Stanford University Press, 2014), argues that instead of focusing either on content related to "identity" or conversely only on experimental form in minority avant-garde writing, these two approaches need to be combined.

61. Epstein, *Beautiful Enemies*, 32.

62. Other helpful terms include, in addition to Alan Golding's "writing *communities*" (*From Outlaw to Classic*, 121), Rachel Blau DuPlessis and Peter Quartermain's "nexus" of Objectivism, Jason Harding's "periodical network" of modernism, Lucy Delap's suffragette "periodical community," Raymond Williams's "cultural formation," and, inspired by Williams, Matthew Chambers's late-modernist "periodical formations." See Rachel Blau DuPlessis and Peter Quartermain, eds., *The Objectivist Nexus: Essays in Cultural Poetics* (Tuscaloosa: University of Alabama Press, 1999); Jason Harding, *The Criterion: Cultural Politics and Periodical Networks in Inter-War Britain* (Oxford: Oxford University Press, 2002); Lucy Delap, *The Feminist Avant-Garde: Transatlantic Encounters of the Early Twentieth Century* (Cambridge: Cambridge University Press, 2007), 26; Raymond Williams, *The Sociology of Culture* (Chicago: University of Chicago Press, 1981), 62; and Matthew Chambers, *Modernism, Periodicals, and Cultural Poetics* (New York: Palgrave Macmillan, 2015), 9.

63. Virginia Jackson, *Dickinson's Misery: A Theory of Lyric Reading* (Princeton, NJ: Princeton University Press, 2013), 6.

64. Ralph Cohen, "History and Genre," *New Literary History* 17, no. 2 (Winter 1986): 203–18, 210.

65. Cohen, 210.

66. Sharon Marcus, Heather Love, and Stephen Best, in "Building a Better Description," *Representations* 135 (Summer 2016): 1–21, outline the many forms description can take, "including observing, measuring, comparing, particularizing, generalizing, and classifying, using words, images, and numbers" (2). In that way "description makes objects and phenomena available for analysis and synthesis and is rarely as simple as its critics imply" (11)—as print scholars would no doubt agree.

67. Pierre Bourdieu, *Distinction: A Social Critique of the Judgement of Taste*, trans. Richard Nice (London: Routledge, 2010), 266, 267.

68. Such competing claims about the value of difficulty as the basis for a poetics have been formative for the network around the British poet J. H. Prynne and the University of Cambridge; for a close examination of such claims see D. S. Marriott, "The Rites of Difficulty," *fragmente* 7 (1997): 118–37. We find a critique of the manipulative power of simple language in the writings of American poets associated with "Language writing." The idea of emancipating the spectator, in turn, was theorized in Bertolt Brecht's Epic Theater, Antonin Artaud's Theatre of Cruelty, Augusto Boal's Theatre of the Oppressed, and the Situationist International's rejection of a "society of the spectacle."

Chapter 1

1. Ezra Pound, "Small Magazines," *English Journal* 14, no. 9 (Nov. 1930): 689–704, 702–3.

2. Alfred Stieglitz, "'291'—A New Publication," *Camera Work*, no. 48 (Oct. 1916): 62.

3. Dawn Ades, introduction to *The Dada Reader: A Critical Anthology*, ed. Dawn Ades (Chicago: University of Chicago Press, 2006), 12–14, 13. The only New York Dada magazines Ades includes are *The Blind Man* and *New York Dada*.

4. Pound, "Small Magazines," 703.

5. Other contemporaneous magazines published in America, which can be seen as part of the proto-Dada movement, include *Maintenant* (1913), *The Ridgefield Gazook* (1915; only a single, hand-drawn maquette was produced, and no further copies were printed), *TNT* (1919), *Rogue* (1915), *The Soil* (1916–17), and later *New York Dada* (1921), *Broom* (1921–24), *Secession* (1922–24), *Aesthete 1925* (1925), *Manuscripts* (MSS) (1922–23), and *transition* (1927–38). *Aesthete 1925*, *Broom*, and *Secession* attempted to instantiate a European version of Dadaism in America.

6. The variant spelling of "The Blindman" seems to be the result of Alfred Frueh's cover drawing. The editors themselves refer to *The Blind Man*, so I will use that spelling throughout. I describe the magazine's production and reception history, its editorial practice, and contributions in my essay "*The Blind Man* Sees the Fountain: New York

Dada Magazines in 1917; An Introduction," in *The Blind Man*, facsimile edition (New York: Ugly Duckling Presse, 2017).

7. Advertisement, *The Little Review* 3, no. 5 (August 1916): inside front cover.

8. William Innes Homer, *Alfred Stieglitz and the American Avant-Garde* (Boston: New York Graphic Society, 1977), 194; David Hopkins, "Proto-Dada: The New York Connection," in *The Oxford Critical and Cultural History of Modernist Magazines*, vol. 3, *Europe 1880–1940*, ed. Peter Brooker, Sascha Bru, Andrew Thacker, and Christian Weikop (Oxford: Oxford University Press, 2013), 160–79, 160; Francis M. Naumann, *New York Dada: 1915–23* (New York: Abrams, 1994); Rudolf E. Kuenzli, *New York Dada* (New York: Willis Locker and Owens, 1986); Arturo Schwarz, *New York Dada: Duchamp, Man Ray, Picabia* (Munich: Prestel, 1973); William Agee, "New York Dada, 1910–1930," in *The Avant-Garde*, ed. Thomas B. Hess and John Ashbery (London: Collier-Macmillan, 1968), 105–13; Ileana B. Leavens, *From "291" to Zurich: The Birth of Dada* (Ann Arbor: UMI Research Press, 1983); Steven Watson, *Strange Bedfellows: The First American Avant-Garde* (New York: Abbeville Press, 1991).

9. See the reprinted manifestos in Mary Ann Caws, ed., *Manifesto: A Century of Isms* (Lincoln: University of Nebraska Press, 2001).

10. Peter Bürger, *Theory of the Avant-Garde*, trans. Michael Shaw (Minneapolis: University of Minnesota Press, 1984), 22.

11. Marjorie Welish, "Wanted," in *In the Futurity Lounge/Asylum for Indeterminacy* (Minneapolis, MN: Coffee House Press, 2012), 50–51.

12. Hopkins, "Proto-Dada," 160. Naumann (*New York Dada: 1915–23*) and Kuenzli (*New York Dada*) have rectified that view with their extensive work on New York Dada, in particular in the visual arts. Others, such as Watson, Churchill, and Tashjian, have followed suit. See Watson, *Strange Bedfellows*; Suzanne W. Churchill, *The Little Magazine "Others" and the Renovation of Modern American Poetry* (Burlington, VT: Ashgate, 2006), 114; and Dickran Tashjian, *Skyscraper Primitives: Dada and the American Avant-Garde, 1910–1925* (Middletown, CT: Wesleyan University Press, 1975), 89–92.

13. Funny Guy [Picabia], "391," *Le Pilhaou-Thibaou: Supplément Illustré de "391"* (July 1921): [3] (my translation).

14. Rudolf Kuenzli, "New York," in *Dada Artifacts*, exhibition catalogue (Iowa City: University of Iowa Museum of Art, 1978), 69–75, 69; Watson, *Strange Bedfellows*, 267.

15. In this focus on canonical omissions, I follow the groundbreaking work of Naomi Sawelson-Gorse, ed., *Women in Dada: Essays on Sex, Gender and Identity* (Cambridge, MA: MIT Press, 1998); Irene Gammel, *Baroness Elsa: Gender, Dada, and Everyday Modernity—A Cultural Biography* (Cambridge, MA: MIT Press, 2002); Amelia Jones, *Irrational Modernism: A Neurasthenic History of New York Dada* (Cambridge, MA: MIT Press, 2004); Shari Benstock, *Women of the Left Bank: Paris, 1900–1940* (Austin: University of Texas Press, 1986); Jayne E. Marek, *Women Editing Modernism: "Little" Magazines and Literary History* (Lexington: University Press of Kentucky, 1995).

16. Agnes Ernst Meyer, "How Versus Why," *291*, no. 1 (March 1915): 2.

17. Jay Bochner "dAdAmAgs," in *Making Mischief: Dada Invades New York*, ed. Francis

Naumann, Beth Venn, and Todd Alden (New York: Whitney Museum of American Art, 1996), 214–21, 216.

18. See Andrew Thacker, "General Introduction: Magazines, Magazines, Magazines!" in *The Oxford Critical and Cultural History of Modernist Magazines*, vol. 2, *North America*, ed. Peter Brooker and Andrew Thacker (Oxford: Oxford University Press, 2012), 1–28, 5; Homer, *Alfred Stieglitz*, 194; Gwen Allen, *Artists' Magazines: An Alternative Space for Art* (Cambridge, MA: MIT Press, 2011), 3.

19. The typographically avant-garde exceptions, outside America, were *BLAST* (1914), *Lacerba* (esp. Marinetti's contributions, 1913–15), the Russian magazine *Futuristy* (1914), and Marinetti's book *Zang Tumb Tuuum* (1914). Most literary magazines, however, continued to use ornamental, symbolist, or art nouveau typefaces and designs.

20. Stieglitz, "'291'—A New Publication," 62.

21. William Wordsworth, "Preface: 1800 Version (with 1802 Variants)," in William Wordsworth and Samuel Taylor Coleridge, *Lyrical Ballads*, 2nd ed, ed. R. L. Brett and A. R. Jones (London: Routledge, 2005), 286–314, 287.

22. A later example is Marinetti's "Une assemblée tumultueuse," a gatefold plate in *Les mots en liberté futuristes* (1919). I am not aware of any gatefolds in literary magazines prior to *291*.

23. The regular edition had about one hundred subscribers, while the deluxe version had only eight. One thousand copies of the regular edition were printed, and one hundred of the deluxe version; see Dawn Ades, *Dada and Surrealism Reviewed* (London: Arts Council of Great Britain, 1978), 33–34.

24. Johanna Drucker, *The Visible Word: Experimental Typography and Modern Art, 1909–1923* (Chicago: University of Chicago Press, 1994), 96.

25. Drucker, 103.

26. Marius de Zayas and Agnes Ernst Meyer, "Mental Reactions," *291*, no. 2 (April 1915): 2.

27. Kathleen D. McCarthy, *Women's Culture: American Philanthropy and Art, 1830–1930* (Chicago: University of Chicago Press, 1991), 183.

28. Agnes Ernst Meyer, *Out of These Roots: The Autobiography of an American Woman* (Boston: Little, Brown, 1953), 102–3.

29. Meyer, 103.

30. Stieglitz, "'291'—A New Publication," 62.

31. De Zayas and Meyer, *Mental Reactions*, National Gallery of Art, www.nga.gov/content/ngaweb/Collection/art-object-page.137583.html.

32. Francis M. Naumann, "Marius de Zayas y Alfred Stieglitz se Separan: La Publicación de 291 y la Formación de Modern Gallery," in *Marius de Zayas: Un Destierro Moderno*, ed. Antonio Saborit, trans. Alberto Román and Luz María Sánchez (Mexico City: El Instituto Nacional de Bellas Artes, 2009), 76–99, 82. For a detailed description of the maquette, see David Stang [entry 58], *Modern Art: Recent Acquisitions*, catalogue 138 (Boston: Ars Libri, 2006), unpaginated.

33. Bürger, *Theory of the Avant-Garde*, 72.

34. Bürger, 73.

35. See Willard Bohn, *Modern Visual Poetry* (Newark: University of Delaware Press, 2001), 136–37.

36. Leavens, *From "291" to Zurich*, 19–37.

37. Bram Dijkstra, *Cubism, Stieglitz, and the Early Poetry of William Carlos Williams* (Princeton, NJ: Princeton University Press, 1969), 32.

38. Editorial, "Simultaneism," *291*, no. 1 (March 1915): 5.

39. Mina Loy, "Gertrude Stein," *Transatlantic Review* 2, no. 3 (Sept. 1924): 305.

40. "Do You Strive to Capture the Symbols of Your Reactions? If Not You Are Quite Old Fashioned," *New York Evening Sun*, Feb. 13, 1917, 10, quoted in Alex Goody, "'Consider Your Grandmothers': Modernism, Gender and the New York Press," *Media History* 7, no. 1 (2001): 47–56, 48.

41. Sarah Hayden, *Curious Disciplines: Mina Loy and Avant-Garde Artisthood* (Albuquerque: University of New Mexico Press, 2018), 74.

42. Mina Loy, "O Marcel . . . Otherwise I Also Have Been to Louise's," *The Blind Man*, no. 2 (May 1917): 14–15.

43. See Stephen Voyce, "'Make the World Your Salon': Poetry and Community at the Arensberg Apartment," *Modernism/modernity* 15, no. 4 (Nov. 2008): 627–46, 642; Carolyn Burke, *Becoming Modern: The Life of Mina Loy* (New York: Farrar, Straus and Giroux, 1996), 402; Marisa Januzzi, "Dada Through the Looking Glass, or: Mina Loy's Objective," in *Women in Dada: Essays on Sex, Gender and Identity*, ed. Naomi Sawelson-Gorse (Cambridge, MA: MIT Press, 1998), 578–612, 583–84; and Hayden, *Curious Disciplines*, 303–4n85. For a detailed discussion of the piece, see Hayden, *Curious Disciplines*, 103–13.

44. On Picabia's misogyny see Jones, *Irrational Modernism*; Drucker, *The Visible Word*; and Sawelson-Gorse, *Women in Dada*.

45. Marius De Zayas, "New York at First Did Not See . . . ," *291*, no. 5/6 (July/August 1915): 6.

46. Jed Rasula's *Destruction Was My Beatrice: Dada and the Unmaking of the Twentieth Century* (New York: Basic Books, 2015) focuses exclusively on male Dadaists.

47. Alfred Kreymborg, *Troubadour: An Autobiography* (New York: Boni and Liveright, 1925), 236.

48. Mina Loy, "Love Songs," *Others* 1, no. 1 (July 1915): 6–8, 7.

49. Mina Loy, "Feminist Manifesto," *Lost Lunar Baedeker: Poems of Mina Loy*, ed. Roger L. Conover (New York: Farrar, Straus and Giroux, 1996), 153–56, 156. It was also through Dodge that Loy appeared in Stieglitz's *Camera Work*, thus establishing her reputation in print before she arrived in New York City. ("I wish you would give me a letter or two to people in New York who are vital." Mina Loy to Mabel Dodge, Feb. 1920, YCAL MSS 196, ser. 1, Correspondence, box 24, folder 664–65, folder 1 of 2. Cf. Mabel Dodge Luhan Papers, Yale Collection of American Literature, Beinecke Rare Book and Manuscript Library. Regarding *Camera Work*, see Mina Loy to Mabel Dodge, April 20 [1914?], ibid., folder 2 of 2.)

50. Kreymborg, *Troubadour*, 223.

51. Kreymborg, 235; Churchill, *The Little Magazine*, 179; Burke, *Becoming Modern*, 196.

52. Kreymborg, *Troubadour*, 235.

53. Carolyn Burke, "The New Poetry and the New Woman: Mina Loy," in *Coming to Light: American Women Poets in the Twentieth Century*, ed. Diane Wood Middlebrook and Marilyn Yalom (Ann Arbor: University of Michigan Press, 1985), 37–57, 37. Alex Goody cites a 1915 *New York Call* article that made this connection explicit in its title: "This Summer's Style in Poetry, or the Elimination of Corsets in Versifying." Goody, "Consider Your Grandmothers," 50.

54. Kreymborg, *Troubadour*, 223.

55. See Martin Puchner, *Poetry of the Revolution: Marx, Manifestos, and the Avant-Gardes* (Princeton, NJ: Princeton University Press, 2006), 2; and Caws, *Manifesto*, xx, xix.

56. One exception is Puchner's discussion of the contradictory manifestos of *BLAST* and the *Cabaret Voltaire*, in *Poetry of the Revolution*, 116–17, 146.

57. Hopkins, "Proto-Dada," 163; Francis Naumann, "New York Dada: Style with a Smile," in *Making Mischief: Dada Invades New York*, ed. Francis M. Naumann, Beth Venn, and Todd Alden (New York: Whitney Museum of American Art, 1996), 10–26, 17.

58. Paul B. Haviland, "When I Arrived at 291 . . . ," *291*, no. 1 (March 1915): 4.

59. Haviland, 4. *Camera Work*'s questionnaire included Djuna Barnes, Charles Demuth, Alfred Kreymborg, Francis Picabia, Man Ray, and numerous others. In it, Stieglitz asked his contributors, "What is 291?" See *Camera Work*, no. 47 (July 1914/Jan. 1915): 3–4, 3.

60. Haviland, "When I Arrived at 291 . . . ," 4.

61. For Charles E. S. Rasay, 291 "is a little 'agora' where men may listen, and may speak freely" ("291—Its Meaning to Me," *Camera Work*, no. 47 [July 1914/Jan. 1915], 12–15, 14); cf. Marius de Zayas, *How, When, and Why Modern Art Came to New York*, ed. Francis Naumann (Cambridge, MA: MIT Press, 1996), 173.

62. Editors, "291 Notes," *291*, no. 1 (March 1915): 5.

63. Meyer, "How Versus Why," 2.

64. Meyer, 2.

65. Meyer, 2.

66. Margaret Anderson, "Announcement," *The Little Review* 1, no. 1 (March 1914): 1–2, 2.

67. Anderson, "Announcement," 2.

68. Anderson, "Announcement," 2; Rosalind E. Krauss, *The Originality of the Avant-Garde and Other Modernist Myths* (Cambridge, MA: MIT Press, 1985), 157.

69. Margaret Anderson, "Our First Year," *The Little Review* 1, no. 11 (Feb. 1915): 1–2.

70. Henri-Pierre Roché, "The Blind Man," *The Blind Man*, no. 1 (April 1917): 3–6, 4.

71. Roché, 6.

72. Roché, 6.

73. Roché, 5.

74. Mina Loy, "In . . . Formation," *The Blind Man*, no. 1 (April 1917): 7.

75. Bürger, *Theory*, 51–52, 55–59; Rosalind E. Krauss, *Passages in Modern Sculpture* (New York: Viking, 1977), 72, 76–81; Arthur C. Danto, *The Transfiguration of the*

Commonplace: A Philosophy of Art (Cambridge, MA: Harvard University Press, 1981), 5, 93–94.

76. Alfred Stieglitz, letter to the editors, *The Blind Man*, no. 2 (May 1917): 15.

77. Stieglitz, 15.

78. William Carlos Williams, "Gloria!" *Others* 5, no. 6 (July 1919): 3–4, 3.

79. Williams, 3.

80. Eric B. White, *Transatlantic Avant-Gardes: Little Magazines and Localist Modernism* (Edinburgh: Edinburgh University Press, 2013), 91.

81. William Carlos Williams, "Belly Music," *Others* 5, no. 6 (July 1919): 25–32, 25.

82. Williams, 26.

83. Williams, 29.

84. Williams, 27.

85. Williams, 27.

86. Margaret Anderson, "On Criticism," *The Little Review* 2, no. 1 (March 1915): 26–30, 26–27.

87. Margaret Anderson, "A Real Magazine," *The Little Review* 3, no. 5 (August 1916): 1–2, 2.

88. Anderson, 2.

89. Note, *The Little Review* 3, no. 6 (Sept. 1916): 1; Jane Heap, "Light Occupations of the Editor While There Is Nothing to Edit," *The Little Review* 3, no. 6 (Sept. 1916): 14–15.

90. "Freudian," *The Little Review* 3, no. 6 (Sept. 1916): 26.

91. Jane Heap, commentary on "Freudian," *The Little Review* 3, no. 6 (Sept. 1916): 26.

92. Marek, *Women Editing Modernism*, 81.

93. Margaret Anderson and Jane Heap, "The Essential Thing," *The Little Review* 3, no. 1 (March 1916): 23.

94. Ezra Pound, "Breviora," *The Little Review* 5, no. 6 (Oct. 1918): 23–24, 23.

95. Regarding the often invoked "dialogic" nature of magazines, see Sean Latham and Robert Scholes, "The Rise of Periodical Studies," *PMLA* 121, no. 2 (March 2005): 517–31, 528; Suzanne W. Churchill and Adam McKible, introduction to *Little Magazines and Modernism: New Approaches*, ed. Suzanne W. Churchill and Adam McKible (Burlington, VT: Ashgate, 2007), 3–18; Alan C. Golding, "*The Dial, The Little Review*, and the Dialogics of Modernism," *American Periodicals* 15, no. 1 (2005): 42–55.

96. Ezra Pound, "A List of Books," *The Little Review* 4, no. 11 (March 1918): 54–58, 57.

97. Pound, 57, 58.

98. Charles Olson, *Projective Verse* (New York: Totem, 1959). Inspired by correspondence with Frances Boldereff and Robert Creeley, Olson published "Projective Verse" in a number of different versions—first in *Poetry New York*, no. 3 (1950), then as the pamphlet *Projective Verse* (New York: Totem, 1959), as well as in numerous anthologies. See also "Projective Verse," in *Collected Prose of Charles Olson*, ed. Donald Allen and Benjamin Friedlander (Berkeley: University of California Press, 1997), 239–49.

99. Marjorie Perloff, *The Dance of the Intellect: Studies in the Poetry of the Pound Tradition* (Cambridge: Cambridge University Press, 1985).

100. J. B. Kerfoot, review of *Others*, *Life*, Sept. 23, 1915, 568; repr. in *Others* 1, no. 5 (Nov. 1915): unpaginated.

101. Alfred Kreymborg, editorial announcement, *Others* 5, no. 1 (Dec. 1918): 1.

102. Kreymborg, 1.

103. Kreymborg, *Troubadour*, 222.

104. Churchill, *The Little Magazine*, 7.

105. Untitled note prefacing Kreymborg's "Overheard in an Asylum," *Rogue* 2, no. 1 (August 1915): 9.

106. John Rodker, "List of Books," *The Little Review* 5, no. 7 (Nov. 1918): 31–33; Rodker, "The 'Others' Anthology," *The Little Review* 7, no. 3 (Sept.–Dec. 1920): 53–56.

107. See *291*, no. 1 (March 1915): 5. A *Little Review* advertising flyer listed all the isms it had published, c. 1920, printed in Mark S. Morrisson, *The Public Face of Modernism: Little Magazines, Audiences, and Reception, 1905–1920* (Madison: University of Wisconsin Press, 2001), 144.

108. Kreymborg, *Troubadour*, 165–66.

109. William Carlos Williams, *I Wanted to Write a Poem: The Autobiography of the Works of a Poet*, ed. Edith Heal (New York: New Directions, 1978), 19–20.

110. The bureau was started with the support of Margery Currey [misspelled Margerie Curries], Elma P. Taylor, Marion Strobel, and Mitchell Dawson, who served as director. Editors, "What Next," *Others* 5, no. 4 (March 1919): 25.

111. Elaine Sproat, "Woman and the Creative Will: A Lecture by Lola Ridge, 1919," *Michigan Occasional Papers* 18 (Spring 1981): 1–23.

112. See Kreymborg, *Troubadour*, 240. Marianne Moore, Vladimir Mayakovsky, Mina Loy, and Emanuel Carnevali read at Lola Ridge's parties. See Burke, *Becoming Modern*, 288, 293; Randy Ploog, "A New *Others*: The Correspondence Between William Carlos Williams and Mitchell Dawson," *William Carlos Williams Review* 30, no. 1/2 (Spring/Fall 2013): 121–36, 123). *Poetry*'s Chicago office was another reading venue; see Lesley Wheeler, *Voicing American Poetry: Sound and Performance from the 1920s to the Present* (Ithaca, NY: Cornell University Press, 2008), 11.

113. "Chance to See Live Poets," *Morning Telegram*, April 18, 1917, YCAL MSS 101, ser. 3, Katherine Dreier: Subject Files, box 62, folders 1683–84 [1 of 2 folders]; Katherine S. Dreier Papers / Société Anonyme Archive, Yale Collection of American Literature, Beinecke Rare Book and Manuscript Library.

114. "Chance to See Live Poets."

115. William Saphier, untitled note, *Others* 5, no. 5 (April-May 1919): 33.

116. See *Others* 3, no. 4 (Dec. 1916); *Others* 4, no. 2 (Dec. 1917); and *Others* 4, no. 3 (Feb. 1918).

117. The phrase "speculative programmes" is from Eric White, "Unfinished Spaces: Aspiration, Incompletion and Speculation in Avant-Garde Journals," unpublished conference paper, BAMS (British Association for Modernist Studies), Institute of English Studies, June 2014.

118. David Lehman, *The Last Avant-Garde: The Making of the New York School of Poets* (New York: Doubleday, 1998), 284.

119. Alfred Stieglitz, "'291' and the Modern Gallery," *Camera Work*, no. 48 (Oct. 1916): 63–64, 64.

120. Marius de Zayas to Agnes Meyer, July 15, 1915, Agnes Meyer Papers, quoted in Homer, *Alfred Stieglitz*, 194.

121. Willard Bohn, "Visualising Women in *291*," in *Women in Dada*, 240–61, 250.

122. Richard Whelan, *Alfred Stieglitz: A Biography* (Boston: Little, Brown, 1995), 386.

123. Meyer, *Out of These Roots*, 102.

124. Tashjian dismisses "Woman" by Rhoades, Meyer, and de Zayas as "only half-heartedly pursued, and scarcely fulfilled" and Meyer and de Zayas's "Mental Reaction" as "a prelude to Picabia's machine drawings." Tashjian, *Skyscraper Primitives*, 33–34.

125. Mina Loy, "Songs to Joannes," *Others* 3, no. 6 (April 1917): 19.

126. Wood, for instance, was the inspiration for the character Rose in James Cameron's *Titanic*.

127. Jane Heap, "Lost: A Renaissance," *The Little Review* 12, no. 2 (May 1929): 5–6, 5.

128. Heap, 6.

129. *The Little Review*'s questionnaire featured Gertrude Stein, André Gide, Ezra Pound, Ernest Hemingway, Aldous Huxley, Constantin Brancusi, Mina Loy, James Joyce, Wyndham Lewis, László Moholy-Nagy, Marianne Moore, William Carlos Williams, Tristan Tzara, and others.

130. Margaret Anderson, "Editorial," *The Little Review* 12, no. 2 (May 1929): 3–4, 3.

131. William Carlos Williams to Stieglitz, Oct. 25, 1931, YCAL MSS 85, ser. 1, Alfred Stieglitz: Correspondence, box 52, folder 1261, Alfred Stieglitz/Georgia O'Keeffe Archive, Yale Collection of American Literature, Beinecke Rare Book and Manuscript Library.

132. William Carlos Williams, "The Advance Guard Magazine," *Contact*, n.s. 1, no. 1 (Feb. 1932): 86–90.

133. Margaret Anderson, "The Germ," *The Little Review* 1, no. 2 (April 1914), 1–2, 1.

134. Jane Heap, "TO," *The Little Review* 12, no. 2 (May 1929): 62; Roché, "The Blind Man," 6.

135. Advertisement, *The Little Review* 3, no. 5 (August 1916): inside front cover.

Chapter 2

1. Aram Saroyan to Vito Acconci, August 31, 1967, *0 to 9* Archive, MSS 026, ser. 1, box 1, folder 9, Fales Library and Special Collections, New York University Libraries.

2. Bernadette Mayer to author, Jan. 2014; Bernadette Mayer, "Rock, Paper, Scissors," in *0 to 9: The Complete Magazine, 1967–1969* (Brooklyn, NY: Ugly Duckling Presse, 2006), 13–14, 13.

3. Jerome Rothenberg, untitled note preceding "Aztec Definitions: Found Poems from the Florentine Codex," *some/thing*, no. 1 (Spring 1965): 1–2, 2.

4. Lucy R. Lippard, ed., *Six Years: The Dematerialization of the Art Object from 1966*

to 1972: A Cross-Reference Book of Information . . . (Berkeley: University of California Press, 1973), vii.

5. Henry Flynt, "Essay: Concept Art (Provisional Version)," in *An Anthology of Chance Operations*, ed. La Monte Young (New York: La Monte Young and Jackson Mac Low, 1963), unpaginated.

6. Sol LeWitt, "Serial Project #1, 1966," *Aspen*, no. 5/6 (1967): unpaginated.

7. Sianne Ngai, *Our Aesthetic Categories: Zany, Cute, Interesting* (Cambridge, MA: Harvard University Press, 2012), 143; Hal Foster, *The Return of the Real: The Avant-Garde at the End of the Century* (Cambridge, MA: MIT Press, 1996), 46.

8. *0 to 9* (Vito Acconci, Bernadette Mayer, 1967–69); *some/thing* (David Antin, Jerome Rothenberg, 1965–68); *Assembling* (Henry Korn, Richard Kostelanetz, 1970–87); *Extensions* (Joachim Neugroschel, Suzanne Zavrian, 1968–74); *Lines* (Aram Saroyan, 1964–65); *Aspen* (Phyllis Johnson, with guest editors, 1965–71); *dé-coll/age* (Wolf Vostell, 1962–69); *S.M.S.* (William Copley, 1968); *Revue OU* (Henri Chopin, 1958–74); *Semina* (Wallace Berman, 1955–64); *Spanner* (Allen Fisher, 1974–2005); *Joglars* (Clark Coolidge, Michael Palmer, 1964–66); *ccV TRE* (George Brecht, 1964–70); *Something Else Newsletter* (Dick Higgins, 1966–83).

9. William Fetterman lists Allan Kaprow, George Brecht, Dick Higgins, and Philip Corner as Cage's students; see William Fetterman, *John Cage's Theatre Pieces: Notations and Performances* (New York: Routledge, 1996), 104.

10. Daniel Kane, "*Angel Hair* Magazine, the Second-Generation New York School, and the Poetics of Sociability," *Contemporary Literature* 45, no. 2 (Summer 2004): 331–67, 355; Ann Vickery, *Leaving Lines of Gender: A Feminist Genealogy of Language Writing* (Hanover, NH: Wesleyan University Press, 2000), 150.

11. Linda Russo, "Poetics of Adjacency: *0-9* and the Conceptual Writing of Bernadette Mayer & Hannah Weiner," in *Don't Ever Get Famous: Essays on New York Writing After the New York School*, ed. Daniel Kane (Champaign: Dalkey Archive Press, 2006), 122–50, 128; Gwen Allen, *Artists' Magazines: An Alternative Space for Art* (Cambridge, MA: MIT Press, 2011), 69.

12. Daniel Kane, "An Interview with Thurston Moore," *Postmodern Culture* 25, no. 1 (Sept. 2014): https://muse.jhu.edu/journals/postmodern_culture/v025/25.1.kane.html.

13. Kane, "*Angel Hair* Magazine," 333.

14. Russo, "Poetics of Adjacency," 124.

15. Lytle Shaw, *Fieldworks: From Place to Site in Postwar Poetics* (Tuscaloosa: University of Alabama Press, 2013); Terence Diggory, *Encyclopedia of the New York School Poets* (New York: Facts on File, 2009), 109, 310.

16. For Rosalind Krauss 1970s conceptual art practices were united by the concept and methodology of the index, which is precisely not a style but an approach. See Rosalind Krauss, "Notes on the Index: Seventies Art in America," *October* 3 (Spring 1977): 68–81, 68.

17. Some exceptions: Hannah Weiner's "Code Poems," in *I'll Drown My Book: Conceptual Writing by Women*, ed. Caroline Bergvall, Laynie Browne, Teresa Carmody, and

Vanessa Place (Los Angeles: Les Figues Press, 2012); and Lee Lozano's "Dialogue Piece," in *Conceptual Art: A Critical Anthology*, ed. Alexander Alberro and Blake Stimson (Cambridge, MA: MIT Press, 1999), originally appeared in *0 to 9*; as did LeWitt's "Sentences on Conceptual Art," which has been reprinted several times.

18. Kenneth Goldsmith and Craig Dworkin's *Against Expression: An Anthology of Conceptual Writing* (Evanston, IL: Northwestern University Press, 2011).

19. Mayer, "Rock, Paper, Scissors," 13.

20. Dick Higgins to Jerome Rothenberg, Oct. 10, 1965, YCAL MSS 299, box 2, folder 29, Dick Higgins Material, Jerome Rothenberg Collection on American Literature, 1959–1995, Beinecke Rare Book and Manuscript Library, Yale University.

21. Bernadette Mayer, email to Gwen Allen, quoted in Allen, *Artists' Magazines*, 69.

22. Dick Higgins, "Intermedia," *Something Else Newsletter* 1, no. 1 (Feb. 1966): unpaginated.

23. Clark Coolidge to Vito Acconci, March 7, [no year], *0 to 9* Archive, MSS 026, ser. 1, box 1, folder 3, Fales Library and Special Collections, New York University Libraries.

24. The "book" is online at http://eclipsearchive.org/projects/REAM/ream.html.

25. Jasper Johns, "Sketchbook Notes," *0 to 9*, no. 6 (July 1969): 1–2, 2.

26. Alan Sondheim, "On Machines," *0 to 9*, no. 6 (July 1969): 4–9, 4.

27. Robert Barry, "The Space Between Pages 29 & 30" and "The Space Between Pages 74 & 75," *0 to 9*, no. 6 (July 1969): table of contents.

28. Adrian Piper, untitled, *0 to 9*, no. 6 (July 1969): 109.

29. Ruth Blacksell, "From Looking to Reading: Text-Based Conceptual Art and Typographic Discourse," *Design Issues* 29, no. 2 (Spring 2013): 60–81, 69.

30. Vito Acconci, "ON," *0 to 9*, no. 3 (Jan. 1968): 4.

31. Craig Dworkin, "Introduction: Delay in Verse," *Language to Cover a Page: The Early Writings of Vito Acconci*, ed. Craig Dworkin (Cambridge, MA: MIT Press, 2006), x–xviii, xvii.

32. Dan Graham, "Poem, March 1966," *Aspen*, no. 5/6 (Fall–Winter 1967): unpaginated.

33. David Antin, *Radical Coherency: Selected Essays on Art and Literature, 1966 to 2005* (Chicago: University of Chicago Press, 2011), 10, 254.

34. Antin, 9.

35. David Antin, "Silence/Noise," *some/thing*, no. 1 (Spring 1965): 60–63, 63.

36. Antin, *Radical Coherency*, 9.

37. Antin, 9.

38. Antin, "Silence/Noise," 60.

39. Jerome Rothenberg, "'Doings' & 'Happenings': Notes on a Performance of the Seneca Eagle Dance Along with the Scenario for Gift Event III, Based on Its Orders," *some/thing*, no. 4/5 (Summer 1968): 112–14.

40. "Aztec Definitions: Found Poems from the Florentine Codex," trans. Charles E. Dibble and Arthur J. O. Anderson, *some/thing*, no. 1 (Spring 1965): 1–7, 3.

41. Rothenberg, untitled preface to "Aztec Definitions," 1–2, 2.

42. Antin, *Radical Coherency*, 251.

43. Carolee Schneemann, email interview with the author, April 8, 2014.

44. Antin, *Radical Coherency*, 252.

45. Antin, 254.

46. Sir Walter Raleigh and Sir Arthur Gorges, "Her Face, Her Tongue, Her Wit," *0 to 9*, no. 1 (April 1967): 3.

47. Peter Wollen, *Paris/Manhattan: Writings on Art* (London: Verso, 2004), 147, 159, 160.

48. Mark Silverberg, *New York School Poets and the Neo-Avant-Garde: Between Radical Art and Radical Chic* (Farnham, Surrey: Ashgate, 2010), 60.

49. Sol LeWitt, "Sentences on Conceptual Art," *0 to 9*, no. 5 (Jan. 1969): 3–5, 3.

50. Rosalind Krauss, "Notes on the Index: Seventies Art in America, Part 2," *October* 4 (Autumn 1977): 58–67, 67.

51. Bernadette Mayer, "One Thing," *0 to 9*, no. 4 (June 1968): 44–48, 44.

52. Mayer, 44.

53. Krauss, "Notes on the Index, Part 2," 59.

54. Krauss, 59.

55. David Antin, "Definitions for Mendy," *some/thing*, no. 1 (Spring 1965): 18–25; George Brecht, "Two Definitions," *some/thing*, no. 2 (Winter 1965): 2.

56. David Antin, "Is There a Postmodernism?" in *Bucknell Review: Romanticism, Modernism, Postmodernism*, ed. Harry R. Garvin (Lewisburg, PA: Bucknell University Press, 1980), 127–35, 131.

57. Bernadette Mayer, "Definitions at the Center of the Newspaper, June 13, 1969," *0 to 9*, no. 6 (July 1969): 75–77, 75.

58. Vito Acconci, "10 (A Late Introduction to *0 to 9*)," in *0 to 9: The Complete Magazine, 1967–1969* (Brooklyn, NY: Ugly Duckling Presse, 2006), 7–11, 9; Themerson, "Theatre of Semantic Poetry," *0 to 9*, no. 2 (August 1967): 65–80, 72.

59. Raymond Queneau, "From *Exercises in Style*," trans. Barbara Wright, *0 to 9*, no. 2 (August 1967): 37–48, 37, 38, 39, 40, 42.

60. Acconci, "10," 9.

61. Bernadette Mayer, "From: A Lecture at the Naropa Institute, 1989," in *Disembodied Poetics: Annals of the Jack Kerouac School*, ed. Anne Waldman and Andrew Schelling (Albuquerque: University of New Mexico Press, 1994), 95–102, 95.

62. Mayer, 95.

63. See, for example, Wim Crouwel, "Type Design for the Computer Age," *Journal of Typographic Research* 4, no. 1 (1970): 51–59.

64. Rosemary Mayer, "Firecrackers," *0 to 9*, no. 5 (Jan. 1969): 74–88.

65. Rosalind E. Krauss, *The Originality of the Avant-Garde and Other Modernist Myths* (Cambridge, MA: MIT Press, 1985), 158.

66. Krauss, 158.

67. Alexander Alberro, *Conceptual Art and the Politics of Publicity* (Cambridge, MA: MIT Press, 2003), 39.

68. Liz Kotz, *Words to Be Looked At: Language in 1960s Art* (Cambridge, MA: MIT Press, 2007), 1.

69. Sol LeWitt, "Paragraphs on Conceptual Art," *Artforum* 5, no. 10 (June 1967): 79–83.

70. LeWitt, "Sentences on Conceptual Art," 3.

71. LeWitt, 5.

72. Lucy R. Lippard, *A Different War: Vietnam in Art* (Seattle: Whatcom Museum of History and Art and Real Comet Press, 1990), 30.

73. LeWitt, "Sentences on Conceptual Art," 4, 3.

74. LeWitt, 3.

75. LeWitt, "Serial Project #1, 1966."

76. Roland Barthes, "The Death of the Author," *Aspen* 5/6 (Fall–Winter 1967): unpaginated; Roland Barthes, *Writing Degree Zero*, trans. Annette Lavers and Colin Smith (London: Jonathan Cape, 1967).

77. Roland Barthes, "Objective Literature: Alain Robbe-Grillet," trans. Richard Howard, *Evergreen Review* 2, no. 5 (Summer 1958): 113–26.

78. Clark Coolidge to Vito Acconci, June 23, [no year], *0 to 9* Archive, MSS 026, ser. 1, box 1, folder 3, Fales Library and Special Collections, New York University Libraries.

79. Coolidge to Acconci.

80. Jerome Rothenberg to Vito Acconci, Jan. 18, 1968, *0 to 9* Archive, MSS 026, ser. 1, box 1, folder 8, Fales Library and Special Collections, New York University Libraries.

81. Jerome Rothenberg to Vito Acconci, Sept. 29, 1968, *0 to 9* Archive, MSS 026, ser. 1, box 1, folder 8, Fales Library and Special Collections, New York University Libraries.

82. Clayton Eshleman to Vito Acconci, Jan. 19, 1969, *0 to 9* Archive, MSS 026, ser. 1, box 1, folder 4, Fales Library and Special Collections, New York University Libraries.

83. Vito Acconci to Clayton Eshleman, March 26, 1969, *Caterpillar* Archive, MSS 010, ser. 2, box 5, folder 2, Fales Library and Special Collections, New York University Libraries. Courtesy of Maria Acconci.

84. Vito Acconci to Clayton Eshleman, March 16, 1969, *Caterpillar* Archive, MSS 010, ser. 2, box 5, folder 2, Fales Library and Special Collections, New York University Libraries. Courtesy of Maria Acconci.

85. John Clellon Holmes to Vito Acconci, August 7, 1968, *0 to 9* Archive, MSS 026, ser. 1, box 1, folder 6, Fales Library and Special Collections, New York University Libraries.

86. John Clellon Holmes to Vito Acconci, April 29, 1967, *0 to 9* Archive, MSS 026, ser. 1, box 1, folder 6, Fales Library and Special Collections, New York University Libraries.

87. Holmes to Acconci, April 29, 1967.

88. Holmes to Acconci, April 29, 1967.

89. Holmes to Acconci, April 29, 1967.

90. Acconci, untitled, *Extensions*, no. 2 (1969): 71.

91. Carolee Schneemann, "Meat Joy," *some/thing*, no. 2 (Winter 1965): 31–45, 43.

92. Schneemann, 31.

93. Yvonne Rainer, "Lecture for a Group of Expectant People," *0 to 9*, no. 5 (Jan. 1969): 12–19, 12, 13.

94. Schneemann's *Interior Scroll* (1975) quotes "the persistence of feelings," "the diaristic indulgence," and "painterly mess" as reasons why male audiences have ignored her

work. Rainer appropriately named her memoir *Feelings Are Facts: A Life* (Cambridge: MIT Press, 2006).

95. Lee Lozano, "Dialogue Piece," *0 to 9*, no. 6 (July 1969): 10.

96. Lozano, "General Strike Piece," *0 to 9*, no. 6 (July 1969): 57.

97. Sarah Lehrer-Graiwer, *Lee Lozano: Dropout Piece* (London: Afterall Books, 2014), 49.

98. Robert C. Morgan, *Art into Ideas: Essays on Conceptual Art* (Cambridge: Cambridge University Press, 1996), 9.

99. Jackson Mac Low, introduction to *Representative Works: 1938–1985* (New York: Roof, 1986), xv–xviii, xvi.

100. Jackson Mac Low, "The Friendship Poems," *some/thing*, no. 2 (Winter 1965): 58–64, 58, 61.

101. Mac Low, 58.

102. Charles Olson, *Projective Verse* (New York: Totem, 1959).

103. Eliot Weinberger, *Works on Paper, 1980–1986* (New York: New Directions, 1986), 142.

104. Weinberger, 141–42.

105. Antin, *Radical Coherency*, 3.

106. Paula Scher, *Make It Bigger* (New York: Princeton Architectural Press, 2002), 56.

107. Jackson Mac Low, "Marines Defend Burning of Village," *some/thing*, no. 3 (Winter 1966): unpaginated.

108. Mac Low, n.p.

109. Kotz, *Words to Be Looked At*, 1.

110. Kotz, 265.

111. Mac Low, "Marines Defend Burning of Village."

112. Mac Low, n.p.

113. Jackson Mac Low, "The Terminology," *Open Letter* 11, no. 3 (Fall 2001): 84–89, 87.

114. Jackson Mac Low, "Some Ways Philosophy Has Helped to Shape My Work," *Poetics Journal* 3 (May 1983): 67–72, 70–71.

115. Lippard, *A Different War*, 31.

116. Benjamin H. D. Buchloh, "Conceptual Art 1962–1969: From the Aesthetic of Administration to the Critique of Institutions," *October* 55 (Winter 1990), 105–43, 141; Bernadette Mayer to the author, Jan. 2014. Mayer also notes: "David Antin was one of the lecturers in the series that was part of that workshop."

117. David Antin and Jerome Rothenberg, editorial, *some/thing*, no. 2 (Winter 1965): unpaginated.

118. Lytle Shaw, *Frank O'Hara: The Poetics of Coterie* (Iowa City: University of Iowa Press, 2006), 20.

119. Lisa Jarnot, "An Interview with Bernadette Mayer," *Poetry Project Newsletter*, no. 168 (Feb.–March 1998): 6–9, 6.

120. Mayer did make exceptions, however, in publishing her sister Rosemary, who was also, at the time, married to Acconci.

121. Andrew Epstein, *Beautiful Enemies: Friendship and Postwar American Poetry* (Oxford: Oxford University Press, 2006), 4.

122. Kane, "*Angel Hair* Magazine," 333.

123. Steve Clay and Rodney Phillips, "A Little History of the Mimeograph Revolution," in *A Secret Location on the Lower East Side: Adventures in Writing, 1960–1980*, ed. Steven Clay and Rodney Phillips (New York: Granary, 1998), 12–54, 14.

124. Daniel Kane, *All Poets Welcome: The Lower East Side Poetry Scene in the 1960s* (Berkeley: University of California Press, 2003), 163, 168.

125. Johanna Drucker, *Figuring the Word: Essays on Books, Writing, and Visual Poetics* (New York: Granary, 1998), 184.

126. Drucker, 185.

127. Drucker, 188.

128. Lehrer-Graiwer, *Lee Lozano*, 22–23.

129. David Campany, "Conceptual Art History or, A Home for Homes for America," in *Rewriting Conceptual Art*, ed. Michael Newman and Jon Bird (London: Reaktion, 1999), 123–39, 131–32.

130. Mayer, "Mimeo Argument," *Poetry Project Newsletter*, no. 90 (April 1982): unpaginated, Franklin Furnace Ephemera Collection, MSS 206, box 66, Fales Library and Special Collections, New York University Libraries.

131. Mayer, n.p.

132. Walter Benjamin, "One-Way Street," trans. Edmund Jephcott, in *Selected Writings, Volume 1: 1913–1926*, ed. Marcus Bullock and Michael W. Jennings (Cambridge, MA: Belknap Press of Harvard University Press, 1996), 444. Having planned the never-published little magazine *Angelus Novus* in 1921, Benjamin here inadvertently writes a manifesto for magazines and signals the first stage of the conjunction between avant-gardes and their medium.

133. Mayer, "Mimeo Argument."

134. Richard Kostelanetz, "Why Assembling," *Assembling*, no. 1 (1970): unpaginated.

135. Drucker, *Figuring the Word*, 175–76.

136. Andreas Huyssen, *After the Great Divide: Modernism, Mass Culture, Postmodernism* (Bloomington: Indiana University Press, 1986), 9.

137. Drucker, *Figuring the Word*, 176.

138. Lucy R. Lippard and John Chandler, "The Dematerialization of Art," *Art International* 12, no. 2 (Feb. 1968): 31–36, 32.

139. Antin, *Radical Coherency*, 251.

140. Kotz, *Words to Be Looked At*, 134.

141. I borrow the expression "making poetry by other means" from Marjorie Perloff, *Unoriginal Genius: Poetry by Other Means in the New Century* (Chicago: University of Chicago Press, 2010).

142. Cornelia Butler, "Women—Concept—Art: Lucy Lippard's Numbers Shows," in *From Conceptualism to Feminism: Lucy Lippard's Numbers Shows, 1969–74*, ed. Cornelia Butler et al. (London: Afterall, 2012), 16–69, 60–61.

143. Mayer, "From: A Lecture," 98.

144. See, for example, Eve Meltzer, *Systems We Have Loved: Conceptual Art, Affect, and the Antihumanist Turn* (Chicago: University of Chicago Press, 2013).

145. See, for example, Mayer has had something of a rediscovery in the art world recently. *Memory* was exhibited again in its entirety at the Poetry Foundation in Chicago in 2016 and then at the Canada gallery in New York in 2017.

146. On April 22, 1979, Susan Howe hosted a conversation with Bernadette Mayer for WBAI/Pacifica, posted on *Jacket2* on May 8, 2015, http://jacket2.org/interviews/bernadette-mayer-susan-howe-1979.

147. Robert C. Morgan, "Carolee Schneemann: The Politics of Eroticism," *Art Journal* 56, no. 4 (Winter 1997): 97–100, 98.

148. Bernadette Mayer, "Experiments," *L=A=N=G=U=A=G=E*, no. 3 (June 1978): unpaginated.

149. Alexander Alberro, "Reconsidering Conceptual Art, 1966–1977," in *Conceptual Art: A Critical Anthology*, xvi–xxxvii, xx; Allen, *Artists' Magazines*, 78; Krauss, *Originality of the Avant-Garde*, 255.

150. Stephanie Anderson, "An Interview with Bernadette Mayer (Part 1)," *Cold Front*, March 24, 2014, http://coldfrontmag.com/an-interview-with-bernadette-mayer-by-stephanie-anderson-part-1.

151. LeWitt, "Sentences on Conceptual Art," 5.

152. Terry Atkinson et al., "Introduction," *Art-Language: The Journal of Conceptual Art* 1, no. 1 (May 1969): 1–10, 3.

153. Joseph Kosuth, "Introductory Note by the American Editor," *Art-Language* 1, no. 2 (Feb. 1970): 1–4, 4.

Chapter 3

1. Douglas Messerli, "Editorial," *Là-bas*, no. 1 (1976): unpaginated.

2. Rae Armantrout, "Why Don't Women Do Language-Oriented Writing?" *L=A=N=G=U=A=G=E*, no. 1 (Feb. 1978): unpaginated.

3. Joseph Kosuth, "Introductory Note by the American Editor," *Art-Language* 1, no. 2 (Feb. 1970): 4.

4. Rachel Blau DuPlessis, "DuPlessis and Eshleman on the Davidson/Weinberger Exchange," *Sulfur*, no. 22 (1988): 188–93, 190.

5. Eliot Weinberger, "Davidson and Weinberger on Language Poetry," *Sulfur*, no. 22 (1988): 180–86, 180, 181.

6. Steve Abbott, "Notes on Boundaries, New Narrative," *Soup*, no. 4 (1985): 79–89, 81.

7. James Sherry, untitled note, *Roof*, no. 3 (Summer 1977): 49.

8. See *The Princeton Encyclopedia of Poetry and Poetics*, 4th ed., ed. Roland Greene, Stephen Cushman, Clare Cavanagh, Jahan Ramazani, and Paul Rouzer (Princeton, NJ: Princeton University Press, 2012), 784–86, which lists these poets as the main group members. It gives *Tottel's*, *This*, *Hills*, and *L=A=N=G=U=A=G=E* as its journals and Roof, Potes and Poets, O Books, The Figures, Tuumba, and Sun & Moon as its presses. McCaffery mentions *Hills*, *Roof*, *This*, *Tottel's*, *Open Letter*, *Alcheringa*, *L=A=N=G=U=A=G=E*,

Tuumba, Burning Deck, and Sun & Moon in Steve McCaffery, *North of Intention: Critical Writings, 1973–1986* (New York: Roof, 1986), 144. Tom Clark lists Watten, Silliman, Perelman, Hejinian, and Bernstein as the "major movers" of the movement; see Tom Clark, "Stalin as Linguist," *Poetry Flash*, no. 148 (July 1985), repr. in *Partisan Review* 54, no. 2 (1987): 299–304, 300.

9. This list could extend to Barbara Barg, Tom Beckett, cris cheek, Carla Harryman, Erica Hunt, Peter Seaton, and others. Georgina Colby, in *Kathy Acker: Writing the Impossible* (Edinburgh: Edinburgh University Press, 2016), is the only other critic I'm aware of who reads Acker's early poetic experiments in the context of 1970s poetry by Antin, Mac Low, and the Language poets.

10. Peter Middleton, "When L=A: Language, Authorship, and Equality in *L=A=N=G=U=A=G=E* Magazine," in *Among Friends: Engendering the Social Site of Poetry*, ed. Anne Dewey and Libbie Rifkin (Iowa City: University of Iowa Press, 2013), 87–105.

11. Susan Vanderborg and Manuel Brito mention other magazines but do not go beyond introductory summaries. See Susan Vanderborg, "'If This Were the Place to Begin': Little Magazines and the Early Language Poetry Scene," in *The World in Time and Space: Towards a History of Innovative American Poetry in Our Time*, ed. Edward Foster and Joseph Donahue (Jersey City, NJ: Talisman House, 2002), 298–320; and Manuel Brito, *Means Matter: Market Fructification of Innovative American Poetry in the Late 20th Century* (New York: Peter Lang, 2010).

12. To name only a few: Marjorie Perloff, "The Word as Such: L=A=N=G=U=A=G=E Poetry in the Eighties," *American Poetry Review* 13, no. 3 (May/June 1984): 15–22; Lee Bartlett, "What Is 'Language Poetry'?" *Critical Inquiry* 12, no. 4 (Summer 1986), 741–52; Jerome McGann, "Contemporary Poetry, Alternate Routes," *Critical Inquiry* 13, no. 3 (Spring 1987): 624–47; Ann Vickery, *Leaving Lines of Gender: A Feminist Genealogy of Language Writing* (Hanover, NH: Wesleyan University Press, 2000); Linda Reinfeld, *Language Poetry: Writing as Rescue* (Baton Rouge: Louisiana State University Press, 1992); Marjorie Perloff, *Unoriginal Genius: Poetry by Other Means in the New Century* (Chicago: University of Chicago Press, 2010); Alison Mark, *Veronica Forrest-Thomson and Language Poetry* (Tavistock: Northcote House, 2001); and Paul Stephens, "Beyond the Creative/Critical Divide: The Metapoetics of Innovative American Writing" (PhD diss., Columbia University, 2005). Critical writings by the poets themselves include Charles Bernstein, *A Poetics* (Cambridge, MA: Harvard University Press, 1992) and *Content's Dream: Essays, 1975–1984* (Los Angeles: Sun & Moon, 1986); Lyn Hejinian, *The Language of Inquiry* (Berkeley: University of California Press, 2000); and Bob Perelman, *The Marginalization of Poetry: Language Writing and Literary History* (Princeton, NJ: Princeton University Press, 1996).

13. Rod Mengham, untitled review of Andrews, Bernstein, Coolidge, McCaffery, and Watten, *Textual Practice* 3, no. 1 (Spring 1989): 115–24, 115; Clark, "Stalin as Linguist," 299 (repr.); Gerald Bruns, "Poetic Communities," *Iowa Review* 32, no. 1 (Spring 2002): 1–38, 22; and Susan Vanderborg, *Paratextual Communities: American Avant-Garde Poetry Since 1950* (Carbondale: Southern Illinois University Press, 2001), 84.

14. George Hartley, *Textual Politics and the Language Poets* (Bloomington: Indiana University Press, 1989), xv; Geoff Ward, *Language Poetry and the American Avant-Garde* (Keele: British Association for American Studies, 1993), 17.

15. Ron Silliman, Carla Harryman, Lyn Hejinian, Steve Benson, Bob Perelman, and Barrett Watten, "Aesthetic Tendency and the Politics of Poetry: A Manifesto," *Social Text*, no. 19/20 (Autumn 1988): 261–75, 261. "A Manifesto" was added by an editorial error and not intended by the authors, as issue 24 explains.

16. Ron Silliman, "from 'Language Writing,'" *L=A=N=G=U=A=G=E*, no. 5 (Oct. 1978): unpaginated.

17. Alan Soldofsky, "Language and Narcissism," *Poetry Flash*, no. 74 (May 1979): unpaginated; Steve Abbott, "Language Poets: An Introduction," *Poetry Flash*, no. 74 (May 1979): unpaginated.

18. Ken Edwards, ed., *Reality Studios* 2, no. 4 (April/May/June 1980); Anthony Mellors and Andrew Lawson, eds., *fragmente: a magazine of contemporary poetics*, no. 2 (Autumn 1990).

19. Charles Bernstein, ed., "Language Sampler," *Paris Review*, no. 86 (Winter 1982): 75–125; Bernstein, "43 Poets (1984)," *boundary 2* 14, no. 1/2 (Fall 1985/Winter 1986); and Silliman, ed., "Realism: An Anthology of 'Language' Writing," *Ironwood* 20, no. 10 (1982).

20. Steve McCaffery's "Language Writing: From Productive to Libidinal Economy" was first given as a talk at SUNY Buffalo in 1980 and then printed in McCaffery, *North of Intention*, 143–58.

21. See Fredric Jameson, "Postmodernism, or the Cultural Logic of Late Capitalism," *New Left Review* I/146 (July/August 1984): 59–92, which compares Lacan's schizophrenic language to Language writing by reference to Perelman's "China," published in *Soup*, no. 2 (1981). Perloff, in turn, taught many critics who would later also write on Language poetry, such as Michael Golston, Brian Reed, and Susan Vanderborg.

22. See, e.g., Clark, "Stalin as Linguist," 300 (repr.); and Bruce Boone, "A Few Remarks on the Perelman/Soldofsky Dispute," *Poetry Flash*, no. 76 (July 1979): 5.

23. Hejinian, *The Language of Inquiry*, 329; and Ward, *Language Poetry and the American Avant-Garde*, 11.

24. Marjorie Perloff, *Dance of the Intellect: Studies in the Poetry of the Pound Tradition* (Cambridge: Cambridge University Press, 1985), 197.

25. Perloff, 192.

26. See, e.g., Linda Kinnahan, *Lyric Interventions: Feminism, Experimental Poetry, and Contemporary Discourse* (Iowa City: University of Iowa Press, 2004); Claudia Rankine and Juliana Spahr, eds., *American Women Poets in the 21st Century: Where Lyric Meets Language* (Middletown, CT: Wesleyan University Press, 2002); Juliana Spahr, *Everybody's Autonomy: Connective Reading and Collective Identity* (Tuscaloosa: University of Alabama Press, 2001); Gillian White, *Lyric Shame: The 'Lyric' Subject of Contemporary American Poetry* (Cambridge, MA: Harvard University Press, 2014); Susan Vanderborg, "'If This Were the Place to Begin,'" 299; and Vickery, *Leaving Lines of Gender*. Even Perloff later disapproved of caricatures of the romantic lyric, which

her own *Dance of the Intellect*, in fact, helped to create. See Marjorie Perloff, "A Response," in *New Definitions of Lyric: Theory, Technology, and Culture*, ed. Mark Jeffreys (New York: Garland, 1997), 243–53; and Marjorie Perloff, "Language Poetry and the Lyric Subject: Ron Silliman's Albany, Susan Howe's Buffalo," *Critical Inquiry* 25, no. 3 (Spring 1999): 405–34.

27. Michael Golston includes figures like Myung Mi Kim in his *Poetic Machinations: Allegory, Surrealism, and Postmodern Poetic Form* (New York: Columbia University Press, 2015). Alan Golding rightly acknowledges that "'Language writing' has never been a homogeneous entity, and . . . always contained dissenting voices." Alan Golding, *From Outlaw to Classic: Canons in American Poetry* (Madison: University of Wisconsin Press, 1995), 151.

28. See Ben Hickman, *Crisis and the US Avant-Garde: Poetry and Real Politics* (Edinburgh: Edinburgh University Press, 2015); and Oren Izenberg, *Being Numerous: Poetry and the Ground of Social Life* (Princeton, NJ: Princeton University Press, 2011). Perloff recently wrote of its "period style" in her *Unoriginal Genius*, 8.

29. Jackson Mac Low, "'Language-Centered,'" published simultaneously in *Open Letter* 5, no. 1 (Winter 1982) and *L=A=N=G=U=A=G=E*, no. 4 (Winter 1982): 23–26, 23.

30. Bruce Andrews and Charles Bernstein, "editors' note," *Open Letter* 5, no. 1 / *L=A=N=G=U=A=G=E*, no. 4 (Winter 1982): 23.

31. Mac Low, "'Language-Centered,'" 26; Steve McCaffery, "The Death of the Subject: The Implications of Counter-Communication in Recent Language-Centered Writing," *L=A=N=G=U=A=G=E*, suppl. 1 (June 1980): unpaginated.

32. Bruce Andrews and Charles Bernstein, untitled editorial, *L=A=N=G=U=A=G=E*, suppl. 1 (June 1980): unpaginated.

33. Charles Bernstein to Tom Beckett, Nov. 15, 1980, YCAL MSS 382, box 1, folder "Bernstein, Charles," *The Difficulties* Records, Yale Collection of American Literature, Beinecke Rare Book and Manuscript Library. Also published in revised form as Charles Bernstein, "Interview," by Tom Beckett, *The Difficulties* 2, no. 1 (Fall 1982): 29–42, 29.

34. Bernstein, "Interview," 29.

35. Bernstein, 29.

36. Peter Bürger, *Theory of the Avant-Garde*, trans. Michael Shaw (Minneapolis: University of Minnesota Press, 1984); Renato Poggioli, *The Theory of the Avant-Garde*, trans. Gerald Fitzgerald (Cambridge, MA: Belknap Press of Harvard University Press, 1968).

37. Michael Andre and Cynthia Logan, "Thou Shalt Not Muzzle the Ox When He Treadeth Out the Corn," *Unmuzzled OX* 1, no. 1 (1971): 2–3, 3.

38. Michael Andre, "Preface," *Unmuzzled OX* 4, no. 4 (1979): v–x, ix.

39. Tom Beckett and Earel Neikirk, untitled editorial, *The Difficulties* 1 (1980): unpaginated.

40. Ron Silliman, "The Dwelling Place: 9 Poets," *Alcheringa* 1, no. 2 (1975): 104.

41. Ron Silliman, "Surprised by Sign (Notes on Nine)," *Alcheringa* 1, no. 2 (1975): 118–20, 120, 118.

42. Barbara Baracks, "Thousands," *Toothpick, Lisbon, and the Orcas Islands* 3, no. 1

(Fall 1973): unpaginated; Marjorie Perloff, *Differentials: Poetry, Poetics, Pedagogy* (Tuscaloosa: University of Alabama Press, 2004), 159.

43. McCaffery, "Death of the Subject," unpaginated.

44. See Craig Dworkin, headnote to digital facsimile of *Toothpick*, Eclipse Archive, http://eclipsearchive.org/projects/TOOTHPICK/toothpick.html.

45. Barbara Baracks, phone conversation with the author, June 9, 2018.

46. Robert Grenier, "On Speech," *This*, no. 1 (1971): unpaginated.

47. Bernstein, *A Poetics*, 2; Charles Bernstein, "Stray Straws and Straw Men," *L=A=N=G=U=A=G=E*, suppl. 1 (June 1980): unpaginated.

48. Bernstein, "Stray Straws."

49. Ron Silliman, "Notes on the Relation of Theory to Practice," *Paper Air* 2, no. 2 (1979): 6–13, 12.

50. Roland Barthes, "Writing Degree Zero," *L=A=N=G=U=A=G=E*, no. 2 (April 1978): unpaginated. Middleton, "When L=A," 94.

51. Lyn Hejinian, "The Rejection of Closure," *Poetics Journal* 4 (1984): 134–43, 134.

52. Bruce Andrews, "Writing Social Work & Political Practice," *L=A=N=G=U=A=G=E*, no. 9/10 (Oct. 1979): unpaginated.

53. Bruce Andrews, "Text and Context," *L=A=N=G=U=A=G=E*, suppl. 1 (June 1980): unpaginated.

54. Tom Savage, note preceding "Kits," *Roof*, no. 2 (Spring 1977): 67.

55. Charles Bernstein, "Artifice of Absorption," *Paper Air* 4, no. 1 (1987): 4–71, 21.

56. Gil Ott, editorial, *Paper Air* 4, no. 3 (1990): 5.

57. Burt Kimmelman, letter to the editor, *Paper Air* 4, no. 2 (1989): 116.

58. Charles Bernstein, "Writing and Method," *Poetics Journal* 3 (May 1983): 6–16, 9.

59. Cf. Reinfeld, *Language Poetry*, 32. The *Paper Air* issue itself was favorably reviewed by Reinfeld in *American Book Review* and by Hank Lazer in *The Nation*. See Linda Reinfeld, "As Slope of Mind: Linda Reinfeld Reviews *The Sophist* and *Artifice of Absorption* by Charles Bernstein," *American Book Review* 10, no. 4 (Sept./Oct. 1988); and Hank Lazer, "Radical Collages," *The Nation*, July 2–9, 1988, 24–26.

60. Bruce Andrews and Charles Bernstein, "Reading Stein," *L=A=N=G=U=A=G=E*, no. 6 (1978): unpaginated.

61. Michael Davidson, "On Reading Stein," *L=A=N=G=U=A=G=E*, no. 6 (1978): unpaginated; Robert Grenier, "Tender Buttons," *L=A=N=G=U=A=G=E*, no. 6 (1978): unpaginated.

62. Grenier, "Tender Buttons."

63. Modernist reprints and reviews appeared in *Montemora*, *Sun & Moon*, *Poetics Journal*, *Sulfur*, *Something Else Newsletter*, and elsewhere.

64. Middleton, "When L=A," 104.

65. Middleton, 88.

66. By 1984, 40 to 50 percent of American authors were using word processors. See Matthew G. Kirschenbaum, *Track Changes: A Literary History of Word Processing* (Cambridge, MA: Harvard University Press, 2016), xiv.

67. Lisa Gitelman, *Paper Knowledge: Toward a Media History of Documents* (Durham, NC: Duke University Press, 2014), 96, 101.

68. Bruce Andrews, Charles Bernstein, and Ron Silliman, untitled note, *L=A=N=G=U=A=G=E* Distributing Service catalogue, unpaginated, n.d., http://writing.upenn.edu/epc/library/L=_Ditr-Svc.pdf.

69. Andrews, Bernstein, and Silliman, n.p. [1].

70. Andrews, "*L=A=N=G=U=A=G=E*," in *The Little Magazine in Contemporary America*, 106–23, 118.

71. Kate Eichhorn, *Adjusted Margin: Xerography, Art, and Activism in the Late Twentieth Century* (Cambridge, MA: MIT Press, 2016), 34.

72. Eichhorn, 34.

73. Bruce Andrews and Charles Bernstein, "The Politics of Poetry," *L=A=N=G=U=A=G=E*, no. 9/10 (Oct. 1979): unpaginated.

74. Charles Bernstein, "The Dollar Value of Poetry," *L=A=N=G=U=A=G=E*, no. 9/10 (Oct. 1979): unpaginated.

75. Bruce Boone, "Writing, Power and Activity," *L=A=N=G=U=A=G=E*, no. 9/10 (Oct. 1979): unpaginated.

76. Boone, n.p.

77. Boone, n.p.

78. Barbara Barg, untitled questionnaire, *L=A=N=G=U=A=G=E*, no. 9/10 (Oct. 1979): unpaginated.

79. Several proto-Language poets were aware of the group's gender imbalance. Steve Benson, for example, urged Tom Beckett to tell him who else would appear in *The Difficulties* issue in which Benson and Carla Harryman were to publish a collaboration: "I need to have a sense of, bluntly, if & to what extent women are involved in the project. . . . I want to know that if I do a work with a woman, it won't stand out as anomalous and peculiar." Steve Benson to Tom Beckett, August 24, 1986, YCAL MSS 382, box 1, folder "Benson, Steve," *The Difficulties* Records, Yale Collection of American Literature, Beinecke Rare Book and Manuscript Library.

80. John Taggart, "Letter to the Editor," *L=A=N=G=U=A=G=E*, no. 2 (April 1978): unpaginated.

81. Loris Essary, "Letter to the Editor," *L=A=N=G=U=A=G=E*, no. 3 (June 1978): unpaginated.

82. Lyn Hejinian, "If Written Is Writing," *L=A=N=G=U=A=G=E*, no. 3 (June 1978): unpaginated.

83. Marjorie Perloff, *Radical Artifice: Writing Poetry in the Age of Media* (Chicago: University of Chicago Press, 1994), 173; Peter Nicholls, "Difference Spreading: From Gertrude Stein to L=A=N=G=U=A=G=E Poetry," in *Contemporary Poetry Meets Modern Theory* (New York: Harvester-Wheatsheaf, 1991), 116–27, 124–25.

84. Sianne Ngai, "Bad Timing (A Sequel): Paranoia, Feminism, and Poetry," *differences* 12, no. 2 (Summer 2001): 1–46, 12.

85. Golding, *From Outlaw to Classic*, 156.

86. Jacques Derrida, *Paper Machine*, trans. Rachel Bowlby (Stanford: Stanford University Press, 2005), 47; see also Jacques Derrida, *Glas*, trans. John P. Leavey Jr. and Richard Rand (Lincoln: University of Nebraska Press, 1986).

87. Gerald Graff, *Professing Literature: An Institutional History* (1987; Chicago: University of Chicago Press, 2007), 240–41.

88. François Cusset, *French Theory: How Foucault, Derrida, Deleuze, and Co. Transformed the Intellectual Life of the United States*, trans. Jeff Fort (Minneapolis: University of Minnesota Press, 2008), 62.

89. Cusset, 54.

90. Ron Silliman, "Canons and Institutions: New Hope for the Disappeared," in *The Politics of Poetic Form: Poetry and Public Policy*, ed. Charles Bernstein (New York: Roof, 1990), 149–74, 164; Ron Silliman, "If by 'Writing' We Mean Literature," *L=A=N=G=U=A=G=E*, no. 9/10 (Oct. 1979): unpaginated.

91. Spahr, *Everybody's Autonomy*, 81.

92. Golding, *From Outlaw to Classic*, 146, 144.

93. Kathleen Fraser, "Partial Local Coherence: Regions with Illustrations; Some Notes on Language Writing," *Ironwood*, no. 20 (1982): 122–39, 128.

94. Clark, "Stalin as Linguist," 300 (repr.).

95. Kevin Killian, *Bedrooms Have Windows* (New York: Amethyst, 1990), 18, 86, 133, 4.

96. Killian, 128.

97. Sarah Schulman, "Lust on Long Island," *OutWeek*, no. 19 (Oct. 1989): 60.

98. Bob Perelman, untitled response, "for *Change*" [a forum of responses by Silliman, Watten, Benson, Hejinian, Bernstein, Perelman], in *In the American Tree*, ed. Ron Silliman (Orono, ME: National Poetry Foundation, 1986), 489–90, 489; and McGann, "Contemporary Poetry, Alternate Routes," 638.

99. Charles Bernstein, "Narrating Narration: The Shapes of Ron Silliman's Work," *The Difficulties* 2, no. 2 (1985): 92–101, 93.

100. Aaron Shurin, a gay Bay Area activist, poet, and *Soup* contributor, explained two decades after the epidemic: "how to write about or into AIDS became, for me, an unavoidable confrontation, and challenged explorative composition with its insistence of thematic content." Aaron Shurin, "The People's P***k: A Dialectical Tale," in *Robert Duncan and Denise Levertov: The Poetry of Politics, the Politics of Poetry*, ed. Albert Gelpi and Robert J. Bertholf (Stanford: Stanford University Press, 2006), 71–80, 78. For a discussion of AIDS writing see Kaplan Page Harris, "Avant-Garde Interrupted: A New Narrative After AIDS," *Contemporary Literature* 52, no. 4 (Winter 2011): 630–57.

101. Kaplan Page Harris, "New Narrative and the Making of Language Poetry," *American Literature* 81, no. 4 (Dec. 2009): 805–32; Kaplan Page Harris, "The Small Press Traffic School of Dissimulation: New Narrative, New Sentence, New Left," *Jacket2*, April 7, 2011, http://jacket2.org/article/small-press-traffic-school-dissimulation#5; and Rob Halpern, "Realism and Utopia: Sex, Writing, and Activism in New Narrative," *Journal of Narrative Theory* 41, no. 1 (Spring 2011): 82–124.

102. Halpern, "Realism and Utopia," 85. The so-called poetry wars concerned

disagreements over the role of the "person" and the authenticity of the poet's voice. Sparked by an event remembering Louis Zukofsky in 1978, they unfolded in the pages of *Poetry Flash* in 1984 and in *Sagetrieb* in 1985. For a detailed account see De Villo Sloan, "'Crude Mechanical Access' or 'Crude Personism': A Chronicle of One San Francisco Bay Area Poetry War," *Sagetrieb*, no. 4 (1985): 241–54.

103. Robert Glück, "Long Note on New Narrative," in *Biting the Error: Writers Explore Narrative*, ed. Mary Burger, Robert Glück, Camille Roy, and Gail Scott (Toronto: Coach House, 2004), 25–34, 25, 26.

104. Glück, "Long Note," 26.

105. Steve Abbott, "Remarks/Hello," *Soup*, no. 1 (1980): 2.

106. Steve Abbott, "Soup Intro," *Soup*, no. 2 (1981): 1.

107. Abbott, 1.

108. Bruce Boone, "Language Writing: The Pluses and Minuses of the New Formalism," *Soup*, no. 2 (1981): 2–9, 2.

109. Rob Halpern, "Restoring 'China,'" *Jacket*, 39 (2010): http://jacketmagazine.com/39/perelman-halpern.shtml.

110. Steve Abbott, "Publisher's Note," *Soup*, no. 4 (1985): unpaginated.

111. Steve Abbott to Tom Beckett, June 4, 1981, YCAL MSS 382, box 1, folder "Abbott, Steve," *The Difficulties* Records, Yale Collection of American Literature, Beinecke Rare Book and Manuscript Library.

112. Steve Abbott to Dennis Cooper, April 20, 1990, p. 7, Dennis Cooper Papers, MSS 85, ser. 2, box 5, folder 218, Fales Library and Special Collections, New York University Libraries.

113. Barbara Baracks, "Content," *Big Deal*, no. 3 (Spring 1975): 2.

114. Kathy Acker, *Rip-Off Red, Girl Detective and the Burning Bombing of America* (New York: Grove, 2002), 53.

115. Kathy Acker, "Devoured by Myths," interview with Sylvère Lotringer, in *Hannibal Lecter, My Father* (New York: Semiotext[e], 1991), 1–24, 23.

116. Glück, "Long Note," 32; and Acker, "First Days of Life," *Soup*, no. 2 (1981): 20–22.

117. Maja Prausnitz, Peggy Pfeiffer, and Richard Peabody, "Interview with Kathy Acker," *Gargoyle*, no. 37 (Winter 1990): 12–23, 16.

118. Prausnitz et al., 17.

119. Chris Kraus, *After Kathy Acker: A Literary Biography* (New York: Semiotext[e], 2017), 83.

120. Kathy Acker, "Interview and Reading at SUNY-Buffalo as Part of the Wednesdays @4 Plus Series, April 12, 1995," *PennSound*, http://writing.upenn.edu/pennsound/x/Acker.php.

121. Acker mentions giving a reading and class in 1974: "Memory [Experiments] II: (extra notes)," Feb. 1–21, 1974, Kathy Acker Notebooks, MSS 434, box 3, folder 10, Fales Library and Special Collections, New York University Libraries. Bernadette Mayer also organized a Wednesday night reading at the Project for her and Hannah Weiner in 1975 (see Kraus, *After Kathy Acker*, 115).

122. The Black Tarantula (Kathy Acker), "*from* I Become Jane Eyre Who Rebelled Against Everyone," *Big Deal*, no. 2 (Spring 1974): 19–21, 20–21.

123. Kathy Acker, "Invisible Universe," published simultaneously in *Open Letter* 5, no. 1 (Winter 1982) and *L=A=N=G=U=A=G=E*, no. 4 (Winter 1982): 83–86, 84.

124. Eichhorn, *Adjusted Margin*, 55.

125. Acker, "*from* I Become Jane Eyre," 20.

126. Prausnitz et al., "Interview," 17.

127. Fraser, "Partial Local Coherence," 126.

128. Ellen G. Friedman, "A Conversation with Kathy Acker," *Review of Contemporary Fiction* 9, no. 3 (1989): 12–22, 15.

129. Charles Bernstein, "Introductory Note," *Paris Review*, no. 86 (Winter 1982): unpaginated.

130. Acker, "*from* I Become Jane Eyre," 20.

131. Robert Glück, "Caricature," *Soup*, no. 4 (1985): 18–28, 28.

132. Larry McCaffery, "An Interview with Kathy Acker," *Mississippi Review* 20, no. 1/2 (1991): 83–97, 89.

133. McCaffery, 89, 90.

134. Gary Sullivan, "Ron Silliman Interview," *readme*, no. 3 (Spring 2000): http://home.jps.net/~nada/silliman.htm.

135. Harris, "New Narrative," 822.

136. "The Flash Mag Survey," *Poetry Flash*, no. 100 (July 1981): 1, 3, 6.

137. Around midcentury, poetry became so entangled with the university partly because of a shift from a literary (and magazine) culture of patronage to one of administration and of governmental, philanthropic, and university funding. See Evan Kindley, *Poet-Critics and the Administration of Culture* (Cambridge, MA: Harvard University Press, 2017).

Chapter 4

1. Abigail Child, "Active Theory," *Raddle Moon*, no. 13 (1994): 12–33, 20.

2. Mira Schor, untitled response, "Forum: On Creativity and Community," *M/E/A/N/I/N/G*, no. 15 (May 1994): 26–29, 27.

3. Beth Anderson and Jennifer Moxley, "Transcending Servitude," *Black Bread*, no. 4 (Feb. 1994): 55–61, 58.

4. Mierle Laderman Ukeles, "Maintenance Art Manifesto: Proposal for an Exhibition, 'Care,'" in *Conceptual Art: A Critical Anthology*, ed. Alexander Alberro and Blake Stimson (Cambridge, MA: MIT Press, 1999), 122–25, 122. Ukeles was also included alongside Bernadette Mayer in Lucy Lippard's *c. 7,500* feminist conceptual art show in 1973.

5. Some related magazines from the same period include *Big Allis* (Melanie Neilson and Jessica Grim, 1989–2000); *Black Bread* (Sianne Ngai and Jessica Lowenthal, 1992–94); *(f.)Lip* (Angela Hryniuk, Sandy [Frances] Duncan, and Betsy Warland, 1987–90); *Re*Map* (Carolyn Kemp and Todd Baron, 1990–2000); *Motel* (Kathryn MacLeod, Lisa Marr, Julia Steele, and Douglas Stetar, 1989–91); *Giantess* (Susan Clark, Lisa Robertson, and Christine

Stewart, 1995); *Tessera* (Barbara Godard, Daphne Marlatt, Kathy Mezei, and Gail Scott, 1984–2005); and *6ix* (Alicia Askenase, Julia Blumenreich, Valerie Fox, Rina Terry, Heather Thomas, and Phyllis Wat, 1991–2001).

6. Rena Rosenwasser referred to *HOW(ever)* as "a marker"; see "Chain/Kelsey St. Press," in "Editorial Forum," *Chain*, no. 1 (Spring/Summer 1994): 92–97, 92. In her review of *HOW(ever)*, the British poet Wendy Mulford called it the first to take contemporary experimental writing by women seriously and to "acknowledge . . . the breakthroughs" of female modernists; see "Wendy Mulford on *How(ever)* Magazine," *Reality Studios*, no. 10 (1988): 94–96, 94.

7. Jane Gallop proposes 1981 as a significant moment in which feminist criticism, especially French feminist theory, gained institutional acceptance. Jane Gallop, *Around 1981: Academic Feminist Literary Theory* (New York: Routledge, 1992). Steve Evans suggests 1989 as another transition in poetry publishing, one that could be identified with the generation following *HOW(ever)*. Steve Evans, "After Patriarchal Poetry: Feminism and the Contemporary Avant-Garde," *differences* 12, no. 2 (Summer 2001): i–v, ii.

8. Maurice Hamington, "Toward a Theory of Feminist Hospitality," *Feminist Formations* 22, no. 1 (2010): 21–38, 24.

9. Eve Kosofsky Sedgwick, *Touching Feeling: Affect, Pedagogy, Performativity* (Durham, NC: Duke University Press, 2003), 139, 142, 144.

10. Sianne Ngai, "Bad Timing (A Sequel): Paranoia, Feminism, and Poetry," *differences* 12, no. 2 (Summer 2001): 1–46, 7.

11. Rae Armantrout, "Why Don't Women Do Language-Oriented Writing?" *L=A=N=G=U=A=G=E*, no. 1 (Feb. 1978): unpaginated.

12. Although "many women remember Andrews and Bernstein as actively encouraging their writing" (Ann Vickery, *Leaving Lines of Gender: A Feminist Genealogy of Language Writing* [Hanover, NH: Wesleyan University Press, 2000], 30), practitioners and critics noted the gender bias of canonical Language poetry. Silliman admitted as much in a letter to Tom Beckett: "I also heard [Hejinian] tell someone else (this was at a reading) that the Bromige issue would be 'more of the boys.' My own guess is that she's feeling that her work, in particular, is not getting the critical response it might otherwise have if she were a man, which is no doubt true generally." Ron Silliman to Tom Beckett, June 1, 1985, YCAL MSS 382, box 8, folder "Silliman, Ron," *The Difficulties* Records, Yale Collection of American Literature, Beinecke Rare Book and Manuscript Library.

13. Joan Retallack, ":Re:Thinking:Literary:Feminism: (Three Essays onto Shaky Grounds)," in *Feminist Measures: Soundings in Poetry and Theory*, ed. Lynn Keller and Cristanne Miller (Ann Arbor: University of Michigan Press, 1994), 344–77, 367.

14. Rachel Blau DuPlessis, *The Pink Guitar: Writing as Feminist Practice* (New York: Routledge, 1990), 3. First given as the seminar "Sexual Difference and Artistic Production: The Debate over a Female Aesthetic" for Workshop 9 at the Barnard College Scholar and Feminist Conference in 1979, the published version blends essay, manifesto, letters, and contributions of workshop participants. The essay led Fraser to invite DuPlessis to become a contributing editor of *HOW(ever)*; see Rachel Blau DuPlessis, "A Few Words About

HOW(ever), 1983–1992," *HOW2* 1, no. 5 (March 2001): www.asu.edu/pipercwcenter/how2journal/archive/online_archive/v1_5_2001/current/readings/however/duplessis.html.

15. DuPlessis, *Pink Guitar*, viii. Taking its cue from Wallace Stevens's "The Man with the Blue Guitar," *Pink Guitar* is a rebuttal to male modernism.

16. DuPlessis, 141.

17. Adrienne Rich, "Blood, Bread and Poetry: The Location of the Poet," *Massachusetts Review* 24, no. 3 (Autumn 1983): 521–40, 535.

18. Christine Brooke-Rose, "Illiterations," in *Breaking the Sequence: Women's Experimental Fiction*, ed. Ellen G. Friedman and Miriam Fuchs (Princeton, NJ: Princeton University Press, 1989), 55–71, 56, 65.

19. Brooke-Rose, 65.

20. Special issues of avant-garde magazines that focused on women include *Poetics Journal* 4: "Women and Language" (May 1984); *Mirage* 3: "The Women's Issue" (1989); and *Tripwire* 3: "Gender" (Summer 1999). There were many "mainstream" magazines and anthologies, too many to list here, but I wish to draw attention to two that were edited by avant-garde writers or had an impact on experimental circles: *Confirmation: An Anthology of African American Women*, ed. Amiri Baraka and Amina Baraka (New York: Morrow, 1983); and *This Bridge Called My Back: Writings by Radical Women of Color*, ed. Cherríe Moraga and Gloria E. Anzaldúa (New York: Persephone, 1981), which also includes a bibliography of work by Native American, Chicana, lesbian, Asian American, Latina, and black feminists.

21. Exceptions include Akua Lezli Hope, who was published in *Confirmation* and *Chain*; and Harryette Mullen, who published in *Chain*, *HOW2*, and *Callaloo*. *M/E/A/N/I/N/G*'s editors appeared in *Heresies*, and both magazines shared contributors.

22. To name only a few: Maggie O'Sullivan, ed., *Out of Everywhere: Innovative Poetry by Women in North America and the UK* (London: Reality Street Editions, 1996); Mary Margaret Sloan, ed., *Moving Borders: Three Decades of Innovative Writing by Women* (Jersey City, NJ: Talisman House, 1998); Lou Robinson and Camille Norton, eds., *Resurgent: New Writing by Women* (Urbana: University of Illinois Press, 1992); Lynn Keller and Cristanne Miller, eds., *Feminist Measures: Soundings in Poetry and Theory* (Ann Arbor: University of Michigan Press, 1994); DuPlessis, *Pink Guitar*; Ellen G. Friedman and Miriam Fuchs, eds., *Breaking the Sequence: Women's Experimental Fiction* (Princeton, NJ: Princeton University Press, 1989); and the journals *Signs*; *Frontiers*; *Heresies*; *Quest*; *Radical Teacher*; and *Black Scholar*. On community and small-press publishing see the special issue "Poetry, Community, Movement," *Diacritics* 26, no. 3/4 (Autumn/Winter 1996). For later feminist anthologies and criticism see note 31.

23. After 2000, conference panels about small-press publishing increased even more—e.g., "Issue Zero: The Literary Magazine Conference," New York (2000) at which the editors of *Big Allis* and *Chain* presented talks.

24. Juliana Spahr and Stephanie Young, "Numbers Trouble," *Chicago Review* 53, no. 2/3 (Autumn 2007): 88–111, 89; and Joshua Kotin and Robert P. Baird, "Poetry Magazines & Women Poets," *Chicago Review* 53, no. 2/3 (Autumn 2007): 226–30.

25. Jena Osman and Juliana Spahr, "Facts," *Chain*, no. 12 (Summer 2005): 4–6.

26. Perloff reviews editors Eliot Weinberger's *American Poetry Since 1950: Innovators and Outsiders, an Anthology* (New York: Marsilio, 1993); Douglas Messerli's *From the Other Side of the Century: A New American Poetry, 1960–1990* (New York: Sun & Moon, 1994); and Peter Gizzi, Connell McGrath, and Juliana Spahr's *Writing from the New Coast*, 2 vols (Stockbridge, MA: o•blēk editions / Garlic Press, 1993). Vol. 1, edited by Gizzi and McGrath, focused on "Presentation"; vol. 2, edited by Gizzi and Spahr, focused on 'Technique." See also Marjorie Perloff, "Whose New American Poetry: Anthologizing in the Nineties," *Diacritics* 26, no. 3/4 (Autumn/Winter 1996): 104–23, 104. Alongside Perloff, Steve Evans and Alan Golding also discuss 1990s anthologizing: see Steve Evans, "Ant[h] slide: Recent Anthologies," *TapRoot Reviews*, no. 6 (1995): 14–15; and Alan Golding, "New, Newer, and Newest American Poetries," *Chicago Review* 43, no. 4 (Fall 1997): 7–21.

27. Juliana Spahr, "Spiderwasp or Literary Criticism," in *Telling It Slant: Avant-Garde Poetics of the 1990s*, ed. Mark Wallace and Steven Marks (Tuscaloosa: University of Alabama Press, 2002), 404–28, 411.

28. Spahr, 409, 411.

29. Harryette Mullen, "Poetry and Identity," in *Telling It Slant: Avant-Garde Poetics of the 1990s*, ed. Mark Wallace and Steven Marks (Tuscaloosa: University of Alabama Press, 2002), 27–31, 30.

30. Perloff, "Whose New American Poetry," 111.

31. See, e.g., Elisabeth A. Frost and Cynthia Hogue, eds., *Innovative Women Poets: An Anthology of Contemporary Poetry and Interviews* (Iowa City: University of Iowa Press, 2006); Laura Hinton and Cynthia Hogue, eds., *We Who Love to Be Astonished: Experimental Women's Writing* (Tuscaloosa: University of Alabama Press, 2002); Lynn Keller, *Thinking Poetry: Readings in Contemporary Women's Exploratory Poetics* (Iowa City: University of Iowa Press, 2010); Claudia Rankine and Juliana Spahr, eds., *American Women Poets in the 21st Century: Where Lyric Meets Language* (Middletown, CT: Wesleyan University Press, 2002); Vickery, *Leaving Lines of Gender*; Linda Kinnahan, *Lyric Interventions: Feminism, Experimental Poetry, and Contemporary Discourse* (Iowa City: University of Iowa Press, 2004); and Elisabeth Frost, *The Feminist Avant-Garde in American Poetry* (Iowa City: University of Iowa Press, 2003). See also note 22 above.

32. See Vickery, *Leaving Lines of Gender*; Megan Simpson, *Poetic Epistemologies: Gender and Knowing in Women's Language-Oriented Writing* (Albany: SUNY Press, 2000); Linda Taylor, "'A Seizure of Voice': Language Innovation and a Feminist Poetics in the Works of Kathleen Fraser," *Contemporary Literature* 33, no. 2 (Summer 1992): 337–72; Redell Olsen, "Strategies of Critical Practice: Recent Writing on Experimental and Innovative Poetry by Women; A Review Essay," *Signs* 33, no. 2 (Winter 2008): 371–87; and Kinnahan, *Lyric Interventions*.

33. Frost, *The Feminist Avant-Garde*, xi.

34. Frost, xiv.

35. Kathleen Fraser, "The Jump: Editing *HOW(ever)*," *Chain*, no. 1 (Spring/Summer 1994): 42–46, 42.

36. Fraser, 43.

37. Daphne Marlatt, "Why?" *HOW(ever)* 5, no. 2 (Jan. 1989): 13–14, 13.

38. Vickery, *Leaving Lines of Gender*, 96.

39. Eliot Weinberger, "A Final Response," *Sulfur*, no. 22 (1988): 199–202, 200. The other three are "the black nationalist poetry of the 1960s," "poetry written against Vietnam," and ethnopoetics.

40. Kathleen Fraser, "Editor's Notes," *HOW(ever)* 5, no. 4 (Oct. 1989): 24–25, 24.

41. Fraser, 24.

42. Kathleen Fraser, "How Error Pops Up: An Interview with Kathleen Fraser," with Robin Tremblay-McGaw, *Poetry Flash*, no. 246 (Sept./Oct. 1993): 1, 6, 9–11, 6.

43. Fraser, 6.

44. Kathleen Fraser, "Partial Local Coherence: Regions with Illustrations; Some Notes on Language Writing," *Ironwood*, no. 20 (1982): 122–39, 137.

45. Fraser, 137.

46. Fraser, "The Jump," 45, 43.

47. Marianne DeKoven, "Male Signature, Female Aesthetic: The Gender Politics of Experimental Writing," in *Breaking the Sequence: Women's Experimental Fiction*, ed. Ellen G. Friedman and Miriam Fuchs (Princeton, NJ: Princeton University Press, 1989), 72–81, 79–80.

48. Frances Jaffer, "Why *HOW(ever)*?" *HOW(ever)* 1, no. 1 (May 1983): 1.

49. We could here think of *M/E/A/N/I/N/G*, *(f.)Lip*, and, slightly later, Bellamy's New Narrative *Mirage #4 / Period[ical]*, which adopted the unusual punctuation humorously; see "Interview: Writer & Literary Zine Editor Kevin Killian Talks Xerox Coup d'État," *Poets House* (blog), Oct. 15, 2018, https://poetshouse.org/seita_killian_interview (originally published by *CLMP [Community of Literary Magazines and Presses]: Front Porch Commons*, Sept. 2015).

50. Ann Vickery describes the revision of a review by Rae Armantrout to be published in *HOW(ever)*, owing to the editors' assumption that their audience might not be familiar with Language poetics. See Vickery, *Leaving Lines of Gender*, 97.

51. Cynthia Hogue, "An Interview with Kathleen Fraser," *Contemporary Literature* 39, no. 1 (Spring 1998): 1–26, 15, 17.

52. Vickery, *Leaving Lines of Gender*, 89, 93.

53. Fraser, "The Jump," 46.

54. Fraser, 44.

55. Mary Jacobus, "The Difference of View," quoted in *HOW(ever)* 3, no. 4 (Jan. 1987): back cover.

56. Jacobus, back cover.

57. Untitled editorial, *HOW(ever)* 3, no. 4 (Jan. 1987): back cover.

58. Fraser, "Editor's Notes," 24.

59. Karen Kelley, "postcard," *HOW(ever)* 5, no. 4 (Oct. 1989): 23.

60. Ruth Stone, "postcard," *HOW(ever)* 1, no. 3 (Feb. 1984): 15.

61. Fraser, "Editor's Notes," 24.

62. Fraser, "The Jump," 44.

63. Mira Schor, untitled response, "Editorial Forum," *Chain*, no. 1 (Spring/Summer 1994): 100–101, 101.

64. Susan Bee and Mira Schor, "A Community of *M/E/A/N/I/N/G*," unpublished essay, unpaginated.

65. Susan Bee and Mira Schor, "Forum 1989," *M/E/A/N/I/N/G*, no. 5 (May 1989): 3.

66. Alison Piepmeier, *Girl Zines: Making Media, Doing Feminism* (New York: New York University Press, 2009), 29.

67. Virginia Woolf, *A Room of One's Own* (1929; New York: Harcourt Brace Jovanovich, 1957), 76.

68. Sandra M. Gilbert and Susan Gubar, *No Man's Land: The Place of the Woman Writer in the Twentieth Century* (New Haven, CT: Yale University Press, 1988), 1:165; Alice Notley, "Doctor Williams' Heiresses," *Tuumba*, no. 28 (July 1980); Linda Kinnahan, *Poetics of the Feminine: Authority and Literary Tradition in William Carlos Williams, Mina Loy, Denise Levertov, and Kathleen Fraser* (Cambridge: Cambridge University Press, 1994), 1. See also Simpson, *Poetic Epistemologies*.

69. Linda R. Williams, "Happy Families? Feminist Reproduction and Matrilineal Thought," in *New Feminist Discourses: Critical Essays on Theories and Texts*, ed. Isobel Armstrong (London: Routledge, 1992), 48–64, 55, 57.

70. Clare Hemmings, *Why Stories Matter: The Political Grammar of Feminist Theory* (Durham, NC: Duke University Press, 2010), 151.

71. Kathleen Fraser, "Editor's Notes &," *HOW2* 1, no. 1 (March 1999): www.asu.edu/pipercwcenter/how2journal/archive/online_archive/v1_1_1999/ednote.html.

72. Kathleen Fraser, "Editor's Note," *HOW(ever)* 1, no. 2 (Nov. 1984): 13. The guide documents a course taught at San Francisco State University in 1982 and features work by guest teachers Carolyn Burke, Rachel Blau DuPlessis, and Frances Jaffer.

73. Fraser, "Partial Local Coherence," 136–37.

74. *0 to 9* printed Apollinaire and Stein; *some/thing* declared the Dadaists and surrealists as their inspiration in expanding the category of poetry; and the proto-Language *Sun & Moon*, no. 2 (Spring 1976) reprinted Loy's commentary on Louis Eilshemius, first published in *The Blind Man*. *Poetics Journal* 4, "Women and Language," posed most questions on poetics through the discussion of female modernists (e.g., Scalapino through H.D., Carolyn Burke through Loy and Riding). DuPlessis discussed gendered influence and reception in "*Pater*-daughter: Male Modernists and Female Readers," *Soup*, no. 4 (1984): 40–54; and "Sub Rrosa: Marcel Duchamp and the Female Spectator," *Sulfur*, no. 21 (Winter 1988): 152–64.

75. Jed Rasula, "A Renaissance of Women Writers," *Sulfur*, no. 7 (1983): 160–72, 167.

76. Rasula, 167–68.

77. Kathleen Fraser, "Response to: 'A Renaissance of Women Writers' by Jed Rasula," *HOW(ever)* 1, no. 2 (Oct. 1983): 13–14, 13.

78. Fraser, 14.

79. Lynn Luria-Sukenick and Marianne DeKoven, "Two Reappreciations of Gertrude Stein," *HOW(ever)* 3, no. 1 (Jan. 1986): 13–14.

80. Luria-Sukenick and DeKoven, 14.

81. Kate Fagan, "'A Narrative in Escaped Places': After Stein," *HOW2* 2, no. 2 (Spring 2004): www.asu.edu/pipercwcenter/how2journal/archive/online_archive/v2_2_2004/current/stein/index.htm.

82. Carla Harryman, "The Mother of Us All," *HOW2* 2, no. 2 (Spring 2004): par. 8, www.asu.edu/pipercwcenter/how2journal/archive/online_archive/v2_2_2004/current/stein/harryman.htm.

83. Harryman, par. 14.

84. Alex Goody, "Gender, Authority and the Speaking Subject, or: Who is Mina Loy?," *HOW2* 1, no. 5 (March 2001): www.asu.edu/pipercwcenter/how2journal/archive/online_archive/v1_5_2001/current/in-conference/mina-loy/goody.html.

85. Hilda Bronstein, "Mina Loy's *Insel* as Caustic Critique of the Surrealist Paradox," *HOW2* 1, no. 4 (Sept. 2000): www.asu.edu/pipercwcenter/how2journal/archive/online_archive/v1_4_2000/current/readings/bronstein.html.

86. Elizabeth Savage, "How to Do Things with Words: Reading Riding's and Retallack's Poethics," *HOW2* 1, no. 3 (Feb. 2000): www.asu.edu/pipercwcenter/how2journal/archive/online_archive/v1_3_2000/current/readings/savage.html.

87. Kinnahan, *Lyric Interventions*, 40.

88. Feminist avant-garde magazines functioned in a way similar to archives: they were not just sites of memory but were "about the work of the imagination," an "intervention" and a "social project" where "collective memory is interactively designed." Arjun Appadurai, "Archive and Aspiration," in *Information Is Alive*, ed. Joke Brouwer, Arjen Mulder, and Susan Charlton (Rotterdam: V2/NAi, 2003), 14–25, 24.

89. On the role of pedagogy for experimental, and especially male, poets see Alan Golding, "'Isn't the Avant-Garde Always Pedagogical': Experimental Poetics and/as Pedagogy," in *Poetry and Pedagogy: The Challenge of the Contemporary*, ed. Joan Retallack and Juliana Spahr (New York: Palgrave Macmillan, 2006), 13–29, 14, 16; and Alan Golding, "From Pound to Olson: The Avant-Garde Poet as Pedagogue," *Journal of Modern Literature* 34, no. 1 (Fall 2010): 86–106.

90. Lynn Keller and Cristanne Miller, "Gender and Avant-Garde Editing: Comparing the 1920s with the 1990s," *HOW2* 1, no. 2 (1999): www.asu.edu/pipercwcenter/how2journal//archive/online_archive/v1_2_1999/current/readings/keller-miller.html#9.

91. Hannah Möckel-Rieke, "Forum," *HOW2* 1, no. 1 (March 1999): www.asu.edu/pipercwcenter/how2journal/archive/online_archive/v1_1_1999/forum.html.

92. Jacques Derrida, *Archive Fever: A Freudian Impression*, trans. Eric Prenowitz (Chicago: University of Chicago Press, 1996), 20.

93. Kate Eichhorn, *The Archival Turn in Feminism: Outrage in Order* (Philadelphia: Temple University Press, 2013), 90.

94. Fraser, "The Jump," 44.

95. Hogue, "An Interview," 18.

96. Fraser, "The Jump," 45.

97. Meredith Stricker, untitled response, "Forum," *HOW2* 1, no. 1 (March 1999): www.asu.edu/pipercwcenter/how2journal/archive/online_archive/v1_1_1999/forum.html.

98. Jena Osman and Juliana Spahr, "Editors' Notes: Frameworks," *Chain*, no. 1 (Spring/Summer 1994): 129–34, 131.

99. Walter Benjamin, "Der Autor als Produzent," in *Gesammelte Schriften*, ed. Rolf Tiedemann and Hermann Schweppenhäuser (Frankfurt: Suhrkamp, 1977), 2:2.688–89.

100. Joan Retallack to Tom Beckett, Jan. 10, 1987, YCAL MSS 382, box 8, folder "Retallack, Joan," *The Difficulties* Records, Yale Collection of American Literature, Beinecke Rare Book and Manuscript Library.

101. Joan Retallack to Tom Beckett, April 18, 1987, YCAL MSS 382, box 8, folder "Retallack, Joan," *The Difficulties* Records, Yale Collection of American Literature, Beinecke Rare Book and Manuscript Library.

102. Julia Kristeva, "Woman Can Never Be Defined," in *New French Feminisms: An Anthology*, ed. Elaine Marks and Isabelle de Courtivron, trans. Marilyn August (New York: Schocken, 1981), 137–41, 137.

103. Lori Cole, *Surveying the Avant-Garde: Questions on Modernism, Art, and the Americas in Transatlantic Magazines* (University Park: Pennsylvania State University Press, 2018), 8, 36.

104. Osman and Spahr, "Editors' Notes: Frameworks," 131.

105. Juliana Spahr, *Everybody's Autonomy: Connective Reading and Collective Identity* (Tuscaloosa: University of Alabama Press, 2001), 6.

106. Jena Osman and Juliana Spahr, "Chains," *Chain*, no. 1 (Spring/Summer 1994), 136.

107. Osman and Spahr, "Editors' Notes: Frameworks," 133.

108. Osman and Spahr, 129.

109. Osman and Spahr, 130.

110. Kathryn Thoms Flannery, *Feminist Literacies, 1968–75* (Urbana: University of Illinois Press, 2005), 54–55.

111. "Forum," *HOW2* 1, no. 1 (March 1999): www.asu.edu/pipercwcenter/how2journal//archive/online_archive/v1_1_1999/whatwhat.html#forum.

112. Jane Sprague, "Forum on Small Press Publishing," *HOW2* 2, no. 4 (Spring/Summer 2006): www.asu.edu/pipercwcenter/how2journal//archive/online_archive/v2_4_2006/current/forum/introduction.html.

113. *Chain*'s "Different Languages" issue has twenty-three co-editors—a direct consequence of the magazine's collaborative "chain" principle.

114. Linda Russo, postcard, *HOW2* 1, no. 2 (Sept. 1999): www.asu.edu/pipercwcenter/how2journal//archive/online_archive/v1_2_1999/postcard.html. Russo refers to the first issue, available online at www.asu.edu/pipercwcenter/how2journal/archive/online_archive/v1_1_1999/index.html.

115. Sheila E. Murphy, "Difficult Made Human," *American Book Review* 27, no. 5 (July/August 2006): 6–7, 6.

116. Johanna Drucker also invited Erica Hunt, who did not contribute in the end,

being "just too busy 'saving' the world," "channeling resources to grassroots organizations pushing for Black community change" in addition to her full-time job and two children (Erica Hunt, email to author, Feb. 11, 2015). MacLeod and Clark invited Julia Steele, and Jessica Grim was invited by Clark. Many thanks to Johanna Drucker for permission to read and cite her unpublished and unarchived materials of the *Raddle Moon* forum.

117. Susan Clark, "Women/Writing/Theory," *Raddle Moon*, no. 11 (1992): 16.

118. Johanna Drucker to participants, Nov. 3, 1990, personal archive of Johanna Drucker.

119. Jean Day, "Response," *Raddle Moon*, no. 13 (1994): 56–61, 56.

120. Chris Tysh, "Critical Theory, or Tooling That Thing," *Raddle Moon*, no. 13 (1994): 44–47, 45, 44.

121. Child, "Active Theory," 12, 14.

122. Drucker, untitled response, "Editorial Forum," *Chain*, no. 1 (Spring/Summer 1994): 37.

123. Drucker to participants, April 12, 1991, personal archive of Johanna Drucker.

124. Drucker to participants.

125. Drucker, "Response," *Raddle Moon*, no. 13 (1994): 48–55, 49.

126. Drucker to participants, April 12, 1991.

127. Drucker to participants, July 1, 1991, personal archive of Johanna Drucker (my italics).

128. Drucker to participants, July 16, 1991, personal archive of Johanna Drucker.

129. Drucker to participants.

130. Day, "Response," 56.

131. Day, 57.

132. Jean Day, email to author, March 12, 2015: "If you want to know whether feminist writers gendered 'theory' male, I think there certainly were some who thought so, and I was probably among them, though that seems far too simplistic now." Jean Day, email to author, March 4, 2015: "What's surprising to me now is what appears to have been my own defensive response, accusing Johanna's piece of 'overtones of mastery and unrevisability'—which I really don't see now. I actually think her response, in retrospect[,] is exactly right."

133. Drucker, "Response," 52–53.

134. Drucker, 52.

135. Marjorie Perloff, "After Language Poetry: Innovation and Its Theoretical Discontents," in *Contemporary Poetics*, ed. Louis Armand (Evanston, IL: Northwestern University Press, 2007), 15–38, 31–32.

136. Cole, *Surveying the Avant-Garde*, 32, 62.

137. Ngai, "Bad Timing," 8.

138. Johanna Drucker, "Exclusion/Inclusion vs. Canon Formation," *HOW(ever)* 6, no. 4 (Jan. 1992): 13–14, 13.

139. Gayatri Chakravorty Spivak, *The Post-Colonial Critic: Interviews, Strategies,*

Dialogues (New York: Routledge, 1990), quoted in Tysh, "Critical Theory, or Tooling That Thing," 44.

140. This anxiety remained a theme for feminist avant-garde magazines throughout the period; for instance, as Spahr and Osman wrote, "We have at various times in working on this issue felt nervous. Nervous because we often couldn't read all the languages. Or nervous that too much work remains in English." Juliana Spahr and Jena Osman, "Editors' Notes," *Chain*, no. 5 (Summer 1998): 3–4, 4.

141. Anderson and Moxley, "Transcending Servitude," 58.

142. Jacques Derrida, "Hospitality," trans. Barry Stocker and Forbes Morlock, *Angelaki* 5, no. 3 (2000): 3–18, 4.

143. Derrida, "Hospitality," 15.

144. Derrida, "Hospitality," 6–7.

Chapter 5

1. Ezra Pound, "Studies in Contemporary Mentality," *New Age* (August 1917 to January 1918).

2. Michael Cross and Thom Donovan, "About," *ON: Contemporary Practice*, https://on-contemporarypractice.squarespace.com/about.

3. Amy Hungerford, "On the Period Formerly Known as the Contemporary," *American Literary History* 20, no. 1/2 (2008): 410–19, 418.

4. Michael Cross, Thom Donovan, and Kyle Schlesinger, "From Center to Margin," *ON: Contemporary Practice*, no. 2 (2010): 7–8, 7.

5. Bruno Latour, *We Have Never Been Modern*, trans. Catherine Porter (New York: Harvester Wheatsheaf, 1993), 73.

6. Latour, 73.

7. Sarah Chihaya, Joshua Kotin, and Kinohi Nishikawa, "'The Contemporary' by the Numbers," Post45, 2016 http://post45.research.yale.edu/2016/02/the-contemporary-by-the-numbers.

8. See Amy Hungerford, *Making Literature Now* (Stanford, CA: Stanford University Press, 2016).

9. Ted Striphas, *The Late Age of Print: Everyday Book Culture from Consumerism to Control* (New York: Columbia University Press, 2009), 4.

10. Roger Fidler, in *Mediamorphosis: Understanding New Media* (London: Sage, 1999), understands mediamorphosis as the transformation of media and communication systems as a result of complex convergences, developments out of earlier or other media, as well as social, political, and technological processes and needs. Jay David Bolter and Richard Grusin, in *Remediation: Understanding New Media* (Cambridge, MA: MIT Press, 1998), understand remediation as the process by which old or original media are present in or remade into a new medium.

11. Ian Morris and Joanne Diaz, preface to *The Little Magazine in Contemporary America*, ed. Ian Morris and Joanne Diaz (Chicago: University of Chicago Press, 2015),

vii–xvii, vii; Brian M. Reed, *Nobody's Business: Twenty-First Century Avant-Garde Poetics* (Ithaca, NY: Cornell University Press, 2013), 1.

12. The term *intermediation* comes from Ted Striphas, who prefers it over *remediation*. See Striphas, *Late Age of Print*, 15–16.

13. Kristen Gallagher, "The Gauss Interview: Chris Alexander Talks to J. Gordon Faylor," *Jacket2*, March 5, 2013, http://jacket2.org/commentary/gauss-interview. Faylor founded *Gauss PDF* in 2010. Its name is a pun on the Gaussian probability distribution function. *Troll Thread* was founded in 2010 by Chris Sylvester, who was soon joined by Joey Yearous-Algozin, Holly Melgard, and Divya Victor (who has now left the project).

14. All three projects move within overlapping circles in primarily New York City, Philadelphia, and Buffalo.

15. Lisa Gitelman, *Paper Knowledge: Toward a Media History of Documents* (Durham, NC: Duke University Press, 2014), 117.

16. Jerome McGann, *A New Republic of Letters: Memory and Scholarship in the Age of Digital Reproduction* (Cambridge, MA: Harvard University Press, 2014), 84.

17. Holly Melgard, Joey Yearous-Algozin, and Chris Sylvester, "Troll Thread Interview," by Tan Lin, *Harriet: A Poetry Blog*, May 4, 2014, www.poetryfoundation.org/harriet/2014/05/troll-thread-interview.

18. Holly Melgard, "Statement of Poetics," *Revista Laboratorio*, no. 8 (2013): www.laboratoriodeescrituras.cl/holly-melgard.

19. Melgard, Yearous-Algozin, and Sylvester, "Troll Thread Interview."

20. Jean Keller, *The Black Book*, www.lulu.com/shop/jean-keller/the-black-book/paperback/product-21008894.html.

21. Holly Melgard, *REIMBUR$EMENT* (*Troll Thread*, 2013), 1. Melgard initially made *REIMBUR$EMENT* for inclusion in the exhibition "Poetry Will Be Made By All! / 89Plus" in Zurich in January of 2014, knowing that this would guarantee at least one printed copy and she would then be "reimbursed." She was not included in the end, being born before 1989, so her "reimbursement" was delayed until the University at Buffalo Libraries Poetry Collection (which now has a standing order for all *Troll Thread* titles) recently ordered a copy.

22. Maker, *Money* (*Troll Thread*, 2012), unpaginated.

23. *Troll Thread* often publishes typographically and conceptually odd work (say, Yearous-Algozin's own *9/11 911 CALLS IN 911 PT. FONT*; or Chris Sylvester's *STILL LIFE W/ BLOG 07/12/13 04:24PM // 05:12PM // 264 PGS MSWORD // 10/18/13 // 3:45PM // 595 PGS MSWORD*) that makes conventional word-by-word reading difficult or impossible.

24. Joey Yearous-Algozin, *HOW TO STOP WORRYING . . .* (*Troll Thread*, July 2016), 1.

25. Amy Hungerford discusses a similarly self-conscious display of publishing economics in *Making Literature Now*. For her, the breakdown of printing, shipping, and other publishing costs in several early issues of *McSweeney's* is a "DIY exhortation" based in "the anticommercial DIY ethic of punk" and zine culture that *McSweeney's* identifies with (26). But when compared to Yearous-Algozin's POD PDF "poem," *McSweeney's* detailing of printing costs and revenue, which far exceeds the "zero revenue" of *Troll Thread*, can seem

like a gimmick; there is little "punk" in the members' benefits for donors who give $10,000 or more to the McSweeney's enterprise, which includes a press, two print magazines, and an online magazine. Unlike *McSweeney's*, which Hungerford shows has "made" the careers of several writers, *Troll Thread* is unlikely to—and does not even care to—do so.

26. See Laurence Sterne, *The Life and Opinions of Tristram Shandy, Gentleman*, 3rd ed. (London: R. and J. Dodsley, 1760), 1:73.

27. Brian Reed and Craig Dworkin, "Untitled Conversation," in *Affect and Audience in the Digital Age*, ed. Amaranth Borsuk (Athens, OH: Essay Press, 2014), 1–16, 5.

28. Holly Melgard, conversation with the author, March 28, 2017.

29. Gallagher, "The Gauss Interview."

30. "Announcing Files 2.0," *Badlands Unlimited*, March 21, 2017, https://badlandsunlimited.com/news/announcing-files-2-0. The files, which can be downloaded for $150–300 to support contemporary artists, include PDFs, a PowerPoint presentation, code in the form of a Perl script, and a newly designed typeface.

31. Feliz Lucia Molina, *A Letter to Kim Jong-Il Looking at Things* (*Gauss PDF*, 2012), 4.

32. Gallagher, "The Gauss Interview."

33. Daniel Wilson, *Files I Have Known: Data Reminiscences* (*Gauss PDF*, 2016): 5.

34. Repurposing the look of old print forms has become popular over the last few years in avant-garde publishing, perhaps spurred by large-scale commercial digitization projects like Google Books, which put out-of-print materials into the public domain, but also by the sheer ease with which old designs can be appropriated digitally. Two recent projects that mimic older print technology and design are the magazine *The Germ* (1997–2005), edited by Macgregor Card and Andrew Maxwell, titled in homage to the Pre-Raphaelite journal of the same name; and the anthology of English-to-English "translations" of Shakespeare's *Sonnets*, published by the experimental translation magazine *Telephone*, ed. Sharmila Cohen and Paul Legault (2010–).

35. *6×6*, no. 5 (Dec. 2001), Ugly Duckling Presse Online Chapbook Archive, www.uglyducklingpresse.org/archive/online-reading-old/6x6-5-our-goal-is-the-victory-of-midnight-and-its-autobiography-of-touch-by-6x6-poets.

36. The letterpress cover and the hand-cut edge, more visible in the intact version, pay homage to Russian Futurist Vasily Kamensky's 1914 chapbook *Tango with Cows*.

37. Gitelman, *Paper Knowledge*, 115.

38. Gitelman, 114.

39. Jacques Derrida, *Paper Machine*, trans. Rachel Bowlby (Stanford: Stanford University Press, 2005), 46.

40. Gitelman, *Paper Knowledge*, x, 115.

41. Melgard, Yearous-Algozin, and Sylvester, "Troll Thread Interview."

42. Hannes Bajohr, "Experimental Writing in Its Moment of Digital Technization: Post-Digital Literature and Print-on-Demand Publishing," in *Publishing as Artistic Practice*, ed. Annette Gilbert (Berlin: Sternberg Press, 2016), 100–115, 101.

43. Nick Thurston, "The Mediatization of Contemporary Writing," in *Publishing as Artistic Practice*, ed. Annette Gilbert (Berlin: Sternberg Press, 2016), 90–99, 93, 96.

44. Melgard, Yearous-Algozin, and Sylvester, "Troll Thread Interview."

45. Walter Benjamin, *Illuminations*, trans. Harry Zohn, ed. Hannah Arendt (New York: Schocken, 1969), 221.

46. "Issues," *Triple Canopy*, www.canopycanopycanopy.com/issues.

47. Editors, "A Note on Unplaced Movements: On the Errant Histories of Flip Books, Cassette Tapes, and Online Publishing," *Triple Canopy*, no. 9 (2010): www.canopycanopycanopy.com/issues/9/contents/a_note_on_unplaced_movements.

48. For a while, UDP published "books which escape attempts to keep them in one place" and which "address the basic assumptions and structures of book distribution and its relationship to how we read." One such paperless project, Julien Poirier and Amy Fusselman's "Phone Books," consists of work written to be performed and received over the phone. See www.uglyducklingpresse.org/catalog/browse/paperless-book-department.

49. Colby Chamberlain, "The Binder and the Server," *Art Journal Open*, Feb. 18, 2012, http://artjournal.collegeart.org/?p=2644.

50. Editors, "A Note on Invalid Format," in *Invalid Format: An Anthology of Triple Canopy* (New York: Triple Canopy, 2011), 2–5, 3.

51. Chamberlain, "The Binder and the Server."

52. Editors, "A Note on Unplaced Movements," 2.

53. Editors, "A Note on Invalid Format," 3.

54. Editors, 3.

55. Matthew G. Kirschenbaum, *Mechanisms: New Media and the Forensic Imagination* (Cambridge, MA: MIT Press, 2008); N. Katherine Hayles, *My Mother Was a Computer: Digital Subjects and Literary Texts* (Chicago: University of Chicago Press, 2005); and Jerome McGann, *A New Republic of Letters: Memory and Scholarship in the Age of Digital Reproduction* (Cambridge, MA: Harvard University Press, 2014).

56. Robert Darnton, "What Is the History of Books?" *Daedalus* 111, no. 3 (1982): 65–83, 68.

57. Hannah Sullivan's *The Work of Revision* (Cambridge, MA: Harvard University Press, 2013) shows in great detail that changes in writing equipment, print technology, and the very understanding of revision have affected how, when, and why authors revise.

58. When Bernadette Mayer and Susan Bee remarked that they did the nitty-gritty work of typing stencils (Mayer) or designing the layout (Bee) for their male co-editors, or in Bee's case, her husband, they revealed a gendered division of labor. In other cases, comments on the labor of printing speak to a magazine's poetics. The magazine editors Tom Raworth and Hettie Jones noted in interviews that hand-setting contributions for *Outburst* and *Yugen*, respectively, made them appreciate short and simple lines, which in turn may have affected their own writing. Stephanie Anderson, "An Interview with Hettie Jones," *Chicago Review* 59, no. 1/2 (Fall 2014 / Winter 2015): 79–90, 80; and Kyle Schlesinger and Matt Chambers, "Tom Raworth: An Interview Conducted by Kyle Schlesinger and Matt Chambers, Poetry Collection, Buffalo, May 22, 2006," *Mimeo Mimeo*, no. 4 (Winter 2010): 7–18, 11.

59. Roger Chartier, "Languages, Books, and Reading from Printed Word to the Digital Text," trans. Teresa Lavender Fagan, *Critical Inquiry* 31, no. 1 (August 2004): 133–52, 151.

60. Sean Latham, "The Mess and Muddle of Modernism: The Modernist Journals Project and Modern Periodical Studies," *Tulsa Studies in Women's Literature* 30, no. 2 (Fall 2011): 407–28, 412.

61. Jessica Pressman, "The Aesthetic of Bookishness in 21st-Century Literature," *Michigan Quarterly Review* 48, no. 4 (2009): 465–82, 466.

62. Pressman, 469, 466.

63. Matthew G. Kirschenbaum, "The RESTful Book: Bibliography and Bookish Media," lecture presented at the A.S.W. Rosenbach Lectures in Bibliography, Philadelphia, PA, 2016, www.youtube.com/watch?v=Wm_DuhVrhGM.

64. Kirschenbaum, "The RESTful book." N. Katherine Hayles, in "Combining Close Reading and Distant Reading: Jonathan Safran Foer's *Tree of Codes* and the Aesthetic of Bookishness," *PMLA* 128, no. 1 (2013): 226–31, even goes so far as to argue that "print books are now so interpenetrated with digital media at every stage of their production that they may more appropriately be considered an output form of digital texts than a separate medium" (226).

65. *Magazine-ish* fits closely with the other terms in this chapter, like *bookish* and *printish*, and it is also a term that already exists, though it isn't widely used. The *OED* credits Samuel Taylor Coleridge with first using *magazinish* in a letter in 1794. See the *Oxford English Dictionary*, s.v. "magazinish, adj."

66. Derrida, *Paper Machine*, 48, 46.

67. Derrida, 30.

68. Poetic Research Bureau, "For an Unoriginal Literature: 'Novelty Is Suicide.' An Introduction to and Dispatch from a Literary Service in the Public Domain," *Invalid Format: An Anthology of Triple Canopy* (New York: Triple Canopy, 2011), 153–56, 155. The PRB is a small collective based in Los Angeles and run by Ara Shirinyan, Andrew Maxwell, and Joseph Mosconi. Shirinyan also edits Make Now Press. Maxwell edited *The Germ* with Macgregor Card.

69. See "Publication Intensive," *Triple Canopy*, www.canopycanopycanopy.com/education#intensive.

70. Editors, "Selected Correspondence of Triple Canopy: The First Two Months; From the Annals of Newhungarianquarterly@googlegroups.com. In Which We Reread *Aspen*, Fight over a Name, and Write an Obnoxious Letter," in *Invalid Format: An Anthology of Triple Canopy* (New York: Triple Canopy, 2011), 318–30, 322–23, 320.

71. Editors, 321.

72. Editors, 330.

73. William Carlos Williams, *I Wanted to Write a Poem: The Autobiography of the Works of a Poet*, ed. Edith Heal (New York: New Directions, 1978), 19.

74. The *CARS ARE REAL* website is now defunct, exemplifying the provisional nature of some digital publishing.

75. Sophia Le Fraga, Facebook status, Oct. 21, 2013, www.facebook.com/photo.php?fbid=10200839941025755.

76. The online magazine *textsound* publishes audio works in often guest-curated "issues": http://textsound.org/. The one-off audio magazine *frequency audio journal* was edited by CAConrad and Magdalena Zurawski in 2004: https://frequencymagazine.blogspot.com/2004/06/frequencys-debut-issue-is-available.html. The UK-based digital *Reductive Journal* (2014–), renamed *Mumei Journal*, presents "*experimental reflections on listening / reading practices*" in PDF-based issues that combine text and clickable MP3s: http://mumeipublishing.com/publication.

77. Danny Snelson, "Live Vinyl MP3: Mutant Sounds, PennSound, UbuWeb, SpokenWeb," *Amodern*, no. 4 (March 2015): http://amodern.net/article/live-vinyl-mp3.

78. Richard Owens, "Misc. Notes on Flarf, Conceptual Writing & C. (Nothing Is Now Clean Slayne but Rotteth)," *ON: Contemporary Practice*, no. 2 (2010): 103–13, 103, 104.

79. Meredith Stricker, "Forum," *HOW2* 1, no. 1 (March 1999).

80. David Lau, "Letter to Lana Turner," *Lana Turner*, no. 7 (Winter 2014): 217–22, 220.

81. Lau, 222.

82. Just as the "interesting" is often prefaced with a "merely" (as Ngai suggested in *Our Aesthetic Categories*), so both avant-garde hard-liners and mainstream critics often attach a condescending mereness to formal innovations.

83. Lau, "Letter," 221.

84. Tyrone Williams, "Notes Toward an American Avant-Garde," *Lana Turner*, no. 7 (Winter 2014): 276–79, 277.

85. Cathy Park Hong, "Delusions of Whiteness in the Avant-Garde," *Lana Turner*, no. 7 (Winter 2014): 248–53, 248.

86. Juliana Spahr and Stephanie Young, "The Program Era and the Mainly White Room," *LA Review of Books*, Sept. 20, 2015, https://lareviewofbooks.org/article/the-program-era-and-the-mainly-white-room; Andrew Peart and Chalcey Wilding, "Sexism and Sexual Assault in Literary Communities: Editors' Statement," *Chicago Review* 59, no. 1/2 (Fall 2014 / Winter 2015): http://chicagoreview.org/wp-content/uploads/2015/05/59-1-Gender-Forum.pdf.

87. Jen Hofer and Sawako Nakayasu, "Can Can," *ON: Contemporary Practice*, no. 1 (2008): 87–98, 92.

88. Derek Attridge, *The Work of Literature* (Oxford: Oxford University Press, 2015), 305.

89. Derrida, *Paper Machine*, 44.

90. Hungerford, *Making Literature Now*, 16.

91. Hungerford, 156.

92. Thom Donovan, email to the author, Oct. 11, 2016.

93. Cross, Donovan, and Schlesinger, "From Center to Margin," 7.

94. Cross, Donovan, and Schlesinger, 7, 8.

95. Donovan, email to the author, Oct. 11, 2016.

96. See the special issue, "The Way We Read Now," ed. Stephen Best and Sharon Marcus, with Emily Apter and Elaine Freedgood, *Representations* 108, no. 1 (Fall 2009),

which discusses and exemplifies these trends. See also Rita Felski, *The Limits of Critique* (Chicago: University of Chicago Press, 2015); and Rita Felski, *The Uses of Literature* (Oxford: Blackwell, 2008).

97. See, e.g., the forums discussed in this book, most recently those in the *Boston Review*, *Chicago Review*, and *Lana Turner*. See also Sandeep Parmar, "Not a British Subject: Race and Poetry in the UK," *LA Review of Books*, 2015, https://lareviewofbooks.org/article/not-a-british-subject-race-and-poetry-in-the-uk; and Andrea Brady, "The White Privilege of British Poetry Is Getting Worse," *The Conversation*, Oct. 8, 2015, https://theconversation.com/the-white-privilege-of-british-poetry-is-getting-worse-48516.

98. Thom Donovan, "Desiring Criticism," *Harriet: A Poetry Blog*, Jan. 15, 2010, www.poetryfoundation.org/harriet/2010/01/desiring-criticism. The blog post spurred a discussion in the comment boxes underneath the essay. A year earlier, *Mayday* published a roundtable on negative criticism in response to an open letter by Kent Johnson: "Roundtable Responses to 'Some Darker Bouquets,'" *Mayday*, no. 1 (Spring 2009): http://maydaymagazine.com/issue1roundtableresponses.php. While hospitable criticism is indeed to be welcomed, negative reviews sometimes help dismantle power relations or at least draw attention to otherwise obscured injurious aspects of a text or author, thus strategically persuading readers to rethink their support or enjoyment of an author or work.

99. Holly Melgard, conversation with the author, March 28, 2017.

100. "Announcing Files 2.0," *Badlands Unlimited* (see note 31 above).

101. I allude here to Hungerford's *Making Literature Now*.

102. Juliana Spahr, "Astonishment and Experimentation," a review of Laura Hinton and Cynthia Hogue, eds., *We Who Love to Be Astonished: Experimental Women's Writing and Performance Poetics* (Tuscaloosa: University of Alabama Press, 2002), *Contemporary Literature* 44, no. 1 (Spring 2003): 172–75, 172.

Epilogue

1. Sianne Ngai, *Our Aesthetic Categories: Zany, Cute, Interesting* (Cambridge, MA: Harvard University Press, 2012), 97.

2. Robert Scholes and Clifford Wulfman, *Modernism in the Magazines: An Introduction* (New Haven, CT: Yale University Press, 2010), 56.

3. Ngai, *Our Aesthetic Categories*, 98.

4. Cid Corman, "Origin," in *The Little Magazine in America: A Modern Documentary History*, ed. Elliott Anderson and Mary Kinzie, *TriQuarterly* 43 (Fall 1978): 239–47, 247.

5. Jacques Derrida, *Archive Fever: A Freudian Impression*, trans. Eric Prenowitz (Chicago: University of Chicago Press, 1996), 68.

6. Rita Felski, *The Limits of Critique* (Chicago: University of Chicago Press, 2015), 146.

7. Eve Kosofsky Sedgwick, *Touching Feeling: Affect, Pedagogy, Performativity* (Durham, NC: Duke University Press, 2003), 130.

8. Sedgwick, 144, 139.

9. Sedgwick, 151.

10. Derek Attridge, *The Work of Literature* (Oxford: Oxford University Press, 2015), 305.

11. Felski, *Limits of Critique*, 128–29.

12. Felski, 188.

13. Walter Benjamin, *The Arcades Project*, trans. Howard Eiland and Kevin McLaughlin (Cambridge, MA: Harvard University Press, 2003), 9.

14. Anne Anlin Cheng, "Skins, Tattoos, and Susceptibility," *Representations* 108, no. 1 (Fall 2009): 98–119, 101.

15. I am thinking here of the readings offered in the experimental journal *Glossator*, https.glossator.org.

16. Sharon Marcus, Heather Love, and Stephen Best, "Building a Better Description," *Representations* 135, no. 1 (Summer 2016): 1–21, 14, 9.

17. Marcus, Love, and Best, 11.

18. Walter Benjamin, "Der Autor als Produzent," in *Gesammelte Schriften*, ed. Rolf Tiedemann and Hermann Schweppenhäuser (Frankfurt: Suhrkamp, 1977), 2:2.701. For Benjamin, the author's role in the revolutionary process is a "mediating" one. A work is only activated by readers. To achieve this, the writer has to rethink "technique" in a revolutionary fashion in order to have any social function. Benjamin borrows Brecht's term *Umfunktionierung* (functional transformation) to demand intellectuals do not serve but change the production apparatus, in accordance with the possible (692).

19. Ralph Cohen, "History and Genre," *New Literary History* 17, no. 2 (Winter 1986): 203–18, 210.

20. Cohen, 210.

21. Jerome McGann, *The Textual Condition* (Princeton, NJ: Princeton University Press, 1991), 62.

22. Bruno Latour and Adam Lowe, "The Migration of Aura, or How to Explore the Original Through Its Facsimiles," in *Switching Codes: Thinking Through Digital Technology in the Humanities and the Arts*, ed. Thomas Bartscherer and Roderick Coover (Chicago: University of Chicago Press, 2011), 275–97, 279.

23. Christian Hawkey, *Ventrakl* (New York: Ugly Duckling Presse, 2010), 5–6.

24. Hannah Arendt, *The Human Condition* (Chicago: University of Chicago Press, 1958), 237.

25. Arendt, 237.

26. Arendt, 237.

27. Morton Dauwen Zabel, "The Way of Periodicals," *Poetry* 34, no. 6 (Sept. 1929): 330–34, 332.

28. Laura Riding, "Preliminaries," *Epilogue: A Critical Summary*, no. 1 (Autumn 1935): 1–5, 3.

Index

Post45

Guy Davidson, *Categorically Famous: Literary Celebrity and Sexual Liberation in 1960s America*

Joseph Jonghyun Jeon, *Vicious Circuits: Korea's IMF Cinema and the End of the American Century*

Lytle Shaw, *Narrowcast: Poetry and Audio Research*

Stephen Schryer, *Maximum Feasible Participation: American Literature and the War on Poverty*

Margaret Ronda, *Remainders: American Poetry at Nature's End*

Jasper Bernes, *The Work of Art in the Age of Deindustrialization*

Annie McClanahan, *Dead Pledges: Debt, Crisis, and Twenty-First-Century Culture*

Amy Hungerford, *Making Literature Now*

J. D. Connor, *The Studios After the Studios: Neoclassical Hollywood (1970–2010)*

Michael Trask, *Camp Sites: Sex, Politics, and Academic Style in Postwar America*

Loren Glass, *Counterculture Colophon: Grove Press, the* Evergreen Review, *and the Incorporation of the Avant-Garde*

Michael Szalay, *Hip Figures: A Literary History of the Democratic Party*

Jared Gardner, *Projections: Comics and the History of Twenty-First-Century Storytelling*

Jerome Christensen, *America's Corporate Art: The Studio Authorship of Hollywood Motion Pictures*

Lightning Source UK Ltd.
Milton Keynes UK
UKHW012237160721
387197UK00010B/437

9 781503 609570